14A

Fire-Power

British Army Weapons and
Theories of War 1904–1945

Fire-Power
British Army Weapons and Theories of War 1904–1945

By

Shelford Bidwell

and

Dominick Graham

London
GEORGE ALLEN & UNWIN
Boston   Sydney

George Allen & Unwin (Publishers) Ltd,
40 Museum Street, London WC1A 1LU, UK

George Allen & Unwin (Publishers) Ltd,
Park Lane, Hemel Hempstead, Herts HP2 4TD, UK

Allen & Unwin Inc.,
9 Winchester Terrace, Winchester, Mass. 01890, USA

George Allen & Unwin Australia Pty Ltd,
8 Napier Street, North Sydney, NSW 2060, Australia

First published in 1982

British Library Cataloguing in Publication Data

Bidwell, Shelford
  Fire-power: British army weapons and theories of
war 1904 – 1945.
1. Great Britain — Army 2. Tactics
I. Title II. Graham, Dominick
355.4'2'0941   U167
ISBN 0–04–942176–X

Set in 11 on 12 point Times by Alan Sutton Limited
and printed in Great Britain
by Mackays of Chatham

Under the effects of long range fire and strong air attacks, baggage and columns rushed eastward in headlong confusion . . . the airmen worked over us like madmen . . . the air activity was enormous.

Extract from a German monograph on the
battle of Amiens, 8 August 1918.
OH *1918, Vol. IV.*

We thought that we were bettering ourselves by leaving Russia for sunny Italy. Little did we know how much more devastating was British than Russian fire. Sixty per cent of our casualties have been from your artillery shells.

A German prisoner on 1 November 1943
in front of Campo Basso in conversation
with Dominick Graham.

Contents

Illustrations

Acknowledgements

We wish to acknowledge our gratitude to all those who gave us advice, lent us papers and photographs, answered many questions and read various chapters in typescript, and whose assistance has been invaluable: Correlli Barnett, Brian Bond, Air Chief Marshal Sir Harry Broadhurst, Major-General W. D. E. Brown, Martin Blumenson, Air Vice-Marshal S. Bufton, Lieutenant-Colonel C. E. Carrington, Field Marshal the Lord Carver, Lieutenant-Colonel Ralph Eastwood, Major-General N. L. Foster, Major-General J. D. Frost, Brigadier P. C. Graves-Morris, Group-Captain E. B. Haslam, Brigadier P. H. C. Hayward, Colonel S. M. W. Hickey, Ian V. Hogg, Colonel P. Hordern, Richard Holmes, John Keegan, Ronald Lewin, Major Kenneth Macksey, Lieutenant-Colonel J. Marriott, Major-General J. M. McNeill, J. R. S. Peploe, Mrs Parham, Peter Simkin, Keith Simpson, Major-General E. K. G. Sixsmith, Roderick Suddaby, T. H. E. Travers, John Terraine, Lieutenant-Colonel P. S. Turner, P. H. Vigor, Brent Wilson and Lieutenant-General Sir John Woodall.

We are also indebted to the librarians of the Bodleian Library; the library of Churchill College, Cambridge; the Imperial War Museum; the Liddell Hart Centre for Military Archives, in King's College London; the Ministry of Defence (Army); the Staff College, Camberley; the Royal Armoured Corps Museum, Bovington; the Royal Engineers Institute; the Royal Signals Institution and the Royal United Services Institution for Defence Studies.

Miss B. D. Wood, Assistant Secretary of the Royal Artillery Institution, has given us unflagging and omniscient support throughout our researches. Carole Hines, Phyllis Miller and Mrs Jean Walter copied our often chaotic and much amended typescripts with unerring accuracy.

Lastly but first in other respects, our wives who cherished us while we wrote and chapters crossed and recrossed the Atlantic for mutual comment, and who listened patiently and critically to us while we read them aloud. Valerie Graham drew the maps.

In making these acknowledgements we must add that all the opinions expressed and any errors of fact are ours alone.

Shelford Bidwell
Dominick Graham

List of Abbreviations

AACC	Army Air Control Centre
AASC	Army Air Support Control
ACT	Air Contact Team
ADC	Aide de Camp to a general officer
AG	Adjutant General
AGRA	Army Group, Royal Artillery
ALO	Air Liaison Officer
ASSU	Air Support Signals Unit
BAFF	British Air Forces in France
BEF	British Expeditionary Force
BGS	Brigadier General Staff (to a corps commander)
BGS (I)	Brigadier General Staff responsible for Intelligence
BGS (Ops)	Brigadier General Staff responsible for operations at GHQ
Cab	Cabinet Office paper at the PRO
CID	Committee of Imperial Defence
CIGS	Chief of the Imperial General Staff
C-in-C	Commander-in-Chief
CRA	Commander Royal Artillery
DMT	Director of Military Training
DSD	Director of Staff Duties
FAC	Forward Air Controller
FAT	*Field Artillery Training* (manual)
FCP	Forward Control Post
FOO	Forward Observation Officer (artillery)
GHQ	General Headquarters
GOC	General Officer Commanding
GOCRA	General Officer (Royal Artillery) at Corps
	CCRA (term used in the Second World War)
	CRA brigadier commanding artillery of a division
	MGRA major-general advising the C-in-C at GHQ or the GOC at Army headquarters
GSO	General Staff Officer (category 1 etc)
HE	High explosive
I	Intelligence (branch)
IWM	Imperial War Museum
LHC	Liddell Hart Centre for Historical Research, the Library, King's College, London
MGGS	Major-General General Staff (to an Army Commander)
MGO	Master-General of the Ordnance
m.v.	Muzzle velocity
OH	*The Official History of the Great War: military operations in France and Belgium*
Ops	Operations
PRO	Public Record Office
p.s.c.	Passed staff college
QF	Quick-firing
QMG	Quartermaster-General

RA	Royal Artillery
RAF	Royal Air Force
RAJ	*Journal of the Royal Artillery*
RE	Royal Engineers
RFA	Royal Field Artillery
RFC	Royal Flying Corps
RGA	Royal Garrison Artillery
RHA	Royal Horse Artillery
RUSI	*Journal of the Royal United Services Institute*
SD	Staff Duties (branch of general staff)
SLE	Short Lee Enfield
TA	Territorial Army
TF	Territorial Force
WO	War Office

Prologue

During the first two hundred years of its existence the British Army was chiefly engaged in small wars in remote territories. Its rôle was to acquire an overseas empire and then police it, varied from time to time by expeditions to Europe, where its contingents formed part of Allied armies. Britain was never deeply involved on land, the forces concerned were small and their casualties low, for her position as a sea-power permitted her to play as great or as small a part in a land war as she chose. This privilege ended in 1914, when she sent an expeditionary force to France on the same principle and in the same hope, only to be drawn inexorably into making a major effort in the bloodiest and most destructive war in her history.

General Sir John French led abroad a force consisting of seven divisions, whose heavy artillery consisted of twenty-four 5-inch guns. In 1918 General Sir Douglas Haig could dispose of over sixty divisions supported by six and a half thousand field pieces from three to eighteen inches in calibre. In addition he had a new form of artillery in the shape of armoured motorised gun-platforms, the 'tanks', and also an air force able to intervene with machine-gun fire and bombs in the land battle. Both these innovations were to dominate future wars.

With these resources Haig was able to play a leading rôle in ending the war. In ninety-five electrifying days from 8 August to 11 November 1918, the British Army in France fought nine great battles, equal to or exceeding any of its operations of the Second World War, capturing as many guns and prisoners as the French, Americans and Belgians put together. It was not these victories, however, that became imprinted on the national consciousness, but the terrible cost of the battles of attrition that preceded them.

The British sacrifice had indeed been great and grievous, but they were by no means the principal sufferers. Their losses were exceeded by those of the Germans and Austrians, who fought on two fronts, the Russians and the French. There is no need to search far for the cause of this slaughter. The generals of that war were men whose military outlook had been formed in the nineteenth century and they were faced with the weapon technology of the twentieth. Modern agriculture provided a surplus of food to put in the mouths of unproductive soldiers, modern medicine preserved the unhygienic masses of soldiery from decimation by epidemic disease, and modern transportation enabled millions of men to be concentrated in the theatre of war. Then modern science and engineering enabled factories to turn out modern weapons to kill them in equally large numbers.

There had been portents. It had been discerned that the killing power of modern weapons would lead to a revival on a large scale of the use of obstacles and entrenchments, and that attacks in the old fashion by means of gunpowder and the *arme blanche*, would be difficult if not impossible. (Not that this was the sole cause of casualties on the horrific scale that were to be inflicted in both World Wars. There was ample room for manoeuvre in the vast spaces of Russia, but even there, where divisions by the hundred grappled with each other, using tanks by the thousand and guns by the tens of thousands, there were losses beside which even those of the earlier war paled.) The American Civil War was the first to presage the bloody nature of future mass warfare. In South Africa Boer marksmen showed the damage rifle-fire could inflict on infantry and that it could even silence the artillery. It was clear that machine-guns could multiply this effect many times. The Russo-Japanese War of 1904–5 emphasised the following points: the importance of machine-guns and heavy artillery; that artillery had to adopt the new technique of indirect fire from covered positions instead of assembling long lines of guns wheel to wheel in the open; the utility of hand grenades and mortars and the importance of signal communications. It was one thing, however, to read the omens correctly, but quite another to change the ideas of men so traditionally conservative as soldiers.

The British, in fact, made good use of their painful lessons in South Africa. It had not been their equipment that had been mainly at fault. The infantry, on whom British generals had always relied, could not shoot straight, its fire discipline was rotten, and its old fashioned reliance on drill precluded the use of field-craft and battle-craft. This was all put right, and the accuracy and intensity of the rifle-fire of the 'Old Contemptibles' of 1914 became a legend, but what was easy to instil into long-service volunteers after much careful training was not possible for the mass armies raised after the outbreak of war. In 1916 a battalion commander, speaking of his New Army soldiers during the battle of the Somme, asserted that they were less effective than the archers of Crécy, because they had not been properly trained to use their Lee Enfield rifles with many times the range and rate of fire of the longbow, neither had they mastered the tactics required to exploit their fire-power.

As regards Manchuria, General Sir Ian Hamilton led a mission to the Japanese Army to study its methods, and had his perceptive report been acted upon the British Army might have been better prepared for positional warfare. However, by 1914 the cavalry had been greatly improved, although it ignored the recommendation by Lord Roberts of Kandahar to throw away its sabres and lances, and the artillery was re-equipped with excellent light guns and howitzers, sighted for indirect fire.

What was lacking was what military men called 'doctrine': the definition of the aim of military operations; the study of weapons and other resources and the lessons of history, leading to the deductions of the correct strategic and tactical principles on which to base both training and the conduct of war – 'Sans doctrine les textes ne sont rien.' A German General Staff officer commenting on the British

Army in 1911 said that '. . . it was not infused with the essential principles of war deduced from history' (these did not appear in their well-known form until the post-war Field Service Regulations were published). It also 'lacked what General Langlois would call "la Doctrine" . . . leaders superiors and subordinates had no mental grasp of the requirements of a modern battle.'[1]

This was so, and it soon appeared that the British could fight doggedly in defence, but were at a loss in the more difficult tactics of attack. They were unaware of the principle of co-operation, and did not grasp how to co-ordinate the different arms. The art of orchestrating the fire of different weapons was not studied and in consequence the close interaction between fire and manoeuvre not understood. Artillery was regarded merely as an accessory, an extra wheel for the coach. The three arms – the cavalry, infantry and artillery – as it were, 'dined at separate tables'. As a result everything had to be learnt during a never ending battle in which many of those best qualified to analyse events were lost. Brian Bond has pointed out that in the small regular army of 1914 there were only 447 officers trained in staff duties (p.s.c.) 'many of whom were killed or wounded in the opening months of the war.'[2] By the end of the war 3,000 staff officers were employed on the Western Front alone. Bearing this in mind – and that the necessary object was to break through a highly organised defensive system protected by fire-power of hitherto unimagined intensity and occupied by some of the best and bravest soldiers in history, coupled with the flow of new weapons, new methods, new inventions, and the base administrative apparatus that had to be built to support the new citizen armies, and the difficulty of training this mass of men who, unlike their opponents, had no military tradition – it is hardly surprising that costly mistakes were made, but truly amazing that the efforts of the staff and fighting soldiers were finally crowned with such an overwhelming success.

In Britain the post-war years were a period of military regression. In terms of military power this was inevitable because of the economic plight of the country exhausted by war. Unfortunately, it was accompanied by mental stagnation. There was reluctance to study past lessons or even to consider doctrine, and a return to the traditional rôle of imperial policing. Not that there was a lack of debate: that was prolonged and vociferous. The advocates of reform now have, deservedly, an honourable place in our military pantheon. Regrettably, though, the very vehemence of their advocacy rebounded and they were driven to exaggerate. Much of what Liddell Hart, in particular, wrote was luminous but too often he led himself into paradox. Everything ordinary officers obediently believed was assailed and stood on its head. Masses of men, and especially masses of guns, were simply obstacles to manoeuvre; manoeuvre was everything and fire-power nothing; offensive action was suspect, at least if it led to a direct assault, and for the principle of concentration, he substituted the principle of dispersion. This obscured his advocacy of mobility and armoured warfare based on the tank, and understandably irritated many conservative officers. In the upshot he achieved little except, eventually, fame.

The second British Expeditionary Force of 1939 was, more or less, a modernised version of its predecessor. Its ejection from the Continent in 1940 proved a great blessing, for it gave time for a new generation of officers who understood both practice and principle to study new methods and construct a war-machine that was far smaller but just as efficient as the one Haig had in 1918.

Much hard fighting showed that the old principles were valid and that fire-power was still lord of the battlefield, and that in the last analysis its success was not based on weapons and machines, but on the application of reason, on the 'still and mental parts'. This is the theme of our study of the British use of fire-power.

BOOK I

The Fire-Tactics of the Old Army: 1904–1914

Sans doctrine les textes ne sont rien . . .

'The British Army . . . was not infused with the essential principles of war deduced from history and lacked what General Langlois would call La Doctrine: the leaders, superior and subordinate (had) no mental grasp of the requirements of a modern battle.'[3]

CHAPTER 1

The Artillery as an Accessory

> *The battle will be primarily the struggle between
> two infantries . . . the army must be an army of
> personnel and not of material. The artillery will
> only be an accessory arm.*
> (General Herr, French artilleryman,
> on the army of 1914)

THE elements that Wellington and Napoleon manipulated at
Waterloo and that Prince Frederick Charles and Marshal
Bazaine rather mismanaged at Gravelotte-St Privat, in 1870,
were fire-power and manoeuvre. At Gravelotte-St Privat,
columns of infantry were slaughtered advancing repeatedly
against storms of fire from men in secure defence positions: the
survivors were counter-attacked by exultant defenders who
swept forward only to be shot down in their turn by men firing
from behind walls and banks. The decisive killers were German
rifled artillery and French Chassepot rifles of superior range to
the Prussian rifle, the Needle Gun. Had the French stayed in
their defences the outcome, a German victory, might have been
different. For the well-entrenched defenders of both sides were
too strong for the attackers.

The weapons that were used at Gravelotte-St Privat developed
and became more lethal in the next thirty years. The rifle was
provided with a magazine which raised its rate of fire, a cartridge
with smokeless powder which helped the owner to hide himself,
and a bullet that ranged further. Infantry fire-power was
increased immeasurably by the Maxim-type automatic machine-
gun, a successor to the mechanical Mitrailleuse of 1870 and the
Gatling gun of the American Civil War. Machine-guns and
improved rifles threatened the artillery's place in the firing line
so that it had to choose between digging in for protection and
adopting steel shields against bullets and shrapnel, or finding
some way to intervene effectively from outside the range of the
bullet. On some terrain the guns could stand back at long range

and engage the opposing infantry, which could not retaliate, and their supporting guns which would. That venerable curtain-raiser, an artillery duel, might then precede infantry bashing before an assault. But if ridges intervened between the guns and their targets it was necessary to find some alternative unless the guns were to share the rigour of the front line with the infantry. The mortar principle had been used from ancient times in sieges to give plunging fire at quite short range and from behind cover. The Austrian howitzer had been used for two centuries for this purpose but it was a slow and laborious business to aim it at a target that was invisible from the gun. A breakthrough came with the French 75-mm gun in 1897. It employed the so-called 'Quick-Firing' (QF) principle. A hydrostatic buffer and recuperator system, hitherto restricted to static guns, took up the recoil and returned the piece to its firing position while the

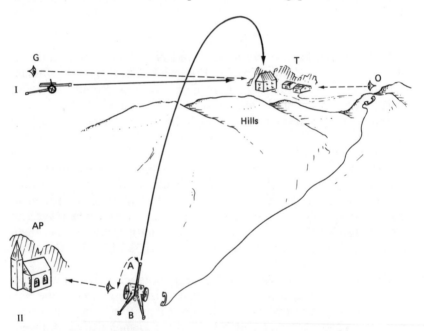

1. *Direct and indirect fire.*
    I. Direct Fire. The layer of the gun G can clearly see the target T through the telescope of his sight. At ranges from point blank to say 1,500 yards, the engagement is quick, accurate and decisive, but the gun is exposed to counter-fire.
    II. Indirect Fire. The target T is invisible to the layers in the battery B so they set the rough range as ordered, and the angle to bring the gun on the correct bearing A, with reference to the arbitrary aiming point AP. Then the observer at O adjusts the fire of the battery by trial and error. It is slower, but so is the process of locating and bringing counter-fire to bear on the battery.

carriage remained stationary and the gun so steady that it stayed aligned on its target. Buffer systems before this took up the force of recoil aided by scotches, inclined planes and spades.

All the tactical implications of this decisive advance over existing field recoil systems took time to assess. The description 'Quick-Firing' meant a high rate of aimed fire due to the gun's stability, of course. A simple dial sight on the gun ensured that successive rounds were actually fired at the range and bearing ordered with only minor and rapid adjustments. Consequently rapid fire could be directed by an observer in the front line, using a telephone or some visual device, while the gun remained hidden behind cover. The QF principle gave howitzers, which were easily concealed, a new importance. A second application of QF weapons was more obvious. Their stability made it easier and safer to fire QF guns from pits in advanced positions, or from behind a shield, since the detachment did not have to leap clear of the recoiling carriage every time it fired. Their high rate of accurate fire, enhanced by 'fixed' ammunition, that is the charge and the shell were in one piece and hence were quicker to load, could be a decisive addition to infantry fire-power. A third possibility was the achievement of surprise by firing concentrations from concealed positions without any preliminary, and warning, ranging rounds. However, first it was necessary to calculate the range and bearing to the target using maps that were accurate and survey procedures carried out by engineers. Various other adjustments were requirement for meteorological conditions and the individuality of each gun to ensure that the rounds fell close to the target. Of these only the provision of accurate maps of continental Europe was out of reach of the Royal Artillery. But this third method was slow, even though it might have the advantage of being independent of observational hazards like darkness, fog and smoke.

These three methods of using QF guns and howitzers were to be called, respectively, indirect, direct and predicted shooting.

Outside the ranks of artillerymen QF implied a revolutionary increase in rates of fire and, hence, prodigious and probably unacceptable ammunition expenditure. Peacetime economy and wartime necessity were antipathetic, as always. What is less often understood is that peacetime habits created peacetime tactics which had to be unlearned when war came. For instance, when training in peace the utmost economy in the expenditure of ammunition is enforced, and the notional casualties likely to result from such a policy disregarded, but in war these values are reversed, and it is learnt, always painfully, that lives are precious, and shells may be squandered to save them.

The description QF concealed the fact that the qualities of the buffer and recuperator systems of guns varied, that none was as steady as the original 75-mm or had as high a rate of fire, and that muzzle velocities and projectile weights varied too. From the tactical point of view, QF was a qualitative rather than an absolute advance. For, although the British had had no QF guns in South Africa, except a few Erhardt 15-pounders of Austrian design, they had used each of the three methods of shooting, including the third, on several occasions. However, QF changed the balance of advantage between each method. It was to decide some of these questions that British and German artillery observers watched the Russians and Japanese handle QF weapons in Manchuria. Naturally, they were more receptive to what they saw than the French, whose secretiveness and satisfaction with their 75-mm closed their minds to innovation or even suggestion.

The Japanese broke new ground in the use of their artillery.[4] At the battle of Sha-ho on 1 September 1904, they deployed their guns on reverse slopes on which they were out of sight not only of their targets and the Russian observers but of their own infantry. From their concealed positions they silenced the Russian guns which were in full view of Japanese observers, in the old fashion, and plastered and silenced the Russian machine-guns. Further, they made good use of concentrations of fire from a heavy artillery reserve which they controlled, like their divisional guns, by telephones.

The Royal Artillery members of Sir Ian Hamilton's mission were convinced that guns deployed blatantly in view of observers, as the Russians' had been, or within machine-gun and rifle range and vision of the enemy, would be destroyed. They concluded that the new conditions enhanced the value of howitzers, provided that they had good telephone communications to connect all observers with their guns and a network of lines laid between batteries and brigades to enable the fire of many batteries to be concentrated on suitable targets. But if telephone lines were obviously necessary they were also a weak link, for they could be cut by shell-fire. Smoke and mist already made visual means of passing fire orders unreliable. Indeed, breakdowns during battles in Manchuria in which the artillery had used indirect fire, led the Japanese infantry to demand that the guns be placed in the forward area amongst the infantry, despite their artillery's successes with concealed positions. After the war, they were inclined to question the courage of gunners who 'hid' on reverse slopes.

British infantry officers who had not been in Manchuria and

had not been convinced by the literature on the subject, expected the guns to be in sight and hearing, too. Many of them expressed the opinion that they expected them to be lined up wheel to wheel, as they had been on occasions in South Africa. And while they could not but be impressed by the power of Russian and Japanese machine-guns, few were prepared to accept as a principle of the modern fire-fight that fire had to be concentrated without concentrating men in proportion. So their own tactics continued to be directed towards obtaining fire superiority at close quarters by methods that overcrowded the battlefield with men. In marked contrast, the artillery recognised the principle that the shell was the weapon, not the gun, and that shells ought to be concentrated but not necessarily the guns themselves. The question was how the artillery could achieve that end in practice with a degree of certainty that would satisfy the infantry. The obvious answer, to improve their communications, was easier said than done.

The French, using their 75-mm guns, chose the direct method of support, placing them in mainly open positions close to the infantry. According to the Royal Artillery lobby at the Staff College, the French method looked deceptively easy on exercises but had proved disastrous in Manchuria on several occasions. A serious doctrinal difference arose over this question and it was aired at the General Staff conference of 1911. In the course of the discussion Brigadier-General Launcelot Kiggell intervened to say that he envisaged a battlefield with lines of infantry pressing forward, bayonets fixed, to close with the enemy. Lines of guns would support them at close range. This vision of the future was so much at variance with the events in Manchuria that two Royal Artillery members of the directing staff at the Staff College, Colonel John du Cane and Lieutenant-Colonel William Furse, took him to task.[5]

Du Cane and Furse argued that QF guns had decisively swung the issue of direct versus indirect fire in favour of the latter.[6] A respected military historian, du Cane pointed out that the methods used by both sides in 1870, even then, were obsolescent; fire effect at close range was so deadly that there ought to have been more concealment and greater extension of weapons and men. For instance, the Mitrailleuse ought to have been deployed outside the range of rifles and in defiladed positions. Manchuria confirmed that lesson. Furse mentioned that in South Africa the guns were driven right up amongst the infantry at Colenso but could not remain in action there and the infantry lost their support; at Pieter's Hill, however, although the infantry never saw a British gun they received heavy support from defiladed positions. Again, at Sha-ho, thousands of Russian shells were fired at four concealed Japanese batteries and only one man was hit by a falsely set fuze! The Japanese had laughed with delight. The Royal Artillery, he argued, ought to improve their observation facilities, particularly telephones as the Germans had done, and the skill of those directing fire from observation posts. As for French artillery tactics, admired by the infantry, they relied on smothering the general area of the target with a hail of shrapnel bullets of questionable accuracy. It was impressive to watch, and perhaps the British were slower, but it should be remembered that French gunnery practice camps were largely tactical, they dispensed with the range details whose job in the Royal Artillery was to check whether a target had actually been hit or not. In war, the effectiveness of French gunnery might depend on whether they survived or were destroyed like the Russians at Sha-ho.

Kiggell had shown himself to be ignorant of modern artillery methods, a fault common enough amongst infantrymen of the time.[7] But he had also misunderstood the character of the modern battlefield and had obviously disregarded the conclusions of the trials at the School of Musketry, Hythe, that had determined with precision the lethality of infantry weapons. (An account of these trials is in Chapter 2.) In contrast, du Cane and Furse had presented an unanswerable technical and tactical argument for the indirect method for QF artillery. But, in practice, the artillery needed first to improve its communications, command organisation and procedures, and the infantry needed heavier direct fire-support from its own weapons when attacking to lessen the call for direct artillery fire support. Neither step was likely to be taken until Kiggell and the other senior General Staff officers modified their opinion that the infantry could attack successfully by using mechanical drills, guts and direct supporting fire that was bound to be inferior to that of defensive fire from entrenchments reinforced by indirect artillery fire. In the meantime, battery commanders were compelled to admit that their communications did not allow them to support the infantry from concealed positions with confidence, particularly in the attack. Many of them were to occupy exposed positions amongst the infantry as a duty, cost what it might, in 1914. For although infantry weapons fire support was widely discussed in 1910 and 1912, in particular at the General Staff conferences in those years, no action was taken on the sensible proposals to increase it. As for the outcome of the debate in 1911 about French artillery methods, the official view became that the French were right. It would have been better had the artillery been enabled to use, with confidence, whichever of the three methods suited the occasion.

If Manchuria provided du Cane and Furse with their tactical ideas about the employment of artillery it had also largely determined the selection of British and German artillery weapons. The French, on the other hand, based their tactics on the personality of their 75-mm gun, which predated Manchuria and South Africa. Socio-political factors were another principal influence on the training and tactics of the infantry of the conscript army of *La République*. Hence, the General Staff pressure on the Royal Artillery to adopt French methods was irrational in the light of British re-equipment since 1904, and it reflected its flirtation with a French Army that was conscript not professional and one that was consumed by an alien doctrine that few seemed to comprehend.

After the South African War it was commonly observed that mobility was fashionable in peace but that more and heavier fire-power was demanded in war. The requirements for 'mobility' and 'fire-power' are usually conflicting. Hamilton, writing from Manchuria to support the choice of the 18-pounder field gun rather than a lighter weapon in 1904, made it clear which he favoured. His attachés were already describing the campaign in terms of the spade, barbed wire, machine-guns and artillery – especially heavy artillery. The same theme about fire-power was heard after 1905 in many lectures and articles.

In fact, the equipment of the divisional artillery, completed by 1911, reflected this sentiment. There were fifty-four field guns firing 18½-pound shrapnel shells, eighteen field howitzers firing 34-pound shrapnel or high explosive, and long guns throwing 60-pound shrapnel or HE. Light 13-pounders supported the Cavalry Division. Obsolescent 6-inch howitzers were intended for the GHQ reserve. The mix of guns, quite different from that of the French but similar to the German, was the artillery's response to recent trends not to the actual tactics of the British infantry. The 18-pounder had been adopted, instead of a 15-pounder like the 75-mm, because artillerymen considered weight of shell to be decisive. The 4.5-inch field howitzer was adopted in 1908 and went into service in 1910 because, after Manchuria, if not after South Africa, the artillery was convinced that plunging fire and heavier shells were needed for destructive shoots. (The new weapons replaced the 15-pounders and 5-inch howitzers used in South Africa. The trust in howitzers was not, therefore, a new fad.) The French had rejected howitzers entirely. The heavy gun, the 60-pounder had a long range and was the only such weapon in the divisional armouries of the first class powers. Its adoption as a counter-battery and harassing weapon showed considerable foresight. (It is interesting to note that a later mark of 60-pounder was still in service during the siege of Tobruk in 1941. A later model 6-inch howitzer was knocking out tanks at about the same time at Fort Capuzzo near the Egyptian frontier.) Thanks alone to the initiative of the Master-General of the Ordnance, Lieutenant-General Sir Stanley von Donop, a 9.2-inch siege howitzer for the heavy artillery reserve was in the design stage. By and large, this family of weapons, reinforced by new heavy howitzers, served the army well during the war. Yet it had been an immaculate conception. And when the pieces were ready to play together in the artillery orchestra they waited in vain for the rap of a conductor's baton.

It was very different in the French and German armies. In basing their infantry tactics on the 75-mm gun, the French accepted the important assumption that the purpose of artillery fire was to neutralise the enemy's fire not to destroy him. The gun's high rate of fire, flat trajectory and light shell made it perfect for temporarily demoralising an opponent by *rafales* of great violence but short duration immediately after which the infantry would close with him at the double. Its characteristics were quite unsuitable for destructive shoots. The keynote of these tactics was surprise and speed. The artillery used the minimum of ranging rounds before firing for effect, which had led, as we have noted, to criticism from British gunnery instructors. In order to ensure accuracy despite rapid ranging, the guns were usually placed in the open, from which direct fire was possible, or in only semi-concealed positions[8] which allowed the observer to be close to the guns.

The comparative imprecision of all artillery had persuaded the French to rely on high rates of fire delivered at short range from their *soixante-quinze* to compensate for it and for some short-comings in their artillery equipment. For they had no other type of gun in their divisions or corps and only about three hundred and thirty heavy guns in the whole army. They had no true howitzers at all. General Herr, who commanded the artillery of the VI Corps in 1912, wrote after the war in his *L'artillerie. Ce qu'elle a été: Ce qu'elle doit être*, that he had recommended the adoption of heavy guns in the corps artillery after he had seen them in action in the Balkan War. But in 1914 a General Staff paper had settled the matter against him by saying: 'A mobile artillery, capable of making good use of ground, will seldom require a long range gun to place itself within effective range of the enemy.' Herr concluded 'The theory of the preponderating power of manoeuvre over fire was thus definitely applied to the artillery. And he described the French view in 1914 of the coming war as: '. . . short and of rapid movement . . . The battle will be primarily the struggle between two infantries, where victory will rest with the battalions . . . the army must be an army of personnel and not of material. The artillery will only be an accessory arm.'[9]

A corollary to speed, high rates of fire, short range and guns placed in the open was simplicity – an absence of calculation. In turn, that excluded howitzers which were essentially weapons for concealed positions, deliberate destructive shoots, prediction and map shooting, on the lines first attempted by Major Hamilton Gordon with 5-inch howitzers in South Africa.[10] The French expected, wanted and needed a short war. They had built their tactics around the simple principle of the 75-mm firestorm and on the seizure and maintenance of the initiative by rapid concentrations of men and fire. Of course, the war was not short. When their opening moves did not give them a winning position they found that their weapons system was too simple. For they had not paid enough regard to infantry weapons and they lacked heavy weapons to which Herr referred. Building a weapons system is like a game of chess. Each weapon has a particular move and in the middle game the side without a Bishop's move or Rooks on the flanks is at a disadvantage.

Wrong though the French proved to be, it was better to have some doctrine and some plan than no doctrine and no plan. General Langlois, the French artilleryman, observed that although the British manuals in 1914 were excellent lack of doctrine made them useless. His admiration for British manuals was excessive, and perhaps the French went to the other doctrinal extreme. But dubious as were its social and political motivation, 'L'offensive à outrance' was based on some verified observations and a superb weapon which the French used very well. For *le soixante-quinze* was the pivot of an organic weapons system in which men, weapons and tactics were wedded to make something greater than each alone. The doctrine to which Langlois referred was the body of ideas that guided the parts of the system. The only guides that he could discern in the British Army were pragmatism and an obstinate empiricism. Of course, the very word 'doctrine' carried with it unwelcome foreign philosophical and political baggage. And neither the German nor the French varieties were suitable to be imported without critical analysis.

As for the French, relations between soldiers and politicians under the Republic, which re-established conscription after the war of 1870 as an article of political and social faith as well as for national survival, had been vexed. Tensions between republicans and monarchists, catholics and masons, colonial and metropolitan soldiers and, simply, politicians and professional soldiers, culminated in the Dreyfus Affair[11] at the turn of the twentieth century. In the following years efforts were made to restore morale in the Army and to keep it out of the political limelight. But Republicans believed that the Army might be a threat to the state unless the conscripted soldier was politicised, educated in his civic duties as much as in his military ones, and trained to have an inquiring mind and to stand up for his rights. Promotion went to officers who agreed, or said that they agreed, with this reliable republican opinion.

As the source of inspiration for the conscript's training in the last few years was political rather than military too little time was spent in hard field training and too much indoors in lectures on civic duties, history and morale. Even when the term of his service was extended to three years from two in 1913, he spent significantly less time in the field, on the ranges and mastering his weapons than the German did in two years. Much of his training was done at schools and very little under his own officers in the units with which he was to fight. In contrast, German training was intensive and all of it was done in the units and under the officers with which the soldiers would have to go to war. The 1914 conscript *poilu* was poorly trained in tactics and weaponry although he may have been tough, typically a peasant and imbued with l'esprit in the attack.[12]

The ideas disseminated by Colonel de Grandmaison's small cell of political soldiers, to whom the motto 'toujours l'attaque' are attributed, subsumed the republican political drive and its corollaries, including over-centralised and poor training. Deft field craft, fire-tactics and marksmanship can no more be taught entirely in a classroom than a World Cup can be won on a blackboard alone. The blackboard is useful to hard professionals to whom the unspoken frictions of real combat, be it in stadia or battlefields, are familiar and whose skills have become instinctive through arduous practice. But untrained, inexperienced and unmotivated soldiers tend, in the field, to bunch together and die in groups. When they are made to fight dispersed they melt away or go to ground. Then they cannot be induced to rise to their feet and advance against fire again. Their leaders die in rallying them. They cannot see the enemy who is firing at them from cover and fail to use their weapons. Until they do so, a kind of paralysis sets in from which the only release is movement. And so a vicious circle results in the death of the herd and the courageous actions of the few who lead it until they are

killed. Republican mythology very plausibly sustained a belief
that the spirit of the nation in arms could rise superior to these
laws of the battlefield. French professionals were less sanguine.
But they determined that with the simple tactics that were best
suited to their semi-trained conscripts they might succeed
provided the men were willing to suffer and showed élan in the
assault. Unfortunately, as Joffre remarked in his memoirs, the
idea got out of hand and into the wrong hands. It acquired
spurious status as a tactical theory per se that it did not merit
and which it was not intended to have. Furthermore, it became
linked with the sound belief that France could not endure a long
war by inspiring the disastrous Plan XVII in which, instead of
waiting for the Germans to attempt to envelop them, the French
themselves assumed an offensive strategy and offensive tactics.

   Earlier, French grand tactics had consisted of a counterstroke
against an anticipated German advance on a broad front through
southern Belgium[13] and north-eastern France. But doubt was
cast on this answer to the attempt of the Germans to envelop the
French left on the grounds that reliable information on which to
base a counterstroke would not reach French grand quartier
general until most of north-eastern France had been overrun. So
Plan XVII was introduced. And, whereas the tactics of the 75-
mm rafale and the inclusion of a reserve of guns under an
artillery commander at corps headquarters had suited the
original grand tactics of surprise counterstrokes against a
manoeuvring enemy in the open, they were inappropriate for
supporting infantry in a broad fronted advance in the hilly and
wooded terrain in the Ardennes, and positively useless against
the prepared defences on the German frontier which Plan XVII
demanded.

   In contrast to the French, the Germans had adopted heavy
mortars and howitzers for dealing with the concrete defences on
the Belgian and French frontiers. After they had seen that guns
in the open were vulnerable to howitzers in Manchuria, they
increased the number of howitzers in the field army to eighteen
105-mm howitzers in each division in 1908–9, twelve 150-mm
howitzers in the corps and an army reserve of 210-mm howitzers
as well. Whereas the French had a corps artillery commander
with forty-eight 75-mm guns, the Germans had no commander at
that level except the commanding officer of the twelve 150-mm
howitzers. German artillery was controlled by divisional artillery
commanders to which additional guns were allotted from the
corps and army howitzers as required. This artillery doctrine
served the plan of the German Army to advance on a broad
front and to envelop the French left wing. The Germans planned

to deploy the maximum force that could be supplied at the start
and to avoid regrouping and husbanding of reserves. The hitting
power of their divisional artillery reflected this principle for it
was much greater than that of the French.[14]

The Germans were not inclined to subordinate fire-power to
manoeuvre and their *Drill Regulations for the Field Artillery*
indicated a preference for concealed positions and indirect fire in
1911. Divisional artillery commanders retained control of their
artillery for as long as possible to ensure that fire was concentrated at decisive points. Far from relying on simplicity in their
artillery methods they paid attention to map shooting, meteoric
conditions, command observation post vehicles, communications
and the co-ordination of reserve artillery regiments to strengthen
the divisional artillery. But although German gunners were
warned that at 'the decisive stage' field guns would have to come
into the open to press home the attack, their preference for
howitzers indicated that they believed in the ability of the
artillery to destroy entrenchments by concentrated methodical
fire if their initial bombardment failed to neutralise the
defenders' fire. In short, the Germans had the kind of all-round
doctrine that du Cane and Furse favoured.

French and German tactical doctrines were distinguished from
the British by clarity of purpose. There was no doubt in the
continental armies where the war was to be fought or against
whom. Consequently, it could be planned down to the last nut
and bolt. Both the Germans and French had a political and
social creed that required the populace to be trained in depth
although they did not accomplish the task equally well. For the
nature of the two peoples was quite different and that affected
their tactical methods as well. In short, France and Germany had
national armies, expressing national purposes in a peculiarly
national way. That was what Langlois meant by the doctrine that
he failed to find in the British Army. Nor was that surprising.
The Expeditionary Force was not firmly committed to fight on
the Continent; its components were assigned to serve all over the
globe. It was a professional force which reflected no conscious
political ideology. It was not a national army and had no
conscripted elements. Furthermore, the British Army played
second fiddle to the Navy in British strategy and was assigned
smaller and smaller budgets annually almost until war broke out.
To an unmilitary people like the British, who had for long kept
themselves apart from the Continent and its troubles, the kind of
all-embracing doctrine to which Langlois referred was both
repugnant and suicidal.

The British Army was a professional force in that they were

volunteers, but were its officers professionals in the German sense? Its rejection of a totalitarian doctrine was sensible but its worship of pragmatism and its almost complete rejection of theory was not. No doubt the rising staff officers who were rebuilding the Army in the decade before 1914 hoped to inspire a balance between the German reverence for theory based on historical analysis and British empiricism. But it was an uphill struggle, for anti-intellectualism was the ruling mode of thought. And, simultaneously, they were challenged to adopt the style of continental war and still left with the burden of their old imperial role. Under the political compromise that masqueraded as a policy, they compromised over equipment, training and tactics between their two roles and gave the appearance, at least, of amateurism rather than professionalism at some levels. The very existence of conflicting French and German answers to every tactical question was a distraction in the face of which they wavered. Lacking a sound doctrine of their own either they hesitated to accept ideas from foreigners or adopted them piece-meal without understanding the purport of doing so. For, although the continental context of the Army's tactics suggested that they ought to take continental ideas seriously, British officers had more campaign experience than continental officers and so they were suspicious of untried continental textbook solutions. A new General Staff,[15] new infantry divisions,[16] falling budgets and indefinite strategic direction from the top were conditions under which this excellent British Army prepared for the war.

The tactical manuals of the period reflect these uncertainties over doctrine. Sir James Edmonds, the historian of the British Army in the First World War, and a man who became almost a symbol of the Old Army as it was later called, remarked that not only were some of the pre-war manuals plagiarised from the German but they were in some cases compiled by staff officers lacking any specific knowledge of the subject. Most tactical manuals were written in very general terms and avoided concrete examples; none defined the circumstances in which the reader was to imagine himself to be placed. The texts were admirable for supporting a prejudice but useless to young officers as guides or even philosophers. They were often out of date in such a period of rapid change. Among those who read them the more sophisticated used the passages that dealt with hard facts, like those in the excellent little *Field Service Pocket Book*, and relied on common sense for the rest.

Field Artillery Training, 1914, showed many weaknesses. It did not define the form of war that it was confronting but tried to reflect the diversity of the imperial experience as well as to guide the would-be continental warrior. Nevertheless, the manual referred mainly to a war of movement and, clearly, one that was on the Continent. In such a war the progressive building up of fire-power was widely recognised as a preliminary to the great battle that senior officers and military correspondents spoke of as inevitable. On it the war would depend. But the manual did not explain that the phases of war that it mentioned, 'war of movement' and 'positional war' for instance, were not discrete situations but merged one into the other. The artillery was particularly affected by such vagueness about the stage in the battle when divisions would have to reinforce each other's fire and would need to be reinforced by reserve artillery, like the French and Germans. In fact, the reserve artillery was virtually non-existent. Further, the machinery within the divisions was incapable of concentrating divisional fire let alone co-ordinating it with its neighbour's.

The control of British artillery, like that of the German, was nominally vested in the divisional Commanders Royal Artillery (CsRA) but neither their small staffs, a brigade major added in 1913, a staff captain and a reconnaissance officer, nor their communications permitted them to control the fire of their guns. There was no artillery reserve under Corps and the Army siege howitzers were not considered on exercises. A firm ruling was not given to divisional commanders or CsRA about the deployment of the three brigades of field guns, one brigade of field howitzers and the heavy battery, available to support the three infantry brigades and twelve battalions of infantry, under their command.[17] Consequently some divisional commanders automatically suballotted field brigades to infantry brigadiers and ignored the CRA in the field, using him as trainer and administrator. Others tended to deploy and control the artillery as they deployed infantry brigades, using the CRA as a channel of command like a brigade commander, although his means and task were quite dissimilar. Yet others kept their artillery as a reserve under the CRA until the battle developed, confusing fire reserves with gun reserves. Each solution was a natural reaction to the notorious weakness of artillery communications, to the conception of artillery fire as only an accessory in the fire tactics of the infantry but not a partner in the planning of operations, and to the novelty of the idea of a CRA who was both an adviser to the divisional commander and the commander of the field artillery brigades and heavy battery of the division.

At the unit level, *FAT 1914* ignored both the unresolved difficulties of the battery commander trying to give his infantry close support and the differences within the ranks of the artillery itself about direct and indirect fire and the German and French models. It paid lip-service to concealment but at the same time spoke of the artillery duel which most gunners knew was a dead-letter against concealed guns. A battery commander was to be conversant with the infantry plan and to control the bursts of fire from his guns so that they were more frequent as the infantry approached the enemy. The manual did not explain how he would overview the battle and control his guns so precisely unless they were almost amongst the infantry, or he had perfect observation, or the infantry conformed to a pre-arranged artillery fire-plan. But arrangements for making fire plans remained ad hoc, for infantry plans were made before the gunner was asked what he could do to help. The new feature of the QF gun was its ability to deliver high rates of fire from concealed positions. Good communications were essential for exploiting its potential. The principle that it most enhanced was surprise. The main function of the guns was neutralisation. None of these pivotal conceptions stood out in *FAT 1914* nor were they impressed on the rest of the Army by the General Staff.

CHAPTER 2

The Tactics of Separate Tables

The full power of an army can be exerted only when all its parts act in close combination.
(Field Service Regulations,
Part I, p. 14, 1909)

TWENTY thousand bullets were fired for each casualty in Manchuria. The statistic was the modern equivalent of the aphorism that it took a ton of lead to kill a man. Both sides found it difficult to see and engage effectively an entrenched enemy and the potential accuracy of the modern rifle was not matched by marksmanship and fire-control of a comparable standard. The British had already discovered this in South Africa where the sections of twenty-five men into which their half companies were divided had proved unwieldy fire units. So the reports from Manchuria served to reinforce a drive in the British Army that was already underway to improve rifle marksmanship and fire control.

Despite poor marksmanship in Manchuria both sides suffered heavy casualties because of the high volume of fire mainly from machine-guns. The Germans concluded that even intense training would not make rifle marksmen out of conscripts, whereas they could teach them to produce accurate fire in great volume with machine-guns. Indeed, the machine-gun on a tripod was almost too accurate.[18] So in 1912 they embarked on a programme to raise the establishment of machine-guns in the army. Instead of the six weapons in their existing *regimental*[19] batteries in 1911, there were to be six gun companies in each battalion. The new scales were well advanced by 1914 and all the Jaeger[20] battalions in the cavalry divisions had been completed.[21] Instead of adding to their scale of two guns in a battalion the British continued to use rifles to raise the strike rate, relying on excellent fire-discipline and individual skill. The German decision followed the positive principles that led them to adopt indirect artillery fire whenever possible. Namely, that fire should be heavy, accurate and generated economically. Indirect fire was potentially more economical, easily concentrated and could be applied in sufficient volume to offset, to a large extent, the natural ballistic limitations of all artillery fire, whether direct or indirect. Machine-guns could fire directly or indirectly like artillery and their fire effect to manpower ratio was excellent. The Germans made it easier to concentrate their fire by organising machine-guns in units of six weapons. In the attack they used their accuracy to strike the objective in enfilade until the moment of the assault. Neutralising fire from the artillery on the other hand had to lift off the objective when the infantry was within two hundred yards of it, just when the crisis in the fire fight occurred.[22]

The British did not think about fire-power in such a rational and co-ordinated way. The Gunners recognised that they needed divisional control to enable fire to be concentrated but they made no progress in achieving it in the last years of peace.[23] They accepted that inaccurate continental surveys placed limits on predicted shooting and that inadequate supplies of telephones and cable inhibited indirect shooting. Treated as only accessories in fire tactics, they waited in vain for the General Staff and the infantry to make up their minds as had the Germans. They could have played a part by analysing the technical factors that had led them to adopt a general policy to neutralise rather than to destroy the enemy and his emplacements. The main ones were the limited accuracy of artillery weapons and methods, limited ammunition supplies and, above all, that siege howitzers were virtually absent from their order of battle. This last factor was important. For it meant that the parameter was reviewed only by the field artillery. The officers of the weak siege and heavy artillery contingent had little influence. On the other side of the coin economy with shells was regarded as the hallmark of sterling artillery work. True, it was inspired about equally by professional principles and sparse peacetime ammunition allotments, but it induced slowness and pedantry. Consequently the infantry made odious comparisons between gallic speed and the Royal Artillery's obsession with accuracy and shooting at long range. Clearly, the French were right that it was the first shell that surprised the enemy and killed him before he could go to ground; surprise was a vital element in neutralising enemy fire effectively. Yet, accuracy at longer ranges was a more difficult technical achievement than at short range, and that reason alone made the Gunners give it attention.

The search for accuracy as an applied science had its home in
the Coast Artillery of the Garrison Branch of the Royal
Artillery, to which siege and heavy weapons belonged. Like the
Germans, they had confidence that the combination of heavy
shells and technical calculations could destroy field fortifications.
For Coastal Gunners were used to dropping heavy shells
accurately at long range on small targets at sea. So it is not
difficult to understand that when large numbers of heavy
howitzers and unlimited ammunition for them were available on
the Western Front, the field artillery officers who had known
nothing about the science before the war should have uncritically
accepted the idea that they could then destroy their enemy in his
emplacements. Nor is it surprising that the infantry in consequence, became hopelessly addicted to massive and prolonged
indirect preparatory bombardments. Unfortunately, the pre-war
Army did not prepare for a siege war and the siege gunners of
1916 were not provided with the necessary aids to accuracy that
they needed until mid-1917. Perhaps it is more important to
grasp that the infantry were the more easily hooked by the
artillery crutch because they had not provided themselves with
adequate fire tactics of their own even for the mobile operations
that were envisaged in 1914.[24]

The school of thought to which Kiggell and his patron, Major-
General Douglas Haig,[25] belonged persisted in condemning the
artillery for trying to achieve 'accuracy at long range' instead of
'effective fire at short range' and argued that guns, like rifles,
were most 'effective' when the trajectory of their projectiles was
flat. They insisted that the problem of co-ordinating fire with
movement, which concerned so many infantry officers, would be
simplified if guns were within sight of their targets like infantry
weapons. There was no need to increase infantry fire-power,
improve artillery communications nor to increase artillery staffs.
Those who advocated a complex system of fire support were
windbags who complicated what was a simple matter explained
in the manuals. Brigadier-General R. C. B. Haking, commander
of 5th Infantry Brigade, a reputable tactician,[26] observed at the
Staff Conference of 1911 that the Gunners ought to adapt their
techniques to the ground instead of wanting the infantry to
conform to their preferred methods. They were probably right to
condemn the French for rejecting howitzers and indirect fire, he
admitted, and for using ammunition extravagantly and
inaccurately. But they should overcome the tactical problems
that made the French school so appealing to the infantry. As for
his own arm, they were slaves to the ground and likely to fall
victim to the fire of the enemy holding it. If they would learn to

select objectives according to the fire support that could be given by the artillery and their own weapons, rather than expecting fire support when the ground did not allow it, they would save casualties. Haking was close to the heart of the matter when he inferred that in no circumstances should the shape of the battle be determined by either the artillery or the infantry alone. Only if infantry fire-power was superior to that of the enemy could advances be made without excessive casualties. He was anticipating the state of affairs in 1916 when British infantry fire was too weak and artillery fire overwhelming. In 1914, that was not the case. Rather it was that infantry commanders were not making the best of the artillery by including them in their plans, and that they had insufficient fire-power of their own.

Haking belonged to the school that believed that infantry weapons should play the key role. That clever Light Infantryman J. F. C. Fuller represented the opposite camp. He presaged the error of 1916 in an article written in April 1914 and published in November with a note to say that his views had been strengthened by the experience on the Aisne.[27] Fuller had visited Salisbury Plain from the Staff College, where he was a student in 1913, to watch a fire-power demonstration. After seeing the well-rehearsed deluge of shells apparently obliterate the targets, he concluded that far from the artillery supporting the infantry it should be vice versa. In 'The Tactics of Penetration: A Counterblast to German Numerical Superiority', he argued that powerful artillery and flanking machine-guns made the penetration of strong defences more promising than envelopment despite the power of modern defences. Yet Fuller had been told at the Staff College that an entrenched enemy could only be destroyed by expending unrealistic amounts of ammunition from existing ordnance as well as time; that he could be neutralised by rapid fire and then overrun by attacking infantry if it could jump on him immediately the fire lifted, although that was difficult to stage-manage.[28] His proposal, which overlooked the crucial difference between neutralising and destructive fire also showed that he did not grasp that he had watched a fire-power and not a tactical demonstration. Many officers were to discover the difference in the coming war when German defenders emerged unscathed from hours of poorly directed but visually impressive British bombardment.

Fuller's article was an example of a literary tradition, which the School of Musketry at Hythe so deprecated, of treating the reader to draughts of ancient history and diagrams instead of hard thinking about tactics. 'Military history is not always a safe guide in problems of fire tactics,' one of its précis warned in

1909. 'It is necessary to supplement the study of military history by continual and close investigation of the power of weapons as demonstrated by peace experiments.'[29] Some such thought was in the mind of the director of the demonstration in 1913. He hoped to convince the mainly infantry and cavalry audience, perched on its shooting sticks in the habitual gale sweeping over Salisbury Plain, that artillery fire should be used not as a substitute for their own weapons, nor as an accessory to them, but in a general fire plan, that included infantry weapons, to permit the infantry and cavalry to manoeuvre by neutralising the enemy's fire in the meanwhile. The demonstration was part of a campaign to bring infantry and cavalry officers to artillery practice camps where they would depict tactical situations for battery officers and make fire plans with them. Senior Gunners, including Brigadier-General John Headlam, then the CRA of the 5th Infantry Division and the future historian of the Regiment for this period, were lobbying for the establishment of a permanent School of Artillery on Salisbury Plain, near the location of the demonstration, where inter-arm studies could be carried on throughout the year. (The school was established only in 1920.)

The need for such studies to formulate fire tactics was evident. The manuals contained a miscellany of statements about infantry fire-tactics, but not a coherent theory of them. The absence of definitions indicated their imprecise treatment. Fire superiority was described as a condition in which the infantry could advance without suffering unacceptable casualties. The suppression of enemy fire was held to be a temporary achievement which could be made permanent only by driving the enemy from his fire position. The number of casualties that were to be tolerated in doing so had to be weighed against those that would be suffered from fire if the enemy's position were not attacked.

As fire superiority was described in terms of casualties it was made relative to the value of the objective and not an absolute condition. Other than the general exhortation that 'to advance is to win', the reason given for attacking an objective was to suppress enemy fire. This negative purpose invited the infantry to pit flesh and blood against fire. It was not stated anywhere that the positive purpose of taking an objective was to establish a new fire base on it from which to continue the fire-fight with advantage. That ought to have been the shared aim of the infantry and the artillery. The infantry would take new fire bases from which to inflict casualties and also observation points to allow the artillery to do so. The existing doctrine encouraged the infantry to attack ground for no better reason than that the enemy was occupying it and firing at them. The artillery became an accessory to this directionless motivation when it bombarded the enemy to enable the infantry to 'push on' regardless of consequences. The downgrading of infantry fire-tactics was made official in 1910. In that year *Infantry Training* was amended with respect to the meaning and purpose of fire superiority by an alteration in wording from 'the decision is obtained by fire' to 'fire superiority makes the decision possible'. The aim of the General Staff was to speed up movement towards the objective. The result was probably to indicate that the advocates of more fire-power were losing the battle against those, like Kiggell, who believed that it was overrated.[30]

The pointless attacking tactics that the infantry pursued in 1916 and 1917 might have been avoided had a clear statement been made in the manuals before the war to the effect that fire-tactics were concerned with the progressive occupation of advantageous fire-positions and their effective use by all arms to inflict casualties on the enemy. Of course, companies practised the positive principle when they moved from fire-position to fire-position in the fire zone. But before the war commanders above them did not envisage attacking defences that were organised in depth. Consequently battalion, brigade and divisional commanders did not regard the infantry battle as a progressive fire-fight. They did not select objectives from the point of view of ensuring continued fire support. In 1915–17, at the highest levels of command, the decisive and compelling facts of ground and fire-control were too often lost to sight when Sir John French and Sir Douglas Haig conceived plans on a larger canvas. The results were disastrous.

Like the artillery the infantry lacked a school where fire-tactics could be evolved and from which authoritative statements could be issued. The School of Musketry did its best but it lacked authority to make decisions. Yet the capabilities of rifles and machine-guns, as well as the possibilities of mortars and grenades had been thoroughly investigated and reported on by the School between 1908 and 1913.[31] From a long series of trials it made some unpopular recommendations. Marksmen were relatively unimportant in a fire-fight. The result was decided by high volumes of fire from average shots trained to hit with the first round somewhere on the target. In one trial 100 élite marksmen had been quickly silenced by 150 second-class shots. This finding was responsible for setting the rapid rate of fire at twelve to fifteen rounds a minute when other armies were expecting no more than eight. Although there was some loss in accuracy at the higher rate the destructive effect was far greater.

Put another way, at six to eight hundred yards against an enemy advancing in short rushes in groups and individually under service conditions, a little over 4 per cent of rounds registered. But 565 rifles, averaging about thirty rounds apiece in three minutes, inflicted 23 per cent casualties. Rapid fire was preferable to deliberate because of its shock effect and because it concealed the numerical strength of the defence as well as the precise location of the firers. But if maintained for more than three minutes at a time at the high rate of fifteen rounds a minute, wood smoke, barrel mirage, oil vapour and fatigue affected results adversely. Because of its wider beaten zone individual rifle-fire was relatively more effective against an extended enemy than machine-gun fire.

The old Maxim machine-gun, in 1908, was roughly equated to twenty-five rifles but the Vickers of 1912 with forty. Such comparisons between rifles and machine-guns are deceptive, however, because of the latter's deeper beaten zone and mode of firing. Its ability to concentrate intense fire over short periods made it a more effective neutraliser of specific targets than rifle-fire. Its narrow front reduced its vulnerability and its fire was, of course, easier to control. Against screen targets, machine-guns

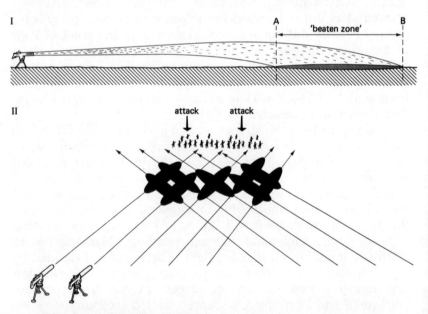

2. *Why the machine gun is deadly.*
    I. The zone of dispersion is a long, narrow ellipse, but filled with bullets at the rate of 400–500 per minute; ground from A to B is lethal.
    II. Guns fire in 'enfilade' at line of attackers, who have to cross interlocking 'beaten zones'.

achieved from 20 per cent hits at 800 yards to 43 per cent at 400 yards using bursts of fifteen rounds. Such an experiment was artificial, in that it took no account of the flat trajectory at the shorter range which would have enabled bullets to strike inter-mediate targets. But the screen represented the kind of bunched target of opportunity favoured by machine-gunners. With its high rate of fire groups of men could be destroyed in seconds before they could disperse.

It was always assumed that advances would be from one covered firing position to another until, close to the enemy, it would be by short rushes. Covering fire from those not advancing would always be given. It is interesting that in 1908 a conclusion was drawn that the stopping power of the defence when outnumbered by two to one or more 'may be exaggerated, and that a rapidly moving line may reach the 400 yards zone without very heavy losses.' This conclusion was affected by the understanding that overhead fire support would be given by machine-guns and that infantry would fire on the move when possible. Experiments against men showing head and shoulders in a trench at between 150 and 50 yards showed that as many as 18 per cent of rounds fired from the hip by men advancing in double time would score hits.

Between 1910 and 1912, the Short Lee Enfield with more powerful Mark VII ammunition and new sights and the lighter Vickers machine-gun were used in the Hythe trials.[32] They swung the advantage in the fire-fight in favour of the defence by extending the effective range of infantry weapons from 600 to 800 yards. A flatter trajectory made them more lethal. When the subject of the fire-fight was discussed at the General Staff Conference of 1910 Major N. R. McMahon, who had been the chief instructor at Hythe, presented his views. He pointed out the importance of high volumes of fire and spoke against the fetish of marksmanship and rifle competitions. The crack shots at Hythe had again proved only marginally more effective than average regimental shots in field conditions, while the nerveless machine-gun in the hands of men with only two weeks training was worth forty rifles. Two such machines had inflicted 60 per cent casualties against men advancing at two paces interval between 800 and 600 yards in one minute. Against such fire, movement by bounds and powerful fire-support was essential. He regretted the General Staff decision to combat the slowness of recent movements under fire by following the French who had abandoned the idea that winning the fire-fight was essential before an advance in favour of treating covering fire as only an essential aid to an advance.

McMahon supported his plea for volume rather than extreme accuracy by pointing out that that was exactly how the British longbow had beaten the crossbow, a more accurate weapon. He went on to point out that in defence they had nothing to fear. It was the attacker who now needed the fire-power. The automatic rifle was already in service in the Mexican Army and he recommended that they should adopt a percentage of automatics to increase fire-support in the assault. The light machine-gun would also shortly appear and they should not be left behind there either, for the Maxim and even the Vickers was too heavy to be used in the assault. Automatic rifles and light machine-guns would enable them to cut adrift from the need to increase the density of men to one a yard in the firing line simply to establish fire superiority. That practice would invite heavy casualties.

On 14 March 1911, McMahon was again present when Lieutenant-Colonel J. Campbell, then chief instructor at Hythe, delivered a talk entitled 'Fire Action' to officers of the 1st and 2nd Divisions at Aldershot.[33] Battles could only be won by advancing, Campbell told his audience. Fire was required for the sole purpose of enabling the infantry to advance. Battles could not be won by playing at 'long bowls' with the enemy. He then rehearsed the generally accepted rules that advances should be from one covered fire-position to another, and that, in training, men should be taught to close with the enemy quickly and to make their bounds as long as possible because once they went to ground it was difficult to make them move again. In Manchuria, he said, the heaviest casualties were suffered when men were lying out in front of the enemy position instead of closing with it. McMahon intervened to point out the difference between rushes in open country, where there were no fire-positions, and movement in bounds. The former should become shorter as the infantry neared the enemy and should take no longer than a rifleman to aim at them. Again he emphasised that the defenders had to be kept under heavy covering fire to avoid the attackers suffering heavily. The main problem in the attack was how that fire could be organised.

Some colourful remarks from a Captain Wetherell of the 1st Bedfordshire Regiment followed. Wetherell took issue with Campbell's remarks that 'to advance is to win' and that 'our energies are directed to getting forward, and the question of fire action is of secondary importance.' In ancient days, he pointed out, the superiority of armour over the weapons of range made it necessary to close with the enemy as quickly as possible. 'To advance is to win' was then considered 'the very latest thing in tactics'. Now, hundreds of years later they were being given the same precept even though weapons had changed. Soon they would be armed with a rifle whose trajectory was flat and whose rate of fire in short bursts was machine-like. 'Yet they were told that the bayonet was the deciding factor of the battle.' They would never send men against fifty machine-guns massed. 'There must come a time when it was madness to send human beings (however willing) to walk up against metal pumped against them from rifles.' He went on to point out the effect of the existing new rifles and ammunition, citing the German Mauser bullet's highest point at 700 metres as 6.23 feet and the Mexican automatic rifle as being able to pump out 600 shots in a minute. The time had come for other methods. Manoeuvre, followed by digging in, together with intense rifle and shell-fire would win fights in the future. Fire had to be beaten down by fire.

Wetherell was congratulated for speaking out but his theme was quietly buried by more senior officers, for a swing against accepting that unsuppressed defensive fire made manoeuvre within 800 yards of the enemy prohibitive was taking place at exactly the time that fire-power was growing. Exercises had shown a tendency for the infantry to engage in fruitless fire-fights instead of advancing: the tempo of field tactics had slowed to a crawl as a result. And the empty battlefield that resulted may have been realistic but it was most unsatisfactory for the umpires. The fear that fire might reduce operations to stagnation took the form of a new concern about morale in such conditions. Sooner or later companies would have to rise to their feet and take their chance in a fire-storm. The most that could be done was to reduce the odds on their being hit. So men must be prepared to take their chance.

Some markers in this apparent swing away from reality may be seen in the following representative pronouncements.[34] In 1907, Lord Kitchener at Meerut said that it was impossible for infantry to advance against artillery and infantry fire over open ground without the use of darkness and the spade. In that year the common opinion was that troops in trenches would suffer very little from the preparatory fire for attacking infantry. Good use of ground by small groups and the rejection of schematic attacks were rules. In 1908, the Inspector General commented in his annual report that infantry were concerned about concealing themselves long after their presence had been detected but then paid too little attention to gaining fire superiority. The School of Musketry suggested that preparatory fire was more effective than was supposed and that infantry ought to fire on the move. In 1909, a Hythe précis pointed out the bright future of automatics as a means of increasing fire-power in proportion to bayonets. In 1910, the CIGS announced the change in policy about fire superiority and at the end of that training season the Inspector General commented that heavy casualties would have been suffered by units that bunched and advanced in the open in dense masses. Simplicity in the French fashion was demanded of the supporting artillery to suppress enemy fire in 1911. In 1912, exercise directors were complaining that troops took little heed of opposing fire and were bad at organising their own supporting fire. In 1913, more attention was paid to supporting fire from infantry weapons and guns but arrangements for ensuring that it came down in the right place and at the right time were ad hoc. Throughout the latter period the directing staffs of exercises failed to depict artillery or infantry fire or to award casualties realistically. Granted fire-effect is always underplayed in peace; but the General Staff appears to have been more afraid of inhibiting the infantry from advancing than concerned to make it adopt proper fire-tactics.

The need to orchestrate shock action and fire action was not confined to the infantry. Traditional users of cold steel, the cavalry had been clearly told by the General Staff that fire action using the SLE rifle, the machine-gun and the 13-pounder would be normal in future and that the sword and the lance should be used only in conjunction with them rather as the infantry used the bayonet. Squadrons were to be trained to fight both mounted and dismounted but shock action was to be used only when the enemy had been shaken by fire or could be taken by surprise. In 1910, the *Memorandum on Army Training* warned commanding officers that the regulations on fire and shock were to be loyally obeyed. In 1912, when it was clear that shock was staging a comeback, they were told that too much time was being devoted to equitation and too little to skill at arms, fire discipline, fire-control and scouting. Henry Wilson, Director of Operations and recently Commandant of the Staff College, remarked that there was some difference between the inside of the heads of advocates of the *arme blanche* (the cavalry sword or lance and hence the cavalry itself) and those who believed in the primacy of the fire weapon. Erskine Childers' critical book about the cavalry, *War and the Arme Blanche*, had been published in 1910, and an official reply from the General Staff had pointed out that the reactionaries in the cavalry did not represent the latest policy.[35]

Lieutenant-Colonel W. H. Greenly[36] made it quite clear, in a series of lectures at the end of 1912, that the cavalry envisaged 'little infantry, much cavalry and many batteries' as the formula for the advance to contact and the retreat. In those phases of war rifles and machine-guns would predominate not cold steel. In contrast to the German and French cavalry, British cavalry shot well and their fire-power was improved by the acquisition, in 1912, of the Vickers in place of the old Maxim machine-gun. The opposition in the cavalry to fire action came from those die-hards who paid almost exclusive attention to horsemanship in training and to the lance and the sword as the primary weapons. From the evidence of Brigadier-General B. de Lisle command-ing the 4th Cavalry Brigade, the trouble was that too many officers were untrained in anything else. They read nothing, could not use a map or a compass efficiently, and ignored the manuals completely. The cavalry, he complained, had no central policy body that could exert pressure on commanding officers except the 'Cavalry Committee' which 'devoted itself to minor changes in equipment, etc.'.

Shock versus fire should not be exaggerated as an issue in order to add a dimension to the later dispute between the cavalry and the Royal Tank Corps when armour was introduced in the 1930s. Perhaps vestiges of shock tactics as opposed to fire tactics can be traced 'inside the heads' of cavalrymen as late as 1942. But in 1912, that was a dead issue if the diehards who 'read nothing' are ignored. In quite another category were those concerned that they might be employed as mounted infantry if their value as mobile fire-power was emphasised. The mounted infantry in South Africa had generally fought on foot using their nags as transport. In contrast, man and horse in the cavalry were a team to be separated as seldom as possible. It was a question how long the cavalry would last if it were habitually used as a reserve of fire-power. The same pressure in the German army had led to the cavalry being trained for dismounted action and to a proposal to arm it with a new rifle superior to the Mauser, but the tide of fashion had turned and in 1914 the cavalry was still armed with a carbine, rather than no rifle at all. To increase its fire-power the German cavalry division had been provided with Jaeger battalions carried in mechanical transport each with a machine-gun company. The French cavalry was unreformed having refused to hold or take ground. An experiment allotting infantry to French cavalry divisions was discontinued in favour of cyclist companies. The French, therefore, had machine-guns and carbines as their source of fire-power. Each army had horse artillery.

The debate that was still alive in the British Army in 1914 was about the employment of the cavalry division and not about the precise point at which the lance ought to enter the unfortunate infantryman's body. Two traditional roles of the cavalry were protection and reconnaissance. The single squadron in the infantry divisions was concerned primarily with the former: the widespread screen of the cavalry division with the latter. However, the cavalry division was also intended to force the enemy to deploy prematurely in a withdrawal and to sweep away his rearguards in an advance. The Germans stressed this aggressive role and employed the motorised Jaeger battalions – the future Panzer Grenadiers – with their machine-gun company, to give the cavalry divisions additional fire-power and the ability to hold ground. The British favoured that idea, too, but had insufficient infantry to carry it out. So they resorted to attaching infantry battalions to cavalry, ad hoc. It never worked well because the infantry, unlike the Jaegers, were restricted to marching pace and were unused to the speed of cavalry operations.

Its lack of infantry affected the performance of the British cavalry adversely in the retreat from Mons in August 1914 and in the advance to the Aisne in September. Without integral infantry protection it was forced to withdraw at night behind the infantry divisions or take a risk, as at Nery,[37] in a gap. Furthermore, it was unable to seize and hold defiles against resistance or to deceive the enemy into wasting his time mounting formal attacks when fighting a rearguard. Their fear of being incorrectly organised for this role but used in it nevertheless, was a reason why cavalry officers were reluctant to emphasise their proficiency with infantry weapons, although they were the only mobile reserve of fire-power the Expeditionary Force possessed.[38]

Age seems to have been a factor in determining the opinion of officers on the relative importance of fire-power in the infantry, the cavalry or the Gunners.[39] Senior officers were concerned about morale in battles that developed into fire-storms. The rising staff officers and commanders, most of whom had seen action in South Africa, were convinced of the need to accentuate fire as the necessary condition for movement – and the more concentrated and heavy it was the better. For junior officers who had not been in action, romance and gallantry may have been more attractive than intellect and science. The cavalry charge, the guns galloping into action with the horses showing the whites of their eyes, and the gallantly led platoon rounding up its demoralised prisoners were appealing pictures in the mind. The Gunner alone of the three visualised a fire fight as the end result of his fantasy. For the others, fire at a distance seemed less sporting than the manly business of running the enemy through with cold steel. To rely on fire support from others hobbled the initiative and interfered with dreams of independent command and individual glory.

Not that there was much glory in the daily life of a company commander in 1913. When the officer commanding E Company of 2 Blankshires could raise his head above the routine of training drafts, attending to 'compassionate' and minor disciplinary cases, inspecting his men's feet and socks after marches, wondering how he would find enough men for the beginning of the collective training season, or simply checking the serviceability of equipment in his company quartermaster sergeant's stores, he was aware that there was much concern in high places about fire and manoeuvre on the battlefield. But all staff 'guff' (loose 'shop' talk or rumour) above brigade level was unreal compared with the mundane problems he had to solve in his company office. An item of 'guff' was that conferences and trials on a new battalion organisation had ended with a decision. Then one morning rumour took material form as a letter from the Adjutant. From 1 January 1914, the Battalion would be organised in four large companies of 200 men each instead of eight companies of 100 men. E Company would cease to exist; he would cease to be a company commander. Suddenly the dreary responsibilities of command seemed less drear.

This scene and the arguments for and against the new organisation help to put the tactical discussion in this chapter in mundane proportions. For the main reason why the battalion had to be reorganised was that the irregular entry of young soldiers into the Army, their training and posting as drafts overseas, the calls on battalions for outside duties, courses and wastage, had made it impossible to field small companies as operational teams. The new establishment of 200 men would be large enough to take to the field. There were tactical considerations, certainly, but the change was primarily in response to the administrative strains that the Imperial commitment was exerting on an Expeditionary Force intended for the continental one. Not surprisingly, the debate in journals and lectures on the new organisation reflected the tug-of-war between the two roles of the Expeditionary Force and stressed administration more than operations.

The strength of the battalion was unchanged by the reorganisation but the fire unit, formerly a section of twenty-five men under a sergeant, two of which comprised a half-company, became a section of ten men under a corporal, of which there were sixteen in the new company. Four platoons each of four sections in a company gave a total of sixty-four sections in a new battalion instead of thirty-two in the old. Captain R. J. Kentish, later to command a brigade of 9th (Scottish) Division on the Somme, and Brigadier-General Ivor Maxse, commanding the 1st

(Guards) Brigade and later an outstanding commander of 18th Division and XVIII Corps and the Director-General of Training in the Expeditionary Force in 1918, took opposite sides over the four company organisation.[40]

The General Staff's statement that introduced the change pointed out that the British were alone in retaining the Napoleonic eight or ten company battalions and asserted that it was not possible to control eight companies on the extended front of a modern battalion. Kentish questioned that assumption arguing that the problem of control had simply been transferred from the battalion commander to the new company commanders. But his main point was that no organisation would work unless battalions were relieved of the tasks of training and draft-finding for overseas. Until the two roles of the Army were divorced no satisfaction could be expected. In the meanwhile the loss of four company commands was going to have a depressing effect and promotion was already slow. Maxse's main point was that the smaller section had sufficient fire-power to act as a unit and was handier than the old one. Modern fire-tactics demanded that the front of a section should be extended and consequently the corporal in command should have more responsibility. Corporals lived with their men and were not taken away for battalion duties as were sergeants. An added advantage of the organisation was that the battalion commander could deploy and control a battalion in depth, use the penetration tactics favoured by the French and retain better control of four companies than of eight.

The Expeditionary Force had barely adopted the new battalion organisation when war began. The Territorials and the overseas battalions remained on the old one for the time being. Clearly, the dominant tactical motivation for it was that in the attack the mass of the new companies would be an advantage. That was not the conception of Maxse. Rather he regarded the creation of the new, smaller section as the basic fire unit of the battalion to be more important. However, the senior staff officers were not thinking about fire units but about building up a firing line by adding men to it as increments. They were still thinking in atomic terms, of so many rifles to the yard, not in terms of increasing the fire-power of small units. Mainly, though, the new organisation was intended to relieve the pressure on battalions which had to provide for the overseas army while, at the same time, they prepared for continental war. The fire tactics of the Army remained virtually unchanged by it.

Some of the pressures for change that have been described come from men whose names have appeared in these pages; Du

Cane, Furse, Headlam, McMahon, Maxse, Haking, Greenly, and the numerous men who wrote in the professional journals. Why were their voices not heard? Finance, politics and the open-ended time scale in which the staff worked certainly blunted the urgency for new weapons and new tactical methods. It was not known that the war would start on 4 August 1914. Again, there were no central schools and no corps foci through which individuals could work. Maxse, for instance, was simply an individual without a wider electorate than his own brigade. The Army was being reformed but some of the powerful political lobbies such as infantry regiments, the Royal Artillery and the Cavalry were inclined to resist all arms doctrines and to cling to their autonomy. But most of all the staff was not able to make decisions alone and no commander-in-chief existed to bring matters to a decision.

It is, therefore, to an examination of the General Staff that we must turn next.

CHAPTER 3

The Still and Mental Parts

> They . . . esteem no act
> But that of hand: the still and mental parts . . .
> hath not a finger's dignity:
> They call this bed-work, mappery, closet war;
> (Troilus and Cressida, Act 1 Sc. 3[41])

THE Old Army that fought the Germans with such stubborn humour in the thunderstorms of August and the cold rain and mud of September and October of 1914 was well led and trained. That is the verdict of history. Yet, when the official account of the operations of the British Army was published after the war, Sir James Edmonds[42] had to defend its regular officers from those who described Lord Kitchener's New Armies as lions led by donkeys. He never convinced the unmilitary but warlike British public that the Regular Army cadre could have been efficient when it had failed to create an equally well-trained and successful New Army. His own volumes had pointed out that the operations with which the war began, in which the Old Army had shone, were very different from those that followed. So it is not surprising that the public believed that 'the donkeys' were professionally incompetent. For had they not failed to foresee and been unable to adapt to the conditions in which the New Armies would have to fight?

In his correspondence and table-talk with Basil Liddell Hart,[43] Edmonds explained that the pre-war leadership was weakened by the deaths of many talented younger men, including divisional commanders, in 1914 and 1915 before they could pass on their experience.[44] The surviving regular training cadre was simply too small for its task. Like Sir Douglas Haig, he did not fault pre-war tactical doctrine,[45] although he remarked that the manuals which the New Armies had to use had been written, in some cases, by tyros and plagiarised from the German. At the Staff College conference of 1913 Edmonds observed that, 'As fast as the German *Felddienstordnung* could be translated, the sheets were handed over to Colonel Frank Henderson and he invested the translation with artistic merit for British use.' He told Liddell Hart after the war that pre-war manual editors were sometimes ill-chosen for their work and used 'scissors and paste' methods. Edmonds admitted that the Old Army was unready for trench warfare in 1914, although the Royal Engineers had studied it and the General Staff had warned the politicians that the Germans were equipped for it. But the Liberal Governments between 1906 and 1914 had been unwilling to spend money on the Army when they were indulging in a naval arms race. It took the wartime governments until the middle of 1916 to provide the Army with the means to fight a war of position effectively. Edmonds concluded that the bloody fiascos of the first two years of the war became inevitable when hastily raised volunteers were committed to battle inadequately armed and supported. The politicians, not the soldiers, were to blame for the high casualties that resulted.

Edmonds spoke for a generation of regular officers who believed that the politicians had let them down. Usually impatient with critical civilians unless they had experienced the frictions of war, he sympathised with soldiers who said that some of their own commanders had failed as well. He was torn, himself, between exposing military incompetence for the good of the British Army and in the interests of truth and protecting the reputation of men who had done their best, although that was often not good enough. In attempting to serve history, the British Army, the General Staff and Sir Douglas Haig in that order of priority, his personal loyalties were conflicting. He had no wish to hand arguments to David Lloyd George or even to Winston Churchill, both of whom were over-critical of soldiers,[46] but when Earl Haig's death in 1928 released him from a curious love-hate relationship he began to recount anecdotes and express opinions about his old Chief which contradicted the official view of him and strengthened the evidence available to Haig's opponents. Edmonds had been a student with Haig at the Staff College and had never thought highly of his intellect since then. His adverse comments on the selection of officers, particularly cavalrymen, for top commands provided further ammunition for the war of words over the capabilities of First World War commanders that still continues.[47]

In his unpublished memoir written in the forties and concerned with personalities and the life-style of the pre-war Army, Edmonds again questioned the competence of some of his contemporaries who had prepared the Army for war. Engineers were inclined to patronise infantry and cavalry officers who lacked the brains or professional dedication to qualify for staff or professional training, but Edmonds revealed personal chagrin that he was unable to rise to the top, despite his brains, because he was in the wrong corps and lacked money and influence. His associates had been the intellectual, not the social elite; the more enlightened commanders and staff officers not the racing and hunting fraternity which 'never looked behind the swingletree'.[48] He regarded himself as one of the Players whose attempts to create an efficient Expeditionary Force had been thwarted by the Gentlemen and the harrying civilians at the War Office. Already an established historian, a good engineer and a German linguist and specialist on the German Army, he regarded himself as part of a vigorous new growth rising through deadwood. His friends had written regularly for the journals and expressed progressive ideas in important committees. And, indeed, the flood of published professional material shows that talented men were leading a renaissance in military science in the six years before 1914.[49] Edmonds was right, too, when he recalled that the professional élite had faced some formidable institutional obstacles in those years.

If Edmonds was justified in attributing the indifferent performance of the New Armies to casualties in this élite, to the Army expanding too rapidly for the survivors to manage, and to the failure of industry to supply sufficient arms and ammunition for the ambitious operations that were undertaken, those particular explanations could have been offered by any intelligent observer. But Edmonds did not connect evidence that when sufficient arms reached the Army they were ill-used, with the thought that anachronisms in doctrine and institutions before the war might have contributed to the mistakes of the cadre during it quite as much as heavy casualties. Yet he pointed in that direction in writing and talking about his experiences just before the war, when he was senior General Staff Officer of the 4th Division, by confirming what published articles, private papers and official documents already suggest. Namely, that in 1914 the British Army was still in the midst of its transformation from a colonial defence force to one capable of defeating a first-class continental opponent and that its institutions were under a particular strain because of the rapid changes in fire-tactics that followed the experience of the war in Manchuria.

Although modern tactical doctrine needed to be based on weapons systems rather than on single weapons each Arm (the Infantry, Cavalry, Artillery and Engineers) still tended to behave as a social and political institution with proprietary claims to certain weapons and no responsibility for the rest. That mode of thinking made Arms Schools to promote and co-ordinate tactical doctrine imperative but, equally, it made them unacceptable to the Infantry and Cavalry, if not to the Artillery.[50] Institutional reform at the summit after the South African War had not shaken, nor had it been designed to shift, the institutional conservatism of the British Army itself. Indeed, the reforms impeded change in that direction. For the Commander-in-Chief's appointment had been abolished but the new General Staff, able and willing as it may have been to co-ordinate and direct the Army's development, had neither inherited nor acquired his authority to change attitudes that were entrenched. A source of the frustration of staff officers, such as Edmonds, was the want of an authority to direct them in their work or to create military institutions with the responsibility and the power to co-ordinate the professional work of the Army.

All Staff work in the decade before 1914 was bedevilled at every turn by the conflict between the new continental commitment and the continuing colonial one. We have already seen that it was the conflict between the Army's rôles, rather than tactical considerations, that caused the new battalion organisation to be adopted in 1914. The units of the Expeditionary Force had to train for a putative continental war to which their political masters had not committed them, and for which the Arms to which they belonged were not adapted. 'The Study of German military organisation and methods was specifically forbidden at war games, staff tours, and intelligence classes, which would have provided the best opportunities for such instruction.'[51] As divisional units they trained for the Continent; as part of the old colonial system they trained drafts for the Army overseas. Seventy-six thousand, about half, of the British Regular Army were located in India alone. Recruits dribbled in throughout the year which wasted the time of the training staffs or that of recruits if they were kept waiting for courses to start. In contrast, the German Army received all its conscripts each October. On mobilisation it had but to recall the last two batches of infantrymen which had completed their two years training,[52] take in some specialists and men whose service had been curtailed because of high educational qualifications, and they were ready to march. German battalions could easily carry the 20 per cent of their strength which may have had less than a single year of intensive training. The German soldier received more training in two years than the British regular in four and infinitely more than a Territorial.[53] All the men were at least twenty years old and selected as physically fit. Many British recruits, on the other hand, needed remedial feeding and physical training before they could start military training. Seventy per cent of regular recruits were out of work and sixty-three were growing lads, under-nourished and under-paid. Only 5 per cent would admit to joining the Army for love of soldiering and adventure. The German Army received a highly selected intake with a much higher standard of education and physical fitness than the British.[54] On mobilisation, a British battalion received 70 per cent of its strength from its reservists, leaving in barracks those serving with the colours who were still under twenty years old. Whereas German reservists were subject to annual training, the British were not and soon fell behind the latest military develop-ments, apart from being unfit for active operations. In peace-time, battalions were never capable of going into the field complete and fully trained and the annual migration of battalions overseas from home stations, and vice versa, further disrupted the training cycle and impeded a division's battle procedures. The staff had to bicker continuously over training funds with the Finance Branch of the War Office whose Treasury-inspired penny-pinching gave way overnight to astonishing profligacy in 1914. Artillery ammunition training scales allowed about twelve rounds per annum per officer for practice. Travel allowances were so miserly that inter-unit attachments and exercises requiring travel were impeded. In these circumstances, trials of new tactics and weapons in the field were difficult to conduct, if not impossible. Infantry battalions concentrated on individual skill-at-arms and on training specialists rather than on their tactical fire teams and their drills for working with other Arms. (It was easier to retain a battalion footballer than a member of the machine-gun section when postings overseas were decided.) The German training routine did not particularly encourage innovation but the creation of a huge conscript army required a training machine. Drills were taught uniformly and efficiently in field units and staff procedures and organisation were directed towards controlling and indoctrinating a mass army of civilians in the shortest possible time. The British lacked a training 'machine' even for the small Regular Army. Theirs was an army of craftsmen rather than of managers and factory workers.

The Regular Army staffs were meagre in peacetime; GHQ of the Expeditionary Force, like a butterfly, came to life for only the few days in the years when it was exercised on manoeuvres. Its performance was then amateurish, as might be imagined. Only one of the three corps headquarters existed,[55] even in skeleton, for it was originally intended that GHQ should control divisions directly. The divisional staffs comprised but two field officers beside the general officer commanding and his ADC;

four extra officers were required on mobilisation. The units, except those of the 1st and 2nd Divisions stationed in Aldershot Command and London District, were so scattered that it was difficult for the staffs to overcome unprogressive idiosyncrasies and to create common doctrines within the Arms and between them. Schools of infantry, artillery and cavalry had not been established on principle because commanders were responsible for training, not the Staff Duties and Military Training branches of the War Office Staff. The latter would have controlled the schools between them, staff duties being responsible for writing and publishing manuals and the co-ordination of doctrine. Indeed, commanders at all levels opposed the conception of Arms Schools or centralised training fearing that either would weaken their own power and responsibilities and encourage a German type of General Staff. The opposition to centralised schools extended to the Territorial Force even though it lacked the skills, resources or time to train part-time soldiers efficiently itself. Vagueness in theory and diversity in practice was one result of this policy which was communicated from the Regular to the Territorial Army, and eventually to the New Armies in France. On the Western Front the New Armies were to suffer from anarchy in training doctrine and from the failure to co-ordinate Home and Expeditionary Force teaching until Sir Douglas Haig, belatedly, created a directorate under Lieutenant-General Sir Ivor Maxse to co-ordinate training doctrine in July 1918. Haig's earlier opposition to the measure rested on his belief in the maintenance of command responsibility.

The War Office General Staff was extended to the rest of the Army between September 1906, when Mr Haldane signed the order, and 1908. An Imperial Conference was held in 1909 and the 'Imperial' General Staff was extended to India in the following year under the direction of Douglas Haig. It is understandable that, barely six years old in 1914, it should lack the professional prestige and political clout of the German General Staff. What is less obvious is that those responsible for the post-South African War reforms did not intend it to become the directing force that it had become in the German Army, in which the relationship between the politicians on one hand and the commanders and the staff on the other was quite different.

The precepts that guided the way the British staff functioned and determined its authority in peace and war, in the field and in Whitehall, stemmed from the Duke of Wellington's staff system in the Peninsular War and the political experience of more than two centuries. In fact, the British and German 'General Staffs' both developed from the Wellingtonian model, although the policies that had shaped their growth since the early nineteenth century were very different. The French system had another provenance. Deriving from Louvois' organisation of 1687, it was adapted by Napoleon into a fighting, a writing and a riding staff united under a chief of staff, Berthier, of whom Napoleon said that although no better staff officer existed, he could not command 500 men. By 1914, three French staff bureaux dealt with Personnel, Intelligence, Operations and Supply respectively, under a chief of staff whose appointment distinguished the French as a unified staff system. A fourth bureau, which dealt with supply alone, was created during the First World War. In the French Army, 'General' referred to the collective staff and not to the operations bureau alone: the principle of unification applied as much to the staff in Paris as to staffs in the field.

It is misleading to apply the same term indiscriminately to the British, German and French 'General' Staffs. For the British staff of 1914 was a triad of which the General Staff was merely the operations, intelligence and training branch although, as it was also responsible for co-ordination, it was the 'senior' branch. The others, the Quartermaster General's and Adjutant General's branches, dealt respectively and autonomously with the supply of materials of all kinds and with personnel in all its aspects. The Prussians had adopted Wellington's system originally but abandoned its most important principles, the autonomy of the administrative and the operational staffs, the supremacy of the commander over both and the separation of political from military administration. The elder von Moltke considered that operations ought to take precedence over administration, in both the military and political senses, in the field and in Berlin. Indeed, after the retirement of Bismarck, the aims of political and military administration had tended to converge. General Erich von Falkenhayn was to retain the office of Minister of War when he became Chief of the Great General Staff in September 1914; to avoid a repetition of the civil-military conflict of 1870–71, he said. From 1916–18, General Erich Ludendorff was called First Quartermaster General but he was virtually Chief of Staff: General von Hindenburg, nominally Chief of the General Staff, was really the commander in chief and played an increasingly political role. The German General Staff, rather than its senior commander, controlled the army; its political influence stemmed from the Kaiser rather than the Minister.

Insulated from the pressure that the requirements of military security exerted on continental policy-makers the British reacted more slowly to changes in the character of land warfare. By effecting compromises between military efficiency and civilian control, political administrators were able to retain constitutional safeguards while they avoided inordinate military expenditure and the kind of national calamity that befell the French in 1870.[56] The separation of operational from administrative policy in the administration of the Army in London, as well as in field army staffs, was a key to their success. But tensions caused by the application of the principle in both places, always present, had become particularly evident at the beginning of the twentieth century when the Army was about to play a major role in strategy. A brief account of the modifications and applications of the principle since Wellington's day will illustrate how it worked and the tensions that it created.

Under Wellington, the QMG's had been the operation staff. It ensured that the troops were concentrated at the right time and place and in a fit state to fight the battle. 'The General's Staff', which helped Wellington to fight his battles, was part of the QMG's staff. The AG's was then the administrative staff which saw to the burial of the dead, attended to casualties and replaced them, handled honours and awards, promotions, appointments and ceremonial. Many of its functions were political. The QMG and the AG were responsible for all staff functions under Wellington and had equal right of access to him. The former's responsibilities included the delicate management of civilian contractors and of the Ordnance whose superior was the Master-General in London.[57] The military worked satisfactorily with the civilians in the field because Wellington ensured that they did. But the disgraceful performance of civilian services in the Crimean War led to their being leached out of the field army. By 1888, the great administrative departments, transport and supply, ordnance and medical, had not only been militarised but had ceased to be commanded like units by the QMG or AG. Policy and command were separated. Then the increasing complexity of the QMG's branch caused the 'General's Staff' to be separated from it. There were then three staff branches instead of two, although the operational link between the General's and the QMG's staffs remained intimate. Throughout this development the principles of equal and separate staffs with right of access to the commander and of command responsibility for decisions were maintained in the field.[58]

The Wellingtonian principle still worked well in the field in South Africa, but at the highest levels, in London, it did not. There the administration of the Army depended on civilians and on politics. Civilians managed industry and commerce from

which arms and clothing had to come, sat in Parliament which
provided money, and a civilian minister in the cabinet presided
over the War Office and was responsible for executing the
defence policy of the government of the day. The Minister
provided the link between the War Office where he was supreme
and the Horse Guards, where the Commander in Chief reigned.
The division between the civilian and military institutions lay
between the institution responsible for planning and administering
a war and that which actually fought it. But when, in 1899,
Britain could not mobilise its economic potential and had no
contingency plans even for defeating those 'cowardly little men
on horses', the Boers, the finger of blame was pointed at the
fuzzy area where civilian and military responsibility met and where
wars were supposed to be planned. It was evident, if evidence
was required, that the British could not undertake even a small
modern war successfully unless it had prepared for it in peacetime.

In 1904 the main proposals of the Esher Committee, which
had examined the organisation of the Army in the light of the
South African War, began to be adopted. Incorporating earlier
recommendations, the War Office was militarised but retained
civilian elements. The appointment of Commander-in-Chief was
abolished. An Army Council, representing the staff branches,
was created with the Secretary of State for War as its chairman.
It included the QMG, AG and Master-General of the Ordnance
as well as the Finance Member, a civilian. Each had right of
access to the Minister as Wellington's staff officers had had right
of access to him. A Chief of the General Staff – originally named
First Military Member, the CGS became Chief of the Imperial
General Staff in 1909 – was responsible for the general super-
vision of all War Office military staffs as well as his own. But
among the members of the Army Council he was primus inter
pares not the Chief; indeed, after the demise of the last
Commander-in-Chief, Lord Roberts, the Army had no
commander. However, the Minister was in a position not unlike
that of Wellington; as chairman of a board of men responsible
for various activities he had the power of decision. The degree to
which he exercised his power, and his methods, depended on his
political influence in the cabinet and on his ability and
judgement in Council.

The role that the CIGS played in Council depended on his
personality and political acumen too. Whereas the Minister had
power without professional knowledge, the CIGS had knowledge not power. In its division of responsibility and reliance on
personality to make it function, the Army Council was an
essentially British political institution. It was not designed to

achieve a particular end, such as military efficiency, but to maintain a balance of power and civilian dominance. Sir Frederick Maurice commented at the end of a lecture given by Sir Herbert Miles after the war:

> I have never been able to see that any system in which there were three, four or five military members of Council each separately responsible to the Secretary of State for War had any principle of military organization behind it. That system, it seems to me, has been solely due to political exigencies . . . to ensure that there shall be a reasonable amount of dissension in the Army Council.

The Army believed that militarising the system would prevent 'the clerks of the Finance Branch freely expressing their opinions on matters of military policy.'[59] No doubt the Ministers knew that by decentralising the system, they retained the real power, even if it was the power not to decide. In fact, in peacetime, the dice were loaded against the General Staff and its Chief, which meant against operational decisions. For most of the General Staff's concerns were easily shelved in favour of the mundane but urgent ones with which the two administrative branches were concerned. Without the time-scale provided by a coherent defence policy the CIGS could never argue that an operational need should take precedence over economy and regulation, the two main principles of administration.

Although the General Staff dominated other staff branches in the field, because there it served a military commander whose aim was to defeat an enemy by his operations, the CIGS's branch was by no means dominant even in the peacetime War Office. In wartime, Letters Patent of 1858 restricted the CIGS's communication with commanders in the field. For these laid down that 'when an Army engaged in active operations in the field the officer commanding the forces reported directly to the Secretary of State for War as the official organ of Her Majesty's Government and takes his instructions.' In 1914, the Secretary of State for War, Lord Kitchener, felt that he had the professional knowledge, the will and the constitutional power under the letters patent to act as the Minister, the late-lamented commander-in-chief and his own chief of general staff, as von Falkenhayn was to do. It was not until 27 January 1916 that an Order in Council was passed to allow the CIGS to issue orders in the name of the government. It was cancelled in 1918.[60]

The War Office was reorganised primarily because it failed to supervise efficiently the transition to war in 1899. The new General Staff was to write contingency plans for war, to direct mobilisation and to provide staffs for the headquarters of the Expeditionary Force. But old ways of thinking died hard, as Capper implied when he quoted Ulysses at Troy to illustrate the British Army's attitude to staffs and staff work. When war came again in 1914 there were not enough officers for all tasks and 'the still and mental parts' took second place to the service of 'the ram that battered down the wall.' Reverting to its former stance as the general's staff at the Horse Guards, the staff marched off to war leaving its place to be taken at the War Office by the over-aged or under-trained. Furthermore, although the mobilisation of the Expeditionary Force was admirably planned and executed the arms industry had been allowed to run down in peace and plans did not exist to mobilise it, despite the experience of the South African war and the recommendations of commissions after it. The civilian branches of the War Office threw up their hands and left the Master-General of the Ordnance, Sir Stanley von Donop, to muddle through as best he could in the face of mounting criticism about the shortage of munitions and arms.[61]

When the direction of the war was scrutinised later, Edmonds and others who spoke for the Army argued that those things that were within the province of the Army alone were well done. But they blamed the politicians for committing the country to war without ensuring that adequate reserves of men, weapons, ammunition and equipment were available for the task. Furthermore, von Donop stated that the MGO included an estimate for a reserve of machine-guns in his budgets for 1913 and 1914 but that David Lloyd George had insisted that the army estimate be reduced and he had had to forgo his reserve.[62] They condemned them bitterly for lacking a defence policy before the war and for failing to provide strategic direction during it. They pointed to the anomalous position of the CIGS, Sir William Robertson, from the time of his appointment at the end of 1915, until he was forced to resign by the manoeuvrings of David Lloyd George in February 1918, as an example of the inefficiency of the defence machinery. The opposition, on the other hand, condemned the Army for neglecting certain weapons before the war, failing, under Kitchener, to provide them after it began, and using them inefficiently and uneconomically in the field when they were provided. While we must suspend final judgement on the charges concerning the war years some preliminary conclusions can be reached about these charges and counter-charges.

It was unrealistic of either side to expect the British, primarily a naval power, to prepare the Army for war on the scale of continental armies. Yet, under Mr Haldane as Minister of War, an Expeditionary Force and a Territorial Force were created amidst remarkable advances in military science. Moreover, Haldane was intended to reduce military budgets and to design reforms to make the Army more efficient, not larger.[63] Faithfully, Haldane spent less each year from 1907 until the outbreak of war on the Army, although the creation of the Royal Flying Corps increased his budget in 1913. There was insufficient money in the eight years between 1906 and 1914 to improve pay and conditions, build up a reserve in the face of variations in the health of the civilian economy, replace old weapons and stockpile new ones, and to provide a reserve of new ammunition. The omission for which he and his successor, John Seely, Herbert Asquith, the Prime Minister, and successive Chiefs of the Imperial General Staff must share the blame is for failing to maintain the arms industry so that it, as well as the Expeditionary Force, had a mobilisation plan. In neglecting this aspect of the lessons of the South African War the administrators, civil and military alike, showed that they had not grasped that the link which joined the civilian to the military institution was the weakest in the chain, and that the effective prosecution of war depended on it more than on any other.

Notwithstanding that preparation for war was a civil-military responsibility, when war began civilians were quick to criticise soldiers for failing to provide an adequate scale of machine-guns and high explosives for the Expeditionary Force. Years afterwards Edmonds persisted in extending von Donop's comment about reserves of weapons into a claim that the Treasury had blocked the adoption of higher scales of weapons in units before the war, and that Sir Douglas Haig, among others, had demanded more machine-guns. No doubt his assertions stemmed from the way that members of the Army Council were habitually forced to trade innovations in one area for concessions in another in the name of economy. Certainly every reform had a sterling price attached to it. But the General Staff rejected a proposal to increase the active scale of machine-guns, although the School of Musketry advised it, for tactical not financial reasons. On the other hand, it is untrue that senior officers despised the machine-gun and refused to increase the scale of them for reactionary reasons. As we have seen, even the School of Musketry considered that there were sufficient in the defence although for the attack the School certainly urged the adoption of light machine-guns. Curiously, light automatics have not featured in the machine-gun controversy although they were to be the pivot of infantry tactics in 1917 and 1918 and they were at the centre of the doctrinal debate before the war, not the heavier Maxim to which Edmonds refers. Therefore, the official version distorts the truth when it says:

> The rapid fire of the British Infantry was a substitute for additional machine guns that were refused to it. In 1909 the School of Musketry urged that each battalion should have six guns instead of two; the suggestion was declined for financial reasons and subsequent reductions of the Army estimates and votes made any such addition impossible. It was therefore decided to raise the rate of fire of each rifle by the special training of the men.[64]

The discussion on machine-guns stemmed from the idea discussed at the Staff Conference of 1909 that the Army ought to modify its tactics for soldiers fresh from civilian life. Edmonds, himself, introduced the question by observing that Napoleon had had to use heavier columns as the quality of his troops declined and that in the later stages of the American Civil War attacks had had to be made in as many as ten lines. In 1870, regular officers who tried to lead levies as though they were trained professionals invariably failed. The superior intelligence of volunteers would make little difference once troops reached the fire zone, he asserted. He thought that they would have to give their troops 'much narrower fronts, very many lines. . .' and that defence 'would have to be in greater depth.'

In the following year the same question was discussed in a different form, this time in connection with the training of the Territorial Force. Colonel John du Cane introduced a discussion on whether it should be trained in units, like the Regular Army, or in central schools. He pointed out that TF commanding officers were inexperienced, brigade majors were not staff-trained and regular general officers commanding TF divisions had much less access to civilian soldiers than to regulars. Furthermore, the Territorials had neither the time nor the inclination to read military literature written in generalities for regulars. Much of it was meaningless to them and the flow of amendments and new editions, with which they were bombarded, deterred them from making an effort to understand them.[65] Clearly, too, central schools could be staffed with good instructors whereas adjutants and their permanent staff instructors were often mediocre and unable to make the literature come alive with examples. The discussion ended in the status quo because not only were there insufficient funds to bring men to central locations but a majority of the commanders preferred the regular system.

At the same conference in 1910, the first after Douglas Haig's departure from the post of Director of Staff Duties to become Chief of Staff in India and the first for his successor Launcelot Kiggell, McMahon had presented his case for light machine-guns in the infantry battalion. His purpose was to persuade the meeting that it was possible to adopt effective and rational as well as simple fire-tactics once the doctrine behind them was clarified and explained. At that moment the manuals were obscurely written and there was no unanimity about what the terms they used really meant. Practice in foreign armies was no better.

'Superiority of fire abroad apparently means little more than a superior volume of fire coupled with complete indifference to heavy losses,' said McMahon. At present, volume of fire was directly related to the number of men in the firing line. Yet a couple of machine-guns could stop an attacking line at about 600 yards, in average visibility, and no increase in mere rifle manpower would ensure that the attackers silenced the fire of the defence. On the other hand, light automatic weapons could provide the attackers with a great volume of very accurate fire from a narrow front. More men could then be released for forward movement, which was the purpose of fire, and many would avoid being casualties in the firing line which had to be heavily manned simply to generate fire. McMahon made the revealing statement that 'In the present day, the firing line is composed to a great extent of men drawn straight from civil life. They have forgotten what they knew about tactics. Therefore it is necessary to have what may be called "tabloid" tactics, so that these men may quickly learn their duties when they return to the colours.' He was referring to reservists, of course. First, though, the purpose, the meaning and the means of obtaining fire superiority and its effect should be clarified. Similar terminology to that in *Field Service Regulations*, 'the assault is made possible by superiority of fire,'[66] had appeared in manuals before the South African War, with the same negative results as in 1910. Infantry fire-tactics must have a focus recognisable by soldiers in the field. And he went on to say that the trials at Hythe showed that with a scale of one machine-gun per company[67] they could 'formulate new ideas about frontages and formations' based on the known effect of their fire. A huge volume of accurate fire from a narrow front at short range from within every company, would make possible the instinctive action and reaction between covering fire and movement that was lacking. The small-unit battle would be speeded up and be comprehensible to reservists and easier to control.

The summing up by Kiggell and the CIGS, Sir William

Nicholson, were both political rather than tactical although they may have reflected the opinion of many senior infantry officers. McMahon's main points were that light machine-guns could produce greater volume of *accurate* fire against *specific* targets than could riflemen lying scattered in the open within four hundred yards of the enemy positions, or even securely in an entrenchment. The present difficulty in combining the fire of one group of men with the movement of another would be eased if light machine-guns, *whose fire was unmistakable* to the ear and eye, were used on a scale of about one weapon to a hundred men. Yet Kiggell stated that fire did not decide combat and that the present slowness was due to troops trying to shoot the enemy out of their positions.

> After the Boer War the general opinion was that the result of the battle would for the future depend on fire-arms alone, and that the sword and bayonet were played out. But this idea is erroneous and was proved to be so in the late war in Manchuria. Everyone admits that. Victory is won actually by the bayonet, or by the fear of it, which amounts to the same thing as far as the actual conduct of the attack is concerned. This fact was proved beyond doubt in the late war. I think the whole question rather hangs on that; and if we accept the view that victory is actually won by the bayonet, it settles the point.

Nicholson summed up next day. He, too, chose to fasten attention on the point that fire alone did not decide the issue, although not to the same absurd degree. But in observing that McMahon had not said that volume was more important than accuracy, to which some people had taken exception, but that he had 'intended to convey . . . that the accuracy of a volume of fire depends upon individual accuracy; and with this view we shall, I think, all agree,' he closed the ranks but missed McMahon's main points.

So 'Tabloid Tactics', of the kind envisaged by Edmonds, were endorsed without the weapon that made them coherent and might have redressed the balance between the defence and the attack. The directors of the General Staff were not prepared to follow McMahon's thinking, even in principle, when he appealed to them:

> There is another reason why the adoption of this principle may be urged, viz. forthcoming developments in connection with automatic weapons. We all have it in our minds that before long an automatic rifle may be in use by all nations. Every nation has been trying to put off the date of its adoption. It was thought that

the French would be the first to be obliged to adopt one, owing
to the defects of the Lebel rifle, but, as it chances, the introduction of the pointed bullet and the new ammunition has thrown
the onus upon us, and we have got to lead the way.[68] This is a
matter in which we shall get no guidance from abroad. No one
abroad can teach us anything about it; we must solve the problem
of automatic weapons and show the way to the rest of Europe.

In examining the role of the General Staff in providing
infantry weapons, including machine-guns and in the evolution
of tactics for them, it is as well to point out that tactics are
developed with actual, not hypothetical, weapons in mind.
Ideally, innovations in weapons and in tactics should go hand in
hand, but they seldom do so. Often, weapons are introduced
only when the old ones are worn out and their maintenance has
ceased to be economical or when they are patently obsolete.
Sometimes they are introduced in response to competition from
another army and that is not unusual in periods of international
tension. In all cases re-equipment tends to be unevenly effected
across the range of weapons and only a general parity maintained with a rival over a period of years. When comparing the
strength of the German Army with its own, the British staff had
to consider the likely role of both armies and the state of
international tension at the time. Even in 1911, the year of the
crisis with Germany over Morocco, the British were not under
the same pressure as the Germans whose Schlieffen Plan
demanded that they have not only quantitative but also
qualitative superiority over the French. A request for funds for
re-armament had no chance of acceptance if it were presented to
the British Cabinet on the professional grounds of tactics and
strategy. On the other hand a political presentation, which
compared the equipment of the British Army unfavourably with
a potential rival, might be successful, particularly if war were in
the offing. If the details of deficiencies were leaked to the press it
would be embarrassing and might lead to a campaign for
equality like the one over naval Dreadnoughts when the slogan
was 'we want eight and we won't wait'. But, even when a
decision had been made to replace a weapon, two or three years
might elapse before the new one was in the hands of troops and
even longer before tactics were developed to exploit its
capabilities. No change of tactics could take root until the
weapon was issued. This consideration would have been evident
to Nicholson, a year after McMahon's presentation.

When Nicholson noted, in March 1911, that British rifles and
machine-guns were inferior to those in the hands of other

armies, the MGO agreed. The Maxim had been in service since 1893, he replied, and most of the guns in battalions had been used in South Africa. No Maxims had been manufactured since 1904 and an Ordnance team had recently condemned about one hundred as unserviceable. In 1910, the MGO had decided not to order the new Vickers Maxim, which weighed only 38 pounds in contrast to the 60 pounds of the old weapon, although other armies had lighter weapons and the Germans were said to be about to purchase the Vickers. His reason was that the British rifle was ripe for replacement as well. It was intended to adopt a .276 or .256-inch weapon which had a superior nitro-cellulose propellent for a lighter round giving it a superior performance to the .311-inch German Mauser, or, indeed, any other rifle. However, the new rifle had not yet completed satisfactory trials, and until a decision was made about its future it was unwise to adopt new automatic weapons that ought to be of the same calibre. A .276 rifle was scheduled to go into production in 1913 and issue to be completed in 1916.[69]

The CIGS's initiative, stimulated by the Morocco crisis, the opinions of instructors at Hythe and by the first indication that the scale of machine-guns was being increased in the German infantry,[70] led to the adoption of the SLE .303 rifle resighted for the new Mark VII ammunition. In August, at the height of the Morocco crisis, the programme for its issue was expedited. The regular divisions actually received it in early 1913. However, to avoid paying overtime to the workforce, the Territorial Force and the Indian Army were not to receive it until 1915.[71]

The decision on the new .303 rifle allowed the Vickers to be adopted and in 1912 it began to be issued to the cavalry which needed a lighter weapon the most. Then, gradually, the infantry received it too as production allowed. In October 1913 the programme for the .276-inch rifle was postponed due to problems with the ammunition. (Overheating of the chamber caused the cartridge to jam. Frederick Myatt, op. cit. p. 36.) Trials for a .303 or smaller calibre automatic rifle were already underway in August 1910, a committee having been formed for the purpose in 1909. The adoption of a weapon depended on the decision about calibre but when trials ceased in December 1913, no suitable weapon had been found. A Lewis light machine-gun had been fired downwards from the floor of an aircraft in 1912 and its mechanical functions had been satisfactory, but it should be remembered that Army weapons had to be suitable for all climates and ground conditions and be able to withstand rough usage. Trials of weapons were inclined to be more rigorous in peace than in war and less intensive. Nevertheless, had the

Germans produced a light machine-gun or automatic rifle the British would probably have adopted one of the available weapons as well.[72]

Democracies normally rearm in times of international tension, when public attention is drawn to their defencelessness, rather than earlier when the soldiers urge them to. The converse is that the absence of a weapon in the armoury does not necessarily mean that the soldiers are incompetent. The re-equipment of the Royal Artillery with QF field guns, field howitzers and a heavy gun between 1904 and 1910 was the result of the public exposure of its obsolescence in South Africa and the demonstration of new weapons and methods in Manchuria. The new weapons and the tactical problems of two wars were then rationally married and, as a result, the artillery acquired a weapons system. Yet, as we have seen, a ferment of ideas circulated among officers about the tactical use of the weapons until the outbreak of war. The delay in confirming the .303 calibre for infantry weapons made Hythe ideas academic until 1913. Then the new rifle led to even greater emphasis on rifle fire and light automatics were seen as rivals, not complements. The old, heavy Maxim section and its inadequate transport persisted, its subaltern in command being too junior to influence battalion tactics towards machine warfare. McMahon offered the infantry a weapons system, like that of the artillery, to suit its tactics. But McMahon's advocacy of light automatics in 1910 came too soon and when the international tension that had provoked the General Staff to adopt the new rifle relaxed it saw no immediate need for further changes. A result was that effective tabloid fire-tactics that were suitable for reservists and volunteers straight from civilian life, and which depended on large numbers of light automatics rather than large numbers of soldiers, did not mature before the war. Indeed, the British Army, in general, did not learn to use the weapon effectively in the attack throughout the course of the coming war.

Nevertheless, there were many officers, besides McMahon, who believed that victory depended on their ability to apply overwhelming fire-power accurately. Lord Roberts was one; the volatile young cavalry brigadier, Hubert Gough, was another. Even Sir John French advocated indirect artillery fire when he was Inspector General. Unfortunately, the fire-power movement had no leader and no institutions with influence adopted and propagated their ideas. Neither the infantry nor the cavalry was a systematic Arm. Unlike the artillery, they were unused to handling a variety of weapons in conjunction. Indeed, the infantry were to be slow to learn when the weapons were available. None of the Chiefs of the Imperial General Staff presumed to direct the Arms. Rather they gave them guidance in the abstract and general manner adopted by manuals. They were, besides, fully employed trying to bridge the gap between the Army's two incompatible roles and attending to whichever was the more important when a crisis arose. None marked 4 August 1914 on his calendar as *der Tag*, by which the Expeditionary Forces should reach the peak of perfection.

The Chiefs were politicians rather than leaders and the system which they served, as well as the task that was given them, made them play the role. Yet the Army needed leadership and was willing to march to any trumpet that sounded a certain note. In the hubbub, the right note was sounded by Sir Douglas Haig and even his successor as DSD, Lancelot Kiggell, expressed clear, if misguided opinions. Haig was DMT and DSD from 1906 to 1909, Chief of Staff in India, where he introduced the Imperial General Staff to the Indian Army, until 1912, and then the commander of I Corps. In that post he was the senior commander of troops with a proper staff in the United Kingdom. Rather than cry for the moon, in the shape of weapons that did not exist and tactics that remained hypothetical, Haig called for simplicity and realism in the use of the weapons in the hands of the troops. He labelled the radicals 'windbags', and urged Kiggell in a letter from India,[73] to have no truck with them. He supported the French 'allez! allez!' school of tactics in which everything had to be quick, simple and practical. Nothing complicated was to be attempted. Like the French he saw his aim to be applying direct fire-power against a visible enemy which would have to be vanquished by cold steel. Fire-power was important but sophistication in its use had to be avoided. Indirect fire, essential if many weapons were to concentrate their fire on to a narrow front, slowed the tempo of the battle and was of questionable reliability with the existing facilities for communications. So the weight of fire that could be applied was limited by the number of weapons that could be trained on the target over open sights. That limitation he accepted for the sake of simplicity, speed and surprise even though it crowded the forward battlefield. In the end the infantryman had to rise to his feet and, advancing into the firestorm, take his chance of survival courageously. High morale and good leadership then became the need, not overwhelming fire.

The Horse and Field branch gunners were inclined to respond to Haig's call for simplicity because they felt more certain of being able to support the infantry that way, even if they should suffer heavily as had the Russians in Manchuria. They were sensitive, too, to the innuendo that they were hiding behind hills instead of supporting their friends wheel to wheel in the open. They were bombarded with instructions to close to 'decisive range' for Haig was convinced that direct fire was more effective – an impression that was not necessarily correct. Yet the artillery had the weapons and skills to adopt indirect methods if the operations and ground called for them and when the additional communications equipment was provided. It had debated the rival merits of the French and German schools of thought and understood them. Only the weakness of infantry fire-power and fire-doctrine tilted the balance in the final years towards a belief that the French method of direct fire would have to be used in many instances.

Haig's vision of a battlefield was rather like that of a fan in the stands of Murrayfield, where his native Scotland played England at Rugby football; or perhaps that of a man looking at the ground between the ears of a horse. His conception of the scale of it was too small, perhaps, and he expected to see too much. He had not commanded a company flat on his belly under fire, nor had he commanded a battery, trying to see his target and his own infantry while passing orders to the guns and praying that he might stay alive long enough to correct his fire. His experience as a cavalryman in South Africa had not taught him how devastating was modern fire-power, and he had not been in Manchuria at all.[74] Yet he grasped well enough that the junior officer's central problems were to see the enemy, to communicate his intention to his men, to make them comply and to muster fire support when he had got them to advance. But rather than make a concession to McMahon's view that fire-power and manpower ought to be reciprocals and that the former ought to be increased, Haig regarded fire-power as limited. Furthermore, he treated it as a potential crutch, too much reliance on which would cause loss of morale, surprise and initiative.

The commanders and staffs of all armies believed that the initial encounter battles would be battalion and brigade affairs in which officers would have to react quickly using the means at hand. There would follow a race to concentrate forces for a decisive battle which would be decided by attrition and superior fire-power. Haig's tactics fitted the first stage admirably; they were unsuited to the second. Indeed, the organisation of the Expeditionary Force, which lacked Corps or Army fire-power reserves, was unsuited to it. Had he been more flexible, recognising the difference between the tactics of the contact battle and those of the decisive phase, Haig might have paid attention to weapons development and to the proponents of fire-power. But in setting his stamp on the pre-war tactics of the Expeditionary Force and its system of manuals, he bore responsibility for the tactics it imposed on the New Armies on the Somme. Furthermore, as one of the architects of the staff system, he ensured that the supremacy of the commanders over their staffs and of the Commander-in-Chief over his commanders was well entrenched. His personality ensured that the ideas that were executed were his.

BOOK II

One Great and Continuous Engagement: 1914–1918

> . . . Neither the course of the war itself nor the military lessons to be drawn therefrom can properly be comprehended, unless the long succession of battles commenced on the Somme in 1916 and ended in November of last year on the Sambre are viewed as forming part of one great and continuous engagement.[75]

CHAPTER 4

Prologue and Retrospect

S IR Douglas Haig signed his Final Dispatch on 21 March 1919, a year to the day after the great German Offensive had opened against his armies. The dispatch was an interesting historical document for it presented his view of the course of the war. More than that, it occupied much of the ground on which the historians and polemicists who disagreed with him would refight the war in print. It was a pre-emptive strike. The soldier was getting his blow in first.

Haig argued that by neglecting to prepare the Army for war the politicians had condemned it to a hasty, ten-fold, expansion and to two years improvising and training even as it fought desperate battles. Not until the beginning of 1917 was the leeway in arms and ammunition made up. The Army's task was complicated by the innovation on the battlefield of what he collectively termed 'mechanical contrivances'. These were, for example, tanks, aircraft, mortars, machine-guns and the techniques associated with heavy artillery firing indirectly. But all of these were auxiliaries. None was a battle winner by itself. Each had had to be used in co-operation with the infantryman whose rifle and bayonet in the end decided the outcome. The techniques that were used in employing these auxiliaries had had to be taught to the New Armies. In fact, they were applications of principles that had been laid down before the war in the manuals of the Old Army for the co-operation of infantry, machine-guns and artillery. The continued relevance of pre-war methods became evident on the Somme, when the period of rigid trench warfare ended and marksmanship and fieldcraft had to be restored to fashion.

Once the initial German offensive had been miraculously countered in September 1914, on the Marne, the war on the Western Front followed the form that had been predicted by the General Staff before the war, although on a greater scale. After a build-up of forces in 1915 it became a single, long wearing battle between equals. Frontal attacks were unavoidable because the trench lines were continuous and the reserves so numerous. The winner was the side which was able to concentrate its efforts on the vital Western Front. In putting that strategy into effect the Entente was at a disadvantage for the Germans were able to concentrate their forces with fewer political distractions.

Considering the stakes at issue – no less than the survival of the British Empire and democracy – the evenness of the two sides and the unpreparedness of the British in 1914, British casualties were not disproportionately heavy. The persistent offensives they undertook in conjunction with the French were essential to help to drive the Germans from French soil and to restrict the Germans' ability to use their interior lines to concentrate against each ally in turn. Initially these attacks were made by ill-equipped and half-trained British divisions. They were necessary, but wasteful and they deprived the Army of future leaders. Later, as their allies weakened, the British had to take the lead until, in 1918, they played the main part in defeating the Germans. Wars could not be won by standing on the defensive, and the casualty figures illustrated that the offensive was not necessarily more expensive than the defensive. The contrary layman's view was a dangerous fallacy which owed its inception to a desire to evade the price of victory and led to the misconception that the German collapse had been a surprise. On the contrary, it was the culminating and predictable result of the previous wearing battles.

Nevertheless, the offensive strategy gave little time for British divisions to be trained and rested, although no effort was spared to run courses of instruction in the numerous schools that were established at all levels of command. Five months before the Armistice, Haig instituted a directorate-general to assist commanders to train their divisions for the mobile warfare that he visualised would soon begin.

The small pre-war body of trained staff officers had been augmented by intelligent civilians and regulars who were hastily, but effectively, trained at the schools. Talent was given every chance, whatever its provenance. Alternation between staff and regimental employment ensured that relations remained good between units and staff and that each was aware of the others' needs. Although senior officers had had no experience of commanding formations larger than a corps in peacetime, their pre-war training and the manuals which guided them stood the test in practice.

Haig's dispatches, his diaries, numerous recorded impressions of him by his contemporaries, and his rock-like performance at the centre of the storm, show him to have been a man who strove to appear as a statesman and a soldier, and to be above politics. Everything that he did or said appeared to be in the interests of his country and the Army. He never apologised and seldom explained his policies, except to assert that they were firmly based on facts and professional principles. Whatever his doubts may have been, he contrived to be consistent and to express confidence that his measures were those most likely to succeed. Indeed, consistency was his fetish. He never admitted to a change of mind, even about people. He had prepared himself for the war: the war had taken the course that he had predicted. He had sustained the faith of his Army in victory throughout a long struggle that could not be avoided. And the Army, which he had had the honour to lead for three years, had won the struggle, despite the meddling of amateurs and the intrigues of politicians.

This is the message of Haig's Final Dispatch. Most of his officers, whatever their reservations about his conduct of particular battles, agreed with his summary. Many others, mainly civilians, some of whom had fired shots in anger on the Western Front, historians and politicians among them, were to take a different view.

The critics pointed to the long series of bloody, indecisive battles as evidence of the incompetence of the higher commanders. They were unwilling to accept the brutal compulsion of the tragedy, as Haig austerely accepted it. Nor would they assume the responsibility for past sins that must accompany a tragic theme. In their opinion, the bitter outcome was not determined by the situation but by the way that it was handled. Suffering at Haig's calvinist Calvary had not been the necessary pre-condition for the victories of the final Hundred Days in 1918.

But had there been any other way?

It is never easy to distinguish the possible from the desirable in war and hindsight is but a mirage; for it distracts attention from the technical, tactical and administrative work that is the daily concern of soldiers and is the stuff of victory. By grasping the working methods of the soldier, the historian may lay his hands on the continuous thread of reason that was real to his subjects at the time and led them through the noise and the confusion. Haig's version of the 'one great and continuous engagement' obscures this practical theme. For although Haig was right to stress it he trivialised it by quantifying and generalising the difficult and continuous process of learning from one battle to another through which the professionals as well as the citizen soldiers passed. Did Haig, himself, learn nothing the reader may ask? But Haig makes one battle look much like the next, except for the steady acquisition of material. As each becomes a monument to abstractions like discipline, courage and timeless military principles, it loses its identity.

Finding no reason in the midst of a uniform and relentless insanity a reader of the literature may embrace sensation and humanity instead. Then he is easily deceived into allowing an extreme experience on a unique occasion to play imposter and to give false colour to the whole. For instance, the recorded memories of the men who walked forward on 1 July 1916[76] may have been shared by thousands on that awful day; but the day, itself, was not typical even of the Somme battles. Nor was the sum of individual experiences greater than its parts. Once a battle started, no one knew much more than was within his sight and hearing; nor would they until an historian reconstructed the scene. Private Bloggs and Lieutenant Smith were participants in but one part of the field. Until something went wrong, they were usually ignorant and uninterested about the professional skill, matured by experience, that had got them to the start-line. They knew for certain only how they, themselves, had been called to the colours, trained and finally brought to the most important moment of their lives. Years later, it seems that the historian's omniscience about the battlefield is not only unreal but privileged, and that it behoves him to handle all his human subjects with equal respect for their frailties, their handicaps and their achievements.

If there were discontinuities during a battle in space, there were also discontinuities between battles due to time. The first historians of a battle are those who survive to fight the next. For more than one picture of a subject must be studied to detect change in it. But between one battle and the next commanders and staff-officers, as well as their men, were wounded, became sick or were pulled out of the line with their divisions, sometimes after only a few days fighting. Improvements in methods between one battle and the next went almost unnoticed because so many survived or fought in but one episode of a long ordeal like the Somme campaign.

In the worm's eye, battles were simply judged 'good shows' or 'bad shows', according to the depth of the blood-bath. Few platoon commanders could say much more than that. They could not write historically about the changes in the way battles were fought. The continuity men were at Corps, Army and General headquarters. The Corps was the lowest level that planned and fought the longer battles like Loos, the Somme, Arras and Passchendaele. It received one division after another in the course of them; saw them arrive, clean and at full-strength; saw them tramp away, a week or two later, dirty, bedraggled and depleted. The professionals of the higher staffs often determined what kind of show it would turn out to be. In failure they became notorious but their work was not memorable otherwise, as the literature of Sassoon and Graves is memorable. They did not record the pilgrimage of individuals from enthusiasm to ennui, and from disillusion to anger. They have not left the taste that lingers last.

The genre of Sassoon and Graves is history; the history of unusual individuals in unusual circumstances. But people who were not unusual passed from the earth as though they had never been. Some of them must be content to be represented by symbols like the Menin Gate or the Thiepval Memorial. Those who did the grinding work of the pen, the conference room, the drawing board and the classroom have some memorial in the appendices, and sometimes in the text, of the *History of the Military Operations in France and Belgium*. But as that memorial is dull and seldom visited it has not preserved the memory of how the victory was won, what it took to win it or why the sacrifice was necessary.

Douglas Haig may have been a biased historian, and no leading actor has not been biased about the parts he played, but his historical sense was shrewd and he showed it in his Final Dispatch. In its pages he anticipated what his critics would say about him, of course, and assumed a position which they have been assailing ever since. But he also began his defence of the memory of those who had fought under him. He was not going to allow posterity to believe that they had died in vain. That would have been the ultimate betrayal. For Haig sought not only to justify his own life but also to preserve and justify the Army that would survive him. Furthermore, by addressing professional matters, which are the meat of military history, he established a chain of cause and effect and a theme that could not be ignored, even if the warning that he issued about the future was ignored.

The themes in the last dispatch of the professional soldier who saw the war from beginning to end, from a Corps, an Army and finally from General Headquarters, are worthy to be studied carefully. Neither political histories nor histories of single battles can do justice to them. But if Haig's purpose is to be served we cannot rest content with his static, professional abstractions. We shall have to present a dynamic account of the Army's professional experience under him. For surely the Army learned from its experience even if it was again neglected when peace returned and had to be taught its business by the same tough enemy a second time.

CHAPTER 5

Many a Doubtful Battle

. . . Sure of himself, steady of poise, knife in hand, intent upon the operation; entirely removed in his professional capacity from the agony of the patient, the anguish of relations, or the doctrines of rival schools, the devices of quacks, or the first-fruits of new learning. He would operate without excitement, or he would depart without being affronted; and if the patient died, he would not reproach himself.

Winston Churchill[77]

But the Great War owned no Master; no one was equal to its vast and novel issues; no human hand controlled its hurricanes; no eye could pierce its whirlwind dust-clouds . . . But . . . the fact remains that no other subject of the King could have endured the ordeal which was his lot with the phlegm, the temper, and the fortitude of Sir Douglas Haig.

Winston Churchill[78]

IN the lines above, Winston Churchill emphasised Haig's steady nerves, even temperament and stamina rather than his judgement, for which he did not have a high regard. When he wrote that Haig was 'entirely removed in his professional capacity from the doctrines of rival schools, the devices of quacks or the first fruits of new learning', no doubt, he had in mind the panacea of the Eastern Strategy, the tank and even strategic bombers. Churchill, himself, had embraced each of them with what Haig considered uncritical enthusiasm. Haig had been right about the Eastern Strategy and the bomber though, and he had not rejected new devices out of hand, least of all the tank. However, he had insisted that they conform to his own scheme of things before he would accept them, and, to that extent, he was remote and his mind was closed, often to reasonable ideas. But it was the soundness of Haig's own ideas when they were tested in the whirlwind of battle that Churchill questioned. He believed that Haig neither directed his battles successfully himself nor allowed others to do so. Every battle that he planned from Neuve Chapelle in March 1915 until Saint Quentin in March 1918 was infected by a germ of doubt which stemmed directly from his personality and methods.

By the end of 1914 the British Expeditionary Force had gained experience in a variety of operations. Smith-Dorrien's II Corps had fought defensive battles at Mons and Le Cateau during the retreat, had attacked the entrenched German defences on the Aisne and had led the fighting advance in Artois during the so-called 'race to the sea'. Haig's I Corps had also fought on the Aisne, and then in the bloody and decisive battle at Ypres in October and November, after which the front became stabilised. During the winter it became possible to take stock of how British tactics and British equipment matched the demands of a campaign whose size and scope had been a surprise, although to those British officers who had studied their profession it seemed only to repeat lessons already learnt and to confirm old theories.

As regards tactics generally the contention of McMahon and the staff of the School of Musketry at Hythe, that the infantry had sufficient fire-power to stop an attack provided they had a field of fire of no less than 400 yards, was supported by experience in action, although this did not preclude a request for more Vickers machine-guns. A proposal was made to the War Office to provide each battalion with four, because in close country it was not always possible to exploit the massed fire of the rifle-men, and also because the German artillery fire inflicted heavy casualties on any exposed troops.[79] It was therefore essential in the defence to pay the greatest attention to concealment and, above all, to seek positions on the reverse slopes of hills or folds in the ground. Trenches on forward slopes might give good command and long fields of fire, but they were exposed to the destructive fire of the German heavy howitzers, but even when out of sight of the German ground observation posts guns and infantry had to conceal themselves carefully from a new menace. On the Aisne they encountered artillery fire directed from the air. (At the same time the Royal Flying Corps began experiments in this vital technique, as will be described in the next chapter.)

The attempt to mount a counter-offensive on the Aisne and the fluid offensive operations in Artois exposed the inability of the British Army to combine artillery support with the infantry advance in a systematic way. In short, it had to learn how to make a pre-arranged fire-plan based on intelligence of the enemy dispositions co-ordinated with the infantry plan. This was to prove a hard nut to crack; indeed, the artillery commanders had found more problems than answers, although it is only just to say they suffered few surprises.

Modern artillery tactics depended above all other considerations on good communications between guns, commanders and observers, and here there was a serious weakness. At Le Cateau, the lack of phones and cable made Brigadier-General Headlam, the CRA of 5th Division, place sections of guns in battalion areas and the remainder in advanced positions. They gave good support but thirty-eight guns were overrun and lost by II Corps in the battle, mainly from his division. The gallantry of the 11th, 37th, 52nd, 80th and 122nd batteries, to mention some of those which extracted guns under fire, earned the admiration of the infantry. But such dramatic methods could not become the rule, for men, horses and the guns so lost could not easily be replaced. 3rd Division used the alternative of deploying guns in concealed positions from which the enemy could not be seen but many of them did not fire for lack of orders to engage observed targets. A solution was to provide more telephones and more forward observers, as Lieutenant-Colonel Furse had recommended in 1911.

The Aisne found the British field guns short of range. The infantry had dug in on the steep slopes of the valley beyond the river and the guns could barely reach them from the near side. Positions beyond the river were cramped, under machine-gun fire and technically unsuitable. Some obsolescent 6-inch siege howitzers arrived during the battle but their range was only 5,200 yards when mounted on their field travelling carriages as compared with 7,000 yards for a 4.5-inch howitzer. (During static operations they could be remounted on a fixed siege carriage which permitted a higher elevation of 7,000 yards.) Only the four 60-pounders in each division could reach the enemy's 150-mm howitzers. An apparently inexhaustible supply of artillery ammunition for all calibres, particularly the 150-mm 'Jack Johnsons' and the 210-mm howitzers, gave the Germans the upper hand which they held throughout 1915. The lack of artillery in the British Corps to match the German heavy howitzers and of a significant reserve of modern artillery under Army control, was sorely felt.

In Artois, a close countryside dotted with villages, II Corps was forced to deploy field gun sections with the infantry and to use them over open sights against houses. The lack of an HE shell for the 18-pounder was then felt, and the 4.5-inch howitzer, already in demand because of its HE, was over-extended.[80]

Such were the bare bones of the Army's appreciation of its experiences in those desperate months, but there was one other factor which made a profound and long lasting lesson on the general into whose hands the fortunes of the British armies in France were to be committed. Until October Haig's I Corps had not been engaged in a decisive battle.

It was to have its chance alongside the French when the new Chief of the German Great General Staff, Erich von Falkenhayn, found Haig's divisions blocking his attempt to drive across Flanders to the Channel and to finish the war in the West before the winter. Ypres was a profound experience for Haig. It was the first and last occasion when he was able to affect the outcome of a great battle by his physical intervention in the fire zone. He never forgot how his stubborn corps saved the day, nor did the impression fade from his mind that the Germans lost their chance by giving up too soon when the British were almost beaten. The famous counter-attack at Gheluvelt of a single battalion, the 2nd Worcestershires, had an effect out of all proportion to its size, for it gave the Germans the impression that the British were still strong. During the fighting Haig experienced and saw the effect of modern heavy howitzers, lost one divisional commander and most of the staffs of the 1st and 2nd Division from a single shell, and by his example undoubtedly steadied those weakened divisions. He learned the importance of depth in defence and the lunacy of siting defences on open forward slopes. He became, like everyone else, eager for more machine-guns, heavier artillery and more shells. But above all else, the battle confirmed his pre-war beliefs that the victor was the one who 'stuck it out'.

The winter months were miserable. Old soldiers, misfits originally left behind in England and very young men, arrived as replacements; many were incapable of standing up to the discomfort and boredom of the winter in the trenches. The enemy threw ten shells for every British one and had devices, from illuminating flares and periscopes to trench mortars and superior grenades, that eased his life and made that of the British hellish. Few soldiers realised how long it took to develop, design, and manufacture the weapons they needed, like mortars and grenades, that were effective, safe and easy to use. Moreover, the weakness of the chemical industry, the narrowness of the armament base and the bottlenecks that were impeding the production of high explosive for shells and the fuses that would make them detonate efficiently, were still to be revealed, but the sheer quantity of material that had been expended already and would be required in the future, and the casualties suffered that would have to be replaced amounted to daunting figures. Despite the returning flow of wounded and some Territorial Force battalions that arrived during the winter, it was clear that the Regular Army Reserve had been exhausted before the Territorial Force was ready for war. Consequently, until the warmth of spring dried the trenches and cheered the men and fresh divisions brought new hope to British commanders there was a serious decline in the morale of the Old Army.[81]

The events of 1915 and 1916 that followed were dominated by brute facts that no commander could ignore. Once the first German rush had been stemmed the French tried to evict the invader, cost what it might, before superior German manpower had its effect. The British had to play their part in the French offensives although they were not properly equipped; they could not stand on the defensive while their allies bled to death. Consequently, until enough guns and ammunition reached the men in the trenches, the British had to fight in support of the French and at the behest of French commanders rather than their own. Haig played the required supporting role much more convincingly than Sir John French, who was half-hearted about sending men to attack prepared defences without sufficient fire support or reserves. Unlike Haig he was unable to dissemble and his doubts were communicated to the rest of the Army.

Haig had foreseen the necessity of a great battle of attrition before the war. He had reduced its complex issues to simple terms. Namely, the maintenance of the morale of his soldiers, the provision of adequate means with which to fight a series of dour battles, and, above all, the master principle of war that victory could only be obtained by offensive action. Finally he believed deeply that everything depended on his will as the commander. His ability to simplify complex matters has been shared by other commanders, Bernard Montgomery for instance, and Churchill recognised it as a source of great strength. But Churchill also pointed to a weakness that flowed from his undoubted power as a leader. For the way that he planned his battles was often faulty and his formidable personality did not make it easy for his subordinates to correct his mistakes. Haig's failures here adversely affected the application of fire-power during the struggle from Neuve Chapelle to Saint Quentin in 1918.

His plans showed that Haig did not understand the *tactical* difference between a break-through battle and the series of battles of attrition in which he engaged by choice or necessity. All battles are battles of attrition in the sense that attrition means the systematic destruction of the opposing force without necessarily making spatial gain. The *modus operandi* is the orchestration of fire-power. By its means limited objectives may be gained and the defender destroyed when he attempts to regain vital ground. Ground is important only if it enables the killing business to be more efficient. To quote a distasteful and unfortunately discredited phrase, the body-count is what matters. Sir Henry Rawlinson, commander of the Fourth Army, laid his finger on the weakness of British grand tactics when he remarked that Haig never fought such a battle of attrition. Sir Neil Malcolm, chief of staff to Sir Hubert Gough, Fifth Army commander, made a similar point when he said that GHQ could not understand the difference between a plan for a breakthrough and one designed to destroy the enemy *in situ* by a series of limited battles. Gough, a most loyal officer, remarked that Haig usually set himself an object beyond his means. Finally, Sir Frederick Maurice, Sir John French's chief planner, emphasised that attrition battles ought to be located where the ground suited the attacker. Breakthrough battles, on the other hand, were mounted on the front of a worthwhile strategic objective. In the siege conditions of the Western Front both types of battle should not be attempted at the same time and in the same place. Haig did so repeatedly.[82]

Sir James Edmonds referred to the Western Front as a protracted siege operation, a form of war which neither Haig nor his staff understood. He meant that in sieges artillery and engineers ought to be dominant. Yet GHQ did not obtain full value from its artillery because it did not plan its battles around it nor exploit its innovations until the Third Army's first great tank battle at Cambrai in November 1917. Haig, a cavalryman, may not have understood artillery techniques but he had successive advisers, H. S. Horne, F. D. V. Wing, H. F. Mercer, John Headlam and Noel Birch, who were all good artillerymen. Surely he took their advice? The answer is that he told them what he wanted. In essence, this was to silence or suppress the fire of the German artillery, breach the ever-deepening belts of wire protecting the German trenches on the sector chosen for attack, and to suppress or silence the machine-gun and rifle fire threatening the assault troops. He did not allow even Noel Birch, who was with him from June 1916 until the end of the war, an equal part with himself and the General Staff in making his plans. The infantry and, later, the tanks were in a worse state. They had no special staffs at GHQ at all, for the General Staff regarded all battles as infantry battles in which all general staff officers were expected to be proficient. Infantry work was not regarded as 'technical'.

In the chapters on the First World War, we shall show that
Haig and his staff did not encourage the use of correct siege
techniques by the artillery and the other arms. Fortunately the
science of gunnery had its own momentum and the artillery staffs
directed it effectively, even if without general staff guidance. An
explanation for the failure of GHQ in this respect is that from
1906 until 1911 Haig had virtually been the creator of the
General Staff system, with Launcelot Kiggell his willing aid.
With the latter as his chief of general staff from 1916 to early
1918, it was inevitable that the system that they had both created
would cast a long shadow. And it did overshadow the relationship not only of artillery commanders with staff officers but
Haig's relationship with his subordinates. Haig insisted that the
commander at each level was entirely responsible for making
tactical plans within the framework of his own general scheme.
In no circumstances could the artillery commander at Army
headquarters issue orders to corps or divisional units. They were
to take orders only from their respective corps or divisional
artillery commanders. Commonality of method was consequently
difficult to achieve. The channel of communication between
GHQ and the Armies that it directed was further impeded by
Haig's tendency to be inarticulate in describing his plans and to
overawe not only his subordinate commanders by brusqueness
but also his own staff. Free exchanges of ideas between Haig and
his commanders about the aims and methods of his battles were
unheard of, and with Launcelot Kiggell as his chief of general
staff he was denied the kind of interpreter and intermediary that
he needed so desperately.

Haig's tactical conceptions were adversely affected by his
belief that responsiblity for what he considered technical matters
ought to be separated from those that were purely tactical.
Unlike Sir John Monash who described a battle as an
engineering matter, assembling materials on site, Haig never
regarded battle as the application of techniques. Consequently
he never shaped his plans to obtain the best results from his
weapons; rather he expected his weapons to adapt to his plans,
and simple though he made war seem when he quoted
principles, he was often guilty of pursuing objects that were
technically and logically incompatible. This was the opinion of
the foremost of those with whom he had to deal in the great
battles on the Western Front. The first of these battles was at
Neuve Chapelle in March, 1915.

In the expansion of the Old Army that took place in the
winter, Haig took command of the new First Army and Smith-
Dorrien of the Second. Both men believed that the only

operations that should be undertaken were tactical ones to improve the generally inferior positions they retained at the end of the autumn fighting. But when French was asked to mount a supporting attack by Joffre, he agreed, and chose Neuve Chapelle, one of the places where the line needed to be improved. Later the French operation was cancelled but Sir John French decided to attack alone. He was sensitive to his ally's suggestions that the British were neither serious nor competent and wished to prove their fears groundless. He also believed that a successful battle would restore the confidence of his own army. The arrival of the 8th Division, made up of regular battalions from overseas, the restored 7th Division, veterans of Haig's Ypres battle, and the Indian Corps which had fought since the autumn, gave him the men.[83] Haig's First Army was to conduct the battle and Sir Henry Rawlinson's IV Corps, containing the 7th and 8th Divisions, was to play the main rôle.[84]

The battle of Neuve Chapelle was the first serious attempt by the British to break the German trench system. It was innovative and became a model for future trench attacks. Detailed trench maps from air photographs, an experimental network of telephone communications as far forward as battalion head-quarters, and wire-cutting by 18-pounders using shrapnel were three novelties. The guns were registered surreptitiously and moved into position at night. Such a concentration of artillery fire on a narrow front was not surpassed even in 1917 and a short, intense preparatory bombardment was not attempted again until the end of that year. Sound though the technical planning may have been, the aim of the plan itself was confused, and in this it set an unhappy precedent.

The confusion stemmed from the belief, reasonable enough at this early stage before the Western Front was understood to be a siege operation, that the plan required a strategic as well as a tactical aim. In this and all the later battles until 1918, the tactical planning was handicapped by the grandiose and conflicting strategic ideas of their setting. At Neuve Chapelle, the original tactical idea was to take the important Aubers Ridge behind the German line, from which the British positions were being observed. But even after the French offensive was cancelled, the British aimed to force the Germans to retreat from their line opposite the French on the right by threatening the main road between Lille and La Bassée. Cavalry was to be released to scour the German rear areas. Haig's ambitious idea was recorded in his diary after talking to Rawlinson on 2 March:

Our objective was not merely the capture of Neuve Chapelle.
Our existing line was just as satisfactory for us as if we were in
Neuve Chapelle. I aimed at getting to the line . . . of the La
Bassée road to Lille and thus cut off the enemy's front. It seemed
to be desirable to make our plan in the chance of surprising the
enemy and with the definite objective of advancing rapidly (and
without any check) in the hope of starting a *general advance*. The
scheme of the 8th and that sent in by General Capper of 7th
Division seemed to indicate a very limited objective. . .[85]

Rawlinson had wanted to take the village on the first day and
then start a second fire-plan and a second advance to take the
Aubers Ridge on the next. A compromise had reserve brigades
leap-frogging through the leading ones to continue the advance
as soon after the capture of Neuve Chapelle as possible. Haig,
on the other hand, had wanted the supporting battalions of the
leading brigades to go straight through to the Ridge. The length

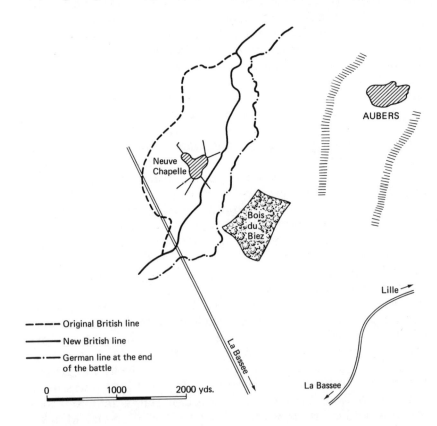

3. *The battle of Neuve Chapelle, March 1915. Opposing lines at the close of
    the battle.*

of the bombardment, too, had been a compromise. Haig had wanted a very short one of about ten minutes: Brigadier-General A. C. A. Holland, CRA of 8th Division acting as artillery commander, had calculated that he needed 2½ hours.[86] Rawlinson proposed a bombardment lasting thirty-five minutes. In truth, no one quite knew how long the bombardment should last for no one knew how accurately the shells would fall, and the purpose of the bombardment, whether to destroy or neutralise the enemy, had not been decided.

When the battle ended the front was just beyond the village. The bombardment for Rawlinson's left brigade was ineffective and the two leading battalions, the Scottish Rifles and the Middlesex, were slaughtered on uncut wire.[87] Afterwards there was a row between the principals about what had gone wrong. Rawlinson blamed his 8th Division commander, 'Joey' Davies, for slowness in leap-frogging his reserve brigade through and appeared to offer him as a sacrifice to an angry Haig by sacking him. In fact, Davies had carried out Rawlinson's orders and had probably saved needless casualties. But when French heard about Rawlinson's behaviour Haig had to step in to prevent French from sacking him in turn. Davies was saved, too, but Rawlinson was placed in an invidious position and beholden to Haig.

Afterwards Rawlinson commented in his diary:

> . . . Douglas Haig was disappointed in this, but I think he looked for too much – he expects to get the cavalry through with the next push but I very much doubt if he will succeed in doing more than lose a large number of gallant men without affecting any very great purpose. I should be content with capturing another piece out of the enemy's line of trenches and waiting for the counter attack. . .[88]

He believed before the battle, and he continued to hold the same view into 1917, that until plenty of reserves and artillery had been accumulated, attacks against the Germans should be deliberate and tactical. The balance in casualties would be favourable only when the Germans were forced to counter-attack at a disadvantage. Haig, on the other hand, convinced himself that a great opportunity had been missed at Neuve Chapelle because Rawlinson had not pushed through his reserves to the Aubers Ridge due to over-caution. He continued to expect that the front would become fluid if only he could push the cavalry through. Rawlinson, an infantryman, remarked 'I am not a believer in the cavalry raid which even if it comes off will not effect very much.'

Fire-Power

Analyses of the battle were written at many levels. But a conclusion was hardly possible when Haig and Rawlinson disagreed fundamentally about what had happened. The short, sharp bombardment and the attempt to achieve surprise had been partially successful. But had the subsequent failure of the infantry to advance much beyond the village been due to their lack of determination, as Haig believed, to the evident failure of artillery support after the initial bombardment, or to the strength of the German machine-gun defences in the houses and copses behind their front system? The failure of the two men to resolve their differences on this occasion led to a tacit agreement

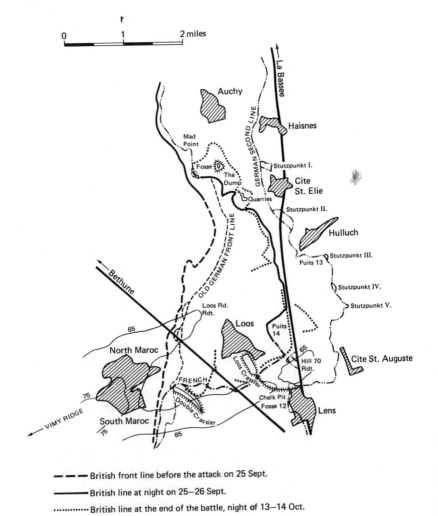

- - - British front line before the attack on 25 Sept.

⸺ British line at night on 25–26 Sept.

·············· British line at the end of the battle, night of 13–14 Oct.

4. *Loos, 1915. The stages of the battle.*

between them to differ. A climate of compromise and obscurity that touched every subsequent battle was created between their respective staffs.

In September 1915, after several unsuccessful but more costly battles than Neuve Chapelle, the British fought the major battle of Loos in conjunction with French attacks on Vimy Ridge and in Champagne. The Germans had built deeper and more complex defences after Neuve Chapelle, and, lacking sufficient heavy howitzers to destroy them in a short, intense bombardment, the British and French had adopted long, methodical ones. At Loos, the pre-bombardment was to last four days. Attacks on narrow fronts had been vulnerable to artillery fire from the flanks, so the frontage at Loos was much wider than at Neuve Chapelle. But much of the British artillery was obsolescent, for the Territorial and New Army divisions that had arrived in France were not yet equipped with the weapons that the Expeditionary Force had had in 1914. There was a severe shortage of heavy calibres, with which the French were already better supplied. Artillery ammunition was unreliable and the standard of shooting of the new divisions unsatisfactory. To compensate for the inadequacy of the bombardment, and rather than narrow the frontage, gas was used by the British for the first time.[89]

If the artillery prospect at Loos was gloomy, no one, from the Commander-in-Chief downwards, liked the ground. The French chose it so that the British attack would supplement their own on Vimy Ridge which overlooked the Douai plain and the sprawl of industrial villages around Lens, one of which was Loos. It was open country, dotted with defended slag heaps and chalk quarries, and the Germans, who had the better observation, were likely to slaughter the British unless they were caught by surprise.

But what was the selected method of achieving the object of the battle, to help the French on Vimy? There could be only two choices. Either, to seize some important positions that gave good observation over the route of German counter-attacks and inflict heavy losses on them; or to achieve a surprise breakthrough so as to destabilise the front and loosen the German hold on Vimy. Rawlinson, who commanded the right of Haig's two corps, confided to his diary that Sir John French's heart was not in the attack and that his pretence to the French that he was serious was dishonest. Haig on the other hand, going boldly for the second possible choice, told his leading divisions to press forward, regardless of loss or progress on their flanks, while the Germans were still shocked from the bombardment. He was determined not to lose a second chance by slowness in committing his reserve, which was to be XI Corps. According to Rawlinson, XI Corps was to move forward behind the leading I Corps of Lieutenant-General Hubert Gough and his own IV Corps, and 'force through by sheer weight of numbers'.[90] This information did not appear in the orders of Rawlinson's leading division, the 15th (Scottish). And although Haig's First Army staff understood that GHQ would put XI Corps under Haig's command at the start of the battle, neither First Army nor GHQ made precise arrangements to receive them or to expedite their march into battle.

Haig's plan depended on surprise, but neither the weight nor the duration of the bombardment could ensure it. The surprise factors were the gas and, depending on its effect, a rapid advance. But cloud gas released from cylinders was a fickle ally for its effectiveness depended on the strength and direction of the wind at the precise moment that the attack was launched. The administrative arrangements for handling the gas, shared by scientists, Sappers and staff officers who quarrelled, and local commanders who were both sceptical and frightened about the effect of the gas, were anything but smooth. Besides, the Germans were well informed and took precautions against a gas attack. When it was released the wind was light and variable, and its direction was almost parallel to the front in places. Some attacking troops were gassed, not only because they ran into the gas but because the gas drifted into salients in their trenches. Its effect on the enemy varied from negligible to considerable.

Despite only partial early success, IV Corps having taken Loos and Hill 70, while Gough's I Corps was making little progress so that the left flank of IV Corps was open to the enemy, Haig decided to commit XI Corps. But its divisions arrived late. They had been delayed at railway level crossings, were unfed, without maps and quite unprepared for their role in the battle. Advancing, too late, under the impression that a breakthrough had been achieved, they walked into heavy fire, became confused and were routed.

The fighting at Loos continued into October. It cost 50,000 casualties and brought the total for the year to 280,000. (The ratio of killed to wounded was usually 1 in 3 or 4, but higher among officers. Between 60 per cent and 70 per cent of the wounded were able to return to the fight from hospital or a dressing station.) The OH remarked that 15,000 men were killed or were never heard of again. 'Such was the tremendous sacrifice made by all ranks to support fully and loyally our French Ally and the price paid in flesh and blood for unpreparedness for war.' Quite so. But the official archives are full of angry correspondence about the destruction of the two New Army divisions of XI Corps, the 21st and 24th. Controversy about it started almost at once between French and Haig.[91]

From within IV Corps, Rawlinson's artillery commander, Brigadier-General C. E. D. Budworth (Budworth was to become Major-General Royal Artillery to Sir Henry Rawlinson at Fourth Army in June 1916) pointed out that the inadequacy of the artillery preparation had been the reason for the initial failure. Gas was not a substitute for adequate numbers of heavy howitzers and modern field guns. In future, either they should prepare their attacks with hurricane bombardments from guns firing at very high rates, or not attempt a breakthrough until there were enough guns and ammunition to destroy the enemy defences. As hurricane bombardments were not practicable at the present stage of training and because the ammunition being supplied was defective, the latter was the sensible course to follow. Dud shells, it should be noted, littered the Loos battlefield.

Before the end of the year French was replaced by Haig as commander in chief, largely because he had failed at Loos.[92]

Rawlinson was promoted to command the new Fourth Army

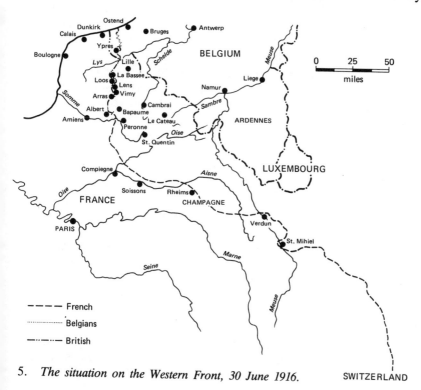

5. *The situation on the Western Front, 30 June 1916.*

in March 1916 and was ordered by Haig to prepare for the great battle on the Somme. It was a limited battle that he wished to fight. On 30 and 31 March, he spoke to Kitchener about the aims and methods of the coming battle. Kitchener said that he preferred small offensives with the sole aim of inflicting casualties. Offensives *au fond* should be avoided since the casualties to men and even material could not easily be replaced. But Douglas Haig had set his heart on a large offensive, apparently, as had the French. Of course, Rawlinson agreed with Kitchener and wrote: 'I shall have to have it out with DH perhaps tomorrow after the Army Commander's Conference.' But he was unsuccessful, for Haig retained his idea of breaking the line and having a gamble on 'rushing the third line on top of a panic'. It was to be the idea of Neuve Chapelle and Loos all over again.

The Somme battlefield was chosen because it was at the junction point of the two armies, where they could attack side by side. However, the facilities for a great battle, a good road and railway system and abundant water, were absent. Furthermore, although the German positions were in a salient they were exceedingly strong, having been developed, unhindered, since 1914. A breakthrough was the original intention. But the German offensive at Verdun, which started in February 1916, had forced the French to reduce their contribution to the Somme plan by the spring. And when the battle started, on 1 July, the primary aim of the French had been modified to that of forcing the Germans to terminate their offensive at Verdun by embroiling them in a wearing battle with the British.

Haig's plan to break through the front had included the use of the new tanks. But they were still not ready in June. He had also assumed that the French would take the leading part. That too was no longer the case. He received no clear approval for an offensive *au fond* from Kitchener, the assumption in London being that he would conform to French wishes which were believed to be to force the Germans to desist at Verdun. The French tactical aim on the Somme was to cross the river south of the British front while the British attacked the right flank of the Germans facing them there. The front would be destabilised and the Germans would withdraw troops from Verdun to re-establish it.

This was the minimum that the French expected from the battle, however. General Ferdinand Foch, who commanded the northern group of armies responsible for the Somme, planned to fight a series of limited battles, using huge artillery concentrations, until he had eaten through the German lines and destroyed their reserves. He would then break through. Except for minor differences over detail and the major differences that Rawlinson did not believe that a breakthrough was practicable, Foch and Rawlinson both regarded the Somme as a siege operation. Haig, on the other hand, intended that there should be a rapid advance. He argued that a series of battles would give the Germans time to build up their defences and, cumulatively, to inflict heavier casualties. Furthermore, he was mindful of the coolness in London to offensives that continued *sine die* and for which unforeseeable casualty bills would be submitted. It was better to aim for quick results.

The planners at Fourth Army and its corps were affected not only by these differences of opinion about the aim of the plan and the method of its execution but also by the procedure for making it which lent itself to further confusion. Rawlinson received a general directive which lacked the all important element, a frank unfolding of the idea behind it. The gap was not bridged by talks between Haig and Rawlinson. They took place but they were about details, never fundamentals. Neither man was at ease with the other. Rawlinson stalked Haig with the respect of a man in the Rockies hunting an unpredictable bear. Haig was wary of Rawlinson because he was afraid of being worsted by him in an argument, for Rawlinson had sharper wits than he, and was articulate, sociable and political. In contrast, Haig's contribution to conferences has been described as a series of grunts, gestures and bold assertions. Concerned, in his first battle as Commander-in-Chief, to retain control of the plan he did not commit himself to anything unless he could foresee the implications of it. Virtually, he never let Rawlinson off the leash. For his part, Rawlinson had no desire to be 'misunderstood' as at Neuve Chapelle. So he followed Haig's directions as best he could, even if they were, in his opinion, misguided. But the advice of his staff and his own knowledge of the technical and tactical details compelled him to challenge GHQ on some matters.

Rawlinson took the advice of Major-General Noel Birch, his artillery adviser until Birch went to GHQ and was replaced by Budworth. He wanted a long, systematic bombardment to destroy the front defence zone as he could not achieve the effect with a short, hurricane bombardment from his existing artillery. There would be a second fire plan, a few days later, to support an attack on the second German defence system. The German defences were strongly built, particularly in the villages of the front system. They were well supplied with mined dug-outs and reinforced cellars and only concentrated, heavy gun fire would demolish them. In contrast, Haig wanted a shorter hurricane bombardment to suit his plan to rupture the front on the left at Thiepval and to overrun the first and second German defence systems in one attack before rolling up the enemy from left to right. His success depended on taking the Germans by surprise, an impracticable idea, and on spreading the initial bombardment over two systems which rendered it inadequate everywhere. Furthermore, neither sufficient concentration of men nor the artillery to support them could be accommodated on the ground opposite Thiepval. This fundamental disagreement between Rawlinson and Haig was not resolved by Birch when he arrived at GHQ.[93] Even Birch, a man reputed to be 'two metres tall', could not prevail. Nor was that surprising for Haig was not in the habit of informing an opponent, in so many words, that he conceded a point. Rather than that he would appropriate his opponent's position as his own. However, that was not his intention on this occasion.

In the weeks before the assault on 1 July 1916 Haig visited all his divisions as was his duty and right. But his procedure fostered an idea that his conception of the battle and Rawlinson's were compatible, which was not so. He passed on his comments about the divisions that he visited when they matched his own ideas of the battle. He did not pursue to an issue some of the vital and disturbing insights that he gained from his visits. These were that the quality of the infantry's patrolling was uneven, that some divisions were aware that the pre-battle bombardment was not being effective in destroying the resistance of the enemy to fighting patrols, that some divisional commanders were concerned about the problem of crossing No Man's Land despite the bombardment and, lastly, that the wide variation in the artillery plans for the actual assault directly reflected the degree of enlightenment of the several divisional commanders on these questions. Rawlinson, for his part, did not enforce a uniform artillery plan and he allowed each corps and division to take a different tack over the crossing of No Man's Land. In short, there was widespread doubt about who was supposed to be master in the house.

The unresolved disagreement about the bombardment resulted in a bad compromise which, in turn, reflected the fact that the infantry plan was neither fish nor fowl. Troops were spread across the front as though for a break-in to the first system only. The deployment was similar to that designed for a river crossing. The artillery effort was spread across the front and in depth, too, being less than effective anywhere. Yet the main thrust was intended to be on the left at Thiepval where no special reserves were positioned to ensure or exploit a success.

Some divisions planned a rapid advance with little hard fighting; others prepared to fight their way through the first German defence system. XIII Corps on the right flank and XV Corps next to them were two corps that treated the German defences seriously. They were the only corps to achieve success. The former reached all its objectives on 1 July.

Out of the disaster of 1 July came the creeping barrage, for it was observed to have contributed to the success of the right wing on that day. Its origins are still debated, perhaps because it was a natural development from the linear concentrations of fire that had been placed on objectives before they were attacked from the beginning of trench fighting. Brigadier E. W. Alexander, Lieutenant-General H. S. Horne's senior artilleryman in XV Corps, wrote that he had used a form of it at Loos, not in close conjunction with advancing infantry but to sweep the area behind the German front. It has been suggested that the French used it first. That was not the opinion of soldiers familiar with

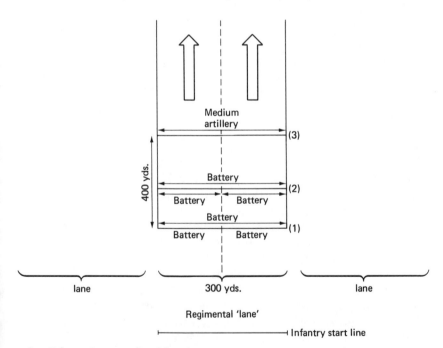

6. *Schematic example of barrage.*
    (1) Affiliated brigade spreads two batteries at twenty-yard gun interval, one battery spread across the whole lane – twenty-four guns.
    (2) Ditto.
    (3) Sixteen medium guns.
    The whole forms a belt of fire 400 yards deep, moving forwards in jumps of 100 yards every 3 minutes.

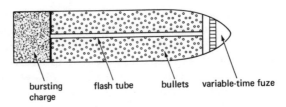

bursting   flash tube   bullets   variable-time fuze
charge

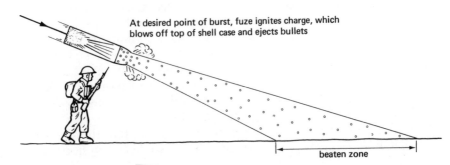

At desired point of burst, fuze ignites charge, which
blows off top of shell case and ejects bullets

beaten zone

7. *Shrapnel relied for its effect on the high velocity of a swarm of bullets
    released at a precise point on the trajectory by the action of a time fuze and
    a small bursting charge. At short ranges and when controlled by observed
    fire it was deadly, but both accuracy and efficiency fell off rapidly as the
    range lengthened. One great advantage as compared with high explosive
    was that the assaulting infantry could move close behind it, as the whole
    effect was forward. Also, as it burst in the air, its effect was not absorbed
    by mud.*

French artillery, nor is it likely considering the distaste of French
field gunners for calculation and the evident admiration of their
infantry for the precision of British artillery, even in late 1914.
The 'creeper' was a barrier of fire, normally of shrapnel, that
rolled forward less than a hundred yards in front of the infantry
as they advanced through the enemy defences at the slow pace
of one hundred yards in three to five minutes. In contrast, the
typical barrage on 1 July fell only on the infantry's successive
objectives. It moved from objective to objective by jumps of five
hundred yards or more and reflected the idea that the advance
would be rapid. It did not protect the infantry in No Man's
Land, let alone in the zones between the German trenches. On 1
July it soon left the infantry far behind.
    Anticipating the problem of protecting his infantry as they
crossed No Man's Land, Major-General Ivor Maxse,
commanding the 18th Division in XIII Corps, asked for a
creeping barrage starting in front of his own trenches. He was
refused; it would be unsafe and, besides, the divisions on his
flanks might be delayed by it. Instead his assaulting troops lay

out in No Man's Land close to the first objective so that they could jump the enemy before he could man his weapons when the barrage lifted. Thereafter he was allowed his creeping barrage to take his infantry through to their next objectives. The 7th Division in XV Corps used a variation of the creeper as well. Although 18th Division suffered about 30 per cent casualties it reached all its objectives and the barrage was recognised as a factor in its success. What was not understood so clearly was that the creeper marked the beginning of the return to emphasising covering fire, designed to neutralise enemy fire until the infantry could close with him, rather than artillery preparation intended to destroy the enemy.

By 14 July, when Rawlinson launched his second attack, the creeping barrage had been accepted as part of the solution to the infantry's problem. By then, Haig's original plan for the left wing had been abandoned and it was the XIII and XV Corps on his right that Rawlinson used. To Haig's surprise, Rawlinson was successful. Unfortunately he was incapable of exploiting his success because of another weakness in Haig's original plan about which Rawlinson had objected. It concerned the control and location of the boundary between the British XIII Corps and the French XX Corps on its right. Haig's plan, and Foch's too, had envisaged the French left and British right as defensive flanks. The function of the French flank was to cover their own crossing of the Somme further south. Haig's original intention was that the British left should make the main thrust north of the river; it would hook round to the right in the second phase of the battle to assist the French on the Somme. The French operations north of the Somme required that they have more room for their XX Corps in a congested British salient round the village of Maricourt. From that village the Anglo-French attack would be eccentric, starting at the centre of a wheel and moving down the spokes, as it were.

Rawlinson disliked the arrangement at Maricourt particularly as the British and French infantry had to attack from the Maricourt Wood at the tip of the salient, at right angles. However, given the plans of Haig and Foch it was unavoidable. Moreover, the only satisfactory observation over the country on either side of the army boundary was from the French side of it, and Rawlinson envisaged the British having to operate without good observation. He also anticipated the French hanging back once they had established a flank guard for their Somme crossings and that when XIII Corps advanced its flank would be open. If the attack on Rawlinson's left were as successful as Haig envisaged, this might not matter. However, Rawlinson's even spacing of divisions across the front showed that he was sceptical of that possibility and he wanted to have the freedom to advance with his right, alongside the French, if that flank were more successful than the other. The Maricourt salient made that flank unsuitable as a main thrust line.

Instead of dealing with this important matter himself directly with Foch, an equivalent Army Group commander, Haig deputed Rawlinson to negotiate. But Rawlinson got nowhere with Foch, so he asked GHQ at least to make his agreement a

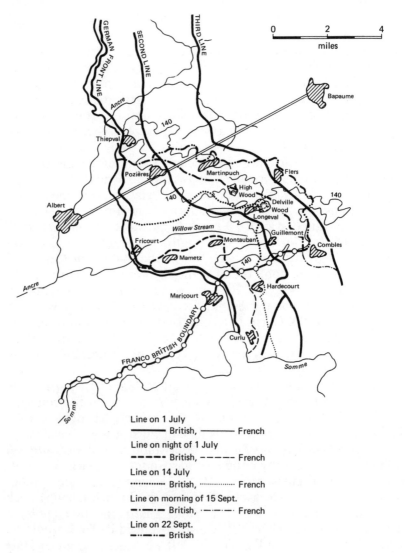

Line on 1 July
———— British, ———— French
Line on night of 1 July
— — — · British, — — — — French
Line on 14 July
············· British, ············· French
Line on morning of 15 Sept.
—·—·— British, —·—·— French
Line on 22 Sept.
—··—··— British

8. *The Somme, 1916.*

favour that the French should repay; the French did so by lending him some batteries of 75-mm field guns and heavy guns. On the first day of battle, on 1 July, the left failed and the right succeeded. A significant exploitation on the right was not immediately possible because neither the French XX nor the British XIII Corps were prepared for it. But, although the main operations took place on that flank for the next two months, Haig did not negotiate a transfer of boundaries to enable operations to be properly co-ordinated. Meanwhile, operations files were filled with acrimonious comments about the refusal of the French to synchronise their attacks with the British and thousands of lives were lost in both armies in July and August and early September around Guillemont as a result of the lack of co-operation between them.

In October, at a time when the French wanted to relinquish line in order to permit divisions to rest and train, Haig agreed to insert an extra British Corps in place of the French XX Corps. By then, deep mud and the exhaustion of British divisions made even Corps commanders outspoken about the need for a protracted period of rest and training. Reinforcements had to be absorbed and the lessons of the fighting to be analysed and distilled into new teaching in the schools. Nevertheless, the fighting continued into December. Joffre's equivocation at this stage must have been maddening, but Haig's extraordinary complaisance towards him made it appear that he was unaware that the army was being asked to do the impossible. He agreed with Joffre to recommence the battle on the Somme in February 1917, leaving barely two months to restore his divisions to health and strength before fighting on in winter conditions. Rawlinson, on the other hand, knew of the conditions of his men from daily contact with them. He and A. A. Montgomery, his chief of staff, were alert to the task of retraining that lay before them by October. But Rawlinson's political sense seems to have overborne his moral courage, for, like all Haig's commanders who survived, Rawlinson learned to handle his Chief with kid gloves and to appear loyal at all times. Outspoken criticism from his senior commanders was not well received by Haig.

The Joffre plan to attack in February on the Somme was cancelled when General Nivelle replaced him as Commander-in-Chief in December. Haig co-operated with the new man as willingly as with Joffre. Indeed he was always able to work with his French colleagues provided they, and not the politicians, determined the plan, and provided he could reach an acceptable compromise between their plans and his. These compromises were not easy to reach and Haig sometimes passed over their tactical implications for his army commanders' plans too lightly. That was the case in 1917.

Haig wanted to conduct a major offensive himself and he had selected the Ypres salient for it. The battle was to be a return match for 1914, and his staff had a series of plans for a third battle of Ypres in their files. In October 1916, the War Cabinet had expressed the opinion that the capture of the Flanders ports was most desirable and the Belgian coast as far as the Dutch frontier was to be the objective of Haig's 1917 campaign. The original Allied plan of operations for 1917 was for a renewed offensive on the Somme battlefield to be undertaken jointly by the French and British with the aim of wearing out the enemy. It was to begin in February and Joffre had agreed that Haig's proposed third battle of Ypres would be its sequel. When the Nivelle plan replaced that one, Haig had his Flanders campaign written into the new plan, too.

There is no need to enter into many details about the notorious and controversial battle of 3rd Ypres, commonly called Passchendaele. The historians concerned, G. C. Wynne and James Edmonds, as well as two of the participants Hubert Gough and John Davidson, the latter being Haig's planner at GHQ, quarrelled over successive drafts of the official account that was not published until 1948. There were gross errors in the eventual compromise version that later historians have repeated.[94] Suffice it to say, on that score, that Haig not only planned for a breakthrough, although every tactical argument was against it, but ignored the recommendations of Rawlinson and Plumer, the two army commanders deputed to direct operations, and then appointed Gough to replace Rawlinson. Minuted papers in the Public Record Office show that Haig did not understand the tactics that the ground enforced, in particular the difficulties in attacking the central part of the German front astride the Menin Road where tanks could not be used and where Rawlinson had commented bitterly that the old Maricourt salient had followed him to Ypres. Plumer pointed out several times that he could not find space to deploy guns for that attack until both Pilckem Ridge and Messines had been taken. When Gough discovered that truth for himself Plumer refused to co-operate by attacking alongside him and joining in what he considered a wrong-headed plan.

These details reveal that Haig, in the first battle of his own choosing, placed his commanders at a disadvantage by his plan. What is of moment here is that 3rd Ypres was the hardest fought battle in the whole history of the Royal Artillery, for whom it started on 12 June, a full seven weeks before the infantry

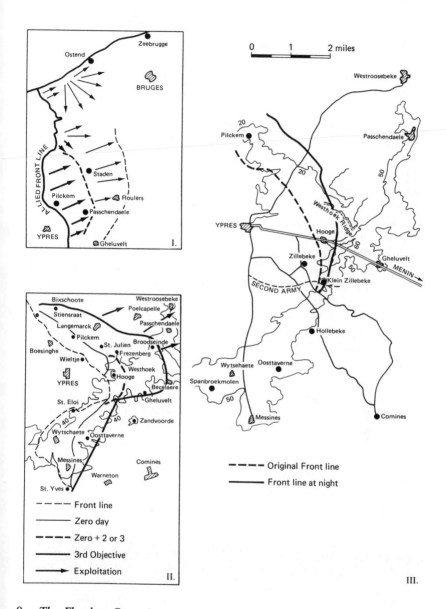

I.

Zeebrugge

Ostend

BRUGES

ALLIED FRONT LINE

Staden

Pilckem

Roulers

Passchendaele

YPRES

Gheluvelt

II.

Bixschoote

Westroosebeke

Stiensraat

Poelcapelle

Langemarck

Passchendaele

Pilckem

Broodseinde

St. Julien

Boesinghe

Frezenberg

Wieltje

Westhoek

Hooge

YPRES

Becelaere

St. Eloi

Gheluvelt

40   40

Zandvoorde

Wytschaete

Oosttaverne

Messines

Comines

Warneton

St. Yves

- - - - Front line

——— Zero day

- - - - Zero + 2 or 3

——— 3rd Objective

——→ Exploitation

III.

0   1   2 miles

Westroosebeke

20

Pilckem

Passchendaele

20

50

Westhoek Ridge

YPRES

Hooge

80

Gheluvelt

Zillebeke

50

MENIN

Klein Zillebeke

SECOND ARMY

Hollebeke

Wytsehaete

Oosttaverne

Spanbroekmolen

50

Messines

Comines

- - - - Original Front line

——— Front line at night

9. *The Flanders Campaign.*
    I. Sketch handed by Sir Douglas Haig to General Pétain, 18 May 1917
(Frontispiece *OH 1917* vol. II).
    II. Preferred plan of Generals Rawlinson and Plumer, February 1917.
    III. Progress of Fifth Army, 31 July 1917.

advanced on 31 July 1917. Its powerful, and equally courageous
opponent disposed of 1,556 pieces of artillery. Against them
H. C. C. Uniacke, a 'Master Gunner' in the old sense of the
title, could pit 2,868. Uniacke, the Major-General, Royal
Artillery to Gough in the Fifth Army, was a man who split no
hairs about the nice paradigms of staff duties; he may not have
been officially a commander, but he felt himself to be a General
Officer Commanding Royal Artillery, and he expected to be
obeyed because he knew what he was doing. Yet he was not
consulted before Gough made his plan, let alone when Haig and
GHQ evolved the outline that Gough received. Had he been
given the option, he would not have fought a battle under such
disadvantageous conditions. It was Uniacke's advice that had
prompted Rawlinson to emphasise the difficulty of deploying
guns within an overlooked salient and strung out in line. The
German heavy guns were hidden behind the ridge and concentrated. For forty-three days the British heavy artillery fought a
bitter duel with the German batteries, and obtained the upper
hand, at a price. On 25 July, Prince Rupprecht of Bavaria
reported that the German Artillery Group 'Wytschaete' had lost
50 per cent of its heavy guns, 30 per cent of its heavy howitzers,
17 per cent of its mortars and 10 per cent of its field guns. It was
by no means a one-sided battle. British casualties were severe.
In some brigades the surviving guns were grouped into a single
battery; others had to surrender all their guns to keep those in
the firing line up to strength.

Uniacke followed the artillery practice of other battles by
studying the lessons of each phase and applying the lessons in
the next. That was one advantage of having artillery staffs and
being a technical arm. Furthermore, despite the exhaustion of
the detachments, the gunners remained in action longer than the
infantry and as there were eight of them for every ten infantrymen, itself a remarkable feature of this battle, their methods
dominated it. However, although improvements were made, the
battle was by no means innovative. Creeping barrages, first used
on the Somme, and counter-battery programmes which came of
age at the battle of Arras in April 1917, were more effective and
complex than before. Some divisions, but unfortunately not all
of them, employed flexible fire-tactics in following barrages,
using fewer troops in the skirmishing waves. The colossal
punishment meted out by the British artillery led to a tactical
game of wits between the Germans, who varied the location
of counter-attack divisions, the timing and strength of
counter-attacks and the strength with which they held outpost
lines, and the British who varied the depth of their initial

objectives and the numbers employed in the first waves.

Terrible as the effect of the British artillery was, however, it was being exerted in what was already an obsolete manner. By the summer of 1917 technical advances due to initiatives by the artillery and engineers such as survey and better maps of the battlefield, air photography, the instrumental location of hostile batteries, and 'predicted' fire, which obviated preliminary registration of targets by shooting in each battery, had all been developed to the stage of full-scale practical application. Unfortunately they were not yet regarded as wholly reliable and were not exploited at the preliminary battles of Arras and Messines. There, as at 3rd Ypres itself, commanders remained addicted to long bombardments with heavy shells whose effect was largely to create a landscape of water-filled craters obstructing movement, as they had in the later stages of the Somme battles. Uniacke himself later stated that in his opinion a change to a policy of short, intense bombardments was necessary, but the circumstances of the Ypres salient made it imperative in the opinion of all the commanders concerned to ensure that the German batteries – whose observers overlooked the British assembly areas and battery positions – and their infantry strong points were silenced before the battle began. The British bombardment, in fact, had to cover the preparations for battle as well as the actual attack. Haig, therefore, by his choice of battlefield, had unquestionably placed his armies at a disadvantage, and at the moment when the new artillery methods combined with the use of tanks was to prove the key to the door of the German defences on the Western Front. This he had not grasped, and it was only made clear to him by the outcome of the local offensive at Cambrai, planned by the Third Army, which he agreed to allow to go ahead on 20 November, ten days after the miseries of Passchendaele had come to an end.

The battle of Cambrai, 20–28 November, was an afterthought or appendix to 3rd Ypres. It was originally conceived by Brigadier-General H. Elles and J. F. C. Fuller, his principal staff officer, as an alternative to Ypres where the ground was unsuitable for tanks. It is justly regarded as the climacteric battle in which the Tank Corps became an arm in its own right. In a broader sense it is the first truly modern battle.

Originally designed as a large scale raid with tanks alone and without infantry or an artillery bombardment that would have created mud-filled craters, it became an infantry and tank battle to break through the Hindenburg line and to seize new positions. But the tank was still an undeveloped weapon, prone to breakdown. Springless and poorly ventilated, it quickly exhausted its crew and it was vulnerable to enemy fire, particularly artillery fire. Fortunately, the CRA of the 9th (Scottish) Division, Brigadier-General H. H. Tudor, one of the leading artillery tacticians, proposed a fully predicted fire plan, without any preliminary bombardment or even a preliminary registration of targets. Even the counter-battery programme was to be predicted. The enemy batteries were not to be destroyed but their fire suppressed or neutralised.

Surprise was complete. The Hindenburg position on the front of Third Army was penetrated to a depth of six miles. Resistance virtually collapsed in some places before the tanks arrived, because of the shock of the accurate artillery fire. In others, 'tank panic' caused mass surrenders. But the Cambrai offensive foundered after a brilliant start. The German soldiers demonstrated their extraordinary ability to recover and to build up a firing line even after being routed. The breakdown of tanks, the exhaustion of the infantry after several days of fighting and a lack of reserves for exploitation showed that despite the new techniques and the tanks, the problem of how to maintain the momentum of the advance once it was inside the enemy defensive system remained unsolved. A new problem had also appeared for the tank in the shape of field guns in the anti-tank role. So while it was apparent that a formula had been found for achieving the break by a combination of tanks and the new artillery methods, the secret of maintaining the momentum of the attack and turning it into a breakthrough still eluded the British.

In the meantime the German tacticians, of whom the most prominent was von Lossberg, devised the antidote to their own defensive doctrine. The spearhead of their future offensives was to be their new élite infantry, the *sturmtruppen* and *sturmabteilungen*. (These honourable titles were appropriated later by the infamous bullies of the Nazi party.) The 'storm troops' operated as small battle groups carrying their own heavy weapons with them, and were trained in the tactics of infiltration. They aimed to bypass any obstinately held centre of resistance, which was left to the ordinary infantry and artillery to reduce by deliberate attack, and go for the enemy artillery and headquarters in the rear. It was still necessary, however, for the crust of the defensive system to be broken open, and the officer on the German side who devised the appropriate method was an artillery colonel, Georg Brüchmuller, nicknamed 'Durchbruch' Müller, or 'Breakthrough' Muller. His system was to assemble a vast mass of artillery with every precaution to ensure secrecy, to fire a preliminary bombardment lasting only about four hours, and using the methods of prediction cover the advance of the assaulting troops with concentrations of heavy artillery on every defended locality, together with a barrage, while the defending artillery areas were drenched with poison gas delivered by shells. It was this method of attack that broke through the recently reorganised and over-extended divisions of the British Fifth Army on 21 March 1918 and caused such consternation, but like any other formula it was not infallible. In any case, the British had already anticipated it. Brüchmuller was an exceptionally able officer, and the British official historians duly recognised his achievement, but it is unfortunately typical of their lack of understanding of the nature of the war that one can search in vain for equal recognition of the work of Birch, Holland, Budworth, Uniacke or Tudor, or that the methods that made Brüchmuller famous at Riga in 1918 had already been brilliantly demonstrated at Cambrai in November 1917.[95]

The Royal Artillery commanders have been criticised for not wholeheartedly embracing the new methods of fire control earlier, but their responsibility was an awful one. Some local attacks had been successfully launched in the ebb and flow of the Somme fighting after only the briefest of preliminary bombardment. This was feasible when the zone of combat was beyond the belt of wire entanglements and complex entrenchments with mined dug-outs, but when the stakes were large as at Arras, it was felt to be too much of a gamble to forgo the certainty of wire-cutting and to rely on prediction to silence the enemy artillery. The memories of the earliest reliance on short bombardments, at Neuve Chapelle, with men hanging on the wire, was still too strong. But the artillery had come a long way since 1914. Passchendaele may have been a bad battle, and Cambrai a great disappointment, but lessons were learned from both. The battles of 1917 had, at least, all been artillery victories, and by the end of the year the new technique of Cambrai held great promise. The 1917 battles had been monuments to the high professionalism of the British artillery arm. In each of them it had been a case of *Ubique* to the rescue.

CHAPTER 6

Ubique

*There's nothin' this side 'eaven or 'ell Ubique
does'nt mean!*[96]

UBIQUE is the motto of the Royal Artillery and the
Royal Engineers. It expresses the presence of guns and
gunners everywhere and the ubiquitous activities of the sapper in
response to technology. The prayer of the infantryman in South
Africa, 'The Guns! Thank Gawd, the Guns!', was echoed many
times before the last SOS was fired in November 1918. 'Modern
War is a piece of engineering, collecting materials at site,'
remarked General Monash, the Australian who was an engineer
and a successful corps commander. Certainly the fighting on the
Western Front was largely a siege operation in which engineers
played as important a role as the artillery. The Royal Flying
Corps sprang from the Air Battalion of the Royal Engineers,
wireless and other communications, survey and the associated
techniques described in this chapter were their responsibilities,
besides roads, railways, bridges and tunnelling. The jingle:

> All things bright and beautiful
> Gadgets great and small
> Bombs, grenades and duckboards
> The Sapper makes them all,

describes their role as maids of all work.

It became obvious in September 1914, on the Aisne, that
artillery superiority was decisive, and it was confirmed at Ypres
in October. By the New Year of 1915 the divisional units of the
Old Army were agreed that many more guns and shells would be
needed to re-open the front. Just how many of each was a
question that no one 'over there' could answer.

Fortunately, Lieutenant-General Sir Stanley von Donop,[97] the
Master-General of the Ordnance in London, was a step ahead of
Sir John French in assessing the requirement. A supporter of the

siege artillery during the rebuilding of the artillery it was thanks to him that a 9.2-inch heavy siege howitzer was ready for manufacture at the outbreak of war. He had already had the first of the six obsolescent 6-inch howitzer batteries sent to France, and it arrived during the battle on the Aisne. He was preparing to replace the obsolescent 15-pounders and 5-inch howitzers, with which the TF was equipped, with 18-pounders and 4.5-inch howitzers. 4.7-inch naval guns, used in South Africa, were to fill the place of 60-pounders until more of the latter had been built. He had been prepared for all this but he had not bargained for the simultaneous demand for equipment from eighteen New Army divisions which Lord Kitchener had raised even before Haig's I Corps fought its stubborn battle at Ypres.

In October, ten years too late, a cabinet committee met to advise von Donop on speeding up the production of weapons and ammunition. The MGO described[98] how two of its members congratulated him, after their first meeting with representatives from industry, on obtaining a large increase in guns for delivery by 1 July 1915. He replied that he would defer judgement until that date as only promises, not guns, had been received. He was right to be sceptical for only the Royal Ordnance Factories fulfilled the quotas. Of the sixteen 9.2-inch howitzers that he ordered not even the eight that Vickers had promised for 15 February 1915 were delivered. The firm explained its failure as due to 'workmen taking holidays from Christmas until after the New Year and since then to very bad time-keeping, which still continues'. In the War Office, the Director of Contracts, a civilian, was responsible for placing contracts with firms. In January, in order to avoid a complete breakdown, this official asked von Donop to take over his function.

Had von Donop's task been only to provide weapons that were already in production he could have handed it over to a committee of production engineers, managers and accountants. Fortunately for the British Army, he quickly realised that the family of weapons had to be extended to meet the conditions unfolding on the Western Front and set the wheels in motion to provide them. A new 6-inch howitzer was designed and appeared in the field in late 1916. An 8-inch howitzer was improvised by boring out and shortening an existing 6-inch gun, and the first battery went into the field in June 1915. His 9.2-inch howitzer, nicknamed 'Mother', went into battery service in May 1915. A completely fresh design for a 12-inch howitzer, an outstanding weapon, was started on its journey from specifications to final trials. The MGO's choice of howitzers rather than guns was a professional judgement made ahead of a later recommendation of the artillery staff at GHQ, in June 1916, which confirmed his decision. All these weapons had to be manufactured in great quantities and it was not until the middle of 1917 that there were considered to be enough. Even then the proportion of heavy guns to field calibres was too low, and lower than in the German and French armies.[99]

Of course, trained detachments organised in batteries and brigades, techniques, tactics and staff procedures, many of them quite new, had to be provided and devised. While these were not the direct responsibility of the MGO they were associated with demands on him for new equipment, modifications and replacements of faulty parts in old ones, and for research into the cause of rashes of dangerous premature shell bursts. Indeed his most vexed and complicated task was to provide sufficient ammunition for the expanding flood of guns, to exert control over its quality, to design new fuzes and explosives that were safe and effective, and new natures of ammunition such as gas and smoke shells. The supply was not satisfactory until the spring of 1917.

In 1915, ammunition was scarcer than guns. Haig sent guns out of the line at 1st Ypres rather than expose men needlessly when they had so few shells. In 1916 the quality of the ammunition and of the guns was unsatisfactory. That British industry could not meet the sudden demand for guns in 1915 was not so surprising as its inability to provide a good supply of ammunition. It was the ammunition shortage on which the politicians and press seized. The so-called shell crisis was one of the factors, although not the decisive one, that led to the formation of a coalition government to replace the Liberal government, in May 1915. In the shuffle, Lloyd George went to the Ministry of Munitions and began the political offensive that led him to 10 Downing Street at the end of 1916. During this period he contributed, by his rough-shod methods, to muddle and bad feeling, as well as a sense of urgency.

The stock of ammunition in 1914 was determined by the Mowatt scale which had been increased at the request of the MGO in 1913. It allowed 1,500 rounds for each of the 324 field guns and 1,200 for each howitzer in the Expeditionary Force. At the end of six months of war, by which time the TF was to be trained, there was to be an additional 500 rounds per gun and 400 rounds per howitzer. To support these scales 18-pounder production was only 10,000 rounds a month, or one round per gun per day, in August 1914. The rate had risen to about 128,000 per month by February 1915, but, owing to Kitchener's New Armies, the number of guns to be supplied had multiplied too.

In retrospect, these scales seem quite inadequate, if not with South African experience in mind, certainly after Manchuria. However, the Army budget did not allow either the production or storage and turnover of a larger reserve in peacetime. Nor had the Cabinet admitted that the TF would be engaged on the Continent, let alone that a huge new citizen army should be raised and sent overseas. In the circumstances of peace it seemed that the TF's old 5-inch howitzers and 15-pounders, for which enough ammunition was available, were adequate for Home Defence. Equally, the General Staff's calculation of the intensity of the fighting proved to be wrong. For it envisaged that although as many as 200 rounds might be expended in a day by a few guns not many would be engaged so heavily, and there would be lulls in the fighting. In the event, the French held stretches of the front, the Vosges for instance, where a gun was not heard to fire for days on end and laundry lines were tied to the muzzles. With a much larger pool of guns and ammunition it proved easier for them to accumulate reserves from production for their great battles in Champagne and at Verdun than for the British who held a generally more active front with a small army. However, it must be pointed out that the French also contrived to maintain quiet fronts in order to rest troops and accumulate munitions, a policy which, unwisely, the British despised.

The MGO was between two fires in 1915 over ammunition supply. GHQ changed its mind about what was required as it learned the job but complained when its demands were not immediately satisfied. The politicians, who had to be taught that a 'shell' was more than just a container for high explosive and could not be manufactured easily and instantly in large numbers, were unreasonably impatient too. The Press was no assistance. *The Times* of 19 May 1915 told its readers that 'men died in heaps because the field guns were short, and gravely short of explosive shells'. Of course, ammunition of all natures was scarce. And, in fact, an early call for field gun HE for engaging houses and woods gave way to demands for more shrapnel to cut barbed wire. Field gun HE was too light to have much effect against trenches, and, contrary to lay opinion, its shrapnel was actually a better man-killer against riflemen exposed on a fire-step. The need for a more effective HE shell for 6-inch and 4.5-inch howitzers and for more of them was desperate. Von Donop tried to explain to GHQ that HE was harder to produce than shrapnel but that foregoing the latter would not enable him to produce more of the former. Politicians were slow to learn that the bottlenecks in production were due to the difficulty in manufacturing fuzes and a satisfactory HE filling for the shell, and in overcoming the resistance of skilled workers to dilution of the workforce by bright, new workers. The Cabinet had permitted skilled men to join the New Armies, which made the labour problem acute. The visible result of national unpreparedness in the munitions industry and incompetence in the Ministry of Munitions was the 25 million unfilled and unfuzed shells in stock by August 1916.

Lloyd George tried to give the impression that his dynamism as Minister of Munition broke a dam of obstinacy at the War Office, so that the soldiers were given the flood of arms and weapons that they deserved. No doubt, he saw himself as the dynamiter. In fact, the technical problems over fuzes and shell fillings were not solved by his actions. The design of a new Fuze 100 removed an initial manufacturing difficulty in January 1915, but in November, when Kitchener was away in the Mediterranean, Lloyd George, as Minister of Munitions, seized responsibility for designs and inventions from the MGO and also removed his responsibility for trials. As a direct result of this step the investigation of prematures was disrupted and the Ministry of Munitions designed and had manufactured a faulty Fuze 101. The new fuze was intended to detonate the shell on impact, in contrast to Fuze 100 which, having a slight delay, made a crater. Not until the spring of 1917 was the safe instantaneous fuze 106 issued. The pre-war HE shell filling was picric acid, called Lyddite after the siege artillery ranges on Romney Marsh at Lydd. But it proved to be uneconomical to mass produce, apart from the unpleasant fact that one third of the nitric acid used in its manufacture came out of the factory chimney and poisoned the neighbourhood. In 1914 there was no government factory that made HE. TNT (Tri-nitro-toluene) was expensive and by itself it behaved unpredictably in shells. The most efficient filling was amatol, a mixture of TNT and ammonium nitrate. But very little ammonium nitrate was made in Britain before the war and most of what was needed came from Norway. Not only had a process for making ammonium nitrate cheaply to be found before a reliable source of HE was assured, but the correct proportions of the mixture determined. Both problems were solved by chemists and chemical engineers, not by politicians and bureaucrats.[100]

Naturally the men in the field were handicapped by the shortage of heavy guns and ammunition, by the lack of an instantaneous fuze, by periodical epidemics of prematures in 1915 and 1916 and by the high proportion of duds in those years. On the Somme 25 per cent of guns were out of action due to design faults, inferior materials and the relative incompetence of unit artificers and officers who had been civilians only a few months before. But although the awful physical conditions in the autumn of 1916 and 1917 on the Somme and at Passchendaele created special crises by exhausting detachments and horses and equipment, the artillery had overcome its initial handicaps and dominated the Germans in weight of shell and in technique by the middle of 1917. It had done it by unremitting toil, certainly, but also by superior command and staff procedures and superior application of available technology. Not the least of the factors was the close co-operation between the technical Arms, the Royal Artillery, the Royal Engineers and the newest recruit and offspring of the latter, the Royal Flying Corps. If the results on the ground fell short of success until August 1918 the causes may be sought in the performance and tactics of the infantry, and in the methods of the commanders and the General Staff, rather than in those of the artillery.

Edmonds often made the point that the Army was engaged in a protracted siege operation in which engineers and artillerymen ought to have been dominant; they should have made the breach and the infantry to have been consigned to enlarge and exploit it. Instead the commanders were inclined to engage in 'open warfare at the halt', as A. P. Wavell described it later, in which the infantry, assisted by the artillery, was expected to 'break through' in order to release a scourge of horsemen on the enemy. The artillery and engineers were simply aids to this murderous process. On the Somme the commanders were not agreed that they were engaged in a complex siege. Indeed, it was questionable, in Edmonds' opinion, whether Sir Douglas Haig ever recognised it. For, while it must be admitted that the techniques and materials for winning such a siege battle were not assembled until the summer of 1917, the engineers, artillerymen and flyers were ready to apply them then, whereas the General Staff and the commanders were still using old methods and techniques in which these arms were subordinates not principals.

The long struggle with the General Staff to ensure that the artillery was consulted before a plan was made, that all the artillery in a battle was controlled, initially, by a single commander who had the right to issue orders down the artillery chain of command, and that there should be an adequate establishment of artillery General Staff officers, is recorded in the papers of several senior artillery officers. In a sense, they had to continue the pre-war fight to have the CRA recognised as a commander with a proper staff. But the CRA had not been given the communications that he needed to command and control his guns in action and was more an adviser, even in 1914, than a commander. As corps artillery appeared, expanded both in numbers and functions – bombardment, counter-battery and harassing – the need to distinguish and to clarify the functions of artillery adviser, commander and staff officer, and to relate these functions to those of the General Staff and formation commanders became essential. The situation in which the engineers and artillery found themselves in 1914, when no commander above divisional level existed, and advisers, nicknamed Tweedledum and Tweedledee, rode around in the same car with neither staff nor communications, was obviously intolerable. Matters improved but the battle with the General Staff was never won.

The General Staff, quoting the Staff Manual, insisted that orders could only be issued through Army, Corps or Divisional Commanders. An artillery officer could only issue orders to the units that were directly under his command. Consequently, on the Somme, Major-General Budworth, Rawlinson's Major-General, Royal Artillery (MGRA), could not compel the Corps artillery to comply with his plan for 1 July 1916, and only XIII Corps actually did so, almost to the letter and with success. At Ypres, in 1917, Major-General H. C. C. Uniacke[101] was prevented from communicating directly with counter-battery groups, although only he had the information from the RFC upon which they were to act. By the time the General Staff had functioned, the weather had closed in and the targets were invisible from the air. He advised Rawlinson, when the latter made the first Ypres plan of 1917, that in a prolonged artillery duel in the Ypres salient the guns would fight at an appalling disadvantage, even with air superiority. Uniacke eventually fought there as Gough's MGRA. But despite the fact that for every 100 infantry there were eighty gunners, and of the importance of the artillery role at Ypres, his view carried little weight when the plan was made by GHQ and Fifth Army.[102]

It would be wrong to conclude that Haig and Birch, Rawlinson and Budworth and Gough and Uniacke, for examples, did not get on very well together. It would also be wrong to suggest that all Gunners thought alike. But the Staff system protected the autonomy of each level of command, consigned the senior artillery officer there to be an adviser rather than an executive and permitted a great deal of variation in the artillery methods that were used at each level. Some of it was not enlightened by science. Most senior artillery officers came from the Field or Horse branches which had been predominant in the Expeditionary Force divisions before the war, rather than from the Garrison Artillery which was mainly concerned with

Coast Defence, although it also handled siege artillery and the heavy guns. Field and Horse officers were usually promoted faster, had a better opportunity to join the general staff and were in a majority among regulars in the Expeditionary Force. Consequently, Garrison officers came to regard themselves as second class citizens and not really part of the field force. Their work in garrisons or as part-time siege Gunners was considered rather plodding, for the pen and the slide-rule were not thought mightier than the sword in war. Nor was the internal combustion engine, on which siege batteries largely relied, as worthy as the horse.

Nevertheless, the siege war required techniques with which Garrison rather than Field artillery officers were familiar, although they may not have been equally familiar with the senior officers and staffs of the Expeditionary Force, nor with tactical problems. Although Uniacke and Budworth, who were all-rounders, learned the intricacies of the heavy artillery game, it was generally believed that had there been more Garrison Gunners in the senior posts the tactical possibilities of the new gunnery would have been perceived sooner. For the techniques first used at Cambrai, in November 1917, might have been applied in April and certainly in June had Birch apprised himself of their possibilities and the MGsRA been of one mind and determination to persuade their commanders of their importance. But, then, the personalities of the Commander-in-Chief and his CGS, Lancelot Kiggell, did not encourage the creation of plans that combined, as opposed to harnessed, the techniques of the Arms.

What were these new artillery techniques? Their starting point and pivot was the Royal Flying Corps pilot.[103-4]

The British first used aircraft to find targets for the artillery on about 13 September 1914, on the Aisne. The aerial observer had two quite separate tasks. First he spotted the target on the ground and located it on a map. Then, he communicated this information to the guns, observed the 'fall of shot' when they fired and made observations about the relationship between it and the target. When the rounds were falling on the target he would periodically return to check that they had not drifted off it again and, if necessary, suggest a correction. Essentially, the observer was not directing the guns but advising them.[105] Fleeting targets, columns of men and guns firing, were the usual ones to be engaged. The latter were called hostile batteries and became the main concern of the pilots and of counter-battery staffs that were formed at corps headquarters.

The need for aircraft arose because parts of the German line, and the hostile batteries behind it, could be seen only from the air. Previously aircraft had been used experimentally on Salisbury Plain in 1912 and 1913 when observations of fire had been sent by smoke signals, wing flapping and simply by landing beside the guns with target data written down on a message pad. But the best means of communication was wireless. A two-way set had been mounted in an aircraft in 1913 but it had occupied the place of the observer and it had been found that piloting and observing was too much for one man. The French and Germans had made more progress along these lines but no British aircraft was equipped with even one-way wireless in 1914.

Two pioneers in the art of artillery observation were Captain B. T. James and Lieutenant D. S. Lewis. The former introduced the infantry clock method for relating fall of shot to the target which replaced the 'Bingo' system – 'under the Y in Vimy' – that was first used in January 1915. Lewis, a Sapper, had already devised a gridded reference system, using letters and numbers, so that a target could be pin-pointed to within a few yards. It was adopted by Major W. G. H. Salmond, then a staff officer at RFC HQ and a Gunner, who had a number of squared maps reproduced by the topographical section for I Corps at Ypres in October 1914. At Neuve Chapelle, Lewis' modified celluloid disc, with hour and distance circles on it, was used. Lined up with its XII to VI o'clock axis along the North-South grid line it enabled fire to be corrected even though the location of the battery was unknown.

From February 1915 a wireless flight was gradually incorporated into every squadron, although the two-way wireless used weighed about seventy-five pounds and still occupied the seat of the observer. Then the Sterling, a transmitter weighing twenty pounds with a range of eight to ten miles, was produced in the autumn of 1915. However, until the Somme, the idiosyncrasies of battery commanders and the want of artillery officers of the right calibre who could be spared for flying obstructed the standardisation of procedures. From the Somme onwards, any observer could communicate with any battery via a telephone exchange and rapidly engage any target that he could identify in pre-arranged zones of the front.

The standardisation of procedures was largely the work of the new counter-battery staffs located at Corps headquarters in 1916, to which RFC flights mainly worked. Their development will be described as we examine two other branches of the art, survey and photography on which the Corps staffs relied for data, which reached maturity in 1917.

Aerial photography had been tried from free and captive

balloons in the American Civil, the Franco-Prussian and the South African wars. The first efficient air camera, a Thornton-Pickard folding camera, arrived in France in February 1915. It was used to take a mosaic to a depth of 1,500 yards at Neuve Chapelle. The photography had to be done by hand over the side of the aircraft and required ten separate – very cold – operations. By the summer of 1915, the camera was being fixed to the aircraft and a semi-automatic plate changing device had been introduced. The photographs were obliques, but at greater heights verticals for map-making were being taken.

The air photographs were supplied to the infantry to show them where the enemy was digging and to enable them to mark in their own work on large scale trench maps. This information could otherwise be obtained only by night patrols and periscope observation. Trench raiders had to be briefed about every nook and cranny in the labyrinth facing them. However, photographs did not reveal whether trenches were occupied or not, and a bombardment was wasted at Neuve Chapelle on a flooded trench. Wire could not be easily identified either, particularly in the rear defences where it was usually overgrown with weeds.

Air photos became the principal intelligence tool of the counter-battery staffs, and furnished a link between the artillery staffs and the General Staffs. Daily coverage of the front and the continual comparison of the photographs taken on consecutive days were keys to their use. As the quality of the photographs improved, it became possible to determine when gun positions were occupied and by what kind of weapon, and to identify the routes being taken to reach them. The location of German communications and headquarters became a further artillery concern in the autumn of 1916, and made possible more intense and accurate artillery harassing programmes. By continuously reviewing the information that they obtained the staffs learned when German guns and headquarters were moving forward or being withdrawn from the front, whether the former were increasing or decreasing in numbers, and thus were able to conjecture what were the intentions and expectations of the German commanders opposite them. So the counter-battery staffs acquired a general intelligence function as well as an artillery one.

The artillery intelligence function was originally assumed by the Aide de Camp (ADC) to the General Officer Commanding (GOC) RA at Corps and he gradually became an unofficial Intelligence Officer (RA). At first, the General Staff was unwilling to allow this new technique to be honoured with General Staff status. Then, when it realised that it had applications wider than counter-battery, GHQ imposed an Intelligence Corps officer on the Royal Artillery.[106] However, he did not prove to be satisfactory since he was not a trained artillery officer. In October 1916, Rawlinson asked for artillery appointments for Fourth Army, saying, 'It is this artillery point of view which is paramount.' But the comments on his letter as it passed around GHQ showed that the staff did not grasp the need for a professionally trained specialist. Charteris' remark 'If we get a trained artillery officer there will be the danger that he will be used solely as an extra staff officer for artillery and not for Intelligence purposes at all', is an indication of his staff's opinion of artillery intelligence. But despite Charteris, the War Office sanctioned artillery appointments at Army, Corps and Corps Heavy Artillery headquarters, although it was careful to name them 'Recce Officers' not 'Intelligence Officers'. Their function was 'to carry out special artillery reconnaissance, to study and collate air photographs and maps so far as they affect the artillery, and to keep in close touch with the RFC'.

This was a step in the right direction, even if it recognised what had been done in an improvised fashion earlier. A systematic procedure for the collection, collation and dissemination of artillery intelligence was to elude the Army until Charteris was replaced as the head of Intelligence. For Birch had not the power to impose a uniform system on the Army commanders or to alter the GS way of thinking. Then, in February 1918, a new BGS (Intelligence), E. Cox, ensured that the GS and the artillery worked together to extract general intelligence from the information available to either of them. However, the War Office would not acquiesce in his proposal to grade the artillery officers as 'General Staff' and continued to refuse to do so until the end, despite appeals from GHQ.

Meanwhile, the sources of artillery intelligence and its usefulness were both increased by the work of surveyors and their association with sound ranging, flash spotting and observation sections at the front. The work began modestly with the topographical section of the GS under Major E. M. Jack RE, who was served by one clerk. In November 1914, Captain H. St.J. L. Winterbotham arrived in charge of a Ranging Section to locate hostile batteries. His method was to fix the position of an aircraft at the moment that it dropped a smoke bomb over a hostile battery. When fire direction by wireless was found to be more effective, Winterbotham's section was used for survey work in the field. By the end of the war the survey staff of the Expeditionary Force had grown to 400 officers and 6,000 other ranks.[107]

A wag once remarked that it was a question whether gunnery

was not a branch of survey, rather than the reverse. Certainly survey was at the heart of the problem of hitting a target that could not be seen but could be located on a map. Surveying means to fix and record the relative direction and distance of two points in three dimensions. That was what artillerymen had been trying to do ever since they were armed with catapults and known as engineers. If they had a map of sorts they could verify it by firing a few ranging rounds to fix and record points that they could observe in the zone in front of them. But to ensure that other batteries could hit the target too, each had to go through the same process of 'survey' by shooting. Not until the relative positions of all the guns and their targets were fixed by surveying instruments and recorded could they expect their rounds to fall close to the target without registration. So the purpose of artillery survey was to make an artillery map of a scale of about 1/20,000 from which the bearings and distances from guns to targets could be measured accurately.

Accurate survey became essential when the target could not be seen but could only be located on a map; for instance, when only an observer in an aircraft could see the other side of the hill. The only way an observer could record what he saw was by locating it on an accurate map or by taking a photograph of it. The photograph, though, still had to be related to an accurate map. And that was where the trouble began: the maps available in August 1914 were on a small scale, 1/80,000, and were out of date and inaccurate.

Staff officers at GHQ and Corps HQ were not disturbed at the thought of using 1/80,000 maps provided they could inspect the ground. They were adequate for marking up boundaries and the various walls of chinagraph on their situation maps. The infantry officer stuffed his map into his pocket and was concerned with only a small part of it: the ground was what mattered to him. He became guarded when asked his location on the map which he still indicated, in October 1914, in the form '300 yards south of the N in Neuve Chapelle'. Maps were not yet gridded as a matter of course. Lewis, with Salmond, was responsible for introducing the grid to allow targets seen from the air to be indicated on a map. The grid also provided the Gunners with a method of locating guns and targets which they did with reference to the western and southern edges of 500 yard squares when they were printed on the maps. Thus a reference such as C5 a 1.9 gave a position, to the nearest fifty yards, near the top left hand corner of square 5a on map sheet C – see diagram 10. (It is pointed out that this was simply a reference grid printed on the map. It was not possible to relate it to one on an adjoining

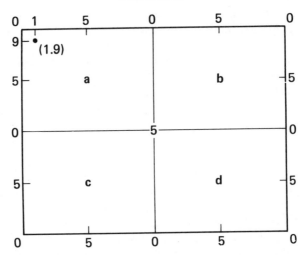

10. *Example of grid reference: point indicated is (big square) 5, (small square) a, (east) 1, (north) 9 – i.e. 5 a 1.9.*

sheet). But references were not much use on a small scale, out-of-date map. So the decision was made to re-map the British zone of operations entirely.

Reinforcements of surveyors, sufficient eventually to form five field survey battalions, were brought to France to establish a matrix of trig points across the British zone, to fit together the manuscript pieces of old surveys where they were confirmed as accurate, and then to use vertical air photographs to fill in the detail between them. The detail included man-made defences, of course. More than one surveyor was arrested as a spy in 1915 for taking bearings on prominent landmarks with a theodolite or for flashing Lucas lamps near trenches. The survey had to be carried into enemy territory so that targets could be surveyed, but the artillery of both sides delighted in obliterating the landmarks that were to appear on the maps and disputes arose about where the missing feature had been. Among the Headlam Papers in the RA Library, Woolwich, was found 'Point 76', a relevant poem by W. C. Eric Radkin:

> In those good days before we fought
> a windmill of the usual sort
> stood on a ridge in Belgium's plain
> with creaking sails it ground the grain
> and steadfastly withstood the strain
> of wind, and storms of hail and rain.

The windmill's lately disappeared
A German 'Johnson' neatly steered
Demolished it – where once it stood
Is now a mass of mangled wood.
Its site on maps one still can fix
It's recognised as 76 . . .

The cameras used for the vertical mosaic were tilted at the moment of exposure and so photographs were slightly distorted. A rectifying camera was used to correct the shape and scale of them. In all 12,000 square miles were mapped. The weak point in the survey was its relief, for the continental survey, based on the one ordered by Napoleon in the early nineteenth century which provided the datum, had not been contoured.

The work continued all through 1915 and 32 million maps were printed of various scales to suit the users. But this was only the beginning, for the artillery positions and targets had to be continuously placed on maps of 1/20,000 or 1/10,000 to an accuracy of fifteen or twenty yards. This required plane-table resection and traverses from known trig points every time a gun position was occupied.

At Loos the 'battery board' was used to ensure that the battery was accurately spotted on the map. 'The map' was actually a sheet of gridded paper fixed to a flat surface, made of zinc or plywood, on which gun positions and targets were plotted. The bearing and distance to targets was measured by a transparent fan and, later, by a metal arm and arc. This was the state of the art on the Somme, but there was still a long way to go. For the accuracy with which the target was plotted, and the confidence with which the data on the sights of the gun, derived from the map, could be depended upon to place the shells on the target left much to be desired. There were improvements on the Somme but it was not until the end of 1917 that the system was matured.

There were two problems at the guns. Survey was not yet fully developed and even if it had been perfected, the guns did not shoot accurately to the map. On the Somme, provided the surveyors had done their work, the gun was correctly plotted on the map. But the survey did not ensure that the bearing recorded on the sights was precisely that on which the gun was pointed when shooting at a target. An error of as little as ten minutes of bearing was enough to make the shell miss a target 9,000 yards away by 25 yards. A line error was much more crucial than a range error, for the natural spread of shells, over and short of the target, would not compensate for it as it would for a range error. The surveyors did not provide precise angular as well as positional data for the guns until the autumn of 1917. They did it by establishing what were called bearing pickets in the gun areas. They ensured that when the guns were initially laid on their aiming points the angle on the sights was correct to an accuracy of five minutes of bearing. The delay in taking this step was not due to technical incompetence but to lack of demand for it. Only when the General Staff saw the advantage of being able to bring fire down on targets without preliminary ranging, which took many days to complete for a big fire-plan and so forfeited surprise did it agree to the adoption of more accurate methods.

An artillery argument against adopting bearing pickets earlier was that greater sources of inaccuracy than line error existed and had not been eliminated.

Every gun was an individual, slightly different from its neighbour even when it emerged from the factory. Its characteristics affected its muzzle velocity and the stability of the shell in flight. Together with the data on the sights of the gun these determined where the shell would fall. After prolonged firing, the muzzle velocity fell and wear in the barrel reduced the stability of the shell. Unless compensation were made, accurate shooting to the map was not achieved. As guns were replaced due to losses in action or mechanical faults, variations occurred between the muzzle velocity and wear of each gun in a battery and between batteries. The effects first became apparent on the Somme where prolonged firing was combined with a great deal of unobserved and uncorrected map shooting. Heavy concentrations of fire were sometimes wasted because they were off the target or widely dispersed. A solution was to encourage battery commanders to shoot at surveyed targets to correct their guns individually. But in 1917, special screens, through which guns fired shells, enabled muzzle velocities to be measured by recording data such as time of flight. Later still, wear measurements of each gun were taken by Ordnance officers and from the combined results individual gun corrections could be calculated.

But calibration was not the end of the matter. For temperature of the propellent, or 'charge', its type, the weight of the shell, and, above all the meteorological conditions at the moment of firing each had an influence on the accuracy of a map shoot. Field battery commanders were often scornful of these details, associated with Coast Defence gunnery, essential though they were for scientific, as opposed to 'bow and arrow', gunnery. Meteorological conditions, in the form of a 'meteor telegram', were issued with increasing frequency during and after the Somme. But the sorting of mixtures of propellents and the taking of charge temperatures in the middle of a wet night, on the second or third day of a battle, was usually cursory. Quality control of ammunition was poor, even in 1917, and gun position officers easily found excuses for ignoring minor adjustments in the middle of a colossal barrage.

Another kind of resistance is represented by a brigadier-general who told H. H. Hemming, one of the pioneers of artillery survey and flash spotting: 'You damned surveyors with your co-ordinates and angles and all the rest, are taking all the fun out of war; in my day we galloped into action and got the first round off in thirty seconds.' Hemming was tempted to reply: 'Yes Sir! and you hit nothing with it except possibly the backs of your own infantry.' Hemming was mainly concerned with the precise location of hostile batteries for the counter-battery organisations at corps by means of sound ranging and flash spotting. By June 1917 his teams of Gunners and Sappers were locating 75 per cent of all German batteries that opened fire almost regardless of weather, the bugbear of the RFC. But all his work was useless if battery commanders ignored 'co-ordinates and angles and all the rest'.

The idea of an artillery duel before a battle had been popular before the war, but it had been conceded that hostile batteries could not be located if they were in concealed positions. Aircraft observation was an answer. The early stages of the war confirmed this but guns remained silent when aircraft were overhead and prolonged bad weather interrupted the flow of information that aircraft gave by photography. So the surveyors and electronic 'blokes' on the ground collaborated to locate the guns that were actually firing by detecting the source of their sound or flash when they fired.

Very little real progress was made in solving the discernible problems in sound ranging in 1915 and 1916. The shock waves of enemy guns, friendly guns, shells passing overhead and shells bursting could not be distinguished by the microphones then being used. Windspeed and direction and atmospheric pressure affected the reception and quality of sound. The flash spotters were not always able to distinguish a reflected sky flash from the real thing, one flash from another, nor to relate bearings reported with the flashes to which they referred. Both systems required a central office where bearings could be plotted to establish, by trisections, a triangle of error within which targets lay.

Sir Lawrence Bragg described one problem and part of the ultimate solution to sound ranging.[108] The microphone was not selective being sensitive to high frequency sounds, like the shell wave made by a gun with the m.v. greater than the velocity of sound, but not to low frequency sound like that of a boom from a gun. He noticed that the gun, but not the shell, had a marked lifting effect on his 'bottom poised over a thunderbox'. Similarly, a jet of cold air came through the rents in the wall of the tarred paper shack in which it was housed. Then 'Corporal Tucker came to our section on Kemmel Hill fresh from experiments with the cooling by air currents of very fine, hot platinum wires' so that their resistance was altered when a current passed through them. 'Somehow we arrived at the brilliant idea of using the jet of air coming through an aperture in the wall of an enclosure to cool Woolaston wire' so that there was a small 'break' in the current for the shell wave, followed by a quite characteristic and definite large one for the gun report.

The rest of the story reinforces this anecdote. For it was a co-operative effort by bright individuals. Lieutenant Lloyd Owen's idea of placing microphones at exactly equal distances in a straight line, ensured that the breaks in the film that recorded the sounds at the central office fell on a smooth curve, enabling the sounds to be correctly matched and those made by friendly guns to be eliminated, and the work to proceed even during a heavy strafe. The problem of meteorological conditions was solved by J. A. Gray's 'wind section' which detonated explosives at surveyed locations at intervals of a few hours so that the sounds could be recorded and corrections of the moment, due to wind and temperature, computed.

Flash spotting was an older game although it had never been systematised. Sections were functioning by the end of 1915, but it was not until the flash and buzzer board of 1916 ensured that all observers concentrated on one and the same target that they were efficient. At the moment of recording a bearing the observer pressed a buzzer that sounded in the computing centre and allowed one bearing to be distinguished from another.

By the summer of 1917, British sound rangers and flash spotters were feared by the Germans.[109] So precise was their data that not only could they determine the nature of the enemy gun firing and its location to fifteen yards, but also locate the fall of shot for British guns and assist in their calibration. In conjunction with the RFC, they enabled the counter-battery organisations in the Corps to win the artillery duels at Arras, in April, and Messines in June. Indeed, one of the marked differences between those battles and the Somme was that more of the guns were consigned, successfully, to silencing the enemy artillery and much fewer to bombarding his trenches. The artillery battle to silence the enemy's guns became an essential prelude to the infantry attack.

The artillery battle was a team effort in which the infantry played no part. But when it came to the bombardment of enemy defences before and during the battle it was the turn of the artillery to have relatively little say in the plan, except to give advice and provide a service. Guns were allotted to counter-battery at the expense of pre-bombardment, so corps commanders, who made the decision, were inclined to disregard their Gunners and favour bombardment throughout the Somme and even in 1917. It was not until astonishingly accurate survey achieved great successes in counter-battery at Arras and Messines, and then ensured the Third Army's tactical surprise at Cambrai that wholesale conversions were made from Somme methods to scientific ones.

The shortcomings of the artillery at the Somme were obvious and perhaps the revolution that took place in their methods after-wards was too silent, and went unnoticed for that reason. In July 1916 there were too few heavy howitzers, serious weaknesses in the 18-pounder recuperator system, faulty ammunition, not enough smoke and no gas shells. The first prolonged operations of the war were bound to expose many faults in equipment and method. The faults in equipment were corrected with time and the co-operation of the MGO, who was William Furse in December 1916 after von Donop's departure. The tactical and training weaknesses, as obvious as the technical ones, seemed to be inseparable from the way operations were conducted. For that reason they were the harder to correct for they were not an artillery matter alone. On 1 July, not only was the preparatory bombardment inadequate to stun the defenders on many parts of the front, but no provision was made for impromptu artillery support when the advancing infantry was held up unexpectedly. Battery commanders in well-placed artillery observation posts were forced to watch the tragedy, knowing that they could have saved lives if they had had guns under their control. But the fire plan moved ahead too fast for the infantry and it was so rigidly planned that fire could not be recalled when they were left behind. Thanks largely to the experience of Ivor Maxse's 18 Division in XIII Corps on the right, and of 7 Division in XV Corps next to them on 1 July, creeping barrages were subsequently devised to move by 100 yard stages in front of the advancing infantry. Instead of a curtain of fire on the objective or on a flank, as at Neuve Chapelle, or one that lifted according to a timetable from objective to objective as most divisions had had on 1 July, the 'creeper' covered the ground progressively in front of and behind the objectives. All the infantry had to do was to stay close to it even if the occasional short round sprayed them with shrapnel.

The barrage was developed further during the next year, and it had both a benign and malign effect on infantry tactics. Usually it was fired with shrapnel because the infantry could approach closer to it than to HE and the shrapnel smoke shielded the infantry from the view of the enemy. Furthermore, HE was inclined to ricochet and short ground bursts were more lethal than short airbursts. When it was learned that the Germans were placing machine-guns in depth to fire indirectly from behind their front trench line, one of the causes of the heavy casualties of 1 July, barrages of several lines of fire were used, the heavier weapons sweeping back and forth over the open ground to search out defenders in shell holes, and to catch counter-attacks as they formed up and moved forward. A standing barrage was maintained in front of objectives after they were taken, sometimes for several hours.

By 1917, Noel Birch was being scathing about commanders who expected a barrage to take them all the way to Berlin. It excused them from studying the ground and the precise location of the enemy and it resigned them to linear tactics behind the linear barrage. Barrages perpetuated the bad practice of selecting linear objectives, either because they happened to be occupied by the enemy or because they were part of some 'Red Line' marked arbitrarily on their maps. Besides, enemy positions faced the wrong way and were seldom suitable as fire bases for future British operations. The preliminary attacks that were undertaken only to square the line to the barrage had proved very costly. Certainly barrages saved lives but they had become such a panacea that the infantry was not having to learn how to move in fire units. In linear waves it could not reorganise under fire when held up by a strong point. Indeed, the infantry had no ability to manoeuvre and use its weapons under fire for it was only trained to walk forward behind a fire roller. W. D. Croft, who commanded a brigade in the 9th (Scottish) Division, remarked that it was ironical that the archers at Crècy had been more effective with the longbow than were his men using modern rifles.

The infantry tactics that developed behind the creeping barrage on the Somme were suitable for assaults on continuous trench lines like those facing the Army on 1 July 1916. With the addition of the creeping barrage and the omission of infantry fire-support to accompany infantry movement, they were the tactics of the assault that were practised before the war. But from 14 July, when the second great set-piece attack on the Somme was mounted, the German defences were not linear but consisted of irregular and discontinuous positions unsuited to linear assault. Had the infantry been trained to fight its way forward with its own weapons it would have preferred accurate concentrations of fire on its flanks and its objectives to barrages in the new circumstances, for they would have enabled it to infiltrate between and around concentrations and to attack the enemy in rear. Those were to be the tactics of 1918, but in 1916 linear tactics predominated because they were simpler. Observed and accurate shooting by the artillery was exceptional; as a general rule, heavy concentrations were fired on areas supposed to be occupied by the enemy by orders given over a telephone in a dug-out at divisional or brigade headquarters. Fire effect was sought by quantity not quality of fire. Consequently, over-bombardment, before and during the battle, turned the terrain into a wilderness in which most landmarks were destroyed. In an attack through a muddy desert, the barrage served as a guide at least. Behind the front trench, supplies and reinforcements were directed by signposts along tracks that were often marked on enemy maps. Such routes were easily seen from the air and harassing fire and standing barrages fell on them, and on the junctions that were inevitably used as rendezvous, with sickening consistency. However, to leave marked routes was to be lost at once. Villages were smashed to brick-dust: woods, Delville being the most notorious on the Somme, were reduced to a stinking tangle of trees and wire hazed with gas and smoke by a perpetual deluge of heavy shells. The shelling was turned on and off like a tap and according to a timetable. Its effect and accuracy were not often monitored. The safest places were those close to the enemy but not honoured by a reference on the map. The huge volume of fire that fell routinely on places that were mentioned reduced their inhabitants to incapability in three days. The physical difficulty of organising an attack when it took six hours to walk from divisional headquarters to a battalion, and telephone lines between them were usually 'out', compelled staffs to centralise and base everything on rigid artillery programmes. Fire-plans were arranged at corps headquarters and the infantry was expected to conform to them. Frequently the orders arrived at a battalion too late for it to react, or fire came down in the wrong place or not at all. The hundreds of minor attacks before and after major operations were particularly prone to such failures. The men in the line who knew, more or less, the enemy's locations, were too weak from continual shelling to attack. Those who came up strong in numbers but physically exhausted before they relieved the incumbents, were disoriented.[110]

Caught in this vicious circle it may be readily understood that, for the infantry, the creeping barrage and the blind concentrations of high explosive was both a life-line and an addiction. The barrage could be identified on the ground and it probably led to where the enemy would be found. But when the programme stopped and impromptu fighting started, command and control broke down. Then the artillery support deteriorated again into the blind shelling of map references and hours of defensive fire in front of supposedly friendly troops. Forward observers' telephone lines were cut by shell fire. A conclusion widely reached during the summer of 1916 was that only major set-piece battles for limited objectives under closely controlled conditions were effective. The small impromptu battles usually failed. Unfortunately, they were always necessary before the big battle to set up the pieces.

The Germans reacted to the unscientific battle of *matériel* that developed on the Somme, for they had no desire to be ground to pieces as they had attempted to grind the French to pieces at Verdun. They ceased to hold continuous trench positions in which they had lost huge numbers of men from artillery fire even before the British infantry reached them behind their barrage. The instigator of the less formal defence system controlled by a Kampf-Truppen Kommandeur and his divisional commander, was Colonel von Lossberg, the chief of staff of Second Army, on the Somme from 2 July.[111] The Kommandeur was the manager of the tangle of shell holes, mined dug-outs, quarry excavations and cellars that formed the German front zone. Regardless of his rank and the troops that were given him he was in charge. The continuity of his tenure usually ensured that he knew more about his front than his opponent. Eventually, at the beginning of 1917, the Germans withdrew from the Somme front to what the British named the Hindenburg position which had been laid out by engineers and designed for defence under von Lossberg's direction. Crude though British artillery on the Somme had been, it had, at least, forced this retirement on the German after inflicting terrible casualties on him.

With experience on the Somme, some British divisions examined their tactics and decided that they had to train for the 'dog fighting' phase that began when the artillery fire programme ended. In that phase they had been thrown on their own resources and had been found wanting. They recognised that the Somme had not been trench warfare but what they now termed semi-open warfare. At the time, in the autumn of 1916, Fourth Army compiled a dossier on the experiences of the many divisions that had passed through their hands on the Somme. The most persistent comments in the file were that semi-open warfare required special training to ensure that the battalions

used the weapons in their hands more effectively. The artillery
ought to be released from Corps control after the initial fire-plan
had been fired so that it could give closer support to the infantry
and the divisional commander should have more artillery under
his command. There was complete consensus that before the
1917 campaign began GHQ would have to collate and
co-ordinate the experiences that divisions reported and
formulate a new tactical doctrine for future operations. The
system in which Armies, Corps and Divisions pursued their own
ideas had to be ended.[112]

CHAPTER 7

Queen of the Battlefield?

*What was siege warfare was called trench war
which came to be regarded as a special problem
to be solved by the bomb and the bayonet.
Instead of gun and mine preparing the way for the
infantry, it was the infantry that was expected to
open a door for an inroad of horsemen against
the enemy rear*[113]

*The British Army . . . in the battle of the Somme
had not yet reached a sufficiently high tactical
standard. The training of the infantry was clearly
behind that of the German; the superficially
trained British were particularly clumsy in
movements of large masses. On the other hand
small bodies such as machine gun crews, bombers
and trench blockers, and special patrols, thanks
to their native independence of character, fought
very well. . .*[114]

IN retrospect, it is clear that the British infantry did not have
the means to breach the siege lines in 1915 nor, had they done
so, the reserves to exploit the breach. In 1916, they were better
equipped and had much greater artillery support, but they used
the methods of Loos to breach stronger German lines on the
Somme. They were not good enough to beat their opponent
even with improved artillery, for the bomb and bayonet trench
fighting of 1915 proved poor preparation for the semi-open
fighting that developed on the Somme. By the second half of
1917, when Passchendaele was fought, the small unit tactics based
on integral fire-support that some commanders were suggesting
after their Somme experiences were still not adopted generally.
For GHQ had not given direction in the matter during the winter
and spring of 1917. Instead of the new methods favoured by the
more enlightened infantry commanders, reliance was still placed
on overwhelming artillery fire power in the Somme fashion. And

when the rains came it was the waterlogged and over-bombarded ground, as much as German stubbornness, that was the real enemy. Elusive, invisible and cowering under pieces of tin in the green slime of shell holes, the German infantryman became the other victim of brute force and ignorance.

By November 1917, infantry battalions were oppressed by the treadmill to which they had been consigned and from which there seemed to be no escape. Then Cambrai brought a ray of hope, for the usual routine had changed: it was the light before the dawn. Not only had the infantry been successful but they had fought in the open, in small fire units against a visible enemy who had surrendered in gratifying numbers. They felt that their humanity had been restored to them; that they were individuals again instead of parts of a mindless wave beating on an iron shore. Afterwards, despite their casualties, that mistakes had been made and that they had failed to reach all their objectives, the divisions were astonishingly effervescent and loud in their approval of the methods that had been used.

Previously, hope had risen as a battalion came out of the line, adopted some quiet village, absorbed drafts, smartened up and trained. In a month it was pleased with itself and capable of doing what was expected of it. In six weeks it had fought, been virtually destroyed again, and, at half-strength, held a 'quiet' sector. There it was visited by the staff of its new Corps Commander whose ideas were quite different from those to which the battalion had become accustomed while training and fighting. The divisional staff had changed, the brigade major – a key personality who affected the health and happiness of the battalions – had been killed, and the battalion commander was new, had not been 'out' since 1914, and could not tell a practical plan from a bad one.   .

If the same men had been fated to survive show after show, like the Flying Dutchman, the morale of the battalion would have suffered more than it did. That is a paradox, perhaps, but it would have fallen to a level at which a relatively few men fought to an objective while the rest dropped off into shell holes on the way there, became stragglers to the rear, or appeared on the objective after the fighting was over. But fresh men in the ranks, ignorant and easily killed though they often were, blended with surviving natural leaders to keep the show going.

The disease of lead-swinging was kept in check by military police who gave stragglers a cup of tea and firmly pushed them forward again. Provided the officers and NCO's did not expect too much of them and the staff did not commit them to battle at an appalling disadvantage, youngsters in their first battle often did a 'very good show'. But by November 1917, the new men were those who had managed to avoid service to date and their hearts had never been in it. The old hands, several times wounded, had been to the well too often to take risks. The methods of Cambrai breathed new life into such men.

The techniques of the trench fighting of 1915 had become ends in themselves and that was one reason why they were so difficult to discard. Specialists in them found plenty of opportunity to shine. The bombers were the élite of these specialists. Organised into company, battalion and even brigade units they were originally trained by the Royal Engineers. The success of the battalion depended on the bombers' ability to throw accurately and far and, no less, on their supporters who were expected to bring up an inexhaustible supply of bombs carried in aprons and a variety of patent devices. 'This bombing business is a desperate form of fighting,' wrote a Coldstream Guards officer at the Hohenzollern Redoubt at Loos in October 1915. 'Twice now we have had more than double the number of killed to wounded. It is practically certain death to the leading bombers and bayoneteers, and yet there seems to be no difficulty in getting men to take it on.'

Snipers were of the élite, too. They carried on a private vendetta against any opponent who showed himself. Their favourite vantage points, reached by careful crawling, were jealously guarded from discovery. Visiting laymen of any rank or arm were discouraged, by rough language, from approaching them. Specialists in night patrolling made the deadly hobby of it that Siegfried Sassoon described so well. They knew every tin can in No Man's Land and every ditch and fold in the ground that could hide them. To watch and see, without being seen, and to jump on the unsuspecting 'tail-end Fritz' of a Bosche patrol was as enjoyable as making 100 runs or taking six wickets in a cricket match.

The 'big shows', though, took you out of the 'safety' and the routine of the trench. Nevertheless, the tactics used in them were mechanical and unvarying. You climbed up a ladder, heavily laden with your share of empty sandbags, grenades, wire, mortar bombs, shovel or pick, two water bottles and rations, a groundsheet, haversack, gas mask, rifle and ammunition, lined up in the open and walked forward in the general direction of the enemy trench. By the time that you reached it, or what you thought was it, you were among strangers. You had not noticed your friends dropping around you. In the captured trench were dead bodies, smashed equipment and a strange NCO who shouted that you were to man the parados at the back of the trench and fire at a counter-attack that was apparently approaching. But you could see nothing of it because the fire-step faced the other way and the German trench was so deep that you could not climb out of the back of it. Suddenly there were explosions further down the trench and Germans were bombing their way up it towards you from the head of a communication trench which no one had noticed and blocked. You had no grenades and forgot to use your rifle in your panic. Everyone else had disappeared and you were alone. So you climbed out of the trench the way that you arrived in it and ran home.

An individual may have had a similar experience in 1916 or 1917, although the fire-power in the hands of his battalion and that employed by the artillery of both sides was much greater. In 1916 he would have walked forward in lines and waves following a creeping barrage which he would have practised with men on horses carrying flags to denote the line of shell bursts. The distances between the lines and between individuals would increase in 1916 and still more in 1917 and, if he were in a follow-up wave, he might have moved in a platoon or section column rather than in line. The appearance of the objective, too, would have changed. Instead of the regular continuous trench line of 1915, with its thick barbed wire entanglements, he would have found scattered groups of battered trenches, a quarry or mine crater, the entrance to a mined dug-out or cellar, or, in 1917, a concrete pill box; and the wire, except in front of the Hindenburg Line, was less systematic.

The confidence of an infantryman in the trenches depended on his learning a job in a team in familiar conditions. Only naturals or professionals could cope with the unexpected. It was the naturals who became the élite. For the rest, the majority, every-thing had to be done according to rules and nothing was to be left to chance. The unexpected was to be avoided since it led to panic. And, for the lad from a factory, the military society was not entirely unfamiliar. Its rules were enforced more strictly and for twenty-four hours a day. If he fell asleep at his post, for instance, he knew that he might be shot by a firing squad instead of being sacked from his job. The discomfort of trench life was more extreme than that of the crowded, two room, back-to-back industrial slum house in which he may have been born, but tomorrow he looked forward to a spell sleeping in a dry barn after an evening's sport with a local 'mamselle' in the estaminet. And the grub was regular and the company was good.

Before the battle the infantryman enjoyed the undamaged villages on the Somme, the trees in leaf and the flowers. The countryside was prettier than in the north, the trenches were dryer and the enemy quieter. But after the first day of the battle, when the shambles prevailing on most of the front would be familiar to him had he been at Loos, the situation and the demands made upon him would have been new. For instance, in the Guillemont fighting in August, after a formal attack behind a creeping barrage, he was isolated with a group of survivors in a smashed up landscape in which he would have been lost had he ventured out of the crudely joined shell holes in which he sheltered. There was no labyrinthine trench system with deep dug-outs, the smell of the recent German occupants hanging over it and pumpernickel and sausage still laid on the table, half-eaten. To withdraw was to run into a 5.9-inch howitzer standing barrage. It was best to keep his head down and not attract the attention of the enemy. Visitors arrived breathlessly 'over the top', usually with bad news. Hot meals were unheard of and reliefs were rumoured but never arrived. His officers were killed or wounded as fast as he learned their names.

A company commander at Guillemont, for whom a day lasted forever, would not have thought at the time, of course, of the long struggle on the Somme as the turning point in the war that it proved to be. If he were a survivor of the divisional stint at Delville Wood, Morval or Flers, he would take part in post mortems when the battle was reviewed and what was to be done 'next time' decided. The mere continuity of his existence made him into an historian of the events through which he had lived and determined to do better next time. He would have agreed with the prevailing view that companies and platoons had to have more of their own fire-power, to be more self-reliant, and to work their way forward without expecting huge artillery bombardments to precede everything that they did. Apart from anything else that was the only way to become master of one's fate. And he would have agreed with the many divisional officers who demanded more time to make their plans and more say in them than they had been allowed on the Somme, where Corps headquarters ran everything, it seemed, without being properly informed. But then he would have glanced at the hairless chins of the latest crop of subalterns who had replaced the ones that he had just lost, and wondered if they would be capable of doing any more than bravely lead men to their deaths behind a barrage planned at corps headquarters regardless of the ground or the location of the enemy.

Major-General R. B. Stephens,[115] commanding 5 Division, addressed the Fourth Army School for Officers, in early September 1916, about the need to retrain the infantry for the new conditions. 'We have to realise that this is not trench warfare. The men are inclined to be trench-bound' he stated. They would take a trench when ordered but having done so were 'quite satisfied to sit in it and hold it very much as if it were part of the old permanent line'. They ought to be gaining and digging new positions that could be used for the next assault. Instead they allowed the enemy to take back key points by infiltration. When the troops ordered to do the next attack arrived they first had to expend their strength capturing a start line. 'Our men do not dig as well as the enemy. Perhaps because the enemy's training is a harder and sterner thing than ours or because they are better trained.'[116-7]

The rest of Stephens' remarks illustrated the transitional stage which tactics had reached by the autumn of 1916. He mentioned that too many men were used in the lines of attack and that chaos ensued when a wave leapfrogged through the one in front of it to continue the advance. He mentioned a new platoon organisation with which his division would shortly experiment. It had two sections of riflemen, each with two rifle grenadiers, a bomber section and a Lewis gun section. Platoon commanders would be taught to find the flanks of enemy positions instead of repeating frontal attacks that had already failed. He did not need to point out that at Guillemont, for instance, the Germans did not hold linear defences, but separate groups of fire-positions each of which defended the flanks of others. An assault on one position was defeated by fire from those not under attack. The new self-contained platoon was suitable for fire and movement against such positions but wasted if the infantry persisted in wave tactics.

Regular soldiers like Stephens may be excused for reiterating that it was pre-war fire and movement tactics that they wished to restore even though they had never been satisfactorily established against strong positions in depth. In the papers of L. L. C. Reynolds,[118] commanding a battalion in 48 Division, is a copy of Sir Horace Smith-Dorrien's Infantry training Memorandum of 20 June 1914 from which Reynolds took a few notes when he was training his battalion in 1916. Stereotyped attacks were to be avoided, Smith-Dorrien had written, particularly those which paid no attention to the physical features and used too many men in the skirmishing line which preceded the main attack. It was the fetish of no movement without fire that was causing them to adopt rigid formations instead of stalking the enemy. In those respects little had changed by the Somme.

It is easy, half a century and several wars later, to point to these insights as evidence for the present historians' views, but they are those that were made at the time in most of the tactical papers that have survived. The writers were grappling with the incompetence of an infantry that would not move without huge preparatory bombardments and had come to believe that stalking the enemy was unnecessary. In the old trench system there was much to recommend pressing on by sheer weight of numbers. The race to get a mass of men across the fire zone before the enemy's defensive fire fell like a portcullis behind them encouraged it. But the situation in the late summer and autumn of 1916 was different from before the war and from 1915. The infantry had the fire-power that earlier it lacked and the enemy no longer held continuous trenches. The semi-open fighting that resulted lent itself to different tactics from the trench phase of the siege war. Hence the widely held conclusion in the autumn of 1916 that the infantry would have to be retrained to make it forget some bad habits that it had acquired in the first year of the war while its fire-power was being built.

It will be remembered that in 1910 Major N. M. McMahon had recommended that each of the eight companies in a battalion should have one light machine-gun. Five years later, in July 1915, the Lewis light machine-gun was issued experimentally on a scale of four weapons per battalion, or one per company. In the meanwhile, the original two Vickers machine-guns had been increased to four and, in October, these were brigaded and began to be replaced in the battalion by Lewis guns. Thus there were to be sixteen Vickers in the brigade and eight Lewis guns in a battalion. At the same time a machine-gun corps was created to handle the Vickers. This organisation was ready for the Somme. Towards the end of the Somme the scale of Lewis guns was increased to sixteen guns, enough for each platoon to have one. However, the Lewis remained a company weapon, officially, until the end of 1917 when platoons acquired an integral Lewis gun section like the one Stephens mentioned in 1916. Meanwhile the company guns were inclined to be allocated to soldiers who were good at stripping them, rather than to good shots and wily stalkers. Consequently, the development of platoon tactics based on light machine-gun fire was impeded.[119]

Before the battle on the Somme started on 1 July 1916, Fourth Army emphasised that Lewis guns were really automatic rifles and that their mobility should be exploited to push them forward early in the attack.[120] Maxse, then commanding 18 Division, rightly refused to use them in his leading waves, since there were few of them and they might be lost. Later, when looser German defences favoured platoon tactics he allotted them to flank platoons and, by the end of 1917, he was asking GHQ to issue a scale of two guns to each platoon and to reduce the number of their riflemen correspondingly. The trend was to increase the scale of light machine-guns, to move them forward in the battle and to use them more aggressively.

As the scale of light automatic weapons increased and they seeped forward into the platoons, the Vickers assumed the role of light artillery and was increasingly used for overhead fire to fill the gap between battalion weapons and the artillery. The Machine-Gun Corps' view that it should have an independent rôle met resistance, perhaps because its young and aggressive officers were not part of an established social and political organisation and were not noted for their tact. The machine-guns, in the opinion of most staff officers at higher levels, ought not to be allowed to behave independently; they were still regarded as infantry weapons not semi-autonomous parts of a weapons system. The Canadians, unhindered by such prejudices, became the leaders in machine-gun tactics, arming themselves with 96 weapons to the British division's 64, and pioneering the use of machine-guns to interdict the battlefield. They rushed them forward to captured ground where they stopped counter-attacks, such as those of the Germans at Hill 70, on which they inflicted appalling casualties in August 1917. The British machine-guns were not outstanding. Uniacke had this to say about them in March 1918:[121]

> In the first place the Germans in 1918 often provided their own machine gun barrage from their forward troops which was successful. Yet our own counterattacks were very often stopped by counter machine gun fire. The whole machine gun question needs to be closely examined to discover wherein our inferiority lies, whether in the number of guns employed, the training of the companies, the technical and tactical training of the officers, or any other cause. The matter is very important; it has been our chief weakness all through the war.

Machine-gun advocates like G. M. Lindsay[122] and G. S. Hutchison placed the blame on dense staff officers and commanders. As the German machine-gunners were primarily infantrymen and fought as a component, albeit an élite one, of the infantry regiment, Uniacke may have been right when he noted that machine gunners were simply not good enough as infantrymen and spent too much time on the technical aspects of their trade and too little on tactics.

Uniacke was one of many who observed that German mobile trench artillery, or mortars, were also superior. They harassed the British at every stage of the 1918 retirements, whereas 'our mortars, after the initial attack have always, up to date, been useless to us.' He was referring to the medium and heavy mortars which were artillery weapons as well as to the Stokes light mortar which was manned by the infantry.

The Stokes 3-inch mortar was a length of water pipe, the bomb being fired when it fell on a striker pin which pierced the primer of a sporting cartridge set in its base. The bomb had either a delay or an instantaneous fuze, a time fuze having proved dangerous. The artillery bombs used a .303 rifle cartridge primer. The Stokes fighting range was about 400 yards so that it was usually located in or just behind the forward trench. There it was unpopular for it attracted retaliatory bombardments from *minenwerfers* which fired 'plum puddings' and 'flying pigs'. Both bombs made a mess of the front trench which required a night's work to repair. Eight men were required to carry forward the thirty bombs which accompanied each tube, an unpopular fatigue for the battalion. The mortar mountings were too heavy for semi-mobile work and were often discarded. The mortar was then slung like a rifle and steadied by hand when fired, a method that did not make for accuracy. The artillery 2-inch and, later, 6-inch Newton mortars did some good work in wire cutting, before the instantaneous fuze 106 gave the artillery howitzers a better performance. But they were too heavy for the mobile operations of 1918 in those parts of the front where the old trench systems were abandoned.[123]

The artillery and the infantry both treated the mortars as Cinderellas for neither was impressed with their value. The Gunner had no wish to leave his horse for 'an old bit of drain pipe'. The battalion commander consigned men to mortars as he did to the Machine-Gun Corps: 'Will you take my award – or go to trench mortars?' It is not surprising that after the war mortars drifted into oblivion for a time, to be revived in 1939–45. But German mortars were again superior to the British in the Second World War. Nor should one wonder why the Machine-Gunners were disciplined by returning them to infantry battalions.

As we have seen, the grenade was the master weapon in the trenches, but the British did not begin to catch up with the German lead until the No. 5 Mills bomb appeared. A 1915 instruction about handling grenades illustrates the variety of them, how dangerous they were and the prevailing ignorance of the infantry about how to handle them. 'Don't force the fuze into the detonator but work it in gently for ¾ of an inch, which is as far as it can go.' 'The safety pin of the No. 5 Mills should not be removed until it is desired to throw the grenade. This should be rigidly adhered to.' 'No. 12 Grenade. This has proved to be most dangerous owing to the heat generated by the lighter, which is too powerful, exploding the detonator.' Grenades had been a Sapper responsibility before the war when it had not seemed so essential to produce a foolproof article. A rash of inadequate weapons, some of them home-made, were released to inexperienced battalions in 1915, with predictable results due to wet weather, bad storage and careless handling.[124]

It was clear, very early, that a bomber needed to be a specialist. A typical grenade school offered a course of nine working days from 7.00 am to 6.00 pm. By the Somme, the original primitive bombs were obsolete but a light bomb that could be thrown as far as the German egg grenade was still required, for the Mills was effective but heavy. Adequate numbers of smoke and phosphorous incendiary grenades were also lacking. But the main requirement for the semi-open fighting on the Somme, apart from good rifle shots and enterprising Lewis gunners, both of whom were rare, was not a grenade that could be thrown but one that could be fired from a rifle. For the enemy was usually at a distance and the rifle grenade was the best weapon for finishing off machine-guns. Rifle grenades had been used in trench fighting but the rod from which they were fired ruined the rifle for normal use and frequently burst the barrel. It was not until the No. 23 Mills rifle grenade and No. 24 rifle bomb with a cup discharger were produced that the rifle grenadier really came into his own. In August of 1918, the Australians who captured Mont St Quentin used rifle grenades covered by Lewis guns to destroy its defending machine-guns.

The divisions that fought on the Somme using these weapons, and were fortunate enough to be able to train during the winter and early spring of 1917, used the period for experiments. They had learned much but some impulse from GHQ was needed to crystalise their individual efforts. With that in mind Brigadier A. Solly-Flood was brought to GHQ at the beginning of 1917 to 'inaugurate a Training Directorate for all arms and services in France. This provided for the co-ordination of all training whether carried out under GHQ, the Armies, the Corps or the Divisions.' But it was sending a boy to do a boy's work and he did little more than 'co-ordinate' and to issue general instructions such as that the platoon was to be organised as a self-contained unit. It finally required a Lieutenant-General, Sir Ivor Maxse, with Major-General Uniacke as Deputy, to compel some uniformity in theory and practice. But even they were not given executive authority when they began, in July 1918, to assist commanders to train their units for open warfare. For the semi-open variety which persisted through much of 1916 and all of 1917, schools were to go without the forceful leadership that both Maxse and Uniacke were capable of providing.

A Fourth Army training instruction, 'Notes on the Lessons of the Operations on the Somme as regards Infantry Attack and the Employment of Specialists' dated 1 December 1916, is disappointing reading. 'Nothing that has occurred during the Somme operation would seem to have in any way affected the correctness of the old principles as regards formations for the attack laid down in our training manuals before the war', it assured its readers. It then plunged into a mass of detail about 'specialists' none of which existed before the war. That it considered everyone but a man with a rifle to be a specialist is an indication that even Fourth Army, widely acknowledged to be 'sensible', and under whom Maxse, Haldane, Watts, Deverell, Furse, Heneker, Stephens and other excellent divisional commanders had served and for whom they had written reports, had not grasped that although Lewis gunners, rifle grenadiers and bombers, required special training they ought and in many cases were being treated as all-rounders and being integrated in platoons. The more enlightened commanders were trying to supersede the old trench idea that they were specialists. Unless that could be done the argument would be raised that casualties to 'specialists' would make a team approach to platoon tactics too fragile to be workable. A. A. Montgomery, over whose signature as Rawlinson's MGGS the instruction had been issued, made no acknowledgement that after the break-in to an enemy position in waves behind a creeping barrage, many divisions used 'worms not waves', as Maxse described platoon and section columns, to continue the attack.

By February 1917, Maxse's XVIII Corps had four identical sections in the platoon each with its bombers, rifle grenadiers and rifle and bayonet men. The Lewis gun sections belonged in company headquarters on the grounds that they could be allotted to platoons if required, and that platoon commanders had enough on their hands to train and administer their sections. The fighting unit was to be the section – a principle that Maxse had advocated in 1913, when the battalion had been re-organised. But that was not the general practice in 1917, when the important reform throughout the Army was simply the restoration of the platoon organisation. Indeed, such had been the state of units on the Somme that platoons had completely collapsed and companies were virtually run by the commander and his company sergeant major who told off men from a company roll to each platoon before a battle. Gough commented at a conference on 28 December 1916: 'I will point out to you the sort of things unearthed at my inspection. In some units not a single platoon was organised.'[125]

A year later, after Passchendaele and Cambrai, the Lewis gun had joined the platoon which consisted of three rifle sections, two of them armed with rifle grenades, besides the Lewis gun section. All were trained as riflemen. But waves not worms were still being taught and the manpower crisis after the losses of the autumn seemed to be leading to a reduction in the size of platoons. Maxse must have been convinced that GHQ would never learn. On 9 December 1917 he wrote to Brigadier Charles Bonham Carter, then at GHQ and responsible for staff duties, tactical doctrine and training manuals:

> Why not consider the future organisation of platoons in 1918, when we shall be worse off for manpower, *now*. Rather than cut numbers in platoons why not double Lewis guns. Train companies to operate on wider fronts and have intervals between fire units. Scrap the idea of shoulder to shoulder. Substitute waves for worms which deploy quickly to fire or to avoid the enemy's fire. Teach each fire unit to keep together and support its neighbour with fire.

The fault with the regulation writers, he went on, was that they had not grasped what kind of men were commanding platoons. 'They try to cram a Staff College education into a pamphlet . . . it is a fine performance but bewilders our platoon commanders and people like me. If they would be simple and teach a few points in each pamphlet I think they would produce better results.'

Maxse commanded XVIII Corps throughout the Passchendaele campaign. He witnessed the confusion between GHQ, Fifth Army and its corps in June 1917, over the plan and the tactical methods to be employed. He knew that instead of using information on German methods that their own infantry gave them to modify their tactical doctrine, GHQ had waited until they received a captured German document that purported to explain it all to them. But German tactics were continually changing to adapt to the advances in British artillery techniques and their fear of tanks. On 7 August 1917, after Gough's battle had already started, GHQ circulated the captured document for the opinion of commanders. They should already have known, for Plumer had told them at the time of Messines, that the Germans had been thinning out their front, deepening their defence zone and holding, well in rear, specially trained counter-attack divisions. Changes in German methods had begun on the

Somme, of course. Davidson's abortive plan for limited attacks that he had submitted to Haig and Gough on 28 June 1917, was actually a rejoinder to the German defence methods of which he was already informed. For by limiting the length of the infantry advance he hoped it would be ready for the counter-attack. A deep advance such as that which Gough planned would cause the infantry to arrive on its objectives weak and disorganised. Maxse's tactics were more aggressive; a response to the problem of fighting through what were now loose defence zones rather than defence lines of the old kind. He wanted to increase the fire-power of the infantry. And Gough, in a less articulate way, also wanted to make them less reliant on a huge artillery plan.

Before the war no staff section at the War Office was responsible, specifically, for tactical intelligence and doctrinal analysis. Since 1914, infantry intelligence had been handled no better than artillery intelligence by the General Staff in France. The matter was in several hands; those of Charteris the BGS (1), Davidson the BGS (Ops) and Bonham Carter the BGS (SD and Training). None of these men had had a direct influence on the Passchendaele plan. With Gough's operation already in trouble, Davidson suddenly had German tactics examined by Army Commanders and asked them to propose how they should be dealt with. His wish, clearly, was that they should suggest that a plan such as he had proposed on 28 June should be adopted.

When the question came to him that same day, Maxse consulted his divisions and on 12 August replied. He agreed with Davidson that initially a short advance of 2,500 yards was enough and that the deeper advance attempted by Gough had been an error. He agreed with Davidson also, 'that ground is gained by artillery, ground is defended by artillery, that battles are won by artillery and that battles are lost by lack of artillery.' But he went on to say that 'our infantry attacks should not be crowded attacks and that infantry in defence should not be in crowded trenches. Thus ground gained should be held lightly in front and be defended in depth with fresh infantry held in readiness for counterattack. Similarly in the attack fresh infantry are required in the day for the purpose of counterattacking the enemy's counterattack. They should start late and not be involved in any other fighting than that necessitated by their special mission of shattering the enemy's counterattack.'

The difference between Maxse's idea and Davidson's which prevailed at the end of the month when Plumer was given the task of fighting his series of limited battles, was important. Maxse, like Colonel von Lossberg who had conceived the German defence plan at Ypres, believed in fighting on the ground and not for it, and in defeating the enemy in the battle by superior tactics. Davidson's was to capture ground and to inflict casualties in doing so. His was the method that ought to have been used on the Somme. It was fundamentally mindless and mechanical and effective only if the enemy were unwise enough to submit himself to the mincing machine as he had, for a time, on the Somme. But that was not von Lossberg's intention at Passchendaele.

In marked contrast to the methods used by Gough and Plumer were those of Third Army at Cambrai on 20 November 1917. Two elements were new there; the predicted barrage and bombardment made possible by scientific gunnery, and the use of large numbers of tanks. The two complemented each other to surprise the enemy as he had not been surprised since Neuve Chapelle. For there was no preliminary bombardment at all and the battle started when the tanks and the infantry advanced and the guns opened fire. Survey and tanks were available to Gough in July 1917, although neither he nor Uniacke were aware of Third Army developments. But the ground at Ypres and Haig's battle plan would have made it impossible for Gough to have used the same methods even had he considered them. Yet it is interesting that although Maxse was not informed about the developments that made a surprise attack at Cambrai possible he wrote a second letter to Fifth Army on 21 August about German methods and the way to combat them. In it he admirably described the ideas that were to be used in the Hundred Days from August to November 1918 and were developed from those of Cambrai.

After describing the new German system of defence in depth with reverse slope positions, its main defended zone in rear of an outpost zone, and counter-attack divisions held ready outside the range of shelling, he observed that five measures should be taken to deal with it. More extensive use of low-flying aeroplanes in the attack; more tanks in the attack; more extensive use of fuze 106 which destroyed wire and men in the open with HE shells but did not crater the ground; instead of the linear formations laid down in the existing instructions 'a more elastic infantry formation for the attack, built up of platoons working in depth rather than battalions stereotyped in waves'; and mechanical carriers for infantry to lighten the men's loads.

Maxse went on to expand these points. Temporary command of the air should be gained in order that strong points, nests of machine-guns, infantry advancing or massing for counter-attack and the personnel of hostile batteries could be attacked. Aircraft were also needed in conjunction with tanks to attack anti-tank guns and forward batteries. To ensure the mobility of tanks, infantry and artillery the ground must not be made impassable by heavy guns in the preliminary bombardment, and smoke should blind the enemy's observation posts. Given these conditions, tanks should be used in sufficient numbers to neutralise strong points and facilitate the task of the infantry. Tanks and infantry should be given co-operative tasks but they should not necessarily move together. The infantry would stalk the objective and arrive within assaulting distance at the same time as the tank. For this they must have more power of manoeuvre than was given by the wave formation. Each section should be a self-contained fighting unit including riflemen, rifle grenadiers and a few bombers. Three such sections would be supported by a Lewis gun section integral to the platoon. 'In conclusion I would venture to emphasise the desirability of recognising more fully that man power will be the deciding factor in this war, either this year or next. The only alternative to man power is mechanical power. The tank, if used in the battle with discretion, is capable of economising man power and minimising casualties.'[126]

CHAPTER 8

A Technical Knock Out

*Four hundred and fifteen fighting tanks went over
the top at zero hour that morning (August 8th
1918) . . . stampeding the enemy forces, circum-
navigating machine-gun nests and receiving as
little hurt from their sting as from ant-heaps in the
path of a rhinoceros.*
David Lloyd George,
War Memoirs, Volume VI, 3136.

*Infantry is the arm which in the end wins battles.
To enable it to do so the co-operation of the other
arms is essential; separate and independent action
by the latter cannot defeat the enemy.*
Field Service Regulations (Operations) 1924, 12.

SIR Douglas Haig described the Hundred Days, between
8 August and 11 November 1918, as the last round of a long
contest in which the British Army gained a technical knock out.
Its opponent was on the ropes but both fighters were exhausted.
The politicians had treated Haig's assurances, that if they
committed their last reserves to it the war could be ended in the
autumn, as yet another of the Commander-in-Chief's routine
expressions of confidence. They were surprised by the success of
his last campaign, misunderstood and ignored Haig's advice that
the civil and military exhaustion of both sides and the deterior-
ation of roads and railways in the autumn weather made an
armistice and a fair peace mandatory before the winter, and
listened to Foch who was determined to extract the maximum
from the Germans and from the British Army whose performance
had been mainly responsible for compelling the Germans to
negotiate.[127] They misjudged the military situation completely.
    After the war writers and politicians belittled British Army
leadership. They emphasised the grinding misery of the earlier
years and remained silent about the Hundred Days treating it as
the culmination of a hateful slugging match. By ignoring the

British Army's professional achievement they reinforced the
German Army's insistence that it had been stabbed in the back
rather than overtaken, in the end, in military science. Consequently it was Loos, the Somme and Passchendaele, with men
stripped to the waist serving guns recoiling from the two
hundredth round of a barrage programme, or plodding in lines
behind the shell bursts through an endless expanse of mud, that
came to typify the war, not the flights of ground-attack aircraft,
deeply penetrating armoured cars with wirelesses and Whippet
tanks, or heavy tanks accompanying small units of well-armed
infantrymen that were the hallmarks of the victories of Second
Amiens and the breaching of the Hindenburg system in 1918. In
remembering the dead and the crippled in after years the British
dwelled morbidly on the bitter defeats of the early rounds and
did not celebrate the technical knock out. Thomas Capper, had
he lived (he was killed at Loos), would have ascribed it to their
failure to understand that wars are won by the still and mental
parts and not the battering ram, and that the former had at last
triumphed over the latter in the Hundred Days.

Whether British men and women understood what had
happened in the months of August, September and October
1918 better than their politicians at the time or not, the end took
them by surprise too. Indeed, the contrast between, say, the
battle for the Westhoek Ridge at Ypres, in August 1917, and the
seizure of Mont St Quentin, exactly a year later by the
Australians, merits both explanation and celebration. The first
feature, a slight swelling below the Menin Road Ridge, was
dearly bought; the second, a notable eminence on the Somme,
was well-defended but went for a song. Yet the British Army
suffered over 110,000 casualties in the victorious fighting on the
active fronts in August 1918, whereas they lost under 70,000 in
the notorious Ypres fighting in August 1917. Clearly, then, it
cannot be that there were fewer casualties in the fighting of the
Hundred Days that is memorable. Quite the contrary. Rather it
is that in suffering them the British Army won the war; and,
more important, that they won it in a style that presaged the
future, not by attacking 'in the same old way'.

The professional military writers of the early twenties, when
the events of 1918 were freshly remembered and the dead hand
of peace routine and political economy had yet to squeeze the
enthusiasm out of the Army, understood the change that had
been wrought in 1918. They believed that the future belonged to
aircraft and tanks operating closely with infantry bristling with
light machine-guns, and even with self-propelled field guns. They
also knew that a severe lack of manpower had been the main

challenge of 1918 and that the use of aircraft, tanks, infantry and artillery in teams linked, in some degree, with wireless had been a successful response. The first had required and the second enabled human resources to be used more efficiently and rationally in 1918 than in the earlier years. It was generally believed that there would be no call for mass infantry to die throwing itself against machines, as in 1916, in future wars.

The model for the future that writers had in mind was tried at Cambrai in November 1917 and improved at the successful battles in August and September 1918. The interval between them was taken up by the desperate defensive battles and retreats of the German offensives from March until June. To celebrate defeat rather than victory the official accounts of those battles were published in 1935, 1937 and 1939: Cambrai had to wait until 1948 and the Hundred Days until 1947. It was as though the directors of the Army, too, wished to forget what they had learned, even if the middle-piece of officers like Alan Brooke and John Dill thought otherwise.

For the British response to the challenges of 1918 was a milestone in the history of land warfare of more significance than Haig indicated in his last dispatch, as it marked the first successful use of high performance teams using high performance machines in the attack. Teams and machines enabled the fighting fronts to be extended, as battalion fronts had been extended when infantry weapons became more lethal after 1900. In aggregate, more fire-power and as many men were engaged in lower density fighting in 1918 than in the narrower fronts of 1916 and 1917. And whereas the dense attacks on narrow fronts had created crises on the roads and railways, converted battlefields into bogs and used resources inefficiently, the wider fronts of 1918, on which the techniques that had been developing steadily throughout the war were brought to some sort of culmination, allowed both administrative and fighting resources to be deployed effectively. The problem of exploiting a breakthrough remained, though, for the infantryman still walked at three miles per hour and the tank at much the same average pace. The roads through the old fighting zones were still too appalling to permit vehicles to carry significant numbers of troops to open country beyond. So Foch, largely at Haig's urging, abandoned the grand tactics of the breakthrough for those that sought a progressive loosening of the front. Strategic aims no longer inhibited tactics in 1918, as they had in every previous British campaign from 1915 onwards. Tactical possibilities were at last allowed to dictate the course of events, as Frederick Maurice had proposed when he was Brigadier General Staff to Sir John French in 1915.

Cambrai was rightly regarded by the Tank Corps as their triumphant coming of age. But it was more than the first demonstration of the capability of a mass of tanks in the attack. The technical capabilities of modern artillery were also exploited for the first time to obtain tactical surprise, and the infantry were prepared to exploit the surprise attack by tanks and artillery by advancing quickly to deep objectives. On the other hand the tactical were not given complete priority over the strategic factors in the plan. Originally J. F. C. Fuller, then the GSO 1 of the Tank Corps, intended to inflict a tactical defeat on the Germans on suitable ground, but not to seize territory. His plan was altered to that of achieving a breach in the Hindenburg defence system and of holding the breach. In that respect the mistake of earlier battles in having grandiose aims but inadequate resources was repeated. The attempt to hold the ground gained led to weakness which the Germans exploited in a successful counter-attack that regained most of what they had lost.

The essential principle of the plan was to achieve surprise, as it had been at Neuve Chapelle. The guns remained silent on their arrival in their battle positions except for normal activity. There was no pre-battle artillery duel to subjugate the hostile batteries, nor was there any pre-battle bombardment of trenches. The operation started with a fast, unregistered barrage in front of advancing tanks. The infantry followed to mop up the surprised defenders of the front system and then other tanks and infantry moved forward in small columns to penetrate the remainder of the German defence system. Survey, accurate location of hostile batteries by air and by flash spotting and sound ranging, calibration of the guns and attention to their calculations allowed accurate and very heavy concentrations of fire on enemy infantry, gun positions, headquarters and communications junctions. Gas shells were used to neutralise battery positions, and in the first few hours of the battle there was very little hostile gunfire.

Infantry were trained before Cambrai to march long distances and were brought up to the front in stages over a period of days. They moved into the line without giving the enemy the opportunity to identify them. During the battle they were expected to fight for several days without relief. Pre-battle training with tanks was undertaken to teach them to work as part of a fire team that might include a single tank. The terrain was slightly rolling farm land, free of the detritus of previous heavy fighting and reasonable going for tanks, even though it was late in the season. Although the German defences were good, the combination of new artillery methods and a very large number of tanks with infantry in close attendance took the enemy completely by surprise. However, as the battle was considered to be an infantry advance with tanks and not a tank advance with infantry, and although many more tanks were available than in any previous attack, the infantry still largely determined the tactics in most divisions. Consequently, there were variations in the way divisions used their tanks, some of which were not designed to maximise the co-operation between the two arms. There was no question at Cambrai of the equality between the arms that existed in armoured divisions in the Second World War. The tanks were an auxiliary arm.

Tanks had been used for the first time on 15 September 1916, on the Somme. Forty-nine machines were allotted to Fourth and Reserve Armies of which 32 reached their start line. Of those 9 subsequently broke down, 5 were ditched, 9 failed to rendezvous with the infantry and 9 reached their objectives and did serious execution. Of those the most famous were the three that supported the attack on Flers when an airman reported that 'a tank is walking up the main street of Flers with the British Army cheering behind'. But later, the divisional commander remarked that one of his brigade majors, who had sorted out the defences just in time to hold a heavy German counter-attack, told him that a disorganised mob of men, some without arms, had followed the tank into the village in carnival spirit.[128]

The first experience with tanks in 1916, and those in 1917 when tanks were used on unsuitable ground at Arras and Passchendaele and tank commanders encountered obstructive infantry officers and even divisional commanders, fostered the view in the corps that tanks ought to be used alone to strike at the nerve centres of the enemy, to destroy him in the open, but not to take or hold ground. Such had been the intention of Fuller's original plan for Cambrai. The divisional commanders who worked with tanks in these years generally agreed that they were a promising development, had achieved miracles in a few cases but would not be the determinant in their plans until they had been made mechanically reliable. They were invaluable in short, set-piece battles, but after forty-eight hours they were spent. Consequently, few divisional commanders modified their tactics to work with tanks until Cambrai and some not even then.

Opinion on using tanks in 1917, and in the twenties too, was shaped not only by the Army's experiences with them but by the three fundamental ideas that inspired their provenance. These were the tank as armoured cavalry, as armoured artillery and as armoured infantry.

Armoured cars that could patrol roads, perhaps in conjunction with cavalry, had been in service at the beginning of the century

and fell into the first category. They were used by the Naval
Division in Flanders in 1914. At Amiens, on 8 August 1918, the
Canadian Independent Force of armoured cars, machine-guns in
trucks and mortars penetrated at least six miles beyond the corps
objectives and maintained communication to Corps Headquarters with Mk III Continuous Wave wireless sets. Its bulletins
were listened to by the French divisions on the Canadian right
flank and by the Australians on the left. On the same day,
Medium Mark A (Whippet) tanks, of which 'Musical Box'[129]
(the famous tank commanded by Lieutenant C. B. Arnold of B
Company 6th Battalion) was one, with crews of three, a range of
eighty miles, a maximum road speed of eight miles per hour and
mounting four Hotchkiss machine-guns, were ranging freely over
the battlefield itself. The wheeled armoured cars were restricted
to roads and were impeded by debris, shell holes and demo-
litions, but they operated in formed bodies, maintained contact
with the main body, and compelled the enemy to react to their
presence by establishing themselves astride road junctions. A
few tanks also fought their way into open country. The Whippets
were mainly intended to work with the cavalry, to assist it to
break out into the open where it could use its speed and range.
But although the cavalry could move faster than the tanks it was
unable to penetrate the enemy machine-gun belt or cross wire
and generally failed in its task. A reason was that the tanks that
were intended to neutralise the machine-guns did not survive in
organised units because of breakdowns, ditchings and direct hits.
Those that survived outdistanced the cavalry when the two arms
worked together under fire. The action of light tanks with
infantry was less than satisfactory because the former demanded
that the barrage move at seventy-five yards in a minute, too fast
for the infantry, in order to make use of their speed. A
conclusion was drawn that light tanks were most effective when
unencumbered by other arms. In Fuller's view the tank, particularly the light tank, was 'in fact, an armoured mechanical
horse' capable of breaking through the front alone. This view
had many adherents after the war.

   The tank as artillery had its recent origins in the provision of
armoured shields to protect field guns from shrapnel and small
arms fire when engaging targets over open sights. The Austrian
infantry had armour piercing bullets in 1914, and the Germans
used them against the tanks, but shields proof against armour
piercing bullets made the guns too heavy for six-horse teams.
The horses were the vulnerable part of the field artillery team
and they suffered heavily, particularly when the guns were
deployed amongst the infantry. Yet the experience of 1914,

reinforced by that of 1918, justified the old belief that artillery firing over open sights at the crisis of a small unit battle was often decisive. On the Somme and in the 1917 battles it had seldom been able to intervene in this way because of obstacles and broken terrain and heavy fire. Those were the conditions in which a tank with a gun that fired HE or a shrapnel-type round could give direct artillery support to infantry that met unexpected resistance. From Neuve Chapelle to Cambrai the artillery had not given such support even with mountain guns and mortars. From this point of view the tank was the self-propelled and armoured artillery piece for which armies had been waiting since Leonardo da Vinci first conceived it.

The immediate inspiration for the tank came from the observation of Lieutenant-Colonel E. D. Swinton[130] that an armoured vehicle moving on tracks, such as were already used for tractors in agriculture and for towing heavy guns, would be able to flatten wire and suppress the machine-guns that were dominating the infantry even in October 1914. After an initial enterprise by the Admiralty Landships Committee, which was already concerned with armoured cars, there emerged the slow machine capable of crossing trenches and carrying either 2 naval 6-pounder QF Hotchkiss guns in side sponsons and 4 machine-guns, or 6 machine-guns, that first fought on 15 September 1916. The former was the male and the latter, designed to protect the male from infantry when it was using its 6 pounder, was called the female. The design was developed until Mark IV and Mark V tanks, with speeds of 3½ and 4½ miles per hour respectively, were the most numerous in 1918.

Between Cambrai and the breaching of the Hindenburg system at the end of September 1918, the tanks were conceived, variously, as armoured cavalry, as armoured infantry and as self-propelled artillery. Visionaries, looking forward to 1919, imagined them as landships employed in fleets. But the dominant fact about the tank was that it was not durable. At Cambrai, 324 fighting tanks were committed, not including supply tanks, wire pullers, wireless tanks and tanks carrying bridging material and cable. At the end of the first day 65 had received direct hits, 71 had broken down, 43 were ditched and many others needed minor repairs. The casualties on 8 August 1918 were higher still and reflected improving German anti-tank artillery. Four hundred and fourteen started, but only 145 were runners on the second day, 85 on the third, 38 on the fourth and 6 remained on the fifth.[131] The crews were exhausted by temperatures of well over 100 degrees Fahrenheit and the fumes and noise from engines and guns. A night on the march before a battle and another spent returning to harbour for maintenance usually meant thirty-six hours without sleep amid the strain of battle. Neither men nor machines were of much use on a second day of fighting.

The supply of fresh crews and tanks was never enough to compensate for the predictable wastage. Consequently, on the extended frontage on which the Army advanced during October and November 1918, the tanks were not the decisive factor that they had been earlier. The Germans held their front with marksmen, machine-gun detachments and field guns in the open. Tanks were seldom available to deal with either. After the war the impression remained among infantrymen that tanks were decisive in set-piece battles but only a useful auxiliary in the extended fighting that followed. This led to the conclusion that tanks should be employed as auxiliary fire-support for infantry on specific occasions.

Tank officers had mixed experiences with the units that they supported in 1917. In the period of joint training that usually preceded a battle, tanks worked best with units that had adopted Sir Ivor Maxse's small unit fire-tactics. For although the platoon commander might be given immediate fire-support by a tank, he was still required to stalk the enemy with his sections using his own weapons, and to be alert to take advantage of the short period for which the enemy's fire was suppressed by the tank. But tactical sense was difficult to teach young officers and section commanders, and those who used ground and their weapons to good effect were rare in 1918. Tank officers were usually of a higher calibre but they often found themselves fighting their tanks alone, like privateers, either because the infantry could not or would not keep up with them or because the other tanks in their section had been hit, had ditched or broken down. Furthermore, tanks drew enemy fire and some infantry were told to hang back to avoid it. Tanks then fell victim to anti-tank guns that the infantry should have engaged. In consequence, there were some notable failures until standard drills were worked out. At Flesquières, on 20 November 1917, German batteries of the 54th Division, specialy trained to handle tanks, executed twenty-six of them without being molested by the infantry of the 51st Highland Division, although low flying aircraft straffed their gun positions. At Fontaine and Bourlon the infantry failed to follow the tanks into the villages on the first instance. In the Arras battles the Australians were angry with the tanks for leaving them in the lurch at Bullecourt. But it was the Australians and Canadians who had the most notable successes with tanks in 1918, largely because they fought better in small groups and, following the tanks more closely, provided the eyes that the slow-moving and blind tanks needed to help them survive.

It was the success of such outstanding infantry as the Australians and Canadians became, and the failures of others, that prompted the Kirke Committee[132] to recommend permanent affiliations between tanks and infantry in preference to the ad hoc arrangements that had led to misunderstandings on occasions. But in 1917 and 1918 neither the stamina of tanks and crews nor the supply of infantry[133] permitted permanent affiliations, although Major-General Elles did propose an armoured corps that would include engineers and services but not integral infantry. So, although the trend in 1918 was towards using a handful of élite divisions in the important battles, and a characteristic of these divisions was their ability to work with tanks, GHQ resisted further pressure that had led in earlier years of siege warfare to specialisation of function, training and equipment in the Army. The strength of the infantry had to be protected, and machine-gun battalions, tank battalions, mortars, gas units and the many other auxiliaries were in competition with it for manpower. An infantry advance would win the war, with or without tanks, it was argued. The General Staff was sceptical, even, about the arguments of General Birch against the reduction of the artillery when divisions were reduced to nine battalions in January 1918.[134]

The staff still thought of the Army as an infantry supported by other arms. Unfortunately, much of the infantry still fought in the frame of mind it had acquired in the earlier years. The need to change tactics to meet the semi-open conditions had been apparent to some commanders in 1916 and 1917 but the majority of the brigade and battalion commanders were not prepared for open warfare. In 1918, they were unduly sensitive about their flanks, although they were exhorted to think more of finding those of the enemy, and were inclined to wait for orders on reaching an objective instead of patrolling forward, making more ground and keeping contact with the enemy. Commanders and staffs did not easily throw off the highly centralised, systematic and bureaucratic methods of 1915–17. Corps HQs were often guilty parties in that respect. In previous years they had controlled the battles because the massive fire-support for the infantry had been directed by them. Now they were slow to devolve responsibility and fire-support to division commanders so that brigades could keep the pressure on the enemy. The brigade commanders, in their turn, had to learn the methods of 1914, when some of them had commanded companies. Not the least of the skills required was to employ heavy artillery at the earliest moment against immature defences before the enemy could consolidate them. The divisions that did manage to use 6-inch howitzers in sections at short range, the New Zealanders for instance, found that it paid dividends. The howitzers prided themselves on deploying in front of the field guns, and their battery commanders acquired that entrepreneurial thrust that prevents a battle from slowing down and slipping away from the control of the local commanders. Infantry that used its own weapons and the few guns at hand in quickly arranged fire-plans usually carried the day. When they waited for fresh fire-plans and reinforcements they often missed the boat, for the enemy withdrew or was reinforced in the meantime.

Those who asserted that the methods of 1914 were again appropriate, and Haig was one of them, were correct. Indeed, in 1918, company commanders now had much more fire-power than McMahon had asked for in 1910. But even the set-piece battles of the Hundred Days followed different procedures from those before the precedent of Cambrai. A large percentage of the enemy's guns were located and neutralised or destroyed, bombardments were predicted and only fired at zero hour when tanks and infantry moved forward under a predicted, fast-moving barrage. The latter was less frequently used than earlier. To increase the surprise effect of a simultaneous assault by tanks, artillery and infantry, the guns fired at higher rates than previously when preparatory bombardments and artillery duels, like that in July 1917 at Ypres, had continued for weeks. The staff was relieved of the heavy demands such programmes made on road and rail facilities for ammunition and the maintenance of guns. But when the hurricane fire-support programmes were completed the local commander of 1918 was still the key influence on the subsequent battle. Without his presence to assess the situation and to goad and encourage, the tempo of the battle slowed up as it had in the pre-war exercises. To his task he could now bring machine-guns, mortars, medium howitzers and surviving tanks, none of which was available as reserve fire-power in 1914. Indeed, rather than adding scarce infantrymen to the fray to influence the decision, he now added fire-power. The improvements in telephony and telegraphy helped him manage this. However, the first and necessary step that commanders had to take was to shift their headquarters right into the battle zone. This had been one of the lessons of Cambrai that had cost some officers their commands.

The senior Old Army officers, J. A. L. Haldane[135] for instance, never failed to be on the spot when trouble brewed.

Haldane, who commanded 3rd Division on the Somme, risked his life at Delville Wood and Longueval as a matter of course. But when artillery fire-power built up and battles were centrally controlled, headquarters had been moved back; commanders like Haldane were rare on the Somme. In the set-piece battles of 1915 and 1916 with their shallow objectives, rearward was more important than forward communication. With a matrix[136] of buried telephone lines at their disposal brigades and divisions were located where they could maintain communication with the higher formation. Telephone links forward to battalions were maintained as long as possible but in the semi-open dog-fighting and heavy shelling on the Somme messages were usually sent by runners and liaison officers.

The need to improve telephone communications was mentioned in connection with the Old Army, and when British officers visited the French Army in 1915 they found machines and personnel superior to theirs. Wireless was slow to penetrate the forward area because the equipment was heavy and the Army lacked trained operators. Furthermore, wireless was insecure unless messages were encoded. Officers were reluctant to take the trouble to become familiar with, let alone adept, at the process. On 1 July 1916, for instance, wirelesses remained open at some brigade headquarters but few of them passed a single message. It was not realised, at that time, that the Germans were using the thermionic valve, which they had discovered before the war, to amplify induction signals from telephones in order to listen to British conversations. The spying mania of 1915 was fuelled by insecure telephone conversations in the front line. The relative success of the power buzzer system in static conditions probably retarded the development of wireless as well. The power buzzer had a range of 2,000 yards in most conditions and did not require a continuous line to be laid and maintained between instruments. Instead it used a base line, 150 to 200 yards long, which could be and frequently was in a tunnel, for transmission, and an induction amplifier at the receiver. But the equipment was heavy and the messages were liable to interference. By the summer of 1917 at Ypres, the power buzzer was not being used very much.

One of the first uses of spark wireless in the forward area was by the Princess Patricia's Canadian Light Infantry machine-gun officer, Major van Den Berg, to control the indirect fire of his guns in March 1916. He used a crossword puzzle code over a phone back to his wireless signaller who transmitted to the guns. This combination of telephone and wireless became the normal practice. Unfortunately for him his signals were picked up by a listening staff officer and he and his team were arrested. In May, again in the Canadian Corps, an FOO from a 9.2-inch howitzer battery sent fire orders over six thousand yards in the Ypres Salient. Yet, during the German attack on Mount Sorrel, on 2 June 1916, although no telephone lines were 'through', no traffic was passed over the wireless until the afternoon.

The Germans used wireless in the forward area earlier than the British, but valuable information was obtained from listening to their company and battalion low-power sets on which the operator had to repeat his message several times. The result of the listening work was improved when the British started to use the valve amplifier in the field themselves. More important, the thermionic valve was used in the first Continuous Wave wireless issued in the field, the Woolwich Set. The Germans never used CW so this was a technical triumph for the British.

CW gave greater range for less power so that the batteries and sets were lighter and the aerials shorter. The tuning was so sharp that four times the number of sets could operate in an area without interference and enemy interception was more difficult. CW was ideal for the artillery with their intricate network of long range communications with aircraft, ground observers and computing centres, and their system of coded fire orders. CW sets were used at Vimy Ridge in April 1917 and operated at a range of 8,000 yards with only five foot aerials at the forward set. In August, the registration of the guns at Hill 70 was done by CW wireless. CW was used extensively at Second Amiens, in August 1918, with sets at divisional headquarters and each artillery brigade, corps survey sections, the Canadian Independent Force and with liaison officers with the French Tenth Army. Sets were opened in Flanders to pass deception traffic when the Canadian Corps moved down to the battle.

Short range spark or loop sets, like those used earlier by the Germans, were designed to replace power buzzers between brigade and battalion and even company. They were supposed to have a range of up to 4,000 yards but were not very successful since the signallers were usually not trained and the sets were too sensitive. Furthermore, like CW sets, spark wireless sets were easily damaged if they were transported in General Service Wagons and tanks. This limited their usefulness in infantry units in mobile operations. However, with the back-up sets that were adopted as a general rule in relays after August 1918, brigade headquarters could be located close to the battalions and use line back to 'wireless head' if necessary. The work of dispatch riders and line detachments was thereby reduced.[137]

Wireless had been used by cavalry headquarters in South

Africa and again in 1914 but it was first used tactically by the aircraft of the corps squadrons which carried transmitters for making observations for the artillery in early 1915. By 1917, as 90 per cent of counter-battery observation was done by airmen using wireless, the success of the artillery battle had come to depend on the weather being suitable for flying, on wireless reception and on a network of telephone lines from the receivers to the users of the airmen's information. Major-General Trenchard and the Commander-in-Chief were agreed that the air battle had to be won if first the artillery battle and then the battle of the infantry were to be successful. So Trenchard was concerned to ensure that his fighter pilots protected the slower aircraft of the corps squadrons, used for artillery work, and drove enemy planes behind their own lines where they could not observe British movement and guns nor direct their own artillery fire so effectively. The success of the RFC in this task waxed and waned with the relative technical efficiency of their aircraft and those of the Germans. The latter concentrated their planes to achieve local superiority and used large circuses like those of Baron von Richthofen to achieve it. Trenchard drove his pilots very hard all along the line, and was criticised for the heavy casualties that they suffered. But thanks to their courage, the RFC training organisation and the aircraft industry, they had air superiority in 1918.

Air superiority was of no use unless it was exploited and there was no doubt that British artillery superiority in 1917 was one of the fruits of it. The artillery was the first to feel the effect when the Germans gained ascendancy in the spring and summer of that year. But another way of exploiting air superiority, ground attack, only came into its own at the end of 1917. The Germans used large formations of close support aircraft in conjunction with their counter-attack divisions in the first days of the Passchendaele campaign, and their bombers were active against rest areas at night throughout its course. But it was not until Cambrai that British pilots were specially assigned and trained for ground attack although on 26 September 1917, in Plumer's offensive, aircraft were very effective against counter-attacks. Before the German March offensive, the RFC was targeted to bomb the German build-up but was only able to fly on five nights between 5 and 21 March because of foggy weather. Although the British gained superiority soon after the battle started, communications with the artillery broke down under the strain of movement. Consequently the Corps SE 5s were switched to additional ground attack which the Germans reported as very effective and GHQ as decisive in delaying the

German advance. In contrast, the Germans missed perfect targets as the British packed the straight roads.

On 8 August, ground attack aircraft were armed with 25-pound HE bombs and smoke bombs but cloud made it difficult for them to liaise closely with the tanks. Their most valuable rôle was attacking anti-tank guns, particularly on the second day when fewer tanks were runners. But without wireless communications they had to rely on visual means to find their targets. Scout planes led the attackers to them or fired Very lights to attract their attention, and artillery aircraft ordered smoke to mark targets. These artillery aircraft reported to a wireless Central Information Bureau at Corps which co-ordinated low level air as well as artillery support. Orders to squadrons were distributed from thence by voice transmission. All that was missing was a wireless telephony set in the tanks to communicate with attack aircraft, and clear weather throughout the day. Seventy-five squadrons were allotted to do this work at the end of August in Third and Fourth Armies.[138]

The new ground attack weapon was grafted on to the existing corps artillery and intelligence organisation, already firmly established and receiving wireless calls from aircraft giving artillery targets. There were various code letter prefixes to denote the targets. 'N' for 'guns in position', 'NF' for 'guns now firing', 'WPFN' for 'many batteries active' and 'GF' for 'fleeting target'. 'LL' called for 'all available batteries and bombing squadrons to engage'. With the general co-ordination of ground attack, wireless interception, and information about the location of our own troops being added to the artillery intelligence function and artillery targeting, the corps centres became hubs of the mobile battle. Wireless from brigades rearward was an essential part of this system. If it did not function the control of the battle tended to gravitate back to corps where the communications did work. A wireless link between tanks, infantry and aircraft at the battalion level had yet to be established to enable the battle to be completely decentralised in its impromptu stages. Nevertheless, imperfect though wireless may have been in the Hundred Days, it came of age by permitting highly organised fire direction centres to function. They anticipated the shape of things to come in the Second World War.

The memory of the invaluable contribution of the RAF and wireless to the ground victory was a casualty of a post-war political struggle between the services. Although *Field Service Regulations*, 1924, made a statutory obeisance towards the importance of air superiority, for all intents and purposes the mechanics of using it in the battle were forgotten. Haig, himself, had emphasised the importance of winning the air battle and that in 1918 the victory in the air had been more decisive than the one on the ground, thanks to a superior supply of pilots and higher aircraft production. The Hundred Days opened the way for a remarkable combination of various types of aircraft, guns, tanks and infantry, all linked by wireless, that was not followed up. Yet the pilots who proved again and again, in 1918, how effective low-flying aircraft could be against troops in the open, heartily disliked the role and did not regard it as a specialty. Unlike the Germans, the RAF did not produce distinctive aircraft for ground attack nor develop the technique of mass machine-gun and bombing attacks. Strategic bombing, ineffective in World War One, appealed more to the post-war RAF than ground attack which had proved itself. The reason was political. In 1917 and 1918, it was the politicians who had overridden the evidence from the field that strategic bombing was a diversion of force from the decisive point and, by adopting it, embraced a fundamentally immoral mode of war.

The army was not guiltless in matters directly within its control. The need to locate the control of a battle at the right level and to give the commander excellent communications had been understood in 1918. Yet wireless was not made a priority after the war. The richness of the human material and the ferment of ideas in the immediate post-war Army is evident from the literature, as it had been before 1914, for the younger men had had experience beyond their years, as was to be the case again in the late forties. Those men raised questions that had been part of the unfinished business of 1914. The need to improve communications, to evolve a common tactical doctrine for all the Arms, and to settle the organisation and tactics of the division were among them.

The experience of the war years could have provided answers to these and other questions. As a start, it would have made sense to commission a rigorous report on the way tanks and aircraft had been used rather than to leave the field to opinion-makers to use imprecise information in support of their prejudices. Even the conclusions of post-war exercises needed to be judged alongside battle experience. The German General Staff, deeply attached to historical method, began its examination of future tactics with the lessons of the war. A proposal that the Historical Section undertake a study was rejected for lack of funds. But the Treasury was only a mote in the eye of a British General Staff that had no historical sense and still, to this day, does not allot sufficient human resources to gather and to analyse its records. So the Army waited until 1932 for the Kirke Report on the lessons of the war. Even then, Kirke's methodology was not historical although his committee's recommendations were sensible. For instance it proposed the inclusion of armoured divisions in the order of battle, and the General Staff accepted the idea in principle but quickly shelved it as inappropriate in the political and economical situation of the country in the Depression.

It was as unsound to have embarked on a new generation of tactics manuals in the early twenties, without analysing the immediate past, as it was to delay the Kirke investigation until the early thirties. That was particularly true of armoured battle tactics of which only a minority of infantrymen had had experience even in 1920. In fact, by November 1918, a minority of divisions had actually attacked with tank support. In the Tank Corps itself, some battalion commanders in the twenties had been infantry officers and had not commanded tanks in battle. Those who had experienced the adventure from the beginning were divided about the possibilities. In truth, the Army directors did not look further than the infantry to determine the meaning of the Hundred Days. They accepted the infantry ordinance that the principles of 1914 had triumphed and that the infantry of 1914 ought to be restored speedily. All other Arms were auxiliaries, as they had been then. That the Hundred Days had been a technical success and a co-operative triumph for the Army and the Royal Air Force and for the Arms within the Army was overlooked. In 1919, the rifle, taught initially in the standing position as though the men were in a trench, was at once restored to its 1914 status. N. M. McMahon's[139] automatic or semi-automatic rifle was not permitted to rear its ugly head until the .280-inch weapon was tried in 1949. Eventually the Army received the Belgian FN rifle in 1955. It is sad to recall that McMahon had exhorted the Army to remember that it had always prided itself on its mastery of fire-power and that it ought to take the lead, in 1910, in the field of automatic weapons.

Underlying most questions was the pre-war one of what to do about the autonomy of the infantry and cavalry regiments and the need for corps schools and corps doctrines. This fundamental issue was trampled under foot in the stampede to 'get back to some serious soldiering' after the war. A School of Infantry had to wait for another war to pass before even the blind sensed that it was necessary. At least a School of Artillery was established. Hythe became the 'Small Arms School' but its activities were split with Netheravon where the Vickers machine-guns found a home.[140] But no infantry doctrine was allowed by those who divided and ruled in the Regiments.

BOOK III

The years between the Wars: 1919–1939

Generally operations of war require one thousand fast chariots, one thousand four-horse wagons covered in leather, and one hundred thousand mailed troops . . . Now, when the army marches abroad, the treasury will be emptied at home.

Sun Tzu, *The Art of War*

Hasten slowly, GFM

Marginal note by General Sir George Milne on a W.O. 'branch memorandum' on armour and mechanisation.

CHAPTER 9

The Swingletree Factor

'Duty.' That is the one secret of success as a
soldier, General Lord Horne – 'our Gunner
General' – insists. To put duty before all else . . .
Pressed to amplify his advice, he allowed one
more word _ 'sport' . . . and particularly to be
fond of horses and of the sports this noble and
sympathetic animal shares with man.[141]

ON Armistice Day, 1918, the Royal Artillery stood at the summit of its reputation. After many vicissitudes and much trial and error its organisation and its technical gunnery had proved strong enough to defeat the scientific arm of the most scientific army in Europe. It was natural enough that as soon as demobilisation could begin this vast apparatus of heavy cannon, together with all the technical and administrative units which supported it, would have to be disbanded. No country could afford to carry such a burden in peace; a peace, it was hoped, that would last for many years. In any case, it did not seem likely that the circumstances for which it was created, the Western Front, would ever recur. But while it was one thing to return manpower and industry to peaceful purposes, and reduce the armed forces to a size that the country could afford, it was strange that the leaders of this great technical arm should allow it to decay into obsolescence for nearly twenty years and the lessons of their great struggle to be forgotten.

The descent into apathy was, at first, gradual. In the years immediately after the war there was a vigorous debate among the Gunners on the future of artillery in the pages of the Journal of the Royal Artillery. A new, permanent School of Artillery was established. Outside artillery circles, the reaction to a war of protracted defence and deliberate attack came as early as 1919, when Fuller's prize-winning entry for the Gold Medal offered by the Royal United Service Institution was published. In 1925 Liddell Hart published *Paris or the Future of War*. In 1926, the

new Chief of the Imperial General Staff, the artillery officer
Field Marshal Sir George F. Milne's first notable action was to
act on Fuller's suggestion and authorise the creation of an
'experimental mechanised force', which included tanks,
motorised infantry and tracked self-propelled artillery, showing
an early promise that he unfortunately never fulfilled. Then
there was a decline, not only in development but in interest. The
reasons were ineluctable. There was the decline in the country's
economy and therefore the reduction of the industrial base on
which any modernisation of the country's defences must rest.
There was, as the euphoria of victory evaporated, a natural and
widespread revulsion from the waste and horrors of mass
warfare. Political opinion had to take note of public opinion,
whose opposition to preparations for war was by no means
confined to an extreme left or pacifist fringe, but was general.
Until the gradual emergence of the Axis powers there was no
palpable opponent. The post-war reductions and economies in
defence and the 'Ten Year Rule' (which governed defence
planning and expenditure on the basis of an assumption that no
major war was likely for a decade, and whose initial date was
moved forward from time to time) were, in retrospect, sensible
and prudent measures. What was not justifiable was the virtual
suspension of any rational analysis of what the future needs of
defence might be. There was no clearly expressed or coherent
policy to guide the armed forces.

It was assumed, rather than stated, that the rôle of the land
forces was, vaguely, the defence of the land frontiers of the
home country and empire, 'imperial military policing' (i.e.
counter-insurgency against tribesmen in Palestine, Iraq and on
the North-West Frontier of India, and riot-control, using armed
force), and the security of naval bases overseas. Milne himself
equivocated. Nothing could have been more extraordinary than
his summing up at a conference of general officers he had called
to discuss the report of the Kirke Committee, in 1933, at the end
of his disastrous reign as CIGS. After a long discussion on how
to organise an attack on a strongly organised modern defensive
position and maintain its momentum using aircraft, tanks, and
mechanised artillery, he gave as his opinion that there would
always be a future for horsed cavalry, that the artillery 'was on
the right lines' (it was almost entirely dependent on horse
traction) and that in any case he hoped that there would never
be a major intervention by Britain in a continental war, and that
the correct task of the army was Imperial defence.[142]

Yet, at the same time, the Staff College was studying just such
problems on the basis of general staff manuals whose content

had been authorised by Milne himself as the Chief of the General Staff. In 1925 Major H. R. Pownall, when reviewing the section on Artillery in the *Field Service Regulations Volume II (Operations)*, was able to say that at last the artillery had the doctrine on which it could base its employment, and which had been so lacking since the end of the war.[143] By 1933 it was not so much that the doctrine was not clear, but the mission, the very raison d'être of the Army, and therefore of the artillery arm. The principles of artillery employment are obvious (centralisation of control, mobility, concentration of fire and so on) but the question was really one of rôle, of what effect the artillery was supposed to have on the enemy. For example, in 1927 Birch recorded that the task he had been given by Haig was to reorganise and strengthen the artillery so that (1) it could defeat the German artillery (2) be able to make a surprise attack at any point in the line 'instead of having to concentrate the whole of his artillery in one place in order to destroy the obstacles on the front of his attack'. In a modified form this was to be applicable in the First World War, but under Milne no such clear definition was possible. But if the rôle of artillery was not something like this, then what? Was it to be an ancillary arm in a 'mechanised' war? Or at most an affair of infantry and light artillery against an unskilled enemy, such as the 'Mad Mullah' in Somaliland, or the Third Afghan War of 1919? No wonder officers were puzzled.

What rationale was there, for instance, behind the artillery order of battle in India in 1933? The only units with a detectable rôle were the coast batteries for the defence of Bombay and Karachi against attack from the sea, (but again, by whom?), and the twenty-four batteries of light mountain howitzers carried in mule pack for operations on the North-West Frontier. There was *one* anti-aircraft battery in the whole sub-continent. There were eight motorised batteries with sixteen medium and twenty-four field guns altogether, but no fewer than *forty horse-drawn batteries* of horse artillery or field artillery, or 264 light guns and howitzers, although it had already been found that the only artillery that was of any use, even in frontier warfare, apart from the mountain batteries, were the mechanised howitzer batteries. ('Medium' was a new category, covering the 5-inch (60-pounder) guns and 6-inch howitzers, classified as 'heavy' until 1924. All the field guns were obsolete models of the type used in 1914. The horse artillery had the 13-pounder (76.2-mm) and the field the 18-pounder Mark I (84-mm) and the 4.5-inch howitzers.) Clearly there were far too many guns for the rôle of imperial policing, and it was equally clear that such a mass of horse-drawn artillery was quite unsuited to even the most conservative and conventional idea of future war. The Army itself had lost direction, and by the year 1933 apathy and reaction had reached their nadir. The only fruitful debate was outside the Army altogether.

There was little the artillery could do in the material sense, for by that year, incredibly, two models of self-propelled field guns and one of a self-propelled anti-aircraft gun had long since been scrapped. A degree of modernisation might have been achieved by getting rid of the horses and disbanding a large number of obsolete units so as to afford fewer but more mobile and powerful ones but that, as was seen when a similar proposal was made so as to create an armoured force, was out of the question. Such obstruction was to be expected in the cavalry and infantry, who were organised on social rather than functional lines, but the Royal Artillery had once prided itself on being an educated, technical, professional body. It is a sad fact that after the great officers who had led it in the war years had left, and the interest in progress during the period immediately following the war had died away, their successors were guilty not so much of a failure in foresight, or of considering the wrong options, or making the wrong assumptions, but of failing to think about anything at all.

Here the historian is faced with a puzzle. In 1933 the Royal Artillery was unmistakably deeply conservative and backward-looking: less interested in its military capacity than its social status and its myth. Its system of officer selection was as narrow as in any fashionable regiment of foot or horse, it had succumbed to the national vice of admiring amateurism, it was suspicious of any innovation, and its officers were expected to conform to a strict social pattern which included an affectation of professional ignorance. One might be looking at the Austrian Army of half a century before. Yet, somehow, in a few years time, these same officers were able to shake off their torpor and recreate an artillery which by 1943 was not perhaps as powerful as the giant weapon of the First World War, but far more mobile and flexible.

The explanation must be sought in the sociological factors which are apt to prevail in any old-established and institutionalised groups. The initiative towards military reform which was begun by Milne and then allowed by him to founder, was not opposed by any rational argument or a rival theory of warfare. For example the infantry and cavalry, entrenched in the 'regimental system', instinctively resisted their supersession by an armoured force, or even the retention of their identities and conversion to motorised or armoured troops. Similarly, to resolve this particular problem it is necessary to examine the origin, education and attitude of artillery officers.

From its foundation down to 1899 the Royal Artillery was a single regiment, unashamed of its professional and technical rôle. Then, when the regiment was split functionally between the 'field' and 'garrison' branches, the new exclusive all-mounted Royal Field Artillery began to move 'up market' and climb the military-social ladder. It became, as was cruelly but justly said, 'the poor man's cavalry'. Cadets at the Royal Military Academy competed eagerly for the Royal Field Artillery and were disappointed if their marks in the final examinations condemned them to the Royal Garrison Artillery, the 'gambardiers', who were condemned to the fixed defences of coastal fortresses or to what was still known as 'siege' artillery, slow moving heavy guns. (The derivation of this curious and derogatory nickname is unknown. Technicians, the 'boffins' of the Second World War, were 'blokes', i.e., rather common.) In the First World War this functional distinction, never very clear, had become meaningless. The garrison artillery became virtually the same as the field. The lighter natures of heavy guns, like the 60-pounders and 6-inch howitzers were, in practice, 'field' guns, just as much as the little 18-pounders and 4.5-inch howitzers. The RGA actually had its own 'field' artillery, in the shape of the 'pack' or 'light' artillery batteries used in mountain warfare. (Why these were given to the garrison artillery is not clear. Perhaps the reason was that the mounted branch considered the care of mules beneath their dignity.) The RGA was technically far more proficient than the field artillery, the result of its four-year long duel with the excellent German artillery. It was the natural choice to operate the new-fangled anti-aircraft artillery, whose employment required the solution of the most difficult technological problems. It was the RGA which constituted the main striking force of the artillery, not the puny cannon of the RHA and RFA. For instance, the 'heavy' component of the artillery of the Fifth Army in 1918 consisted of 244 pieces of artillery of the calibre of 5-inch (60-pounder) up to 15-inch, apart from 230 mortars of 6-inch and 9.45-inch.

In 1924 it was decided to re-amalgamate the two branches, but amalgamation was not what took place. In effect, the Royal Garrison Artillery was abolished. Apart from the coastal 'fire commands' and their batteries of fixed armaments, the only ex-garrison units which remained were twenty-eight medium batteries (112 guns and howitzers), the mountain artillery, one anti-aircraft brigade of three batteries (twenty-four guns) for the whole army and a single survey company, responsible for topographical survey, and for all sophisticated means of locating enemy batteries and other targets. Its retention at least kept these techniques alive. No mobile heavy artillery was retained. The mounted branch consisted of fourteen batteries of Royal Horse Artillery (eighty-four guns) and 112 batteries of field artillery (four mechanised, the rest horse drawn) 448 guns at peace establishment, or 672 after mobilisation. The imbalance was too great, as the mounted branch remained the posting most sought after, and so it was the ethos of the horseman, not the professional artilleryman, which thenceforth dominated the re-amalgamated Regiment.

Taking the year 1933 as the mid-point between the wars, artillery officers occupied a number of positions of great power and influence, both in the War Office and in India (where the staff structure was duplicated under a Commander-in-Chief, in Delhi.) Major-General W. H. Bartholomew, one of the most able officers of his day was Director of Military Operations and Intelligence, General Sir A. A. Montgomery-Massingberd was the Adjutant-General and about to take up the appointment of Chief of the General Staff in succession to Milne, and General Sir William Thwaites was Director-General of the Territorial Army. Brigadier A. F. Brooke, the future CIGS under Churchill, was the Army instructor at the Imperial Defence College, responsible for the education of officers likely to reach the highest posts in the Army, and Colonel Sir Ronald Adam, later to be DCIGS and the most enlightened officer ever to hold the appointment of Adjutant-General, was a senior instructor at the Staff College. In India artillery officers held the appointments of Deputy Chief of Staff and Director of Staff Duties, Adjutant-General (General Sir Alexander Wardrop, whose claim to fame was the authorship of the definitive work *Pig-Sticking, or Hog Hunting*) and the Master-General of the Ordnance.

Above them all was Field Marshal Sir George Milne, who from 1926 to 1933 was, as CIGS, the professional head of the Army for a crucial period, and as Master-Gunner, St James's Park (the ancient title of the senior Colonel-Commandant of the Royal Regiment of Artillery) from 1929 to 1946, the ruling authority over the whole Regiment; from the one position on its operational role and fitness for war, and from the other on its domestic affairs, its manning, its morale and its whole attitude and outlook. Milne's reputation has been treated harshly by historians and deservedly so, for putting his hand to the plough of army reform and the cause of mechanisation and armoured warfare, and then timidly retreating in the face of a counter-attack by the entrenched representatives of the regimental system. It is difficult to discover what he really thought about anything, but we know what he said. He agreed that progress was necessary, to please the reformers, but did nothing about it so as not to offend the regimental colonels. He held conferences to discuss modernisation, and then poured cold water on it. In the last year of his reign he gave as his opinion that the Royal Artillery was 'on the right lines', at the moment when it had no rôle and all its equipment was obsolete or obsolescent and its collective mentality embedded in horseflesh. He looks out of his portrait, calm, handsome, covered with decorations, with an air of profound wisdom and authority, the *roi faineant* of the British Army, who has the doubtful honour of being, with the Duke of Cambridge as his only rival, the greatest reactionary in its history. With such a man at its head, the first cause of the mental stagnation inside the Royal Artillery is obvious. Certainly no initiative could come up from below with any hope of prospering.

In the huge Regiment of which he was the head in 1933, 2,081 officers of the rank of lieutenant-colonel and below were at regimental duty, or in staff appointments, at the School of Artillery, the Military College of Science, or in technical staff appointments in the department of the Master-General of the Ordnance. There was no lack of potential talent. Among the captains and majors there were, for instance, Kirkman, later the leading artilleryman of the Second World War, Campbell Clarke, the gifted Director of Artillery who held office during the period of rearmament and the war, and Parham, the inventor of the quick response system for the control of massed artillery fire that came into general use in 1943. The best officers tended to be siphoned off from the mainstream of the Regiment to the Staff College, through whose portals lay the only guaranteed route to the higher appointments in the Army, or to the exclusive Royal Horse Artillery, or to be instructors in Gunnery and members of the Gunnery Staff. The more adventurous officers managed to obtain postings to the mountain artillery, for there was always the prospect of a small war on the North-West Frontier of India. Others, like Wingate, preferred secondment to the various colonial gendarmeries, such as the West African Frontier Force, the Somaliland Camel Corps and the Sudan Defence Force. With all these lively characters out of the way insufficient leaven remained in the dough.

All the same, there was no lack of ability, or brains. Admittance to the Staff College was partly by qualifying examination[144] and nomination on the basis of having obtained a high grading in the annual report made on every officer, and partly by straight competition in the examination. The academic standards of the Royal Military Academy, Woolwich, where all artillery and engineer cadets received their training was far higher than that of the Royal Military College, Sandhurst, and it was found that the numbers of their successful candidates was so great that vacancies had to be rationed so as to give the cavalry and infantry a chance. Yet inside the Regiment there was no ferment of ideas, no debate about rôle and really very little interest in the technique of gunnery, which after all was the artilleryman's bread and butter. For this there were several reasons.

All the majors and many of the captains were veterans, who found the routine of peacetime service in a garrison boring in the extreme. In India the batteries were kept operational at two-thirds strength, (four instead of six guns), but in England the situation was desperate. Horses and men were so far below strength that the resources of the whole brigade had to be combined to enable one battery to be formed for a day's exercise, and the manpower was only just enough to carry out administration, which included the time-absorbing care of the horses. The units in England were expected to be no more than holding units for reinforcements for those overseas. Artillery officers could just live on their pay, but it was very poor, and the prospects of advancement beyond the rank of major remote, except for those with staff training, or with a horse artillery background. There was little incentive, indeed there was a feeling that there was no moral obligation to do more than the minimum required. The sole exception, which claimed the ungrudging attention of all the field artillery was the care of the horse. The *History of the Royal Artillery 1919–1939* says: 'The most all-pervading feature of regimental life . . . was the total dependence of nearly all the Regiment on the horse.'[145] Major-General Harrison, whose distinguished career spanned both wars, says of this period: 'Certain it was that a battery whose horses always looked well was a good battery, whether they (sic) *could hit a target or not.*'[146] Horses and horseflesh have always been an English and Irish passion, but with the field artillery it was an obsession. General Harrison uses a telling phrase of those days, by no means derogatory in intention, to describe the artillery officer whose interest was confined to his horses: 'He never looked behind the swingle-tree.' (The swingletree was the point of attachment of the traces connecting the team of horses to the gun limber.) How this absurd attitude grew up is not at all clear. The Royal Field and Royal Horse Artillery officers of the war period understood their business as gunners very well. By 1917 when field gunnery had become complicated the battery commander was often the only officer who could act as gun position officer.

It may have been due to the belief, widely held in the 1920s and 1930s, that in any future war the sole requirement for horse or field artillery would be to gallop or trot into action as quickly as possible and engage the target with observed fire adjusted by eye, and that elaborate calculations and scientific methods were useless, a relic of trench warfare – but this is only partly the explanation. The attitude was adolescent, a hangover from the contemporary public school attitude towards anything that hinted of cleverness or intellect. The atmosphere in a typical battery is nearly caught in a nostalgic reminiscence describing a day at practice in the 1920s. The exercise set for the day involves survey and predicted fire. The battery commander confesses that he knows nothing about it, all the officers affect good humoured if tolerant derision, and the conversation turns away from the problem to the prospects of sport. The execution is left to the junior subaltern, who actually hits the target with the first round, but honour is saved, for it must have been a fluke.[147]

It was not enough for an officer to devote his whole attention merely when on duty to the horses used to pull the guns. He was expected, indeed it was his duty as much as pleasure, to devote all his leisure to some form of mounted sport. Par excellence it had to be fox-hunting, believed to teach both moral virtues – 'to ride straight' – and martial ones such as an 'eye for country', courage and the ability to take quick decisions. When the commanding officer of the 9th Brigade, part of the Experimental Mechanised Force, was asked to lecture on mechanised artillery at the Staff College he solemnly assured his distinguished audience that it was essential for the officers to be allowed to keep their chargers, and that they should spend half, if not three-quarters of their time hunting.[148] In most batteries, in fact, officers who could afford to hunted three days a week. In India there was only a little hunting, with jackals taking the place of foxes, but the principal mounted sport was pig-sticking, hunting the fierce Indian wild boar mounted and using only a spear. Polo came third, as artillery officers could not compete with the long purses of the cavalry in such a highly competitive and expensive game.[149] The accent was on manliness – on *machismo*. Leave had to be spent tiger-shooting or stalking in the Himalayas. For an officer to elect to idle away his time in a house-boat on a Kashmir lake 'poodle-faking' or playing golf, says Harrison, 'would have meant ostracism in a Gunner mess.'[150] Captain O. G. Body, in an article on 'The Human Element in Peace Time Training', said that some 'messes . . . present an air of manliness, dignity and responsibility . . . others an air savouring of the light novel and the cinema'. He warned officers not to cultivate an 'air of foppishness and indolence', adding, percep-

tively, 'that we grow into what we pretend to be'.[151] This seems
to be exactly what happened.

The Journal of the Royal Artillery in the years immediately
after the war are full of articles on technical gunnery, tactics, the
lessons of the past war and the nature of the next. The Duncan
Silver Medal essay competition of 1921 was on the subject of
mechanisation.[152] Both the choice of the subject and the
arguments of the winner were remarkably far-sighted. Among
other contributions are articles by Ironside, Pile and Pownall,
but the keynote was struck by Herbert Uniacke, the British
Bruchmüller, in an 'Address to Young officers on Joining the
Regiment' published in the Journal in 1920. Predictably it is full
of stern Victorian values but every word is applicable today:
'You now belong to a fighting caste: you are an officer in the
Royal Artillery – and – *noblesse oblige*.' 'A great and sacred
trust is in your hands.' He spoke of courage, the tradition of
service, constant care for the well-being of the men, leadership,
courage and self-sacrifice, but also, 'finally, bear in mind that
you can *never* learn too much about your job . . . you can never
pull your weight until you *do* know your job.' There is no
nonsense there about hunting three days a week or an affectation of ignorance of guns and gunnery, but by 1934 the content
of the Journal has changed. It has become a sort of house
magazine rather than a serious professional journal, with articles
on pig-sticking, shooting, and even a motoring holiday in Spain.
An article exemplifying the change of mood was by a Major
E. W. M. Powell, Royal Field Artillery, who took as his subject
'Hunting as Training for War' – fox-hunting, that is – containing
such jewels of knowledge as 'take your hat off to the Master
when you first see him. . .' The harvesting of the lessons of the
war, the keen professional interest that pervaded the Regiment
and the urge for progress had died away. Body, now a
lieutenant-colonel, was by then a senior instructor at the Royal
Military Academy, Woolwich, responsible for the education of
cadets. He, commissioned in 1910 was, like Uniacke, a man of
integrity and Victorian virtues, but he personified reaction. His
favourite character was the Duke of Wellington, and in his essay
submitted for the Duncan competition of 1921 he argued that
'horses have permanent advantages', that there would be no
change for a 'generation' and what he called 'tank batteries', i.e.
self-propelled guns, must evolve separately, and become an arm,
outside the Royal Artillery.

So, by the mid-point between the wars the horsemen had won
the day. Both new ideas and professional knowledge had
become unfashionable. The affectation, as Body himself had

warned, had become real, and the 'swingletree' factor prevailed. There was nothing of Uniacke's philosophy in the indignant exclamation of a senior subaltern in a field regiment when he learned that the new commanding officer proposed to hold a weekly 'officer's day' and regular study groups to improve and broaden their knowledge: 'He's trying to turn us all into professionals like those continental officers.' That was in 1933.[153]

The cause was partly in the system for educating officers. In peace to make good wastage the Royal Artillery required approximately seventy new officers a year. In the 1930s about ten a year were graduates of Oxford or Cambridge who, if they had joined the senior branch of the Officers Training Corps, were commissioned directly into their batteries. The remainder were trained as cadets at the Royal Military Academy at Woolwich, founded in 1741 for the education of officers of the Royal Artillery and the Royal Engineers. In those days the syllabus included mathematics, map-making, freehand drawing, field engineering and fortification. The two technical arms then had much in common, especially in siege warfare, but in the twentieth century their requirements diverged. The engineers were sent to Cambridge to obtain a degree but artillery officers, except those whose future career lay in design and weapon procurement, required only a reasonable proficiency in mathematics and more of a broader tactical military education. General Harrison recalls that on being commissioned into the Royal Garrison Artillery in 1913 he had learnt nothing that was to be of any use to him. Even in the early 1920s the course was very similar; an odd mixture of practical field engineering, mathematics, dynamics, ballistics, carpentry, the work of a shoeing-smith, map-making, a little practical work on internal combustion engines, field sanitation and a great deal of riding, infantry ceremonial drill and physical training.[154]

In 1926 the two year course was shortened by six months and the newly commissioned artillery officers spent the time saved at the School of Artillery. (The engineers attended their own depot before going up to Cambridge.) The course was broadened to include military history (the Peninsular War, the opening phase of the First World War in Belgium and France, Napoleon's Italian campaign of 1796) tactics, military law and a little economics and political theory. The level of instruction varied widely. Ragging and disorder were the general rule in the science classes, so much so that at one period a uniformed officer had to attend them to protect the wretched civilian teachers. The officer instructors too often had had no formal qualifications in the subjects for which they were responsible,

such as military history, and did not know how to teach or
lecture; the Royal Engineer officers being the exception. The
weakness of the system of instruction was that apart from such
subjects as digging trenches of First World War pattern, or
practical map-making, all instruction was in the classroom in
which the future officers, already young men, were treated as
schoolboys. By contrast the man at a university had the benefit
of the tutorial system and was taking his first steps, as a man,
recognised to be such, in the discipline of self-education. He
soon learnt that questioning facts and assumptions is part of the
educational process. At Woolwich the cadet was taught to accept
what he was told without argument.

The cadets were not stupid; far from it. In academic terms it
was in those days easier to obtain a place at Oxford or Cambridge
than at Woolwich, which admitted only those who obtained the
highest places in the fiercely competitive Army Entrance Examination, the standard being about the same as a good Advanced
Level of today. The one benefit of the academic course, monitored throughout with written examinations to test progress, was
that the cadets learnt to work hard at their books, for long hours,
and sometimes late at night when physically exhausted after the
daily periods of drill, riding, games and work in the gymnasium.
Lack of progress might mean expulsion or relegation. (And also
financial hardship to their parents, who had to pay substantial
fees for attendance, only waived for the sons of officers who had
lost their lives on active service, or for the few cadets who won
scholarships in the Army Entrance Examination.)

Here was the heart of the matter. The first lesson a cadet
aspiring to be an officer must be taught is that all the demands
on his intellect and physical endurance are a necessary
preparation for his high calling. His discipline must be self-
discipline. He must not be imprinted with the attitudes of either
a schoolboy or of what was once deemed appropriate in a private
in the nineteenth-century battalion of foot. The first term was a
breaking-in process, as is not uncommon at military academies.
At the United States Military Academy it was ferocious, but
there it was compensated by pride at being admitted, a sense of
privilege in being allowed to serve the flag, all expressed in the
three words of the West Point motto: '*Honour, Duty, Country*'.
No such noble or inspiring sentiments greeted the 'snooker' on
his arrival. A sense of unworthiness, of the great deal there is to
learn, is no bad attitude in a newly joined member of any
honourable profession, but Woolwich simply reproduced the
narrow ethos of the public school by reducing aspiring young
men of eighteen and nineteen once more to the lowly status of a

'new boy'. It may have been an extreme example, but the harangue by the cadet senior under-officer to the incoming term of January, 1932, was to remind them that whatever success they may have had at school, here at Woolwich they were 'just dirt', and went on to outline the various ways that they might offend, after which he warned them against cheating in the examinations.

This was bad, but the disciplinary system was worse. The cadets were legally civilians, unconstrained but also unprotected by the many provisions of the Army Act and military law which in two years time they themselves would be responsible for justly administering. What they encountered was a version of the school prefectorial system they had left behind them. Discipline was almost entirely in the hands of the senior term. Each term, or intake, formed a company and the Academy was organised as a battalion of infantry whose discipline was the responsibility of the whole senior term. The equivalent of a head prefect was the senior under-officer, assisted by a cadet adjutant and an under-officer in charge of each company. The remainder of the senior term were all appointed corporals, who, together with the cadet under-officers, all had the power to award summary punishment. This would have been sound enough in principle if it taught the seniors responsible leadership, but unfortunately they had received no preliminary instruction or guidance in that difficult art. There was no question of their setting an example or of acting as the guide, counsellor or even friend to cadets, as the more senior subalterns in a good regiment were for the second-lieutenants. Conversation with a senior, or even between members of different terms, was forbidden.

There was a whole list of crimes of which a cadet could be guilty, ranging from imperfectly cleaned buttons or a wrongly threaded bootlace to an untidy bedroom or minor unpunctuality. For these the corporals were on the look-out, and all were empowered to order a 'hoxter', half an hour's 'extra drill', or what the soldiers of those days called 'fatigues' – such as rolling the cricket pitch – held before breakfast. These punishments were awarded summarily, on the spot, without the requirement to hear any explanation or defence, in complete defiance of the code of military law. Submission without any argument was all that was required. One offence which earned another 'hoxter' was an error, even in punctuation, in the form a cadet had to fill and render on being awarded punishment. The code, in fact, was crime-creating. Many reckless or indifferent cadets, some to become distinguished officers, accumulated so many that they left Woolwich without working off their debit balance. It was a perfectly futile system and it taught a bad lesson, not to the victim but to the cadets empowered to apply it. They were after all not being trained to be corporals, and in any case in a good regiment real corporals and sergeants do not behave in such a fashion. The lesson was soon unlearned after joining, for the Royal Artillery had a tradition of good behaviour, and its daily routine was never absorbed, as in the infantry, with 'commanding Officer's Orders' and the procession of 'defaulters' coming up for summary judgment and minor punishment.

What was far worse was legitimised bullying and hazing of cadets by the senior term. By some process whose origins are now lost, the seniors had become the guardians of the 'tone', or standard of behaviour, of the corps of cadets. What this was depended on the caprice of the under-officers. The method of enforcement was by humiliating physical punishment, inflicted quite arbitrarily. It was condoned by the commandant and staff, who had, in effect, abdicated from their own responsibilities. The most notorious case recorded was the 'running' of O. C. Wingate, the future creator and leader of the Chindits, in 1922. He was without doubt an awkward and unsatisfactory cadet, but it is questionable whether the cure was to make him run the gauntlet in the style of the army of Frederic the Great, stripped naked, between two rows of seniors while they beat him with canes, and then to fling him into a tank of cold water. It is also questionable whether the cadets responsible for decreeing and carrying out this punishment were themselves fit to be commissioned.[155]

The real object of this code was to stamp out any spark of rebelliousness, originality or departure from what the seniors considered was the norm. Part of the treatment intended to subdue the new intake was known as 'snooker-dances', once, long before, real dances or concerts, but which had degenerated into mass bullying of the snookers by the senior term. Bullying is a risky process, however, when the victims are equal in number and are strong and fit young men who are prepared to fight back. In 1930 the scandal became public, when in the course of a resulting brawl a cadet was seriously injured. 'Running', 'snooker-dances' and illegal punishments of all kinds were banned. Nevertheless, as late as 1932 four snookers of a newly joined term were subjected to a milder form of 'running' for the sole offence of being Old Etonians, and another, in his second term, for having a vase filled with flowers in his bedroom.[156]

The young second-lieutenants who emerged from this extraordinary establishment, therefore, had twice been profoundly 'socialised', first at school, and markedly so if they came from Wellington, Cheltenham, Clifton or Haileybury, the great Victorian public schools founded to provide soldiers and civil servants for the Empire. After a second dose they were thoroughly converted into 'authoritarians', in the sense that they did not so much delight in the *exercise* of authority, but sought the corsetting support of an authoritarian regime. They were still redeemable, however, and now all depended on their reception in their batteries, the next step in their education. They had, so far, never enjoyed a scintilla of independence of action or thought, had no training in leadership, and were totally unacquainted with the men of working-class origin whom they had to train in peace and lead in war. This had to be learnt on the job. In the best batteries the new second-lieutenant was welcomed, and then given a thorough grounding in his duties, his footsteps being guided usually by the senior subaltern. He was made to work a stint in the battery office, the quarter-master's store, the farrier's shop, learning to make a shoe and shoe a horse, pass a test in gun-laying and, in some batteries, clean a set of harness that had been thoughtfully left in the water-trough against his arrival. Then, at last, he was entrusted with the glorious command of two guns, with their men, horses and ammunition wagons, and was an officer at last, with an officer's responsibilities.

If he was unlucky he had inflicted on him for the third time in his short life the status of a 'new boy' at school. No one spoke to him in the mess and he was expected not to speak unless spoken to, he was left to his own devices and to pick up such information as he could from the two sergeants who commanded his gun-sections. The only instruction he received was by rebuke for his errors or omissions. A great deal depended on the senior subaltern who, as the majors and captains for the most part had lost all interest, exercised an influence beyond his rank. Sometimes they were bachelors, living in the mess, and as they had no hope of promotion before they were thirty-three they had become progressively more jaundiced and bored with their simple tasks. Too often the older men, either by choice or lack of practice, affected ignorance of any military subject except horse-mastership, and were grimly sitting out their time for their pensions.

It was a dreary scene, but it had some bright colours. The great officers who had created the war-winning artillery weapon of 1917–18 had left the Regiment two priceless legacies before they disappeared from the scene. One was the artillery chain of command. The other was the School of Artillery with its cadre of highly trained instructors, known as the 'Gunnery Staff'. As has been told, Birch and his chief of staff Rawlins, had, under

Haig, created an artillery hierarchy, not for command, for that must always be the responsiblity of the commander-in-chief and, by his authority, of the General Staff, but for 'control', which is a different matter, and for dealing with all questions of artillery policy, doctrine, manning and training. In the post-war period the elaborate organisation of armies and corps, and divisions in India had been largely dismantled. Except for the 'Commanders, Royal Artillery' in the few surviving regular divisions, all based in England, all that remained of the vaguely defined but very effective artillery hierarchy were the 'Brigadiers, Royal Artillery' at the headquarters of the territorial commands at home and in India, who were, strictly speaking, only specialist advisers. Fortunately, the General Officers Commanding-in-Chief and their Staffs rarely had any knowledge of and little interest in them, except the fitness of the horses. They were only too thankful to delegate all purely artillery affairs to their advisers.

The Brigadiers RA assisted by their artillery staff officers and by the Gunnery Staff supervised all training including the camps of practice which were the culminating event of the artillery training year. All were outstanding men, veterans of the Western Front, and intolerant of any slackness or professional ineptitude. Some, in the fashion of those days, were irascible and rough-tongued, and their set-downs were famous. One, observing with mounting disgust the wildly scattered salvoes of a brigade attempting to concentrate the fire of its batteries, said to the wretched commanding officer: 'Damn it, man, you might as well take out you p . . . and p . . . at the enemy.' Another, at one of the public post-mortems held after every firing exercise, said to an erring battery commander: 'You are paid a large salary by the Government of India to despatch, when required, eighteen pounds of steel and high explosive to its correct destination. In my opinion you are defrauding them.' It would have been regarded as very drastic in those days for a battery commander to be relieved for inefficiency (it was more dangerous to neglect the horses), but the wrath of the Brigadier RA was feared, and many a hippophile was forced 'to look behind the swingletree' whether he liked the view or not.

During the war a number of temporary schools of gunnery had sprung up, but in 1920 a school with the charter of teaching all aspects of field artillery, not only gunnery but tactics, methods of employment and artillery staff duties was set up at the site of the war-time camp of practice and artillery range at Larkhill, on Salisbury Plain. The charter of the School of Artillery eventually became a wide one, and its Commandant, in the absence of a Director of Royal Artillery, a man of power and influence. It was his business to ensure uniformity of methods in operations, and therefore in training, and a high standard of technical gunnery throughout the Royal Artillery. This was achieved by the creation of a corps of 'Instructors in Gunnery' – the 'IGs' – who with their non-commissioned assistants formed the Gunnery Staff. A small, subordinate, School of Artillery with a detachment of the Gunnery Staff was also established in India. The 'IGs' attended a stiff two-year course, beginning with four and a half months at the Military College of Science[157] and the rest at Larkhill. Many of them were qualified in all three branches of artillery – field army, coast and anti-aircraft – and had also attended the long survey course. The position of these highly qualified captains and majors was one of those working British anomalies. They had no executive power of any kind, and their ultimate allegiance was to the Commandant at Larkhill. Their mission was not only to instruct along the lines the Commandant laid down for use throughout the Army, but also to report and criticise. Where the artillery in peace differs from the other arms is that its performance can be exactly judged by the criteria of speed of response to calls for fire and the accuracy of the fall of shot. The annual practice camp was therefore not only the climax of training but also a test of fitness for operations. The Brigadier, Royal Artillery, who supervised the practice, had an IG at his elbow to set the exercises with an AIG watching the detailed work in the command posts, who submitted written reports on each unit. These were merciless, and could not be suppressed, watered down or shelved. It was important that the IGs were not a race apart of 'blokes' or pedants. They were all good regimental officers, specially selected, sharing the regimental outlook and as devoted to field sports and equitation as all the rest, but demonstrating that such interests were far from incompatible with efficiency.

The other great benefit conferred by the School was the introduction of the Young Officers Courses in 1926. This ensured that they joined their batteries with a thorough grounding in the equipments they were likely to meet in the field artillery (but without practical instruction in wheeled or tracked vehicles: it was all horses), able to act as section commanders and gun position officers and also to carry out simple fire missions at the forward observation post. The odd consequence of this was that the subalterns were, as a whole, better qualified than their seniors who, if they were wise, delegated to them the basic tasks of training the gun 'detachments', or crews, the command post specialists, the surveyors and the signallers. Batteries were often underposted in officers, and in those days there was a generous amount of furlough (two months annually and one period of six months during each India posting), so subalterns gained frequent experience in responsibilities above their rank, which was greatly to their benefit. Many were to find themselves in command of batteries in war before they had reached their thirtieth birthdays.

It could be said of the Royal Artillery, therefore, that by its own blinkered standards it was efficient. In times of great difficulty it had preserved its warlike skills. Its institutions were sound. Its officers were professionally superior and better educated than the average of the other combat arms, and included much unexploited talent. What it lacked was direction. It resembled a very large and run-down company with a loyal work-force containing many potential managers, but dominated by obsolete ideas and with obsolete plant, inviting a take-over bid by some ruthless entrepreneur. It was hardly likely that he would emerge from within its ranks, with the 'middle management' bored and the young entry ruthlessly socialised into obedient authoritarians. Of all that vast mass of officers only one rebel emerged in the inter-war years, Wingate, and his destiny was to take him outside the sphere of artillery altogether. Not until the incubus of the horse had been removed and the shock of war was felt was the Royal Artillery collectively able to rouse itself from its apathy.

This, of course, could be said of the army as a whole, but the Royal Artillery was a special case. For over two centuries it had been an educated, scientific, forward-looking arm. On the Western Front it had responded brilliantly and on a grand scale to the challenge of modern warfare. Yet, betraying its traditions, it approached the Second World War with lethargy. The Royal Artillery is sometimes accused of obstructing the progress of mechanisation and modernisation in the inter-war years. It did nothing so positive. The sin of which the Royal Artillery was guilty was of doing nothing at all, with one notable exception – the group of officers engaged in weapon design in the Department of the Master-General of the Ordnance. Very little material progress was possible until the decision to re-arm was taken in the mid-1930s, but this did not preclude thought. No Hobart, no Pope emerged from its ranks. Broad and Pile, also pioneers of armoured warfare, had left the Royal Artillery for the Royal Tank Corps, both perceiving it to be the arm of the future. There was only mental stagnation and a nostalgic attempt to recreate the sort of life that the older officers had enjoyed before 1914. In consequence, when it finally set out on the road to modernisation it fumbled. Its early experiences were dire, and were to cost it, and the whole army, some bitter lessons and some humiliating defeats.

CHAPTER 10

Policies, Theories and Weapons

An Army cannot be run according to the rules of etiquette.

Sun Tzu, *The Art of War*

WHEN General Sir George Milne became Chief of the Imperial General Staff in 1926 one of his first actions was to draft a memorandum requesting the Secretary of State for War to define the tasks for which the Army existed. This seems to have been perfectly logical. At that time all plans for modernising the Army were constrained by the financial situation of the country, which precluded any policy involving lavish re-equipment, and the Ten Year Rule, which stated that military plans should be based on the assumption that the country would not be involved in a major war for the next ten years; the starting year of this decade being advanced from year to year so that the undefined threat always lay ten years ahead. All the same, the Army vote was a substantial fraction of the national expenditure, and without a proper definition of the Army's rôle it was not easy for the Army Council to plan for its best use.

The constitutional position of the CIGS has always been perfectly clear. Although selected on the basis of being one of the ablest officers in the Army, he is only a member of the Army Council functioning as a board of management, whose chairman is the Secretary of State for War, through whom its advice reaches the government. The CIGS is at best only the first among equals, although by virtue of his responsibilities, which included war plans, 'doctrine', intelligence, training and all the organisational matters embraced under the title of 'staff duties', in short, all warlike affairs, as compared with the supportive roles of his fellow Army Councillors, his post was the most influential one. (In practice the status of the CIGS varied according to his relationship with the government of the day.) A CIGS was therefore precluded from pressing his own ideas as distinct from the collective opinion of the Army Council, but there was nothing ultra vires in any member of Council posing a question to his own chairman, the only member of the government he was allowed formally to approach. In the event, the members of Council, on the initiative of the Quartermaster General, objected strongly and the question was withdrawn. It was, perhaps, not possible for the government to give a definite answer at that date, but the absence of one was to make the process of modernising the Army difficult, to say the least.

The real reason, or reasons, for the blocking action of the other Council members, apart from the flimsy procedural objection, can only be a subject for conjecture. It may have been the fear that too rigid a definition might later tie the hands of Council; politically there is a lot to be said for vague or no terms of reference. They may have been, as is not unknown in such bodies, testing the nerve and authority of a new chief. They may have suspected that Milne nursed dangerous radical ideas. He was associated with the proposal to set up the Experimental Mechanised Force, agreed by the Secretary of State before ever Milne had taken up his appointment, but it was the company Milne kept, the men, not his measures, that his colleagues may have found alarming. He hobnobbed with the young Captain B. H. Liddell Hart, a newspaper correspondent who had first suggested the creation of an experimental force and was the leading advocate of military reform, but what was even worse was his choice of Colonel Fuller as Military Assistant, also suggested by Liddell Hart. J. F. C. Fuller, nicknamed 'Boney', for 'Bonaparte', by his contemporaries, and not altogether irreverently, had in 1916 been a staff officer with what was to become the Royal Tank Corps and had brought all his great gifts to bear on the subject of tanks and their tactics. He enjoyed an extraordinary and privileged position in the British Army, one that would be impossible today for any serving officer, however brilliant, so strict is the censorship now imposed on public servants or officers. Fuller, an arch-radical and the prophet of wholesale mechanisation and tank warfare, poured out a series of dazzling, irreverent and revolutionary books and articles which shocked the establishment to the core. (When his winning RUSI Gold Medal Prize Essay, on the application of science to the technique of warfare and its consequences was published, General Lynden Bell rushed into his room crying out: 'Boney, Boney, what have you done?')[158]

A 'military assistant' to a high official is no more than a

superior secretary with a thorough knowledge of the substance and context of his master's work, arranging his business, preparing abstracts and obtaining briefs from the appropriate staff officers or heads of departments for all the many papers his master has to assimilate. By custom he is a young and promising staff officer, usually a major, who while serving as office manager (he is much less than a chef de cabinet) obtains valuable experience. He is not in any sense a consultant, nor is his advice ever asked. Equally it would be very improper for him to offer it. Fuller, a veteran, highly articulate, outrageously outspoken, the leading authority on armoured warfare, with his own constituency inside the Army and commanding a wide audience outside it, was forty-seven years old, a full colonel and far too heavily gunned for so minor a role. Obviously Milne had appointed him to serve as his 'ideas-man' and eminence grise, and not a particularly unobtrusive one, at that. Milne's colleagues may well have felt that this un-British demand to define the Army's tasks could lead to all sorts of measures too horrible to contemplate, such as the abolition of the cavalry. Be that as it may, the members of Council pressed their objection, and Milne yielded, revealing for the first but not the last time his fatal lack of backbone.

Milne's reign as CIGS lasted until 1933, so for seven long years the Army was without any sense of mission. This depressed its morale and made any continuous or constructive policy for its modernisation impossible. In the Royal Artillery it appears to have been the prevailing impression that the Army's rôle was 'to police the Empire and undertake small colonial wars.'[159] Certainly such an impression was justified by experience. Between 1919 and 1924 the Army had been involved in the Anglo-Irish struggle, the Third Afghan War of 1919, the suppression of an Arab rebellion in Iraq in 1920–1 and another by the Kurds in 1923, and in the chronic counter-insurgency operations against the Pathan tribes on the North-West Frontier of India. The Royal Artillery Journal continued to publish a flow of lively and forward-looking articles, but their emphasis was on the techniques of gunnery, weapon specification and organisation, and though much of this was of value there was no attempt to examine fundamentals. Some of the ideas advanced were eventually to bear fruit ten years later, but they excited little interest in the Regiment at large, where 'shop' was never talked, and in any case to write for the Journal was regarded as eccentric, or a form of showing off, if not actually subversive. Reading was not regarded in a much better light unless it was 'Marco' (Lord Louis Mountbatten) on polo, Wardrop on pig-sticking or some authority such as Best or Dunbar Brander on shikar, or hunting for big game. We can compare the Royal Tank Corps: during Hobart's command of the 1st Tank Brigade shop was talked, even in the officer's mess![160] Nothing happened, and the Duncan Prize Essay for 1930 concludes with the cri de coeur:

> I cannot understand why we have so few guns in a division, why I get so little training with other arms, why I am made to talk through an abominably inefficient telephone, why we have not got our own Gunner aeroplanes and what would happen if my battery had to engage half a dozen enemy tanks which had broken through the forward zone.[161]

Such questions could not be answered until the various tasks of the artillery were defined. The need for coast artillery and anti-aircraft defence was obvious enough and presented purely technical problems. It was the field rôle which was baffling. Was it man-killing, and if so was the target in the open, or under cover? Was it for use against earthworks and obstacles organised in depth, and if so was the task suppression of fire or the actual destruction of the defence system, or a combination of the two? How far could the responsibility for counter-battery fire and long range 'harassing' fire against installations on the rear edge of the combat area be transferred to light bomber aircraft, so reducing or obviating the need for super-heavy artillery? And what about tanks? The consensus of opinion in the RA Journal was that enemy tanks having broken through the front would charge into the gun line at speeds too great for guns on normal land-carriages to engage with any hope of success. Was it an artillery task to prevent tanks penetrating the front, or simply to defend itself in its indirect fire positions in the rear, and were the field guns adequate for the task, or was a special equipment, similar to those used in coast artillery against fast moving targets necessary? Would friendly tanks themselves require artillery covering fire against the enemy anti-tank weapons? And how could this question be answered until the characteristics and function of the tanks themselves had been analysed? None of this could be decided until the nature of the possible opponents in a future war had been studied, and this in turn could only be based on speculation until an answer had been given to the question which Milne had shrunk from asking.

In the absence of an answer it was only natural to listen to other voices. The official manuals were of no assistance. *Field Service Regulations*, supported by the several arms manuals –

*Infantry Training, Cavalry Training, Tank and Armoured Car
Training, Artillery Training* – provided impeccable guidelines for
the conduct of operations, but they were abstractions, treating
the arms as pieces on the chessboard of war with characteristics
as unvarying as chessmen. The so-called 'principles of war', first
adumbrated by no less than Fuller, were soundly based on the
lessons of military history, but they were so general that they
afforded no guidance in a situation in which long-cherished
assumptions were being brutally upset by technology.[162] Neither
the Field Service regulations nor artillery training offered an
answer to the question posed by Captain R. D. Foster in his
Duncan prize essay, but the answers were there to be read by
those who understood the language. All were concerned with
the production and application of fire-power.

   Fuller, in an article called 'The Army of the Artillery Cycle'
wrote: 'The superior weapon of the future is the *gun*, the
superior soldier is the *gunner*, and the superior army is a force
based on mechanically propelled artillery.'[163] This is one of the
flashes of insight which so distinguish his work. Unfortunately, it
is immediately marred by his technological conclusions. Fuller's
attitude towards the usefulness of massed heavy artillery was
coloured by his experience of the long preliminary bombardments
used in the middle period of the war to suppress hostile artillery
fire, to batter the defences and above all to cut the deep belts of
barbed wire. The morass which resulted when it rained during
3rd Ypres especially stuck in his mind, or vice versa.[164] In this
particular article he argued that 'long range guns and heavy
howitzers will (in future) play a very secondary role', and
specified the useful shell-weights or calibres as 3 or 6-pounder
guns and heavy machine-guns of 0.5 or 1.0-inch calibre. Fuller
intuitively grasped that fire-power was the key to modern tactics
but, like his great coeval Liddell Hart, he understood neither the
technology nor the principles of its employment.

   (In 1944 Liddell Hart published his *Thoughts on War*, a
selection of all his most significant observations on strategy,
tactics and weapons, which the events of the three previous years
had done as much to confound as to confirm. The passage on
artillery is wrong in almost every particular; the inevitable result
of special pleading in favour of the tank and against artillery,
except for self-propelled guns. To any one who was at Alamein
the sentence 'To load an at *present helpless* mass of infantry with
a *cumbrous* mass of artillery is likely to produce a fiasco'
(author's italics) must have read strangely, while the field
gunners, who had fought many a fierce battle against tanks,
would have been surprised to read that 'to have a chance the gun

must have a fixed mounting with an all-round traverse – in which case it is no longer a field gun unless it is fitted in a tank!' The 25-pounder with its 360° traverse was introduced in 1939.)[165]

Yet the lessons of the First World War were plain for all to read. There were altogether six major inventions or developments which mark the watershed between the wars of the eighteenth and nineteenth centuries and modern warfare, of which the 'tank' is only one. They are the scientific application of long range, massed artillery fire, its opposite the 'tank', or mobile armoured gun-platform, aircraft, the machine-gun, the revolution in infantry tactics and – the thermionic valve. In the Uniacke papers there is a reference to a new development in 'wireless' called 'CW', or 'continuous wave', which enabled ordinary speech to be used, with all the advantages in the way of ease and speed of communication that conferred, and Herbert Uniacke immediately grasped its significance. All the great battles from 1916 to 1918 followed the same course until the Germans finally cracked under the remorseless attrition of the Allied offensives. It was always possible to break into the crust of the enemy defences, but once the assaulting troops had disappeared into the smoke clouds they were out of control and beyond the reach of any assistance they needed in the desperate battle inside the enemy position. Telephone lines were cut to pieces by shell fire as soon as laid, runners were killed and visual signalling not always possible.

In 1918 both Morse and speech radios were extensively used, but what was lacking was a portable 'soldier-proof' set, capable of being so sharply tuned that many frequencies could be used and so permit not only headquarters to be linked, but all the parts of a battalion. By 1931 this was possible and Broad demonstrated how a whole brigade of tanks, 180 in all, could be controlled by radio down to individual tanks. Two brigades of artillery were issued with radio equipment for trials as early as 1928. In 1933 Milne held a high level staff conference to discuss the report of the Kirke Committee (see chapter 11), and in the discussion on maintaining the momentum of an offensive after the initial break in one speaker emphasised the need for universal radio during the fighting on the objective (later termed the 'dog-fight'), but there was a general reluctance, outside the armour and artillery, to rely on radio as the primary means of communication. This was partly because, even in 1938–9, when radio sets became a general issue, they were still far from reliable, and also because of the fear of interception. The marching, as opposed to motor infantry, were slow to come to terms with radio, understandably, as they were completely exposed to fire, and the early sets were an awkward load and not robust enough to withstand the shocks of infantry fighting. The artillery, by contrast, saw it to be the obvious answer to its communication problems, not only to the vexed one of continuous support during the advance but for speeding up the whole process of deployment and fire-control generally. Adoption of radio went hand in hand with mechanisation, as sprung vehicles provided a stable platform for the sets of those days, so easily jolted off frequency. The artillery soon found out what could be achieved even with imperfect equipment if the determination to make it work is instilled into the operators.

There still remained the question of mobility; of moving the guns into the combat zone so as to keep in range. Horses have a good cross-country performance, and mules are even better. One solution to the problem of continuous support was to use 3.7-inch mountain howitzers carried on mules, but the main disadvantages of animal traction is that it is very slow and vulnerable to enemy fire. Mechanisation was, however, imperative, not because of these objections but because of the disappearance of the right type of horse, the 'light vanner', from civilian transport. There were nowhere near enough in the country to mobilise the Army. Wheeled traction was at first rejected because of memories of the morass of shell craters of the Western Front. In the first phase of mechanisation both infantry and artillery experimented with tracks, but tracked vehicles were more expensive than wheeled, slower over long distances and more liable to break down, so in the final stage of mechanisation the artillery adopted wheels. Rightly, as it turned out, because in mobile warfare in well-developed countries with a good road network there was no difficulty in reaching suitable gun positions. As for rough country, it was soon found that four wheel drive vehicles with trained drivers could negotiate almost every type of ground.

There still remained the need for armoured artillery to operate well forward in the actual combat zone, especially, but not exclusively, for the support of tanks. It so happened that in 1925 Haig's principal artillery officer, General Sir Noel Birch, had become the Master-General of the Ordnance and President of the new Ordnance Committee, and his talented staff officer, S. W. H. Rawlins, was serving under him again, this time as Director of Artillery. (There were two Ds of A at that time. Rawlins dealt with cannon, except for tanks, which came under S. C. Peck, later to become Director of Mechanisation. The Ordnance Committee was set up in 1924.)[166] At that early date Rawlins had already a project for a self-propelled tracked gun mounting. This was a complex and unsuitable weapon. The presence and effectiveness of aircraft over the battlefield from 1915 onwards had made the need for an effective anti-aircraft gun perfectly clear, and it was thought that the divisional artillery should be able to protect itself and also, from its normal area of deployment – roughly along a line 1,500 to 2,000 yards behind the front – to provide a barrier of fire against bombers. The gun chosen, an 18-pounder therefore required a double system of sights and be able to elevate up to 90°, which created great difficulties of design and offered no protection to the crew. The next version, designed to act purely as a field gun, looked very like a tank, with the 18-pounder in a revolving turret. The 18-pounder gave it a powerful direct fire capability and could smash any known or projected tank, but a howitzer would have been better for indirect fire in the support rôle. However, it was a bold and imaginative step forward, and came to be known as the 'Birch' gun. (It may well have been that the original idea was Birch's own.) The first trials showed that the turret limited the elevation and so the range and the total weight was too much for the engine. The next version had no turret and the 18-pounder gun complete with its shield was mounted on a pedestal in the turret ring. Six were made to equip a battery of the 9th Field Brigade, Royal Artillery, the unit selected to form part of the Experimental Force.

Things might have gone well had the Royal Tank Corps and the Royal Artillery been able to pull together. In the same year as Rawlins gave his lecture on future artillery design at the Royal Artillery Institute P. C. S. Hobart, an engineer officer of immense drive and imagination who had transferred to the Royal Tank Corps and had just been appointed an instructor with responsibility for tank warfare at the Staff College, was drawing up notional specifications for what was later to be called an armoured division. This included a 'Royal Tank Artillery', 'designed for the support of tanks just as RHA was for the support of cavalry'.[167] This agreed with official thought. *Tank Training* Volume II of 1927 was quite specific: 'In all circumstances the primary duty of supporting artillery is the protection of armoured fighting vehicles from observed fire.' Hobart, at the Staff College, could only theorise. The practical investigation proved a sorry affair. Fuller, who had been designated commander of the Experimental Mechanised Force, resigned over a difference in the interpretation of his responsibilities. The officer appointed in his place lacked his fire and vision and there was effective resistance to the conversion of infantry or cavalry regiments to tanks. The experimental force was broken up in

1930 without any useful conclusions being reached and the Birch guns were scrapped. Liddell Hart, who cannot be relied upon when he speaks of artillery matters, suggests that Birch was hostile to the idea, that its being named after him was a piece of flattery intended as a sop, and that 'it was too radical a departure for the majority of Gunners, who were inclined to feel that if it matured it would be absorbed by the Royal Tank Corps.' There is no evidence for this. Apart from the fact that the pilot models were produced on the initiative of two artillery officers, its rôle was supported by the winner of the Duncan Silver Medal Essay for 1926–7, and also in 1930 by Major-General S. C. Peck, Director of Mechanisation. Captain Body in his Duncan essay actually recommended that it *should* be taken over by the Royal Tank Corps, a very different thing. Body, when lecturing to cadets at the Royal Military Academy in 1932, may have expressed a more widely held opinion when he said that the objection to a self-propelled gun was that if the running gear broke down the gun was also out of action, whereas a towed gun could always be hitched up to another towing vehicle and brought into action. There was something in that argument, but the indications, such as they are, point to a rejection of artillery support by the advocates of the tank.

In 1929 the War Office published a provisional pamphlet entitled *Armoured and Mechanized Formations*. The author was Colonel C. N. F. Broad (later General Sir Charles Broad), an able and experienced artillery officer who had transferred to the Royal Tank Corps as he perceived that the tank was the arm of the future. Broad, with Fuller, Lindsay and Hobart, was one of the great British tank pioneers, militarily well educated and intensely practical; a man of detail, the opposite of the visionary Fuller. His pamphlet is a milestone in tank development. In it appears a 'close support tank battery', i.e. a 'Birch' gun and clearly a Royal Artillery Unit, because in the detailed table of organisation the corporals are called by their peculiar artillery title of 'bombardier'. Broad's intention was for the guns either to give close support singly, firing direct like the assault guns of the future, or to act in battery as normal field artillery. In 1931 there appeared a revised and watered down version of his pamphlet, with a foreword by Milne himself: *Modern Formations (1931)*. This was also a document for discussion, not a manual laying down doctrine. It included among the 'modern' formations a horsed cavalry division, supported by a horsed brigade of the Royal Horse Artillery. There is no other mention of artillery, except five lines stating that if tanks were ordered to attack a 'prepared' position they would require artillery support. (And this in a pamphlet sponsored by the Master Gunner!) The 'tank battery' has disappeared, and instead there is a note that some tanks in a battalion might be armed with 15-pounder mortars.

Broad's post in the Staff Duties Directorate was later occupied by P. C. Hobart, as a brigadier Deputy Director with responsibility for Armoured Fighting Vehicles. He never pressed for the re-introduction of self-propelled artillery; on the contrary, his thoughts moved in the opposite direction. In 1926 when he was lecturing at the Staff College his sketch of a suitable organisation for an armoured division included a 'fire group' with infantry supported by towed artillery, and a 'tank group' with 'tracked' artillery. This was almost exactly the organisation arrived at after much trial and error in 1943, but by 1937 Hobart had changed his mind. When he became a deputy director in the Staff Duties Branch in the War Office with responsibility for the tank doctrine (DDSD, AFV) he submitted a paper suggesting a tank division of two tank brigades unadulterated by supporting arms – 'pure in race', as the Germans were later to describe it; they themselves preferring to fight in mixed battle-groups. He relegated all the infantry and artillery to a 'holding group', later the 'pivot' group, and later still the 'support group' with a purely ancillary function. Its tasks were either to hold a base in which the administrative and supply vehicles were protected, or to secure the objectives captured by the unaided effort of the tanks. This was perverse, because ten years before Hobart had grasped the potential of close support aircraft as a substitute for heavy artillery, going so far as to include three squadrons as organic to one of his notional organisations of a tank division,[168] but by 1937 it must have been clear to him that the Royal Air Force had neither the resources nor the intention to provide aircraft for any purpose of the Army's except reconnaissance and artillery spotting. Artillery, therefore, was the only substitute, but at that date no one in the tank corps or the artillery had grasped that long range artillery combined with forward observers using radio control could support armoured attacks without the necessity to motor along behind the tanks.

The tank-artillery relationship is an example of the rigidity of British military thinking. The Royal Artillery preferred indirect fire, except for the purely defensive rôle against tanks; except much later in South-East Asia, where guns firing direct at short range were occasionally used for 'bunker-busting'. It never used its anti-tank guns offensively, in the German fashion. The Royal Armoured Corps never followed the logic of 'going it alone' to the obvious conclusion of mounting really heavy guns on tank chassis to act as assault guns, as did the Germans and later the

FOUR LEADING ARTILLERYMEN OF THE FIRST WORLD WAR

1. Haig's MGRA, General Sir Noel Birch, wearing the full-dress uniform of the Royal Horse Artillery.

2. Major-General Sir Herbert Uniacke, MGRA Fifth Army at 3rd Ypres.

3. Lieutenant-General Sir Arthur Holland, GOC RA VII Corps, MGRA and later Commander, Third Army.

4. Major-General C. E. D. Budworth, MGRA Fourth Army under Rawlinson.

5. 18-pounder stuck in artillery-generated mud, 1917.

6. 18-pounder in action in hastily occupied position, March 1918.

7. Three-man portable 'wireless' station, May 1917.

8. British Mark V tanks in close co-operation with Canadian infantry clearing out a pocket of resistance, 1918.

9. The experimental, self-propelled field/AA 18-pounder 'Birch' gun, far ahead of its time, 1926.

10. Early experiments in all mechanised, tracked draught: Austin 7, motor cycle orderly, tracked 'dragons' towing command post and a 4·5-inch howitzer.

11. General Sir John Woodall, designer of the army/air co-operation system.

12. Major-General J. H. Parham, proponent of the Air OP and inventor of the system for radio-controlled massed fire.

13. General Sir Brian Horrocks, who employed it to 'blast his way through'.

14. Air Chief Marshal Sir Harry Broadhurst who, on the air side, perfected the Woodall system.

15. Model 68R portable radio, 1944, one of the many types of mobile sets making universal radio control of the battle possible.

16. The mainstay of the British infantry in two World Wars, the Vickers ·303-inch medium machine-gun, with crew and mascot, Africa, 1943.

17. 25-pounder Mark I showing the turntable platform permitting rapid traverse for engaging tanks.

18. The excellent 5·5-inch gun, with the 25-pounder, the basic British artillery equipment, seen here engaged in the VERITABLE fire-plan.

19. Hurricane 'tank-busters' of the Desert Air Force engaging German tanks, reputedly at El Hamma, 1943.

20. HMS *Warspite* bombarding enemy defences on the Normandy coast, June 1944.

Russians. The feeling among the Gunners seemed to be that anything like a gun on tracks for direct fire was the business of the tank people, and among the armoured officers that their weapon was a tracked vehicle with a revolving turret; anything else was a Gunner affair.

It is, of course, unfair and also unhistorical to condemn the men of one period for not adopting the mode of thought of another. In the 1930s the discipline of 'operational analysis' had not been conceived, and the notion that mathematician or scientist could contribute anything to the study of tactics would have been regarded as droll. Nevertheless, the arguments of the armoured pioneers were blatantly inconsistent in themselves. On the one hand, the tank was asserted to be the dominant weapon, able to sweep guns and infantry irresistibly from the field. Lecturing to an artillery audience F. A. Pile, a former artillery-man himself, said: 'You may expect to be attacked by large numbers of fast-moving tanks . . . they may appear on your front or flanks, they may even appear suddenly far in your rear. . .' He then goes on to say that the best antidote is a half-inch (12.7-mm) heavy machine gun, using a 'hose-pipe' method of fire control.[169] As late as 1938 a tiny gun firing a 2-pound weight shell was deemed to be effective against all known tanks. But surely, if tanks could be knocked out by such weapons so easy to operate and so much cheaper than tanks, then (a) the balance between infantry and tanks could be swiftly restored (b) artillery covering fire would be required to suppress these ubiquitous and easily concealed weapons, on the analogy of the infantry and machine guns (c) and therefore either self-propelled guns or tanks equipped with a large calibre gun capable of firing a high explosive shell would still be required as part of the tank inventory. No one asked the question *how* tanks were supposed to defeat emplaced infantry. Did they crush them with their tracks? Did they painstakingly locate their entrenched positions while keeping out of range of the 'hose-pipes' of anti-tank fire, and then shell them into submission? With what weapon, when the lesson of the Western Front was that the smallest British piece in service which was fully effective against such targets was the 4.5-inch howitzer? (The tank designers of the Soviet Union found the correct answer. By 1939 they had adopted a 3-inch (76.2-mm) for their medium tank and had fitted 152-mm howitzers to their heavy support tank.)[170]

The three leading advocates of the armoured cause – Fuller, Liddell Hart and Hobart – were men blessed with vivid and creative imagination backed by the aggressive drive without which nothing is ever achieved, but they all shared one disabling

habit of thought. Their reasoning was never empirical. They
were all highly articulate, and their polemics are full of vivid
metaphors and similes. Their arguments were backed by
historical analogies. They were, in short, *literary* in their
approach to any problem. In their own minds their metaphors
began to assume the character of statements of natural laws,
whereas in practice a flanking movement on a curved track is not
in the least like the blow of a scythe, nor does the fraught
advance of any assault, however well executed, into the heart of
a defensive position alive with counter-attacks and criss-crossed
by defensive fire in any way resemble the rush of a flooded river,
tearing inanimate clods from its banks and pouring round and
over obstacles. ('The expanding torrents' of Liddell Hart.) For
them, even Hobart the engineer, a 'tank' was an abstract entity,
a concept, with essential attributes transcending any physical
properties it might have conferred on it by technology. A tank
was armoured, whereas infantry was not, therefore the tank was
invulnerable and infantry would disappear from the battlefield,
except for certain humble duties. It moved, and a moving target
was difficult to hit, from which it was but a short step to argue
that tanks, unsupported, could safely attack artillery in position.
Liddell Hart went so far as to suggest that the tank's mobility
would enable it to dodge air attack. All counter-arguments that
properly designed anti-tank guns might neutralise the tank were
regarded as reactionary and special pleading for the retention of
the old arms. At the same time it was assumed that the defence,
due to the development of such weapons, was inherently
superior to any form of attack, as if the 'defence' and the
'offensive' had immutable properties or essences. Therefore only
evasion, envelopment, the attack on the defender's supply
system and the psychological attack on the mind of the
defending commander had any hope of success, and the only
instrument at hand for such manoeuvres was a tank –
unhampered by infantry or guns, scything round the baffled
enemy, pouring through his positions like a river, or entangling
him like the net of a retarius. The opposing generals would
collapse with nervous breakdowns imposed by the shock.
Pursued to the limit these flights of fancy resulted in the
conclusion that the land battle of the future would be between
fleets of tanks on the analogy of naval warfare. The role of the
artillery would be merely the defence of the safe harbours where
the tanks could rest and replenish, while the infantry were only
for garrison duty or to act as 'tank marines'.

Admittedly much of this was rhetoric, and provoked by the
resistance of the diehards, but the debate, increasingly heated,

became especially bitter when it was the turn of Hobart to carry the torch of the reformers after Fuller and Broad had left the scene. His saga lies outside the scope of this book, but in the course of his struggle he was to clash with artillery officers, Haining, when Director of Military operations and intelligence, Alan Brooke the future CIGS, and Major-General R. G. Finlayson, who played a leading part in his downfall. Hobart's great gifts were marred by an emotional and aggressive character. Gunners, he concluded in his violent way, were emissaries of Satan bent on frustrating him at every turn, and he extended his dislike of them to their arm.[171] He made a fatal error in which lay the seeds of future tribulation and many defeats. The outcome of future battles, he believed, would depend on combat between tanks. The armour of the tanks of the day was of the order of two inches (50-mm), which could be defeated by a small calibre high velocity gun, a 40-mm firing only a solid armour-piercing shot weighing 2.4 pounds – the notorious 'two-pounder', obsolete before the blitzkrieg struck. There were difficulties in fitting anything bigger in the existing design of tank turrets. Hobart accordingly recommended this as the main tank armament and it was rational to choose the same weapon as the infantry anti-tank gun.[172] In addition he left as a legacy a dislike, even a distrust, of artillery support for tanks, persisting among some commanders of armoured forces until as late as 1944.

In the meantime artillery development was left in the hands of the designers, known disparagingly as the 'blokes'. As far as there was any doctrinal background, it was that the next war would be rather like the mobile phases of the last. The three arms would continue to exist, with the cavalry carrying out its classic roles of reconnaissance, protection and pursuit, either horsed, or as 'dragoons' mounted in vehicles, or in light tanks. The scope of the heavier tanks was to act as a break-in force, or to provide close fire-support for the infantry. This was the view of General Sir Hugh Elles, the first commander of the Tank Corps and Master-General of the Ordnance in 1935. There were schisms inside the armoured school. The Duncan essays published in the Royal Artillery Journal showed that the Royal Artillery was fully aware that in future war the field artillery would be the objective of tank attacks and that air attack would threaten both the army in the field, its bases and the home country.[173] Air defence presented purely technical and complex problems whose solution was independent of tactical doctrine, so the more scientifically trained Royal Artillery officers were able to grapple with them without waiting for precise specifications, and very fortunate it was that they did. Without their efforts there would have been no foundation on which to build the great apparatus of Anti-Aircraft Command which found itself in the front line of the battle for survival, and was perhaps the most sophisticated and efficient branch of the land forces.

The only guidance the field branch artillery had were the recommendations made on the basis of the technical lessons of the past war. Briefly, these were for greater mechanical reliability of the recoil gear and carriage, longer range and greater shell-power and better fuzes. There was in those days no Chief Scientific Adviser, no Director of Combat Development and no operational research establishment. Such doctrine as emerged was the joint responsibility of the Director of Staff Duties (DSD) and the Director of Military Training (DMT), whose advisers did not always agree. Weapon development therefore proceeded in a doctrinal vacuum. Suitable areas for research were decided by an interlocking hierarchy of committees and design and experimental establishments. At the top was the CIGS's committee, with the CIGS himself in the chair, the DSD as vice-chairman, the DMT, the Director of Artillery[174] and the Inspectors of the Royal Artillery and Royal Tank Corps, with the Director of Military Operations on call. Its terms of reference were 'to define the general policy regarding the conduct of research connected with the arms and equipment of the fighting troops, including transport vehicles.' There was an Ordnance Committee with representation from all three services to consider all questions of research and design, and a purely army Royal Artillery Committee linked to the Ordnance Committee through a common chairman whose terms of reference included new designs, trials, the consideration of new inventions and reports on foreign equipment. These committees tasked the Design Department in Woolwich Arsenal, the artillery Experimental Establishment at Shoeburyness, the Air Defence Establishment at Biggin Hill and the Research Department at Woolwich.

A detailed history of the process of re-equipping the Royal Artillery would be both long and have to dwell on many highly technical questions. To the uninitiated a cannon is simply a tube supported on a wheeled carriage, but in reality it is a complicated piece of machinery incorporating delicate optical appliances and required to perform with precision under violent and repeated stresses. (If we take the shell alone, it is a steel case filled with high explosive required sometimes not to explode until it has penetrated a foot or so of concrete, or at others if it hits a blade of grass, and at the same time be perfectly safe, not only to store and transport, but also to withstand a sudden punch with a force of many thousands of pounds to the square inch, spun like a top and accelerated up a barrel eight or ten feet long to emerge at a velocity of over 1,000 miles per hour). The basic requirements of longer range, a more powerful shell and better mechanical reliability than the field artillery of the past war conflicted with a demand for mobility, which meant no great increase in weight, but it took some time for the General Staff to grasp the fact that with the advent of mechanical traction mobility depended on horsepower, not horses. For some time the possibility of a dual purpose field anti-aircraft gun was researched.[175] A 4.1-inch howitzer was designed and discarded; a model which both the United States and German armies were to standardise with a 32 and 35-pound shell respectively. Economy demanded that some use be made of the vast surplus of First World War equipment, for after the war there were 4,000 18-pounders and 4.5-howitzers and 10,000,000 rounds of ammunition in stock surplus to establishment, with smaller numbers of medium and heavy equipments. The 4.5-inch howitzer was discarded, but the later marks of 18-pounder were retubed to take a larger shell. The need for the field artillery to defend itself against tanks demanded a gun-like rather than a howitzer-like solution, and it had to traverse (switch its line of fire) easily and be light to manhandle. There were serious delays because the General Staff specifications were apt to change without regard for the progress made in design and trials. For instance, there was a demand for the range of the new field gun to be increased from 12,000 to 15,000 yards. It was demanded that the new standard 5-inch medium gun was first to have a range of 16,000 yards and a shell weight of 85 pounds, then later 18,000 yards with a 78-pound shell, only for the whole project to be cancelled in December 1938 after an order for fifty guns had actually been placed at the Royal Ordnance Factory, in favour of a completely new design, the 5.5-inch 'gun-howitzer'.

In the upshot the Royal Artillery had to fight the earlier battles of the Second World War with the first mark of the 25-pounder, the retubed 18-pounder on an improved carriage, with a limited range of 11,800 yards, and obsolete First World War equipments, which included even the 18-pounder Mark I and the 60-pounder, which dated back to 1914.[176] However, the new inventory which began to arrive in the hands of the troops in late 1941 was a credit to its designers. The 25-pounder Mark II with a range of 13,400 yards fitted with an absurdly simple light turntable, or 'platform', was both a highly effective light howitzer and a good anti-tank gun, although its shell-weight, sacrificed for range, was inadequate in the opinion of many users. For long range counter-battery there was the new 4.5-inch gun with a 55-pound shell and range of 20,500 yards, but best of all was the new general purpose medium 5.5-inch gun with a range of 16,000 yards with a 100-pound shell and 18,600 with an 80-pound shell. Successful designs can only result from much patient work and the contributions of many brains, but there is no doubt that the leader in the long haul to re-arm the artillery was E. M. C. Clarke (later Major-General Sir Edward Campbell-Clarke) who spent most of his service in the design department and became Director of Artillery at this crucial period. His active and fertile mind ranged over the whole field of artillery, including tank armament, and he was not afraid to take an initiative. There were only seventy-six 60-pounders available for conversion to the new calibre of 4.5-inch. Perceiving this to be inadequate he went ahead on his own initiative with the design of a completely new gun, the 4.5-inch, which had a common carriage with the 5.5-inch, so rationalising design and manufacture. He also saw that the proposed 2-pounder anti-tank gun was altogether too small but he was not able to influence policy until 1940, when he successfully pressed for the 57-mm 6-pounder on which the technical staff had been working to be adopted, and also to be fitted in all new tanks.

The one failure was the 2-pounder anti-tank gun and this was a failure of analysis, and not of design. It was not foreseen that the armoured protection of the turret and front plate on tanks would go up to four inches and that with improved armament they would be able to engage at ranges of 1,000 yards and more. Before 1940 it was believed that tanks would charge into the defended areas as if they were cavalry and the decisive range would be 500 yards or less. (It must be said that the panzers fell into exactly the same error, and had rapidly to modify their tactics.) Pre-war practice was against screens carried in sleds towed at high speed at the end of long wires by lorries out of the arc of fire, which approached the battery from all quarters, jinking like snipe. The obvious gunnery solution to adopt was the one used in coast artillery against fast motor torpedo-boats: a light, rapidly traversable weapon on a pedestal mounting, but with a low silhouette so that it could easily be concealed in the forward areas. The result was the tiny, beautifully engineered 40-mm 2-pounder, resembling a Dinky toy, travelling on wheels which were detached in action so that it was supported on a Y-shaped platform of three spars radiating from a central pivot. It had a muzzle velocity of 2,650 feet per second (809 metre/secs), excellent sights and could punch a hole through two inches (50-mm) of armour plate at 500 yards and an inch and a half

(40-mm) at 1,000. Either a naval historian or a Gunner could have arrived at a different solution, and two Gunners did. Major G. E. A. Granet, who won the gold medal for his Duncan prize essay in 1929, discussing this very subject, showed that the 18-pounder was by no means too heavy a weapon for direct fire against tanks, and the runner-up, Captain R. G. Cherry who won the Silver Medal, suggested a combined anti-tank/anti-aircraft 6-pounder gun on a self-propelled chassis for forward area defence.[177]

Dual purpose guns were an unprofitable line of research, as was pointed out by another Duncan Gold Medallist,[178] partly because of conflicting technical requirements, and partly because their rôle required different patterns of deployment, and it was abandoned. (The use by the Germans of their 88-mm FLAK as an anti-tank weapon was an inspired improvisation, and discontinued as soon as they had enough 88-mm barrels to use on field carriages.) The 3-inch 20 hundredweight AA gun left over from the war was modernised, but its ceiling of 17,000 feet and its small lethal burst radius was inadequate against modern aircraft. A 4.5-inch gun for use in fixed emplacements and a mobile or fixed 3.7-inch, both with effective ceilings of 25,000–30,000 feet, were fortunately ready by 1939, because when the decision to re-equip was finally taken defence of the home air space was given the first priority. In addition a light gun with a high rate of fire for point defence in forward areas was purchased from the Swedish arms firm of Bofors. This was the immensely effective 40-mm, firing a high explosive shell with an effective ceiling of about 3,500–4,000 feet at a rate of fire of 120 rounds per minute, which in gradually improved forms was retained in the British service until superseded by the Rapier guided missile system in the 1970s. The design of guns presented no unusual technical difficulties. The key to air defence was early warning, the gathering of firing data concerning a target travelling at three or four miles a minute, the mathematical solution of complex equations and the passage of firing data to the gun before the target was out of range.

There remained the question of traction. Field guns continued to be coupled to ammunition limbers, with pairs of coupled limbers as 'wagons' to provide ammunition on the gun position, exactly as was the practice in the days of the horse. Indeed, the new tractor, a four-wheeled drive made by Morris was punningly called a 'Quad'. (From 'quadruped', the facetious slang for a gun-team horse.) The medium artillery was towed by a lorry-type four-wheeled drive diesel AEC *Matador*, which also carried forty rounds of ammunition which gave it a mobility fully equal to the 'field' artillery, and the few heavy pieces by the powerful *Scammell*. All supply and staff vehicles were wheeled except for the observation posts, which were carried in 'Bren carriers', a little open steel box with more or less bullet proof sides, on tracks. The only serious gap in this inventory was an armoured self-propelled field gun for co-operation with tanks.

In 1942 some 25-pounders were mounted in a slab-sided steel box perched on a slow 'Valentine' 'infantry' tank chassis but they were soon discarded. When a good American SP, the M7 105-mm howitzer was finally obtained, it was used simply as conventional artillery piece, deployed in indirect fire positions well behind the tanks.

There was also a lack of any modern weapon heavier than the 5.5-inch, as all attempts to adapt the old heavy guns such as the 6-inch gun and the 8-inch and 9.2-inch howitzers had, predictably, proved abortive. A new design had been delayed for lack of a clearly defined staff requirement. It was not until November 1940 that approval was given to develop a mobile howitzer by tubing down the existing 8-inch howitzers to 7.2-inches and fitting it with giant pneumatic tyres. This was an astonishingly primitive weapon which bounded about like a rubber ball on firing, but it fired a 200-pound shell to a range of 15,500 yards and was a triumph of rapid improvisation.

So it was that the 'blokes', beavering away in their offices and on the trial ranges, did in fact serve the Royal Artillery and the Army well. They had provided an armoury which, in spite of its gaps, was as good as anything possessed by either their future enemy or their allies. They had done their part. The important problem that their unscientific colleagues now had to solve was how it was to be organised and employed. Here, at first, there was nothing but naïvety and poverty of thought.

CHAPTER 11

A Fairly New Model Army

*Nevertheless, I continued to the end obsessed by
the iniquity of a policy which accepted for the
army a most exacting and hazardous commitment, and at the same time denied to it the means
of making itself fit to meet it.*
General Sir John Burnett-Stuart, *c.* 1937

THE Ten Year Rule was abrogated in 1933, and at last the
way seemed clear to begin to modernise an Army whose outlook was as obsolete as its equipment, or so it seemed, but the
politics of defence are never simple or easy. The most important
question of all, the rôle of the Army, was not decided until early
in 1939, when the task of providing an expeditionary force to
operate on the Continent of Europe was raised from the last to
the first priority. There its scope was to be in conformity with
French strategy, which was a virtuous, non-aggressive defence of
French territory. In any case the French Army was believed to
be the most powerful and efficient in the world. The British
presence was merely a demonstration of political solidarity or, as
the French put it more brutally, the British had to be seen to be
prepared to make an *effort du sang*. From the first, therefore,
there was the clash of opinion between the advocates of
armoured mobility and of a mobile, offensive strategy, and the
more cautious and conservative generals who considered that
formations better suited to hold ground were preferable.

The next obstacle to rapid rearmament arose from the whole
question of air power and the function of the Royal Air Force.
Unlike the Army, the Royal Air Force had a doctrine, which
was 'Trenchardism'; in short, that the most effective and
economical method of waging a future war was by the offensive
use of air power for strategic bombing of the enemy homeland.
As a matter of principle, the principle of concentration of effort,
the air force chiefs opposed the allocation of any aircraft other
than reconnaissance to the direct, tactical support of army

operations. This inhibited, to say the least, the development by
the British of the sort of mobile operations conceived by Hobart,
in which ground attack aircraft were to take the place of heavy
artillery. The Air Staff's view of air defence of the home base
was even more doctrinaire. Offensive action was the best
defence; any diversion of resources allotted to purely defensive
measures would also be a violation of the principle of concentration. There could not, perhaps, be two better examples of the
dangers of a slavish, literal interpretation of the 'principles of
war'. As it turned out the Air Staff pressed its case too well and
it rebounded. If it was true that a few air raids could bring a
country to its knees and if, as the Prime Minister, Baldwin, had
declared on professional advice, 'the bomber will always get
through', then in the event of war this could also be the fate of
the United Kingdom. Political and public opinion, more sensible
than the Air Staff, held that this was not a satisfactory state of
affairs. It was not reassuring to be told that attack was the best
means of defence, or that while England was being bombed the
Royal Air Force would be inflicting similar suffering on the
enemy, especially when professional advice to the government at
the time of the German invasion of Czechoslovakia, in 1938, was
that the German Air Force would be able to keep up bombing at
the rate of 500–600 tons per day for two months, and that the
resultant casualties would be of the order of 1,000,000 killed and
another 3,000,000 psychiatric casualties.[179] Even before the
Czech crisis, in November 1938, the Committee of Imperial
Defence recommended that the air defence of Great Britain
should have absolute priority over all other requirements.[180]

In 1933 there were only twenty nine anti-aircraft batteries in
the Royal Artillery, six manned by regulars intended for the
protection of the field army, and twenty-three by the Territorial
Army for home defence. All had obsolete equipment. The first
appreciation of what was required to implement the CID's
recommendation was 76 batteries and 108 searchlights. This was
followed by the 'Ideal' scheme; 158 batteries and 196 lights.
These were bare equipment figures, and excluded such essentials
as predictors, height-finders, signal equipment and transport,
including gun-tractors. The obsolete 3-inch 30 hundredweight
gun would have to be replaced by the new 3.7-inch, the 40-mm
Bofors brought into service for low level defence, and, of course,
large stocks of ammunition built up. The bid for 3.7-inch guns
alone, with their elaborate sights and mounting, may have been
as much as 1,500.

None of this included air defence for the army in the field or,
if there was an expeditionary force, for defence of its overseas

bases and communications. In addition, a due proportion of the capital expenditure allotted for defence and industrial capacity had to be allotted to increasing the defensive capacity of the Royal Air Force, for in 1938 of the existing fighter squadrons only five were equipped with modern (Hurricane) aircraft. All the deficiencies of equipment which were to bedevil Army operations in the early part of the war must be seen in the light of this necessary deflection of military production to the air defence of Great Britain.

The third obstacle was created by the Army Council itself. No attempt had been made to evaluate the lessons of the Great War until 1931, when the task was given to a hastily assembled committee. As to the nature of a future war, no proper staff machinery or agency existed to study it. Hobart, writing to Liddell Hart in 1937, complained, 'I can never get anyone to paint any sort of definite picture of what the battle area might look like (in their opinion) in the next war.'[181] Liddell Hart, taking up this theme in October of the same year, wrote: 'The War Office has organs for research into weapons, etc., but not into the conditions of future warfare . . . There are no means for the comprehensive analysis of past experience, and thus no synthesis of adequately expressed data to serve as a guide in framing policy . . . At present the investigation of problems is pushed on to officers who are occupied with current military business. That task ought to be given to a body of officers who can devote their whole time to exploring the data on record, collecting it from outside, and working out the conclusions in a free atmosphere. Such a body should be composed of the best intellects in the Army, with a good blend of practical experience, and in selecting them particular attention should be given to originality of thought or critical powers. It is very desirable that they should be supplemented by a permanent nucleus consisting of some first-rate university men who have been trained in scientific inquiry.'[182] Here, surely, is Liddell Hart at his best, years ahead of his time, but who, in the 1930s, was going to pay any attention to such a body?

The handling of the report of the 1931 'Kirke Committee' gives an answer. This was a high-powered team consisting of five major-generals and two brigadiers, with Lieutenant-General W. M. St G. Kirke as its president. Its terms of reference were to answer two questions:

1. What are the principal lessons to be derived from our experiences in the several theatres of the Great War, as disclosed by the official histories and reports? (At that date the

official histories so far published had only reached 1916, but the committee members, judging from their comments about tanks, for instance, also drew on unpublished reports and their own great experience.)
2. Have these lessons been correctly and adequately applied in the Field Service Regulations and other training manuals, and in our system of training generally?

General Kirke was ordered to report within the year, so he divided the work between the members, with two for the Western Front, éach to report on a particular campaign. Their conclusions were in close agreement and the summary, the *Report of the Committee on the Lessons of the Great War* was signed on 13 October. It was graded Secret and its readership limited to senior members of the General Staff. On 11 January 1933 Milne held a high level staff conference to discuss its findings, after which it was effectively shelved. In April 1934 a bowdlerised version, with some of the Committee's forthright views removed and without a security classification, was circulated throughout the Army; to encourage thought and discussion but not action, like *Modern Formations*.

The Kirke report is so compressed that it is difficult to summarise it further. It is a remarkable piece of work, and goes far to rebut the over-simple notion that the pre-1939 reorganisation was a struggle between the advocates of armoured mobility and a host of blimps. It hit a large number of important nails hard on the head, such as the army's need to keep itself constantly informed on all scientific developments that might affect the art of war. It went straight to the heart of the matter, asking in effect what the Army was for:

'We have no specific war problem as we had in 1913.'
'Our organisation and equipment are in a state of flux and obviously unsuited for war against a first class of even a second class enemy.'
'The comparative value to be attached to the various arms is the subject of controversy.'
'Is the great lesson of the war that we should always try to act on the defensive, whatever the fifth principle may say to the contrary?' (The 'fifth principle' was that the final and successful operation of war was *offensive action*, and that all other phases were but preparations for it.)

Kirke answered this last rhetorical question himself. 'As the attack is by far the most difficult operation of modern war our small army should be able to strike quickly and effectively . . .

and therefore a full measure of reorganisation and re-equipment should be directed towards its solution.' The core of the problem was how to maintain the momentum of the advance after the main defensive position had been breached and so avoid the endless and costly battles of attrition of the Western Front.

The Kirke report embraced both principles and much detail (it even commented on the utility of the infantryman's entrenching tool) but its main thrust was directed at the problem of converting the 'break-in' to the 'break-through'. Among its recommendations were that command and control at brigade level and below should be based primarily on radio, the infantry must be made more mobile; the number of weapons used in the battalion reduced, and there should be arrangements to give it close fire-support by heavy weapons. The artillery must speed up its technical procedures, with the same object of giving continuous support to the infantry during the phase of exploitation. There was a need for fire-support from a medium gun or howitzer. 'The moral and material effect of the German 5.9-inch howitzer will not have been forgotten by anyone who experienced it.' On the subject of tanks Kirke said that their performance on the Western Front 'placed their value beyond doubt' and went on to say that infantry-tank co-operation was seldom effective unless the two arms had trained together, and that there should be permanent affiliations. In this context the shape of an armoured division was vaguely but presciently sketched. Because the design of tanks was constantly improving 'was not an adequate reason for delay' in expanding the tank arm. On the delicate subjects of horsed cavalry and direct offensive air support Kirke was understandably guarded or silent (air support lay outside its terms of reference) but all in all these recommendations were both far-seeing and daring in 1931.

Milne was now confronted with a report that he felt was not mistaken, he was far too intelligent a man for that, but embarrassing, if not actually dangerous. The many senior officers at his January 1933 conference broadly agreed with Kirke's conclusions and the whole subject of maintaining the momentum of the attack was thoroughly discussed with many thoughtful additions, but in his closing address Milne gave as his own opinion that the various arms were being developed along the right lines, that the Army as a whole must be given time to adjust itself to change and to digest new ideas, and that there was still a rôle for horsed cavalry. He then dismissed the whole subject by asserting that the Army was not intended for use in another war on the Continent of Europe: its primary function was Imperial defence and Imperial policing. What that distinguished gathering felt at this sublime dismissal of all that they had left their busy desks to discuss is not recorded.[183]

Milne has been much abused, and perhaps deservedly, because if he had a 'principle of war' it was the one later recommended by Mao Tse Tung: 'If the enemy advances we retreat.' In mitigation, though, he sincerely believed that a Fabian policy was the only possible one in the circumstances. The horizon was possibly a little dark, but war was not imminent. Nothing should be done to upset the Army, which meant in fact the colonels of regiments and the more senior officers in their messes and clubs. The cavalry lobby in particular was very powerful. Their case for the mounted arm and the *arme blanche* was not entirely frivolous. Mounted regiments had done well in the Palestine campaign, and the British cavalry had proved useful during the retreat and confused fighting of March 1918. (The last mounted charge by British cavalry was on 24 March at Villaselve, when a small force made up of detachments of the 3rd Dragoon Guards, the Royals and the 10th Hussars supported by 'O' Battery, Royal Horse Artillery. It cost 73 out of 150 men, but inflicted some 70 to 80 casualties, and captured 3 machine-guns and 96 prisoners.) The cavalry were able to point out that the March offensive might have fared better if the Germans had had a force of cavalry to exploit the infantry breakthrough. Faith in cavalry as opposed to mere mounted infantry persisted. In 1933 the senior cadet term of the Royal Military Academy, encamped near Aldershot to be shown the various arms in action, was treated to a demonstration of the mounted charge, sabres drawn, by a full regiment of cavalry. When war broke out a Yeomanry Division, all mounted, was mobilised and sent to Palestine.

There were also objections to plunging on the tank which could not lightly be dismissed. The running-gear was unreliable, indeed, all experience so far had shown that losses in tanks were as much due to breakdown as to enemy action, (but that as Kirke felt, would be put right in due course) and, more important, the only experience of large scale tank warfare had shown that tanks were extremely vulnerable to directly aimed artillery fire. Tank losses in the final offensives of 1918 were severe and casualties among crews a third of the strength of the Tank Corps. These were only countervailing arguments but they carried weight at that time.[184]

This dubious military reasoning was reinforced by that combined blessing and bane of the cavalry and infantry in the British Army, the 'regimental' system. The cavalry as a whole and each of the cavalry units ('regiments') were closed military societies whose officers were recruited on a basis of class and wealth. They were fiercely exclusive, and their colonels were men of influence connected with the 'establishment' by ties of class and marriage. (It should be explained that the 'colonels' of regiments have no command responsibility, which is the duty of the commanding officer, a lieutenant-colonel. The post is honorary, held by a senior and respected member of the regiment, usually retired, often a general officer, who looks after the well-being of the unit, its charitable funds, dress, bands and so on, and approves the applications of newly commissioned officers to join their regiment.) The cavalry colonels formed a powerful, political pressure group united in its resistance to change. The opposition to the mechanisation of the Royal Scots Greys was carried into Parliament and the columns of *The Times* as late as 1938. Milne, with his highly developed sense of what was possible coupled with his dislike of confrontation was unwilling to clash with it, preferring to let the cavalry come to accept mechanisation gradually, as it did. There was one inescapable factor affecting the future of all mounted troops seldom mentioned in accounts of the long controversy over mechanisation – the lack of a reserve of horses.

The long, bitter ideological battle between the 'apostles of mobility' and the more work-a-day officers who held key posts during the modernisation of the Army in the 1930s has been described too often to require repetition here: it will be sufficient to describe the outcome.

In the end both sides had their way. The official line, adopted when General Sir Cyril Deverell became CIGS, and supported on the tank side by Generals Elles and Martel, was that the basic formation of the Army would continue to be the marching infantry division, its transport and artillery mechanised, but with its battalion organisation improved in a number of important details. The Royal Tank Corps was equipped with small, slow, heavily armoured Infantry tanks or 'I' which would support the infantry. In 1937 a single 'mobile division' was formed; in effect a mechanised cavalry division with light, fast tanks – the cavalry units naturally preserving their identity. Its function was to be the traditional light cavalry one of screening and reconnaissance. This had a short life and was overtaken by the armoured division proper, organised on the lines fought for by Hobart in defiance of official policy, with two tank brigades and a mixed brigade of artillery and infantry successively entitled the 'Pivot Group' and the 'Support Group'.

Except for one early model with one machine-gun only, both fast tanks and infantry tanks were initially armed with the

2-pounder gun for use against hostile tanks and one or two machine-guns as the primary anti-infantry or anti-artillery weapon. The 2-pounder proved a mistake, but the reasoning in its favour was that it was easily accommodated in the small tanks of those days. It was effective against any tank then known, and as the round of ammunition was small a large number could be carried, thus obviating the need for early replenishment. (All the emergent armoured corps in other armies followed suit except the Russians, who at an earlier date chose the 76.2-mm (3-inch) gun as their main tank armament.)[185] In British opinion a tank with a big gun would lack the mobility for its rôle of deep penetration. (Long afterwards, on 1 July 1966, General Sir Charles Broad said emphatically that modern tanks with their huge cannon were far removed from his own idea of armoured warfare, which was based on the forays behind the lines of the cavalry of both sides in the American Civil War.) All the British tanks were gradually up-gunned, and in 1942 the Army was largely re-equipped with the US Sherman tank armed with a long 75-mm gun.

The adoption of the machine-gun was better based. It was a versatile weapon, used in 1918 by both German and British infantry as a close support, attacking weapon. Obviously it was better to put it in an armoured vehicle than carry it in mule pack or manhandle it forward. In the 1920s a future Director of the Royal Armoured Corps, G. le Q. Martel, an engineer officer, experimented with a tiny tank armed with a machine-gun and a crew of one which, after various mutations, became the light machine-gun, or Bren carrier, of the Second World War. Liddell Hart over-hopefully suggested that 'every anti-tank gun . . . would be smothered in a thick spray of aimed machine-gun fire from the tankettes . . .'[186], not to be borne out in real tank fighting, in which the heavy anti-tank gun soon gained the upper hand, but the tank-borne machine-gun remained an important secondary weapon, especially in close country, until the end of the War. (It returned to fashion in Vietnam, and also in the Sinai Desert in 1973 when short range, infantry-operated guided missiles became a threat to even the heaviest tanks.)

The net result was that the army in the field had one kind of tank suitable only for infantry support – and a tank formation almost 'pure in race' as the Germans were to call it later – highly mobile but weak in fire-power for far ranging armoured operations. This state of affairs was only remedied later after harsh experience.

Less controversial, but equally important, was the reorganisation of the infantry battalion. Those who perceived that the marching infantryman would continue to be one of three principal arms in a future war were proved entirely correct. The infantryman as a vehicle for fire-power has the disadvantages of being fragile, prone to fatigue and a slow mover, although these inherent characteristics can be relieved by transporting him to the scene of combat in an armoured vehicle, or by air. These inherent shortcomings are more than compensated by his tactical mobility in any terrain from ice-clad mountain to tropical swamp. The fact that he presents only a small and inconspicuous target (the dread 'unlocated machine-gun' noted by Kirke as *the* great obstacle on the battlefield), can easily hide himself and, given a little time, can burrow underground like a mole. He also has, as nature's gifts, excellent optical and acoustic sensors and a small but unsurpassed neural computer, one fitted to each model.

The object of the reforms of the 1930s was to make the infantry more mobile and more self-supporting, but also to simplify their tactics by reducing the number of different weapons in the battalion. After the disbandment of the Machine-Gun Corps in 1919 each British battalion had been given a company of twelve Vickers machine-guns, and two of the four sections in each platoon had a Lewis gun. Kirke suggested recentralising the Vickers guns and equipping the infantry with only light machine-guns and mortars, but this merely substituted one weapon for another, and in addition the 2-pounder anti-tank gun was to be an infantry weapon. A difficulty arose here from the peculiar organisation of the British infantry. In all other armies the basic unit is the 'regiment', a permanent grouping with its own identity, usually cantoned in one town or barracks, consisting of three battalions together with a number of specialist companies equipped with support weapons; heavy mortars, light howitzers or guns, anti-aircraft machine-guns, signals equipment and anti-tank guns all manned by members of the regiment. The regimental commander has, therefore, at his own immediate disposal fire-power for concentrated use or for decentralisation to the battalions. (Significantly, in the German model the battalions were not called Batallionen, but Abteilungen, or 'detachments'. They were tactical entities, but not independent, exclusive units, as with the British.)

In the British Army battalions, partly for traditional reasons and partly for the need to deploy small units widely for 'Imperial policing', were (and are) discrete units belonging to a 'Regiment' of a different sort. This is a non-tactical entity based on an obsolete function ('fusilier', 'grenadier', 'rifleman') or on the area of recruitment (the Highlands of Scotland, or English counties) or both. The tactical organisation corresponding to the

Continental 'regiment' is the looser 'brigade', made up of battalions from different regiments.[187] Outside the infantry organisation specialist weapons and functions are the responsibility of Corps. Novelties in the British Army have either to be accommodated in some corps deemed capable of handling them, such as the Royal Engineers, who in times past have been made responsible for aviation, the army post, chemical warfare and signals communications, or if no suitable or welcoming corps existed one had to be created. As we have seen, the machine-gun and the tanks had been formed into specialist corps. Heavy support weapons, therefore, either had to be grouped into some suitable corps, or given to the infantry battalions, for independent weapons companies in the brigade organisation would be homeless, masterless, cap-badgeless pariahs. The Royal Artillery's own solution to the problem of providing continuous close support for the infantry was by providing a 'light brigade' of three batteries of six 3.7-inch mountain howitzers for each division, carried on mule pack. These could be decentralised by batteries to brigades or sections of two guns per battalion, which they could accompany during the advance over any terrain.

The reforms inflicted on the infantry in the period 1937–9 followed Kirke, up to a point. The machine-guns were segregated in ten special battalions of infantry, with 48 guns each, and the infantry rearmed with one of the new Bren light machine-guns for each rifle section, simplifying training. The new machine-gun battalions (in effect a revived machine-gun corps, the distinction was purely nominal, but the new organisation preserved the identity of the sacred infantry cap-badges) were grouped either under army or corps headquarters for sub-allotting to divisions and brigades. This system, adopted perforce in the absence of a true, tactical regimental organisation, ensured that the gunners would be total strangers to the infantry among whom they would be intimately deployed in the hour of battle. The infantry were devoted to their Vickers guns, and were able eventually to claim them back. The machine-gun battalions were then converted to dual purpose pools of reserve fire-power (still, of course recognised as infantry) composed of Vickers guns and 4.2-inch mortars.

Again, because there was no other place for them to go, the infantry battalions were given platoons of 3-inch mortars, some 2-inch mortars for each company (really no more than a discharger for little smoke or high explosive bombs), a platoon of 2-pounder anti-tank guns and a platoon of 'Bren Carriers'. These last were descendants of the Martel's 'tankettes'; little steel boxes on tracks, each armed with a Bren gun for use mounted or dismounted. They were to have a long life as a sort of useful petrol-driven mule, but as miniature armoured fighting vehicles they were to prove hopelessly vulnerable to artillery air-burst, any kind of anti-tank fire and especially to anti-tank mines. The aim was to convert the battalion into what we would now term a 'battle-group', with its own miniature artillery and 'armour'. It was altogether too much, so looking round for something to discard the infantry picked on the 2-pounder guns. Guns were clearly a Royal Artillery weapon. Therefore, at the shortest notice, and much to the surprise of the artillerymen, who were already trying to cope with an unwanted and ill-thought out reorganisation that had been foisted on them, they found themselves responsible for anti-tank defence. All they could do in the time, and with the resources available, was to convert all the light and some of the army (i.e. reserve) field brigades to anti-tank. This was not a satisfactory arrangement either. Once the infantry had had some first-hand experience of panzer attacks they demanded their guns back again. In an emergency there is no substitute for having the necessary weapon close to hand and manned by men trained in the unit. The converted Royal Artillery regiments, however, were retained as divisional or corps units but equipped with heavier anti-tank guns, some self-propelled.

The field artillery itself was to be thrown into confusion, from which it had barely recovered when, in 1940, it faced the blitzkrieg. Everyone agrees that during the earlier war the artillery had become supremely scientific and mastered the arts of counter-battery and the break-in battle. Kirke rightly perceived that its procedures should be speeded up so that it would react to the ever changing situations of the break-through battle, but on this question Kirke was uninspired. Crassly, it said of 'survey' – the blanket term then used for modern, scientific fire-control, and the only means by which the fire of more than the six guns of a single battery could be concentrated rapidly on a single, important target – that though it was a 'valuable adjunct', it should not be regarded as 'a primary method to be used on every occasion'.

This was not based on the experience of the Western Front, where predicted fire and massed fire was first introduced, but reflected the impatience of old fashioned artillery officers with the tests of survey at post-war practice camp, when they usually took two or more hours to complete observations and make the calculations, grumbling as they worked. In the 1930–1 Royal Artillery Journal the opponents of survey, arguing that better results could be achieved by the simple, old fashioned observed fire from a single battery (galloping into action with a cry of 'halt, action front!') which was more effective than all this trigonometry, initiated the 'Mutt and Jeff at War' controversy.[188] The defender of survey in a telling phrase appealed to his opponents – 'if . . . the reactionary will drop his attitude of stubborn prejudice . . .' – to try and make the system work. Both the underlying principles of artillery survey and the mathematics involved were simple, and the rather absurd 'Mutt and Jeff' controversy reveals the extent of the grip of the 'swingletree' obsession, bearing in mind that the 'reactionaries' had passed through Woolwich, where they could not have escaped the strong mathematical content of the curriculum.

It is necessary at this point to pause for a brief technical explanation of a process central to all field gunnery practice and therefore to understanding its wider tactical application. The process of artillery survey is nothing more than making a map in which the only features are battery positions and targets. The object is twofold. Originally, on the Western Front, where the engineer survey produced maps of 1:20,000 scale or even larger overprinted with trench lines and hostile battery positions, it enabled fully predicted fire to be brought down at short notice, and it also made possible the huge barrage plans of that war. Its other use was to enable the fire of several batteries to be brought down at the shortest notice on a target of opportunity detected by a forward observer and fixed either by map-reading or by registering his own battery, after which the data was circulated to all other batteries. It was this second capability which was so essential in maintaining the momentum of the attack. In a mobile war no such elaborate mapping would be available. Kirke's artillery advisers adopted the pessimistic standpoint that there was no way of speeding up the process, while the swingle-tree faction for quite other, psychological reasons mocked the whole process as a waste of time.

One of the obstacles to simplification was the doctrine put out by the School of Artillery itself, which insisted on the pursuit of extreme accuracy. Predicted fire and the concentrated fire of a number of batteries was only permissible if either large scale maps were available or if full survey had been completed. When it had the target could either be fixed by survey methods from the observation post or posts, or it could be registered by firing, after which the data was laboriously computed and circulated through the inefficient telephone network of the day to the guns. It was all very slow. The system was called 'brigade control' and there was, inevitably, an army form to be filled in to ensure that the correct procedure was adopted. 'Brigade Control' exercises were greeted with groans of boredom and left to the adjutant and the junior officers.

'Survey' in reality was a process initiated from the moment that the first battery dropped into action. The gun position officer fixed his position from a 1-inch map using a compass, while the observing officer at the same time plotted likely targets on his map. The process of mapping was then extended, first to embrace all the battery positions in the regiment, which were seldom more than a few hundred yards apart, and gradually the whole divisional artillery. At the same time the specialist survey sections responsible for this process were progressively improving its accuracy. All mapping related the gun positions to a rectangular grid (familiar to anyone who uses a sheet of a 1-inch British Ordnance Survey map sheet), and the map co-ordinates, finally refined to an accuracy of the order of five or ten metres, were a currency common to all batteries and regiments from which the firing data specific to each individual battery could be computed. The mathematically minded will perceive that gun data, bearing and range are polar co-ordinates and the grid references Cartesian co-ordinates, and the process involves converting one from the other either by elementary calculations or by graphical means, involving no more than the ability to plot the data on a blank grid and the use of a range scale and protractor.

In India a very simple procedure had been evolved by which the fire of two adjacent batteries could be controlled as if they were one from either observation post, thus providing the fire of twelve guns on any important target while the process of survey was going forward.[189]

Suddenly, at short notice the whole well-tried organisation and technique was scrapped in favour of a fire-unit which was to consist of a continental-type regiment of two battalions each of three batteries, of which there would be three in the divisional artillery. (The artillery adopted the term 'regiment' from then on for an artillery unit, but following the British practice of adopting the most confusing nomenclature possible, called the 'battalions' 'batteries', and the 'batteries' 'troops'.) Survey and the survey parties were abolished. Instead the troops were to be so closely located that their relative positions could be fixed from a single, central point and their fire concentrated by a simple graphical method. Its originator and sponsors are not known for certain, but it was adopted against the advice of the School of Artillery on the orders of the War Office.[190] It was badly thought out and caused a great upheaval, but as it was tried and found wanting in the 1940 campaign in France and Belgium there is no need to discuss it further. It is of more interest to describe what followed.

Many officers would have preferred to return to a regiment of four six-gun batteries, but under dive-bombing six guns presented too dense a target, unless the battery frontage was made so great that it became difficult to control. To change to four-gun batteries either reduced the divisional artillery to forty-eight guns, which was unacceptable, or required an extra regiment, which made for too many staff overheads. (In the continental artillery regiment the fourth unit or battalion consisted of heavy howitzers, but Kirke had recommended a single type of gun throughout the division.) The solution adopted was for regiments of three *eight*-gun batteries, each of two four-gun 'troops', using the Indian method, known as 'linking', to shoot as one. This proved manoeuvrable and had the great advantage of fitting the triangular infantry brigade, there being a battery to affiliate to each battalion in training and war. The survey party was restored. It was a change of heart, however, not a change of organisation that was required. The officers of the new citizen army were free from affectation and took their gunnery seriously, and also the standard of intelligence of the new rank and file was far superior to that of the tough and loyal but dim 'old sweats' of the horsed, pre-1939 Royal Artillery. The disappearance of the horse, whose care took up half the day's work, made it possible to concentrate on the proper business of artillery training. The single survey company which was all that existed in England in 1933 was expanded into a number of survey regiments, including as well as the surveyors a battery each of flash-spotters and sound-rangers for the location of hostile batteries. With the will to make the system work and improved procedures the target times for bringing a regiment on the grid was reduced to one hour in open country and for the whole divisional artillery more than three was considered bad. Survey ceased to be a bogey, and it can be safely asserted that in the whole war the survey preparations of the artillery were always completed before those of the troops they were supporting.

The real problem was not survey but command and control: the system for collecting information, transmitting it and retransmitting the necessary orders. It was radio that revolutionised modern warfare. In the nineteenth century a general *watched* the battle, in the early twentieth he stared at an empty landscape wondering what was happening on the other side of the hill or inside the smoke-screen into which his troops had disappeared, but in the 1940s he could *listen* to the battle. From the armoured cars, from the tanks, and above all from the twenty or more expert observers of the Royal Artillery detached from the combat but close to the units they supported, came an unending flow of information about the progress of the battle in clear speech. Mobile observers who moved with the infantry and tanks controlled the fire of guns with double the range of the old 18-pounders and 4.5-inch howitzers. The fog of war which cloaked the battle soon after the break-through was dispelled, and 'close' support became possible, not through the proximity of the gun but of the forward observing officer. The next step was to find a means of firing rapid concentrations from whole regiments.

This was to be solved by H. J. Parham. He was a horseman with the coveted letters *'Eq. v.'* after his name in the regimental list, meaning that he had passed the equitation course and one in practical veterinary science, but he not only looked 'behind the swingletree', but all round him. He had an amateur pilot's licence and, as will be related in the proper place, was concerned in the development of the artillery air observation post and helped to push through the scheme for its adoption.

In 1940 Parham was commanding a field regiment engaged in the confused fighting in Belgium, when German tanks were observed moving into a wood. Ignoring all the 'rules of ranging' taught at Larkhill, Parham ordered all three of his batteries to fire ten rounds per gun, without further ado or preliminary ranging, on the six-figure reference of the wood as deduced by eye from a 1-inch scale map. His well-trained regiment responded promptly, and the observers were rewarded by the sight of a huge explosion. 'It made quite an impression on the spectators,' said Parham. (He surmised that the panzers did not know that they were near the British position, and were in the act of refuelling under cover of the trees.) It also made an impression on Parham and caused him in due course to reflect on current conventions for the engagement of targets.

In 1941 he was back in England and a brigadier. The lessons of the disastrous campaign in France were being earnestly studied, and one of the questions raised was why the British Army could not have the same support in the field from their air force as the Germans. This was something the Royal Air Force resolutely opposed but, thought Parham, what could dive-bombers do in the actual zone of combat that artillery could not? A 25-pounder battery from a normal position a mile behind the front line with a 60° arc of fire can command rather more than twenty square miles of enemy territory.

Next, what was the point of this extreme pursuit of accuracy? Accuracy of fire is limited both by the accuracy of location of the target and the zone of dispersion of the gun. The 'unlocated machine-gun' specifically mentioned by Kirke as one of the primary obstacles to be overcome was never likely to be accurately located in the noise and confusion of battle; only its general area. A regular exercise at practice was to set the observing officer the task of hitting a located machine-gun, or 'pin-point target', using one gun and the technique known as 'adjusting the mean point of impact', and there was a calculation used to predict how many rounds would be required after this was completed to ensure at least one dropping in the gun-pit. *How* the target was 'pin-pointed' or located was never explained. The simplest plan was to drench the area with fire. This principle applied to targets generally on a real battlefield. Moreover the shock effect of a large number of rounds arriving simultaneously was far greater than that of a prolonged bombardment of a few guns. The Parham system, to be adopted in all the Commonwealth armies, was to fire every gun that could bear as soon as it could be laid and loaded.

The key to the whole affair was the structure of the communication network. If the observing officer was empowered to call for fire from every gun in the division and had a radio link which bypassed the breaks in the ordinary command chain it would immensely accelerate the response to any emergency call for fire.

One of Parham's virtues was an instinctive preference for experiment as opposed to arguing about principles. He decided to put his scheme to a practical test. The crux of the question was how far he was correct in assuming that a six-figure map reference picked by eye was sufficiently accurate for his purpose. By 1941 Parham was Commander, Royal Artillery (CRA) of the 38th Infantry Division and he held an exercise for his three regiments on the downs above Worbarrow Bay in Dorset, using buoys moored in the sea as targets. The results were positive. (The exercise caused considerable local alarm and the Royal Navy in nearby Portland, who had not been alerted, were not amused when reports arrived that massed artillery was thundering away at targets out to sea. They wanted to know whether the invasion had begun, and if so, why they had not been informed.)

The next step was a more elaborate test under the critical eyes of a number of distinguished persons on the Larkhill ranges of the School of Artillery. There a flaw in Parham's original system for moving the mean point of impact which had near fatal results was revealed. The fire of one battery dropped among the spectators in the VIP stand and Parham always remembered the awful occasion of the day when 'we nearly killed all those generals', but his system, after some necessary refinements had been made, was fully accepted, and it became one of the most powerful instruments lying ready to the hand of an artillery commander.[191]

It must be understood that the 'U' target system, as it came to be known, superseded neither accurate survey, which was essential in the preparation of large, predicted fire plans, nor the normal engagement of targets of opportunity nor the registration of local fire-plans by battery observers using the 'rules of ranging'. It was simply the means of producing, in a matter of minutes, a hammer blow to meet an emergency; to repel a counter-attack, or to smash unexpected resistance.

We have now run somewhat ahead of events and must return to the moral and physical impact of the new German system of war – the blitzkrieg.

BOOK IV

The Second Round: 1939–1945

Renown awaits the commander who restores artillery to pre-eminence on the battlefield.
Attributed to Winston Churchill, *c.* 1942

Artillery is the God of War.
Stalin

CHAPTER 12

Blitzkrieg

Armour and movement are only two of the important characteristics of the tank; the third and most important is fire-power.

Heinz Guderian

IT is, perhaps, significant that the expression *blitzkrieg* does not appear in the autobiography of the great tactician who proved its most brilliant exponent.

Heinz Guderian, a product of the German system of military education and a member of the German General Staff, was a man unlikely to be seduced by any military catchword, however vivid, or to believe that there was any simple formula for success in so complicated and chancy an affair as war. His system was based on sound and well-known military principles leading to obvious conclusions. Had Guderian seen the Kirke Committee's report, or the transcript of Milne's staff conference, he would have endorsed all their recommendations. In Britain the debate languished in the absence of a continental commitment. In Germany, where there was a specific military aim, the habit of clear and rational analysis examined the possibilities of a combination of the tank, radio communications and air power in the light of the ancient maxims of offensive action, speed in decision and concentration of resources. The result was a military instrument perfectly suited to the strategic aim.

The idea of blitzkrieg was far more than a technique; a matter of novel weapons and tactics. It was also, and primarily, a strategy whose parent was Hitler himself. Hitler's policy, that cloudy melange of German hegemony over Europe, race, a *drang nach osten* and *lebensraum*, was pursued, according to the dictum of Clausewitz, by any suitable means. If one of these was military action he saw that it had to be rapid, so as to present the rest of the world with a fait accompli. Above all, he had to avoid anything in the nature of a prolonged war of attrition which in the long run could only go against Germany. The English prophets of armoured mobility spoke of paralysing the opposing armies by attacking their headquarters and therefore the very will of the commanders to continue the struggle. Underlying the purely tactical proposals in Fuller's 'Plan 1919', of a vast onslaught by thousands of tanks, and Liddell Hart's theories of the 'indirect approach' and 'strategic dislocation', there was a basis of psychology. Hitler raised this idea to the political plane. His target was the will of the victim country's government, not merely the opposing generals and the morale of the people as a whole. The way was prepared by propaganda, intimidation and subversion, followed by a lightning blow. For this the air arm was as useful for terrorising the civil population as for the orthodox support of the ground forces. Guderian tells the story, often quoted, of how when Hitler saw the first demonstration of a mechanised force complete with tanks, he exclaimed that it was exactly what he wanted and what he must have. This was the rationale of the blitzkrieg, which must be kept in mind if both its formidable nature and its undoubted weaknesses are to be understood.[192]

The term blitzkrieg in the strictest sense, therefore, describes a particular strategy of conquest, adapted to the political situation in Europe at a particular time, and effective only when directed by a Hitler. It has, however, also conveniently, if less exactly, come to be applied to the technique of 'lightning war'. There is in English military terminology no word for that part of generalship which lies below 'strategy' and above 'tactics'. 'Strategy' has come to mean 'grand strategy', as opposed to the old fashioned meaning of the manoeuvres leading to battle, 'tactics' has the limited meaning of the technique of combat, and the useful 'grand tactics' is obsolete. The German words *operation* and *operativ*, can be translated as 'tactics' and 'tactical', but they can also connote the plan and conduct of 'operations' on a large scale and at a high level of command.

While the Kirke Committee Report was being circulated for consideration the more advanced thinkers in the German Army were also pondering the question of how to maintain the momentum of the offensive on a modern battlefield, theoretically dominated by defensive weapons, but they arrived at a practical conclusion. They already had a model. In 1917 they had devised a system of attack relying on deep infiltration and used it effectively in 1918. It had failed for lack of a mobile arm. Now, they saw, the source of mobility it had lacked in 1918 could be the petrol engine instead of the tired legs of the infantry. In their new form of war the ordinary marching divisions would be preceded by an élite force of tanks and mechanised infantry and artillery and a powerful air force properly equipped for the task of ground support. In a sentence, the modus operandi was to break the crust of the forward defences, drive through with this mobile force and fight a battle of manoeuvre in the depth of the victim's defensive system. Speed and the maintenance of momentum of the attack was to be the key of the whole business. Like the *sturmabteilungen* of 1918, the spearhead troops were to press on disregarding the security of their rear and flanks, bypass hard centres of resistance and leave them to the marching infantry following in the rear. The defending commander was to be given no respite to reorganise or establish a fresh defensive front. The scheme of manoeuvre was to chop his defences up into fragments, envelop them and destroy them piecemeal. This was the blitzkrieg on the operational level, using the word in its German connotation, and in the sense of this chapter.

The problem facing the British defence planners after the withdrawal from France was not how to create a blitzkrieg army of their own, although the army succumbed to the understandable temptation to demand weapons similar to the enemy's – dive bombers, for instance. Certainly there was much that could be learnt, but the first priority was to examine how such an onslaught could be first checked and then broken up. It was a rational and intellectual process which had to be undertaken by the same men who, in the fraught period after Dunkirk, were frantically striving to re-equip the veterans of the blitzkrieg and equip and train the mass of green units in Britain against invasion, while at the same time the Battle of Britain was being fought. Their hopes of arriving at a solution were, fortunately, not depressed by fresh applications of blitzkrieg formula in Africa, Greece and Crete, admittedly on a miniature scale, leading to the defeat or repulse of moderately well-equipped and stout-hearted British and Commonwealth troops, on the similar tactics used by the Japanese in Malaya and Burma.

The difficulties and distractions were daunting. It is greatly to the credit of the soldiers and airmen that the way to tame the blitzkrieg was discovered (or rediscovered, it is a point of view) and applied in August 1942, after which there was no going back.

It must be added here that what the British had to do on a small scale had also to be attempted on the largest scale by the Russians while they were suffering invasion of their territory and a series of military disasters, and that they too first checked and eventually rolled back the invader in total defeat, but the circumstances in Russia were different. There was ample space to recoil, the Soviet Union had vast and undamaged resources awaiting mobilisation and a population large enough to enable it to resort to the brutal responses of outnumbering the aggressor and meeting every attack with counter-attack, but this does not diminish in any way the extent of the Soviet's achievement. The great battle of Kursk in 1943 was a milestone in the history of defensive warfare against tanks. The British problem was the more acute because they possessed neither a strong industrial base nor reserves of manpower. For them it depended more on economy of force and the dexterous use of fire-power, small in volume compared with the enormous amount available to the Red Army.

It is tempting, therefore, to look more closely at the German invasion of Russia, but there the blitzkrieg was a strategic failure. For our purpose the campaign in France and Flanders in 1940 is a more compact example. It is also more relevant, as it was the British experience. Its course is too well known to require more than the briefest recapitulation. The Germans attacked on 10 May 1940, the perfect weather favouring the three limbs of their new tactics, the air force and the armoured divisions, coupled with a surprise parachute and air-transported attack. On 14 May Kleist's Panzer Group (in effect a panzer army) of seven armoured divisions, whose thrust was the essential manoeuvre of the whole operation, crossed the Meuse, routed the French Second Army, made a sweeping, scything stroke *(sichelschnitt)* to cut the British and French armies to the north of its axis from their base, reaching Boulogne and the Channel coast on the 25th. The Dutch were overwhelmed in five days, the Belgians capitulated on the 27th, Paris fell on 14 June and all resistance in France ceased on the 21st. Hitler's strategy achieved in six weeks what Germany had previously failed to do in four years and three months.

If there was one, ineluctable condition for a successful war of this kind it was not the possession of novel weapons, dazzling tactical skill, a good plan, able commanders or any other of the traditional requirements for military victory. It was the choice of a suitable victim. The French, apparently so strong and with great military traditions, might have been expected to fight desperately when defending the sacred soil of their country, but Hitler intuitively perceived that France, a reluctant belligerent, was politically feeble, ripe for the blitzkrieg treatment and its army could be toppled, for all that he and one or two of his senior commanders nearly lost their nerve during the execution of the hazardous sichelschnitt. Indeed, in view of the odds, no one could have criticised them for insisting on a slower advance and progressive consolidation of the gains of the panzer divisions. At one stage, crucial to the whole manoeuvre and therefore to the whole war, the map revealed a tentacle no more than 30 miles wide and 200 miles long open to attack from either flank, while the same map revealed French and British divisions by the score to the north and south. Nor was this menacing object in any way solid. The fighting echelons of a panzer division could occupy 50 miles of road space marching in peace-time conditions. In operations there would be traffic jams in some places, columns vastly strung out in others, and long gaps between the panzers and the supply columns and the infantry of the marching divisions toiling on foot far in the rear. The whole advance was exposed to air attacks made in deadly enfilade along the length of the columns, especially if aimed at the columns of motor infantry, artillery and the unarmoured supply vehicles, stretched along the roads, or to ground thrusts made at right angles to them. The small attack by a handful of British tanks and infantry on 21 May failed, but its moral effect was so great that it imposed enough delay to make the uninterrupted British retreat to the beaches of Dunkirk possible. Nothing greater was attempted: the French commanders were indeed paralysed.

The whole debacle seemed at first to be inexplicable, and the first excuses and explanations, like more considered ones made in the years immediately after the war, did not get to the heart of the matter. A number of conventional factors not peculiar to the blitzkrieg must be given due weight. The Allies, for political reaons, felt that their stance must be free of any taint of aggression or provocation: 'On land it had been agreed that Anglo-French strategy should aim primarily at maintaining the integrity of French territory. Should the Low Countries be invaded the Allies will attempt to stop the enemy as far forward as conditions permit.'[193] What the French, who dictated this strategy, expected to happen next is not clear, but what is clear is that their whole doctrine was based on the defensive and that they firmly believed that in modern war offensive action of any kind was too costly to undertake. The result was the long period of inaction – the *drôle de guerre*, or 'phoney war' – from September to April, unrelieved even by any large scale manoeuvres or mobile training, which had so depressing an effect on the morale of the French troops. The British were more stoical, but they too spent most of their time in billets or in digging defences along the Belgian border instead of training. (There was an absurd order forbidding the use of radio for training the operators. In consequence when the advance into Belgium took place and events moved too fast to lay telephone lines there was a communications failure at unit level; most seriously in the artillery.)

The whole French command system was abysmally bad. Its structure was defective and its communications rudimentary. General Gamelin, the Commander-in-Chief, was without a radio network. He afterwards admitted that any order from his headquarters was unlikely to bear fruit for forty-eight hours. French generals, perhaps obsessed with purely defensive tactics, proved unable to make up their minds or give orders, and failed completely to use their ample reserves to counter-attack in the crucial early phase of the break-through, or later, for that matter. The employment of the air forces was equally dilatory.

For many students of warfare the success of the blitzkrieg was a vindication of the radical doctrines of the apostles of mobility and of the tank. If ever a campaign was decided by strategical dislocation and loss of will of the higher command it was certainly that of 1940. General Georges is said to have broken down completely at the news of the German break-through at Sedan and the panic flight of the French divisions from the left bank of the Meuse. At a conference on that day (14 May) 'most of the French officers were in tears, some quite openly sobbing . . .' at the news.[194] General Ironside found General Bilotte 'completely demoralised with no thought of a plan, (he) shook him by the coat and forced him to make (one)'.[195] Generals, however, should be, and usually are, made of sterner stuff. Nor was the principle of the 'indirect approach' in evidence, unless it is assumed that it includes every manoeuvre except a frontal attack. The vital move, the forcing of the passage of the Meuse, was a frontal attack. The German objective was the classic one of destroying the opposing armies, which was successfully accomplished piecemeal, or 'in detail', beginning with all those trapped in Belgium, and finishing with those standing uselessly behind the Maginot Line. There was no dispersion, no widely flung net of small units. The main thrust was a concentrated blow by some 1,500 tanks on a twenty-five mile front.

Others attributed the German success simply to superiority in the number and quality of equipment. This is a view that has had to be modified. On the ground the key weapon was the tank. The total strength of armoured fighting vehicles of all kinds possessed by the French was 4,000. Of these some 2,000 were fit for modern warfare, and of these in turn a good proportion were S-35s (or 'Somua's', from the initials of the manufacturer), with a 47-mm turret mounted gun, one of the best tanks in service at that date. There were also a number of the slower but heavily armoured and formidable Char B1 with a short 75-mm gun in the hull and a 47-mm in the turret. The French tanks were grouped in three 'light mechanised divisions' (*Divisions Legères Mécanique*, or DLMs) which resembled the German light divisions in being basically motorised infantry with a strong tank element, and three armoured divisions (*divisions cuirassées*) containing the heavy tanks. These armoured divisions, however, had been only recently formed and had done little or no collective training. The DLMs were allotted to separate armies, and the divisions cuirassées to the reserve; one to the general reserve and two to the reserves of the French First Army Group in the centre, where the main blow of the panzers was to fall. They were used up piecemeal instead of for a concentrated counter-punch.

The Germans deployed 2,539 tanks for their offensive, but this is a deceptive figure. Of these 1,478 were the already obsolete Mark Is and Mark IIs, armed only with machine-guns or a 20-mm gun. The only battleworthy tanks were 349 Panzer Mark IIIs with a 37-mm gun, 334 Czech tanks with 37-mm guns and 278 Panzer Mark IVs, later, when upgunned, to be the mainstay of the panzer armies in the mid-war period, but in 1940 armed only with a short 75-mm and intended as a close support tank for the Mark IIIs.[196]

All these types, French and German, were vulnerable to all the artillery deployed by either side, except for the two battalions of British tanks of the 'infantry' type with the British Expeditionary Force, which were so heavily armoured that they were proof against the German 37-mm gun, and Char B1. Experience in France and later in Africa showed that tanks could be destroyed by 2-pounders, 75-mm and 18-pounder field guns, 105-mm field howitzers, 3.7-inch mountain howitzers, 25-pounder (3.45-inch) guns and the well known 88-mm anti-aircraft guns, all using direct laying.

No tank of the Second World War was proof against a direct hit by a 'medium' artillery shell (90 pounds from a 155-mm howitzer, or 100 pounds from a 5.5-inch gun) and when these larger calibres were included in artillery concentrations tanks could be set on fire, their tracks broken by splinter or their turrets jammed. What was equally if not more important was that such concentrated fire could halt and severely punish the unprotected infantry and towed artillery which closely accompanied panzer attacks, and drive the tank commanders inside their turrets; the more battle-hardened in those days usually preferring to sit on the rim of the hatch to obtain a clear view of the battlefield. Tanks were also vulnerable to air attack, both from bombers, cannon-fire from fighters and the 'tank-busting' weapons fitted in fighter-bombers later in the war, such as 40-mm Bofors and high-explosive rockets.

The first sight of an enemy tank in battle was enough to alarm anyone, but if the gun crews were well trained they were proof against what the Russians called 'tank panic', and field artillery batteries if well sited could repel a tank attack. The British, who had exercised their field branch against simulated tank targets regularly before the war did so, repeatedly. The French 75-mm field gun was also an excellent anti-tank gun. It is not to underrate the tank as a weapon to say that in 1940 the German panzers obtained their effect more by moral effect than by fire-power.

It was moral effect that achieved the larger victory. Between them the French, Belgians, British and Dutch could put 142 divisions into the field, the Germans 126, of which 32 marching infantry divisions were retained in reserve. Had the contest been between these old fashioned divisions the Allies might have maintained a successful defence, although French insistence on static methods and their reluctance to counter-attack makes this doubtful. But it was not this mass of infantry that counted. The cutting edge of the German Army was formed by the ten panzer and three light divisions.

In addition there was another new arm – the airborne formations. Airborne attack was to prove extremely risky and extremely costly, so much so that Hitler discontinued its use after the Pyrrhic victory of the German airborne troops in Crete, but the sudden descent of masses of troops far behind defended frontiers had a profound effect on the morale of troops and civilians. It was the quintessence of blitzkrieg. A parachute infantry regiment and a regiment of infantry in gliders followed by the infantry of a normal division flown in by transports to captured airfields, coupled with some terror bombing by the German Air Force, achieved the downfall of the Netherlands. The main line of Belgian resistance on the Albert Canal was broken by 400 gliderborne assault engineers who captured the bridges and the fort at Eben Emael by coup de main. Once the German commanders had by such means seized the priceless advantage of the initiative they never relinquished it.[197]

The success of the German airborne troops emphasises the fact that if there was a single, key factor in the secret of the blitzkrieg it was air-power. The Germans perceived that their air force was not an ancillary or supporting weapon but that it and the army were equal partners in their war machine.

The Luftwaffe was in fact outnumbered by the combined Allied Air Forces, but was better commanded and also qualitatively superior, although both the British and French possessed some aircraft, notably the Spitfire fighters thrown into the air battle late in May, that were fully a match for the Germans. An effective figure for the French first line strength committed to the battle for France is hard to arrive at. A very large number of undamaged aircraft were surrendered, and it appears that some hundreds of good fighters fresh from the factories were held in store and never issued to squadrons during the battle.[198] British Air Forces in France (BAFF) consisted of an Air Component for the British Expeditionary Force of five Lysander reconnaissance squadrons, four Blenheim bomber squadrons and six Hurricane fighter squadrons, exclusive of the Spitfire and Hurricane squadrons from the metropolitan air force committed to the rescue of the BEF. In addition there was the French controlled Advanced Air Striking Force of ten squadrons (160 aircraft) of Battle light bombers; perhaps 450 aircraft altogether. Of these the Battles and Lysanders were to prove useless against the German fighters and anti-aircraft defences.

Two 'air fleets' were deployed by the Luftwaffe, one for each of the two Army Groups attacking in the north, with a total of some 1,000 fighters and 1,700 bombers (the combined fighter/ground attack aircraft had not yet been developed). In addition the army and air force between them provided ground cover in the shape of excellent, modern low and medium altitude anti-aircraft batteries, freeing their fighters from purely defensive duties for air control and covering their bombing sorties – being wise enough, having invented the poison, to provide themselves with the antidote. They were very effective, on one occasion shooting down 27 out of 37 of the remaining British Battles when they made a heroic and sacrificial attack on the German crossings over the Meuse. The French, by contrast, had virtually no effective cover against the 400 'Stuka' Ju-87 dive-bombers which made such an impression on their victims.[199] The Ju-87 was in fact already obsolete and an easy target for either rapid fire from guns like the Bofors 40-mm, or any fighter. Again its effect was moral. To be observed and attacked from above, and be naked to such attack, combined with the din of aircraft diving on one vertically and the crash of bombs, arouses atavistic fears and can try the nerves of the best troops. If there was a turning point in the battle of France it was when the air attacks, concentrated on the front of Guderian's Corps at Sedan, made the gunners of two French divisional artilleries bolt before a single tank had crossed the river, at a moment when the German columns were in full view from the west bank and crowding down to the river with their bridging equipment.

The Luftwaffe system of command was based on universal

radio (many of the French aircraft lacked radios), and simplicity. Co-operation with the Army was complete. The operation orders for the divisions crossing the Meuse tabulated air and artillery targets in parallel columns, a degree of integration the British were unable to arrive at for two years or more.[200] The British intercept service heard clear messages being passed to German aircraft at the height of the battle: 'All bombers to Cambrai'; 'All fighters to Arras', followed by 'All fighters on the way' ten minutes later.[201] The system was important, but what was crucial was the perfect sympathy between the ground and air commanders. There was dismay in the British camp when squadrons of Bomber Command, committed to the battle of France, instead of attacking German army units or the German Air Force bases in the field, bombed Essen; an extreme example of Bomber Command's doctrinaire policy. The French procedure for tactical operations, followed perforce by the British, when information of a juicy target or a call for air attack in an emergency was received, was to send out a reconnaissance sortie to examine the situation. If it survived the enemy fighters and returned to report the staff discussed the appropriate response and a strike was finally dispatched. There were no army liaison officers at the airfields, and the briefings and debriefings required motor journeys from headquarters to airfield. Three hours was a good response time. Fortunately the British officers concerned, Air Marshal Sir Arthur Barret, and the Army liaison officers on his staff, read the lesson of France correctly and were to design the admirable British system for army/air co-operation whose beneficial effects were to be felt in North Africa in 1942.

It was to prove a question of education. The British, in all their political and civil activities so imaginative, so pragmatic and so flexible, for some reason always seemed to have adopted extreme positions when faced with military problems. The Regimental system was useful, and suited the British, but though it had (and has) its disadvantages it is sacrosanct; no breath of criticism must ever be uttered to disparage it. It gave rise to the habit of 'separate tables', as we have called it. The Royal Air Force adopted Trenchardism and no alternative air strategy was allowed to be considered. The doctrinaires in Bomber Command opposed army co-operation root and branch from start to finish. The Germans and the Russians had no difficulty in grasping that the tank was a highly versatile form of *artillery* – of fire-power – combining the properties of an assault gun, 'infantry tank', assault weapon in its own right, mobile, armoured anti-tank gun and a weapon for pursuit. The British proponents of the tank argued among themselves about the nature of the tank as if its rôles were mutually exclusive, whereas common sense should have made it clear that sometimes the tanks required the support of the infantry and sometimes the infantry that of the tanks. The result was that when the British finally put an armoured division in the field in its original form it was what the Germans were later in Africa to describe as 'pure in race'. It had two brigades of six regiments (battalions) of tanks, and a support group; a brigade of one regiment (battalion) of field artillery, one of anti-tank guns, one of infantry and one of light anti-aircraft artillery, which was used either for protection when the tanks were in harbour or to secure ground captured by the tanks.[202] Wavell once condemned the relegation of infantry to the rôle of 'scavengers after the artillery or the jackals of the tanks', but when the British finally seized the armoured idea they decided that the infantry and the artillery were fit only for the latter rôle.

By contrast the original panzer division was a 'division' in the strict sense: a self-sufficient formation of all arms. It was equally strong in tanks and infantry, and had a full divisional artillery of light and medium howitzers, light and medium anti-aircraft guns, anti-tank guns, a reconnaissance battalion, engineers complete with a bridging train and second line supply columns. Notably, it had a flight of light aircraft (the short take-off Fieseler Storch) for communication and personal reconnaissance by commanders; something that the Royal Air Force opposed and only agreed to after a long and sterile argument with the Army. The German belief in the interdependence of the arms was further reflected down through the regimental organisation. The regiment had a heavy howitzer company, and the battalions their own light howitzers, machine-guns, mortars and anti-tank guns.

Given an understanding of the principle of co-operation and a little military knowledge it is not difficult to arrive at a correct organisation. What made the new tactics work was the German soldier. Every officer and man was imbued with the doctrine that his first duty was to obey the call of his leaders, as it was also the duty of every man, private first class or general, to *lead* if the situation demanded it. This was an ancient tradition. In August 1914 a paunchy, 49-year-old colonel on the staff, Ludendorff, at a loose end and up at the front, came upon a column of infantry scattered and shaken by enemy fire. He unhesitatingly placed himself at its head and led it successfully to its objective. What is remarkable is not Ludendorff's action, but that the men responded immediately to the leadership of an officer personally unknown to them, in the dark amid the confusion of a night attack. Leadership of the practical sort is not magical or charismatic: it is a state of mind, formed by training and permeating both leaders and followers. It was fortified by teaching every man that the supreme act of combat was to attack: to fire at the enemy with whatever weapon he possessed, and always to press forward. (As is revealed by the prefix 'sturm', which recurs so often in the German military vocabulary: *Sturmtruppen, Sturmboot, Sturmgeschutze.*) The basic defensive tactic was a counter-attack. (British troops were to learn quickly, albeit painfully, that their fight only started *after* they had thankfully reached their objective.) So we see defensive weapons being used aggressively, as when the 1st Panzer Division crossed the Meuse, and the anti-tank and anti-aircraft gunners came into action in full view and shot point-blank at the French emplacements on the far bank.

German soldiers were not without esprit de corps, but their true spirit was the esprit d'armée. They thought of themselves first and foremost as Germans, and as soldiers. All were comrades, comrades who owed loyalty to each other. It was this deep-seated feeling that enabled small groups of men from different arms to coalesce into 'battle groups' *(Kampfgruppen)* like iron filings obeying the pull of a magnetic field. (The British Army in Africa believed that the German success was due to this facility for combination, and sought to copy it by forming their own 'battle groups' and introducing the term, but they mistook the result for the cause.)

The builders of the new German Army did not subscribe to the idea that the tremendous fire-power conferred by modern weapon technology made offensive action unprofitable, nor did they regard the experience of the Western Front as confirming it. When they had been forced on the defensive they had devised a defence that was essentially based on the counter-attack and the counter-offensive, with an elastic front covered by intense artillery and machine-gun fire, and whole divisions arranged in great depth ready to riposte. Their tactically successful offensives of 1918, using élite troops to thrust deep into the enemy defences, turning or bypassing strong resistance, were the prototype of the new panzer tactics, but mobility and skilful tactics are only a means toward an end. Increased fire-power, given air mobility and tank mobility, could be concentrated to such a degree that it was possible to burst through any purely static defensive system and then keep on attacking and advancing. The Germans, in short, believed in the 'fifth principle', and constructed their military instrument and indoctrinated their soldiers accordingly.

The blitzkrieg was an attitude of mind. It also required a suitable victim, as has been said, and the concept of the armoured attack in depth as a psychological attack on the mind of opposing commanders was startlingly vindicated in 1940, but it is not a factor on which it is wise to plan. The British generals in 1940, and the Russians in the midst of the appalling reverses of 1941 when whole armies were cut off and surrendering, kept their nerve in a most praiseworthy manner. There is another, more 'mechanical' way of looking at a blitzkrieg's effect on the command structure. Consider a crude and simple model like the French in 1940, based on a rudimentary telephone system backed up by written orders sent by dispatch rider, and occasional conferences requiring senior officers to motor about from headquarters to headquarters. The information chain is like a family tree, with a break at each command level. All the information going up from the line of contact has to be edited, checked and retransmitted. All the orders going downwards have to be read, rewritten and elaborated at each command level and retransmitted. There is a calculable time-lag between the higher command perceiving a situation and the appropriate action being taken. In a slow-moving battle of attrition this is not significant, even at moments as dramatic as March 1918, for today's information is used for tomorrow's battle, or even later. In any case, in a well-trained army subordinate commanders are expected to take vigorous action without waiting for orders or permission from above. It is the business of the staff to find out what is happening so a new plan can be made, and in this connection it must be emphasised that it is often as difficult to ascertain the position of friendly troops as of the enemy's. All previous experience was that eventually a break-through would slow down, from sheer fatigue and lack of supply, but a panzer thrust actually gained momentum as it proceeded. What happens in such a situation is that the information flow is too fast for the machine to handle, and then, as the machine itself is damaged by the attack, it dries up altogether.

There is a graphic example of such a situation in the memoirs of Marshal Zhukov. The resumed German offensive of October 1941 dislocated the Russian defensive system so thoroughly that Stalin was unable to extract any information from the various headquarters, some of which were out of touch altogether and their locations unknown. Zhukov is sent forward to investigate and report, and motors off into the empty Russian vastness, uncertain whether a front exists or not, and whether he will meet Russians or the enemy first. He first finds the headquarters of the Briansk Front (group of armies), to learn of chaos everywhere; the Front split in two, no reserves left to block the gap, and the position of the enemy unknown, but believed to be pressing on towards Orel, far in the rear. Four armies are either encircled, or about to be encircled. Zhukov then goes off to find General Budyenny, of the Reserve Front, and discovers his headquarters through a fortunate encounter with two (!) signal-men laying a cable to its new location, but Budyenny is not there, he had gone forward to visit one of his army head-quarters, now out of contact, and Budyenny is missing. Zhukov motors on for another twelve kilometres and, by another lucky chance, finds Budyenny alone in a village, lost, for his own headquarters has moved since his departure without being able to tell him where. He is delighted to hear that Zhukov had found it. Zhukov goes off once more into the void and by a third stroke of luck comes across an intact reserve tank brigade, waiting for orders but completely out of touch harboured in a forest. Zhukov sends it off to block a gap, and gradually the situation is pulled together. Reserves are brought up, defensive positions hastily constructed and, here is the heart of the matter, a counter offensive is launched.[203]

What had happened was that the deep panzer thrusts affected not so much the mind or brain of an army, but its nervous system. The analogy is not exact because an army is not a unitary system. It is hydra-headed, and even if its nervous system is severed in places, parts of it will go on working perfectly well until they can be knitted up again. Indeed, there is a lot to be said for the 'hierarchical' chain-of-command type of army. If its subordinate commanders keep their heads and continue to fight an army can survive a good deal of disruption. What was required was not the abolition of the simple hier-archical system, but its reinforcement. Radio was the key to the problem of constructing a command and control system capable of rapid response and proof against the shock of battle. It can be strengthened by additional networks, so that a single failure does not cause a complete blockage, and it can be speeded up by superimposing extra links connecting the area where the flow of information is generated directly to the superior headquarters where it is urgently needed, bypassing altogether the retrans-mission points in the basic hierarchical system.

One of the most acute problems for the commander of a modern army was where to position himself. Much has been written, and most of it unperceptive, about the habit of the generals of the Western Front to command from comfortable headquarters far in the rear. Even in the later war a commander as able as Douglas MacArthur was unfairly nicknamed 'Dug-out Doug', but in operations taking place over a frontage of fifty or a hundred miles, as on the Western Front, or a thousand, as in the

Pacific, the only place for a commander was at his main head-quarters where the flows of information converged. Radio communications made alternative solutions possible. Guderian is credited with the invention of the forward, mobile headquarters; what the British were to term a 'tactical headquarters'. It is interesting to note that Guderian spent his formative years as a young officer seconded from the infantry to the German equivalent of the Royal Corps of Signals; commanding a field radio station with a cavalry division in 1914 and rising to the post of Signal Officer of the Fifth Army on the Western Front before joining the General Staff in 1917. His habit of commanding from the front arose from more than the traditional German attitude. He knew that he could not control such fast, fluid operations as he intended using only the stale information trickling up to his panzer group headquarters after retransmission from regiment to division to corps. The fronts on which his formations advanced were so narrow that it was perfectly possible for him to focus his attention on the vital *schwerpunkt*. All that he required was contact with his own headquarters; and through it with the intermediate ones, for nothing is more confusing for divisional commanders of subordinate formations or irritates them more than an army commander on the loose up in front counter-manding their orders or giving fresh ones unknown to them, although Guderian's were always perfectly predictable. They were invariably to keep advancing. The soldiers nick-named him 'Hurry-On Heinz'. Accordingly he equipped himself with a car and a radio vehicle fitted with cypher apparatus and in this way he was able to keep in continual touch with his chief of staff. In the British Army 'tac HQs' were only used regularly by divisional commanders and below, using clear speech whenever possible to save time; and a simple code, changed daily, to conceal only locations and unit names. British senior commanders were not in favour of interfering with the actions of forward troops in the German manner, preferring to trust the commander on the spot, but they visited regularly. (In the writer's experience Generals Harding, Loewen, McCreery and Allfrey could all be encountered in the forward areas. The late Field Marshal Templer, when a major-general in command of the 6th Armoured Division, had the disconcerting habit of going off for an early morning walk round the line of contact to check if the positions coincided with the 'last light' situation reports sent during the night.)

The alternative to the general himself going forward was to send specially trained liaison officers equipped with a direct radio link to report on the situation at the front. The prototype was set up by Air Marshal Sir Arthur Barret, commanding the British Air Forces in France, in 1940, in the form of a group of army and air force officers equipped with armoured cars fitted with long range radios and motor cycle dispatch riders, to provide him with information normally taking hours or even a whole day to percolate up the French command chain.[204] This was the germ of the elaborate and successful 'air support signal units' linking armies with their tactical air forces, whose evolution will be described later. Other variations were the Army's 'GHQ Reconnaissance Regiment', using radio patrols to report directly from the area of contact to army or any group headquarters, and General Montgomery's team of personal liaison officers who had much the same function. Alternatively, there was the 'J' service of the Royal Signals, which monitored the transmissions of friendly units in contact with the enemy and so was able to provide immediate but unprocessed information about the progress of a battle. Eventually the army in the field was served by a complicated but logically constructed network of radio circuits providing a copious flow of information from every source. It was entirely an organisational matter, of specialist interest only and much neglected by military students, but in it lay the first step to meeting and beating the blitzkrieg. All the new weapons, all the new tactics would have availed little if a compatible command and control system had not been devised at the same time.

This had to include a solution to the vexed problem of air support. As well, a coherent theory of armoured warfare had to be agreed upon, the infantry reorganised so as to take their part in the new warfare, the threat of the tank met, and the problem evaded by Kirke, of adapting artillery procedures to mobile warfare, faced and solved. None of this could be done in a moment, and in the meantime the Army had to contend with another artist of the blitzkrieg, Erwin Rommel.

CHAPTER 13

The Sand Model

> To what then are we to ascribe the brilliant
> successes of the Afrika Korps? The superior
> quality of our anti-tank guns, our systematic
> practice of the Principle of Co-operation-of-
> Arms, and – last but not least – our tactical
> methods . . . although generally inferior in
> numbers of tanks, our tactical leadership usually
> succeed in concentrating superior numbers of
> tanks and guns at the decisive point (i.e. the
> schwerpunkt).[205]
>
> Generallmajor F. W. von Mellenthin

ONE of the elementary training devices used by soldiers is
the sand model. It has the merit of simplicity and is far
better than a map, on which is recorded all the obstructive clutter
of houses and forests, metalled roads and power-lines likely to
complicate the 'lesson' and confuse the pupil. A sweep of the
hand can create a simple topography; a coloured tape or two a
road or a river. The theatre in which the Commonwealth armies
were to meet one of the most gifted opponents of the tactical
blitzkrieg was just such a model. The 'Western Desert' was
barren, unpopulated and with the most rudimentary communications, but it offered almost infinite scope for manoeuvre. The
topography could not be altered, but the tactician could, as it
were, always select a fresh venue if so inclined.

There are many interesting parallels between the Peninsular
War and the Desert War. Both served as a training and proving
ground and helped to form the traditions of the British Army. In
both a small army was able to engage more or less in isolation a
fraction of the army of a great continental power. In both its
success, indeed in Africa its very survival, depended on command of the sea, and in the later war, that and command of the
air. In both, an army composed of valorous but dissociated
regiments and corps was gradually welded together and learnt its

business, as an *army*. Both were marked by victorious advances and disappointing retreats. The only difference was that the able and autocratic leader who commanded and supervised the class arrived in the Peninsula at an early date, while General Montgomery began his lesson only after twenty months, a period in which the British and Commonwealth forces were twice ignominiously routed after a successful advance and in May and June 1942 suffered a disastrous defeat, worse than the one inflicted on the Fifth Army in France in March 1918.

The Desert War has been the subject of intense historical scrutiny and has generated a vast literature. There can now be very little doubt about the course of events, or the ability and character of the leading actors.[206] The British, who provided the high command, were in many respects better off in weapons and resources than their opponents but, following their own theories (if theories they were), went badly astray to the point at which they almost lost control of the Mediterranean and the Middle East. Then, in August 1942, there was the well-known change in command and a reversion to older but sounder principles and methods. The battle of El Alamein was a battle on the pattern of 1918, without the horses. The only radical change was the greatly increased importance of direct air support, introduced in the earlier war, but by late 1942 with a sophisticated apparatus for control.

The malaise of the middle period was dispersion and fragmentation of units, with its inevitable consequence when facing a capable and mobile adversary. As Montgomery said in his staccato and repetitive fashion to his new staff when he first met them: 'Well, gentlemen, you've been defeated. Badly defeated. You've been defeated in detail – in detail!'[207] This, however, was perhaps the symptom, not the disease itself, although he had put his finger on the important point.

The British commanders, for one reason or another, had embraced a theory of war which virtually discarded regular divisional organisations, and the principle of concentration, to rely on manoeuvre and extreme dispersion. In the Gazala position defended localities held by never more than a brigade were separated far beyond the range of mutual support, even by artillery fire. The locality held by the 150th Infantry Brigade, for instance, was some ten miles from its neighbour to the north and twenty from the Free French at Bir Hacheim in the south. (See diagram 11.) The underlying idea may have been borrowed from classical eighteenth-century strategy; these 'boxes', as they were called, being the fortresses, and the armoured formations representing the field army. In the event they were either over-

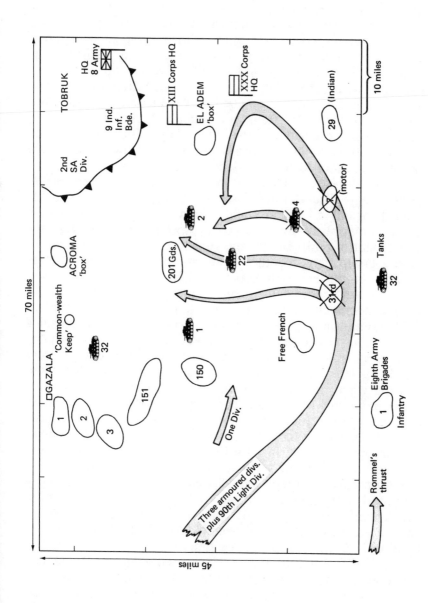

11. *Eighth Army defence layout, 27 May 1942.*

run or slowly battered into submission by whole enemy divisions, one by one.

The attacking formation adopted by the British was seldom bigger than a 'brigade group' of all arms acting at some distance from its neighbour, and sometimes small mixed groups, often no more than a company of infantry in lorries accompanied by a troop or so of towed field guns, with a troop of light tanks. These were used to observe or harry the enemy. Originally an expedient adopted in a period when the British were numerically painfully weak, the 'Jock Columns', named after their famous leader Brigadier 'Jock' Campbell, V.C., became an established part of the tactical system, no doubt because of the seal of approval of the paladin of the Desert War. They were, in fact, no more than mobile batteries for harassing fire from a safe range, but came to be regarded as miniature 'battle-groups'.

It would be as well here to explain the confused British terminology. The Germans used the term *kampfgruppe* (battle group) for any ad hoc grouping within as established formation made temporarily for a separate specific mission, e.g. the attachment of tanks and 88-mm guns to an infantry regiment, *or* such a group flung together in an emergency made up of stray details. At the end of the battle of El Hamma, for instance, General von Liebenstein, then commanding the Desert Afrika Korps, personally collected some stragglers and a number of field and anti-tank guns to form a gun-line to check the pursuing British tanks. In either sense the British 'brigade groups', the term is in any case tautological and the Jock Columns were 'battle groups', as was the support group in the armoured division when, as was too often the case, it was not supporting the armour but acting independently. The British have always been addicted to forming ad hoc groupings which they variously termed 'forces', or 'columns', a hangover of nineteenth-century warfare in India, e.g. in Africa there were 'Gazelle Force', and 'Robcol', a shortening of 'Rob Waller's Column'. In July 1942 the term 'battle group' was slipped into a paper outlining a proposed reorganisation written by General E. Dorman-Smith, which confused everyone; it being believed that some radical change was being made. Far from it. The Eighth Army had been fighting in battle groups all the time.

The fundamental difference between German and British tactics, however, lay in the fact that the Germans, however grouped, manoeuvred in large masses at close intervals so arranged that tanks, guns and motorised infantry could all support each other without need for elaborate redeployment. Time and again during the Desert War the isolated British columns were overrun by a whole division or more. As a general rule the British infantry brigades stuck closely to their field guns and, when they had them, their tanks, as it was the secret of survival when at any moment a great mass of enemy preceded by fifty or sixty tanks might descend on them. By contrast, in the armoured division, the 'support group' of infantry and artillery operated independently, sometimes, as at Gazala, holding static 'boxes' and sending their transport to the rear. In the attack they were often left out of battle altogether with their anti-tank guns.

Possibly the most serious consequence of this policy of dispersion was the fragmentation and decentralisation of the British field artillery; acknowledged by the Germans to be their most dangerous and efficient opponent. This deprived divisional commanders of the most flexible source of fire-power in their armoury, seventy or more guns concentrated on a single target. Equally serious, the whole difficult art of identifying targets and making a co-ordinated fire-plan to suppress enemy weapons *before* they did any damage was gradually forgotten, or fell into disuse, and with it a great deal of essential skills in technical gunnery. The armoured units never did understand it. Nor did they understand elementary tactics.

To quote Lord Carver:

> Our real weakness was the failure to develop tactics for a concentrated attack employing tanks, artillery and infantry in depth on a narrow front. Time and time again tanks motored or charged at the enemy on a broad front until the leading troops were knocked out by enemy tanks or anti-tank guns: the momentum of the attack immediately failed. Such artillery as was supporting the tanks indulged in some spattering of the enemy . . . after which the tanks motored about or charged again with the same results as before . . . the infantry taking no part, their task being to follow up and occupy the objective after it had been captured by the tanks.[208]

Another and distressing example of lack of tactical nous was recorded by a battery commander, who was sent off in a hastily assembled 'column' composed of his battery, a company of Scots Guards in lorries and an anti-tank battery, in the middle of the Gazala battle, in the dark, to pursue what was vainly believed to be a beaten enemy. He lost 127 men and twelve guns, including seven of the precious new 6-pounders.[209]

The British policy which led to these setbacks and defeats marked an extraordinary break with well established principles and the precepts laid down in the manuals, and the fact that it was not having any success was emphasised by the equally

obvious fact that the German methods were exactly the
opposite. There is no simple answer to the question of why the
British commanders behaved in this way. What can be ruled out
is stupidity. None of them was stupid. Inexplicably, generals
who had already fought successfully, and in a more rational
manner, either fell into these practices once they reached
the desert or acquiesced in them. Tacticians in any case do not
have to be intellectuals but only to have a clear view of the aim,
an understanding of the tools – their weapons – and a sense of
what is practicable; a description which fits the majority of the
desert commanders.

Four strands went to the making of this situation: the troops,
the weapons, the factors and perceptions affecting the
formulation of policy and, reverting to the human factor, the
generals who had to conduct what all agree was a novel, complex
and difficult series of operations. It is notable that when the
British commanders were in circumstances familiar to them, with
a tangible objective, a naturally narrow front and secure flanks
and the main arm being infantry, they were almost uniformly
successful. It was the fluid, open battle in the flat desert that
baffled them.

The British and Commonwealth infantry varied widely in
quality, compared with their German opponents. This is hardly
surprising because the British and Indian regiments had to try
and combine some sort of training for a war that had not been
defined with internal security duties and 'imperial policing',
while suffering from a chronic shortage even of training
ammunition. By contrast the Germans, who had been training
their infantry for war for six years, cutting out frills and
concentrating on weapon skills, minor tactics and élan in the
attack, found in Poland that many battalions lacked the spirit of
the soldiers of 1914–18.[210] Rommel certainly complained about
the lack of skill of his infantry in the Afrika Korps. The best
British and Indian battalions became a match for any troops and
the Australians and New Zealanders were superb.

The artillery was highly professional, for a number of reasons,
in spite of its pre-occupation with horses. Indeed, many argued
that the qualities of the fox-hunter or the hog-hunter were
exactly those required for the Desert War. That is as may be,
but the Desert's most dashing leader, Campbell, and its ablest
professional artilleryman, Kirkman, were both horse artillerymen with the same tastes. The existence of a central school to
impose a common doctrine, the selection of officers from over a
wide field for command and the fact that the Territorial and
wartime intake were of a superior mental capacity produced a

well-trained arm of high morale. Its sin had been its apathy in the pre-war period, and its weakness in the Desert was that in the early period its senior commanders lacked the status to challenge the obvious errors in employment; indeed, as will be related, they themselves were nearly abolished.

The new Royal Armoured Corps was the weakest of the three British arms. Ideally, the best course would have been to have built it up on the Royal Tank Corps, whose officers were single-minded in the pursuit of their profession and accustomed to machines and machinery, and to have disbanded the cavalry, but this had not been politically possible. The cavalry, having resisted conversion for as long as possible arrived in the armoured world rather late. It was not a question of aptitude and intelligence, for the mechanics were not difficult to teach and the gunnery simple, but one of motivation – of the cavalry-man's whole attitude to his profession. Some regiments became very good: but they were among the few who, however 'cavalier', were determined to excel in everything they did. The rest fell below this standard by varying degrees.

It is a hard saying, but the wholesale conversion of the cavalry regiments had the unfortunate result of handing the new, decisive arm of the future over to the most mentally inert, unprofessional and reactionary group in the British army. The Foot Guards managed to overcome the practice of recruiting their officers from a narrow social class of independent means by their ferocious discipline and meticulous training, whose object was to produce the most determined infantry in the world. Not so the cavalryman. His regiment was not only an exclusive club, but an expensive one. He had sunk a considerable capital in equipping himself for the obligatory equestrian sports. The founding regiments of the 7th Armoured Division, for instance, were upset when General Hobart demanded a full working week, and the abandonment of polo as the first priority.[211] Soldiering for them was a secondary occupation whose details were of little interest.

It was an attitude which led to arguing about inconvenient orders, and contributed to the system of command by conference and discussion which grew up in the Eighth Army, and their mindless persistence in tactics that proved to be futile, if not suicidal. Their worst peacetime characteristic was social exclusive-ness. They were at ease only with their peers, the Guards and the Greenjackets – it was no tactical or military consideration that led to the Rifle Brigade and the 60th Rifle's conversion en bloc to the motorised infantry who worked with the armoured brigades. They did not mix with lesser beings, and in India did

not even 'call' on them, making exceptions only for the Indian
Cavalry and the Royal Horse Artillery. Before the Battle of El
Alamein a cavalry brigadier attempted to refuse the attachment
of an extra field regiment, of the Royal Artillery. 'We only
accept support from the Royal *Horse* Artillery,' he said loftily.[212]

Such soldiers were the prisoners of their class and their regimental upbringing. They could not suddenly on the outbreak of
war change their deeply engrained attitudes and develop a keen
interest in minor tactics, or that friendly intimacy with the
ordinary infantry and artillery essential for good co-operation. It
was the reconnaissance regiments in armoured cars, working on
their own in a traditional cavalry role, like the famous 11th
Hussars, who did best. It was the former Royal Tank Corps
men, like Gatehouse, who had served in the earlier war, and the
younger Roberts, who worked out the methods of using tanks
and field artillery together to defeat the anti-tank guns.[213] When
the armoured regiments were re-equipped with the M4 Sherman
with its turret-mounted 75-mm gun and so were at last able to
engage the German anti-tank guns at a matching range this only
fortified the habit of some of the cavalry regiments to go it
alone. The professional tank-men had the knowledge, but the
cavalry set the tone.

Both sides in the Desert War were constrained by its unusual
logistic problems. It was well put by a German commander, 'The
Desert was a tactician's Paradise, but a quartermaster's
nightmare.' Everything the British forces required had to be
transported across rocky or sandy terrain where the lorries
grinding forward in low gear themselves consumed the precious
petrol they were carrying forward to the tanks and the hundreds
of wheeled vehicles in a Desert formation. Forward dumps and
'field maintenance centres' were always exposed to enemy raids
in a war without a continuous front or secure flanks. The British
administrative staff and the supply services performed marvels,
but in mobile operations the supply of the two vital heavy
commodities, field artillery ammunition and petrol, were a
constant anxiety. The first was aggravated by the policy of
dispersing the artillery, as the greater the shortage the more
important it was to use what ammunition there was economically, accurately and in concentrated form. The converse of the
second was that the strategy adopted by the Royal Air Force was
to attack the enemy supply convoys in the Mediterranean with
priority over direct air support for the field formations.

The desert was not only a nightmare for quartermasters. It
presented the Royal Corps of Signals with some acute problems.
The most reliable and quickest form of communication was cable

(telephone, morse key, and teleprinter for the level above army headquarters), but what with headquarters moving – sometimes in a headlong rush to escape enemy attention, or 'flap' – or being overrun, both sides relied to a great extent on radio. The British equipment then in service had, unfortunately, not been designed to use the best frequencies, or to bridge the distances between division and brigade headquarters and units imposed by the British habit of wide dispersion. As a result commanders were frequently out of touch with their own units and the situation, and as is so often the case in war this occurred at the most crucial moments.

These difficulties were gradually overcome as the newer sets became available, but while the fastest way to control mobile operations is by voice radio between officers, it is also the most insecure. Ideally, all sensitive matter should be transmitted telegraphically in high grade cypher and voice restricted to immediate tactical orders, but this was not practical. To improve voice security a number of simple substitution codes were used, but they were cumbersome to use and were repeatedly captured. Officers who could not bother to use them resorted to curious jargon of private allusions and hints. (Some Indian Army officers resorted to Urdu which, though baffling, immediately identified the unit or headquarters.) All this provided a rich harvest for the German intercept service. The Royal Signals, responsible for army policy as well as the provision of communications, had a long struggle to impose radio discipline on the wayward or impatient regimental and junior staff officers of the combat arm. These faults were by no means confined to the British side. The Royal Signals and the intelligence staff combined to produce an interception and decryption that successfully penetrated the Axis dispositions and intentions and made a decisive contribution to the conduct of British operations.[214]

As regards weapons, every British commander was obsessed by the relative strength of tanks available to each side. (Which, if Lancaster's Law is applied, gives the larger side favourable odds of winning proportional to the squares of the relative strengths, but only if maximum concentration is achieved.) Numerically this varied a great deal from day to day, owing to casualties and breakdowns, but if the opening date of the Gazala battle is taken as a datum, the Eighth Army was substantially superior in numbers. As regards their relative gun-power measured in terms of the ability to penetrate armour plate, a detailed analysis made by Lord Carver has shown that the advantage slightly favoured the British.[215]

The Germans dominated the armoured battle by their aggressive use of anti-tank guns. Like the British they had at first settled for a tiny anti-tank and tank gun of 37 mm, and they still retained a number of these in the desert, together with a curiosity in the shape of an unpleasant ultra-high-velocity light-weight gun with a 28/21 mm conical bore. Their mainstay was the long 50-mm (4½-pounder) PAK, and a number of 88-mm FLAK converted for anti-tank work by ripping off the sophisticated electronics and fitting a shield.[216] Later the German divisions were reinforced by a few of the new German 75-mm PAK and a number of captured Russian 76.2-mm (3-inch) field guns, both of which had a good performance and were frequently mistaken for the deadly 88-mm.

The Eighth Army did not receive the 6-pounder, a gun superior to the long 50-mm PAK, in sufficient quantity to affect the battle until April 1942, the reason being that 509 2-pounder guns had been lost in France in 1940. The 6-pounder was ready to go into production, but the difficult choice had to be made between retooling the factories, or continuing a run of production of 2-pounders to make good the loss first, so as to avoid a period in which there were only a few anti-tank guns of any kind. The 17-pounder (77-mm) was not fully in service until 1943. The trouble with the 2-pounder was lack of penetration at long range, unless it could hit the turret or obtain a shot at the side of a tank. Once the Germans had learnt to stand off and suppress the 2-pounders with machine-gun and artillery fire they ceased to be of much value. This had two consequences. The 25-pounder field gun was drawn into the anti-tank direct-fire battle to protect the infantry. Its indirect fire role was not abandoned, but as every infantry brigade demanded its share of the guns the artillery effort was dissipated. The infantry formation commanders also demanded that some tanks should also be decentralised to them for protection, especially when moving in the open desert, or at any rate march close to their motorised columns.

There was much argument at the time, and since, over the refusal to use the British 3.7-inch (95-mm) heavy anti-aircraft gun in the same way as the Germans used the 88-mm FLAK. Although to a non-artillery eye it looked very similar to the 88-mm FLAK it was in fact a much heavier gun altogether, depended on a more sophisticated fire-control system and was without a telescopic sight, but these technical disadvantages could have been overcome. The real reason for retaining it for its proper rôle was that the outcome of the Desert War depended on the winning of air control by the Royal Air Force. This required that its fighters should be freed as far as possible from the close defence of the base installations, vital to all three services and the airfields. Air defence was based on a combination of guns and aircraft, so clearly any reduction in the number of guns would require an increase in the number of fighter aircraft reserved for a purely defensive role. It was a question of priorities. The number of guns required to make a significant impact would have been two regiments, or forty-eight, plus perhaps 50 per cent reserve, as casualties in gun versus tank engagements were always heavy. These two units would have required complete retraining and reorientation, for the two types of work require different patterns of deployment, different attitudes, perhaps even different commanding officers, for one demands initiative and decentralisation; the other centralisation, the strictest fire-discipline imposed from the operations room and meticulous accuracy. In any case, even if the guns had been made available it is doubtful if the desert commanders would have used them correctly, in view of the hash they made of the employment of all their other artillery.

As it happens, there was an alternative solution. The arrival in service of the 3.7-inch heavy anti-aircraft made the 3-inch 30-cwt medium anti-aircraft gun, with its excellent anti-tank potential, redundant. A conversion was put in hand, in England, the plan being to fit fifty 3-inch pieces on Churchill tank chassis to provide a self-propelled model, and fifty on field carriages. Unfortunately progress was so slow that it was overtaken by the production of the 17-pounders and the project abandoned.[217] It would have been better to have shipped as many unmodified guns as possible on their wheeled anti-aircraft mountings out to Egypt. They would have been no more vulnerable than the unmodified German 'eighty-eights', or the British 2-pounders, which were habitually fired over the tail-boards of their 'portee' trucks.

Any discussion, therefore, of British tactical doctrine in the desert must take into account the disadvantage under which the Eighth Army operated until the infantry were made tank-proof by the belated reformation of their anti-tank gun platoons, discarded in 1938, and equipped with the 6-pounder. The 25-pounders were not deployed in a purely anti-tank pattern but, uncomfortably, in a dual rôle, the gun areas being often well forward in open positions sometimes in front of the infantry. At Alam Hamza, in December 1941, in one of several instances, the 25th Field Regiment was deployed forward to act as a screen behind which the infantry could debus and form up for an attack, while at the same time the batteries registered in preparation for the fire-plan. This was forestalled by a strong German counter-attack. The infantry in their lorries were withdrawn behind the protection of the batteries while the guns fought off the tanks, losing heavily in the process. The 31st Regiment was destroyed completely in another exactly similar situation.[218]

This does not account for the extreme dispersion adopted by the Eighth Army, its tactical bad habits, and its failure to draw the correct deductions from observation of German methods. More than one explanation has been advanced for its unorthodox policy and the likeliest answer is that all of them are correct. There was the ratio of troops to space. Anyone who has had to deploy so much as a battalion for defence has felt the tug to cover every approach or occupy every commanding feature, and spread it ever wider. This temptation was at its greatest in the open desert, where there were few commanding features or clearly defined lines of approach. The weakness of these over extended positions was not obvious when plotted on a 1:100,000 scale map with the ovals representing defended areas strongly blocked in with coloured pencils: 'the great wall of chinagraph', as some wit once called it, that looked so solid and reassuring. The same tendency was observed in Tunisia. It is a common enough fault.

Then there was the belief that the desert environment was unique, and imposed its own rules on tactics. The British Army at home and abroad was perhaps at that period overtrained in 'passive air defence', the result of the experience of 1940 in France. There was great insistence on dispersion and concealment, but in the desert there was no natural cover. The only course was to spread out as widely as possible. Accordingly when on the move units travelled in 'desert formation', widely dispersed with even the vehicles a hundred yards apart or more, and harboured in the same way. Drilled to regard it as a crime to be too close to a neighbour, it required a mental effort to concentrate when concentration became necessary. Newcomers to the desert, with their 'white knees', were urged to become 'desert-wise' or 'desert-worthy', to learn to navigate, to cook for themselves, to conserve water, to 'harbour' or 'leaguer' in the accepted way. At the same time they absorbed a healthy, or unhealthy, respect for Rommel and his tanks imparted by the old desert hands. (One general after being sent home in 1942 was given the task of lecturing to units on German methods in the desert. He gave the unfortunate impression that they were invincible after a very accurate description of how they attacked, and concluded . . . 'and then you are *Rommelled*', without any hint on how to avoid this fate.)[219] It was natural enough to regard the desert soldiers' peculiar tactical habits as part of the mental readjustment required to survive in the desert.

This, unplanned, trend was fortified by theory. Lord Carver, without identifying them, says that there were some commanders who, influenced by Liddell Hart, '. . . relied on movement and dispersion for its own sake, believing that its effect on the enemy's mind was the decisive factor.' He quotes an a propos passage from one of his articles of 1935: 'The dangers of air attack, the aim of mystification, and the need of drawing full value from mechanised mobility, suggest that advancing forces should not only be as widely distributed as is compatible with combined action, but should be dispersed as much as is compatible with cohesion . . . Fluidity of force may succeed where concentration of force merely entails a hopeless rigidity.'[220] The first part of this passage is qualified out of meaning by the escape-word 'compatible', and is only an inflated version of the old adage 'march divided' – to conceal the objective for as long as possible – and 'fight united'. The second part is nonsense, and pernicious nonsense at that. How Liddell Hart had the effrontery to claim after the war was over that the German generals were among his disciples, when in fact in the desert they adopted an exactly opposite policy and disproved his fanciful theories by repeatedly and bloodily crushing the widely dispersed units of the Eighth Army one by one is difficult to understand; as, indeed, it is difficult to understand how the British generals, or some of them, could fall for them. Not all of them did; certainly neither Tuker nor Morshead, nor some of the senior staff officers, such as de Guingand, as Montgomery found when he consulted them on taking up his appointment. It is possible that the Eighth Army's peculiar desert tactics were a locally produced heresy, but the coincidence between Liddell Hart's theory and the Eighth Army's practice is, however, too close to be fortuitous.

Fortunately there is a record of the view taken of operations in the desert. From 1940 onwards the training branch of the General Staff of the Army worldwide collected, collated and analysed post-operational reports, which in due course were printed and published by the War Office, and a rain of pamphlets began to descend on the troops, some of whom may have read them or even acted on them. Most of the matter contained was practical and useful and of interest to the individual arms, ranging from the correct use of the radio to the continued usefulness of the bayonet. The more general lessons appeared in *Notes from the Theatres of War*, which were followed later by the equally interesting series *Current Reports from Overseas*. *Notes No. 1* is entitled 'Cyrenaica November 1941' and was published in February 1942, and contains two significant statements. _'The armoured division (operates) organised in brigades of all arms including a proportion of infantry'_, and _'Mobile desert warfare appears to be largely a matter of columns of all arms which may work over long distances widely separated.'_ (Author's italics.) These pamphlets were published in London and it is stated on the flyleaf that they were 'prepared under the direction of the Chief of the Imperial General Staff'. They were, therefore, an authoritative guide to correct methods, and we can be certain that the theatre reports on which they were based had the approval of the theatre commander-in-chief, in this case General Auchinleck. This was the official Middle East and Eighth Army view as seen after CRUSADER but before the battle of Gazala. The success of CRUSADER was taken as confirmation, whereas in fact the victory had been won by the determination of the troops and in spite of the doctrine.

While the units of the Eighth Army continued to muddle on its staff, and the staff in Headquarters, Middle East Command, continued to report with both accuracy and perception on the tactical details of the fighting. That the support of field artillery 'is an essential adjunct to the operations of armoured fighting vehicles in armoured engagements' is stated in _Notes No. 1_, together with a radio net diagram and the recommendation that the observation posts should be mounted in M3 (Stuart) light tanks and travel with the leading armoured squadrons. Also included is the first accurate account of how a German armoured formation of all arms attacked a defended position, and German methods are fully covered in later issues. There is a graphic report by an unnamed British officer who was in German hands for some time and travelled with a German formation. He says that it moved in a dense phalanx, regardless of the threat of air attack: 'The light AA defensive fire put up by German columns has to be experienced to be believed . . . columns of four guns on the move put up a wall of light FLAK . . . the armoured columns did not slacken speed or disperse on the arrival of our bomber formations but forged ahead at full speed.' _Notes No. 2_ 'Cyrenaica November–December 1941' confirms the German habit of attacking in mass – fifty to eighty tanks – and it states clearly something the armoured commanders continued to ignore for a long time: that the Germans relied on their anti-tank guns to kill tanks, not the relatively feeble tank guns, using them well forward in the attack and in company with them. It recommends that the British do the same. _Notes No. 10_, 'Cyrenaica January–June 1942', returns to the subject of German attack tactics in greater detail. As far as possible, it says, the division was employed complete, although the infantry, tanks and guns would be combined in battle groups within it for convenience and better co-operation, usually two, made up of a battalion of each. When on the move the division was preceded by the reconnaissance unit, with the main body following in a regular, almost parade-ground formation. The tanks led, moving in several ranks with some artillery, 88-mm and 150-mm *sturmgeschutze* close behind. The rest of the artillery followed in column on the left and right flanks, the whole forming a square inside which travelled the motor infantry, many of their vehicles towing more anti-tank guns. (The establishment was fifty 50-mm PAK, but many of the obsolescent lighter guns were retained.) Headquarters and 1st line supply vehicles were in the rear, but all commanders rode in front. When the enemy position was located it was closely reconnoitred by the battle group or the divisional commander and the defending anti-tank guns located. This was done methodically and the preparation of the attack might take three hours. In the first phase the anti-tank guns would be silenced by field artillery fire, the shell-firing 75-mm of the Mark IV tanks, and often by long range fire of the 88-mm and the 50-mm guns as well. When the enemy fire from the 25-pounders, fully visible in their direct fire positions, had slackened sufficiently, the tanks and the motor infantry in their vehicles charged, some tanks going straight through the gun line, while others helped the infantry mop up. The tanks then rallied to the rear to refuel and rearm, the infantry put the captured locality in a state of defence and the anti-tank guns came up to join them.

If a strong force of British tanks was encountered the battle group sometimes adopted the ruse of ordering the infantry and anti-tank artillery to form a defensive line, and when this was ready to draw the British tanks on to it by a feigned withdrawal; the panzers slipping between the gun intervals to take up positions among the infantry ready to counter-attack once the British had, as usual, fallen victim to anti-tank fire.[221] In a withdrawal the order of march was reversed, the procedure for fighting a defensive battle remaining the same, but if the British were judged vulnerable all units were in position for a rapid right-about turn and for a limited but destructive counter-attack; as used at the end of the CRUSADER operation against pursuing brigade groups, usually with devastating effect.

Of British operations, *Notes No. 4* describes in full detail the highly orthodox plan made by the 7th Indian Infantry Brigade for the successful attacks on the strongly held Omar positions; the preliminary patrolling to locate the enemy and the minefield

12. *Panzer tactics in the desert.*

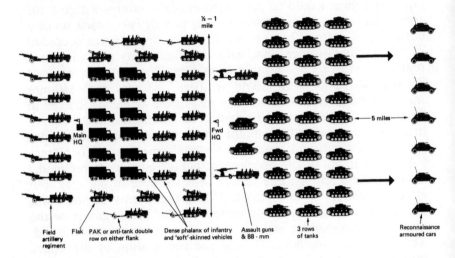

NB Symbols represent types only and not the details of specific equipments

I. Division or Battle Group on the march. From this tightly packed formation it could easily deploy for defence or attack. When retreating, the order of march is simply reversed.

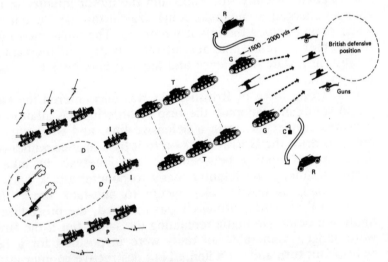

NB Symbols represent types only and not the details of specific equipments

II. Fire fight and reconnaissance. C – commander reconnoitres enemy position. RR – reconnaissance units clear left and right. GG – line of Mk IV tanks and 88-mm and machine-guns engage British anti-tank guns and 25-pounder batteries. TT – Panzer regiment waits in rear. II – Panzer infantry form up. DD – rest of group. PP – screen of anti-tank and anti-aircraft guns. FF – field batteries of 105-mm and 150-mm guns deploy.

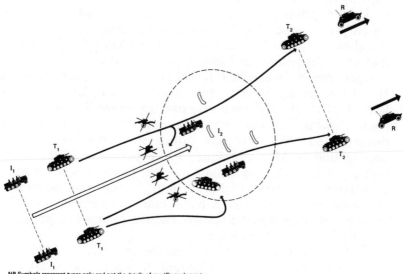

NB Symbols represent types only and not the details of specific equipments

III. The assault. T_1 – tanks take out defending batteries and sweep through position to T_2. I_1 – I_2 – infantry mop up. RR – reconnaissance moves out, preparatory to continuing advance.

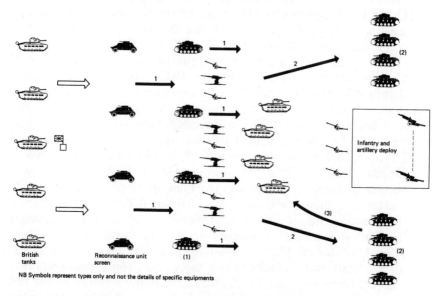

NB Symbols represent types only and not the details of specific equipments

IV. Mobile defence. 1 – Reconnaissance and tanks withdraw, unmasking anit-tank guns (G–G). 2 – Further withdrawal onto infantry and guns. 3 – Counter-attack as opportunity offers.

gaps by the infantry, and the co-ordinated attack by infantry and
tanks supported by covering fire from the field artillery in a
timed programme. The techniques were there, and well understood by the *infantry*. The 4th and 5th Indian Infantry Divisions
had used them time and time again in Eritrea.

Notes No. 6, issued in July 1942 covering the same period as
No. 4 (but based on views that could not have left Cairo much
later than May), contains a long passage on the limitations of the
Jock Column, all but recommending that its use should be
discontinued. Not that any notice was taken of it during
the fighting of May and June. The experiences of the Gazala
battle made little impression on the hard-pressed formation
commanders of the Eighth Army. It was not possible to
eradicate so deep-rooted a habit until the fighting on the El
Alamein position had died down, and the change in command of
August had been completed.

In the end everything hinged on the generals, and ultimately
on the Commander-in-Chief himself. Someone had to lay down
a doctrine and then enforce it. Auchinleck's own views seem to
have been gradually changing, or evolving, as he surveyed the
armoured battles. *Notes No. 1*, as quoted, is evidence that the
doctrine of dispersion had his approval. There is evidence to
support this in the biography of General Messervy. Major-
General E. Dorman-Smith (he later adopted the Irish style of
Dorman O'Gowan) had been an influential figure in the Middle
East since the first offensive against the Italians; first as a sort of
consultant and ideas-man to Wavell and then to Auchinleck.
(He was at the time Commandant of the Middle East Staff
College located at Haifa.) In July 1942, when Auchinleck took
command himself in the field he employed Dorman-Smith as a
deputy chief-of-staff in Headquarters Middle East (Operations)
and his chief-of-staff in the field. In July Messervy, who had
been summarily relieved of the command of the 7th Armoured
Division by Ritchie, was temporarily employed in Cairo also as a
Deputy Chief-of-Staff. There, he told his biographer, he was
shown a paper written by Dorman-Smith concerning desert
tactics. Its theme was the utility of small forces acting widely
dispersed, and it reminded Messervy of a paper entitled
'Extended Warfare' concocted by Dorman-Smith when he had
been Director of Military Training in India. Messervy, who for
all his dash and panache was a thoroughly sound and orthodox
soldier, wrote a paper in rebuttal, advocating a return to the old
divisional organisation and its use as a compact battle formation.
He showed this to Auchinleck, who was furious, and tore it up
in front of him.[222] Yet, puzzlingly, Auchinleck by his actions

rather than a statement of policy was to show that he at least half agreed. (Messervy, may, of course, have misunderstood Dorman-Smith's object, and confused it with his unfortunate adoption of the term 'battle group', while Auchinleck may have been angered by an implicit criticism of his former methods, and of his great friend of many years.)

Auchinleck's successful defence of the El Alamein position was not only the decisive battle of the Desert War, but is also extremely instructive. He resisted the temptation to try and provide a continuous defence line from the sea to the Qattara Depression, and concentrated the whole of the 1st South African Infantry Division in the north, and in consequence its complete artillery, reinforced by a British medium regiment – a full establishment of a total of eighty-eight guns – and was thus able to cover the main axis of Rommel's advance. Auchinleck continually reinforced it as fast as regiments of artillery could be brought in from other parts of the theatre. These, grouped with such infantry units as could be hastily collected were thrown piecemeal into battle, for at that desperate moment there was no other course open to him.

The intensity of the bombardment by these massed batteries rudely halted the advance of the Germans and broke the spirit of the Italian Trieste and Savona divisions, which fled. It reminded German veterans of the *Trommelfeuer* – like a roll of drums – they had endured on the Western Front. The British artillery fire was equalled in intensity by the direct air support of the Royal Air Force, now operating from its permanent airfields close behind the front and working with the army through a specially designed communication system. It is difficult to judge whether the artillery or the air force made the greater contribution. However, the question at the heart of the matter, as to how weapon-system centralisation of resources for both was reconciled with a prompt and flexible response to their demands, is a general one applying to our whole theme.

Auchinleck's major counter-offensive was a failure. The same faults were repeated. The 23rd Armoured Brigade lost 140 tanks, almost all its strength, when with great courage it hurled itself against the waiting gun line unaccompanied by infantry and without artillery support. It was newly arrived from England and was put into battle in advance of its parent formation. (It appears, therefore, that faulty tactics were not confined to the Middle East. As late as April 1943 the armoured brigades of the home-trained 6th Armoured Division as well as the desert-trained 1st both made costly and abortive attacks without using their infantry and artillery to clear away what was only a desperate defence by an attenuated German gun line. This was duly commented on in *Notes No. 16.*)[223] Neither Auchinleck nor the generals in the field should, perhaps, be condemned too severely for failing to correct these errors amid the hurly-burly of the Desert War. Not everyone was clear or in agreement about what was happening. Occasionally the desert air was clear and the observers were lucky to be on commanding ground affording a good view of the battle. More often the ground was flat and visibility distorted by heat-shimmer, making it impossible to distinguish one type of vehicle from another, or obscured by the clouds of dust thrown up by bursting shells and the churning of tank tracks. It was difficult to recognise friend or foe, let alone make a nice appreciation of whether the shot and shell arriving with banshee howls from every quarter came from artillery or tanks.

What was required, and at that time impossible to obtain, was a period for rest, reflection and re-education. Tactics cannot be imposed by decree and acted on in mid-battle. The behaviour of troops is governed by training, and a great deal of time is required to teach the complex and difficult task of 'laying on' an attack, doubly difficult in the face of the enemy and the friction of war. It has to be instilled in exercises endlessly repeated until it is second nature to everyone concerned, and the procedures must be reinforced by discipline. It was not until Montgomery took over that any commander had the time or the authority and character to impose his ideas, brutally if necessary.

All this is true, but what reveals the shallowness of military thought in Middle East Headquarters in mid-1942 are the measures proposed to put things right. As the various issues of *Notes from the Theatres of War* makes clear, a part of the General Staff, presumably 'G' (Training), had discerned what had to be done. No great level of military knowledge was required to see that what had to be done could only be done by a revision of tactical doctrine and by retraining. Instead, the futile expedient of tinkering with organisations was adopted. (It is a vice of young, clever but inexperienced staff officers without enough to do.) Some of these possibly originated in the brain of Dorman-Smith, of whom it was justly said that he could produce four or five solutions to any one military problem, 'one of which might be a winner'. Those that can be attributed to him are not altogether unsound. He wanted to substitute a single 'mobile' division of tanks and motorised infantry for the separate types of a fully armoured division and marching infantry divisions. He also advocated the formation of battle groups ad hoc brought from other parts of the Middle East Command to meet the losses of June and July. He believed in concentrating the fire of artillery and his tactical advice to Auchinleck during the fighting on the Alamein line when he was chief-of-staff in the field was shrewd; notably to concentrate his attacks on the Italian-held sectors.[224]

Who was responsible for some of the other proposals is now unknown. One was to institutionalise the 'brigade group' and to form divisions of brigades complete with their own artillery, the armoured division to consist of one armoured and one infantry brigade. (That at least had the merit of abolishing the support group and became the basis of the reorganised armoured division. Its final form closely resembled that of the panzer division, and it was used successfully for the rest of the war.) The divisional artillery as such was to be abolished and with it the commander, Royal Artillery. The anti-tank regiments were to be broken up and the guns absorbed into the field regiments in the brigades. The commander of the corps artillery was to be abolished, and the corps artillery to become a sort of pool, allocated to divisions as necessary. Any artillery advice to commanders was to be provided by the operations branch of the General Staff. (Whether this was to be from staff-trained artillery officers, or staff officers of the other arms, so notoriously, indeed wilfully, ignorant of artillery matters, is not clear.) There was also a proposal to develop a self-propelled 95-mm (3.7-inch) howitzer to be operated by the infantry, already short of manpower and who already had three other heavy weapons in the battalion.

The weirdest suggestion, owing something to the Jock Columns, was to abolish the conventional infantry division altogether and form it into motorised 'battle groups' of one battalion, less two companies, plus an attached artillery battery, these being grouped together under brigadiers; some unspecified number of 'brigades' to make up a 'division'. The detached companies were to be used to escort the artillery observation posts, or established 'fortified OPs'. What does seem strange is that these ridiculous proposals, which ignored a whole range of new problems they themselves would create, caused great alarm and absorbed much valuable time in argument, were not firmly stamped on from the beginning. One undoubted benefit of the sweeping changes in command of August 1942 was that after the arrival of Alexander and Montgomery nothing more was ever heard of them.[225]

One question that does emerge here is when should a commander be dismissed, and how far should he be given a chance to benefit by his mistakes; for heaven knows if every commander had been sacked after his first failure there would be no 'Great Captains' left to study.

The desert generals were not wanting in ability, nor was the arm of their origin significant, although the loss of Caunter and of the gifted and strong-minded Pope, both formerly of the Royal Tank Corps, one posted away and one killed in an air crash on the eve of taking command of XXX Corps (the Armoured Corps) was serious. Beresford-Peirse, Campbell and Cunningham were artillerymen. Ritchie, O'Connor, Gott, Tuker, perhaps the best tactician in the desert, Harding, a bright star who did not attain command until later, Godwin-Austin, the real victor of CRUSADER and Dorman-Smith were, like Rommel (and Guderian and Balck), infantrymen. Norrie served in the earlier war in the Tank Corps, returning after it to horsed cavalry, but he hardly shone as an armoured commander or as a corps commander, a rôle thrust on him too early as a result of the death of Pope. Messervy was a cavalryman who was brilliant as a commander of infantry, but failed disastrously during his brief period in command of the 7th Armoured Division, although there were extenuating circumstances. One cannot help feeling that they should all have been handled differently. The successive dismissals of Cunningham, who was felt by his Commander-in-Chief to have lost the battle in his mind, and of Ritchie, whose appointment was a mistake, were undoubtedly necessary. But for the rest, one is reminded of the constant procession of generals who commanded Union armies in the American Civil War. For one reason or another, Creagh, Beresford-Peirse, Messervy, Norrie and Godwin-Austin were all relieved, as was Dorman-Smith, who was dismissed ignominiously from his influential position. The effect on the command level immediately below was certainly unsettling, as it probably was on the troops as a whole.

A successful army requires something else besides a successful theory. There has to be firm and consistent direction from the top, discharging an energising current to provide the subtle magnetism that binds it together. This had existed in the little Western Desert Force that had defeated the Italians. O'Connor and Dorman-Smith, Creagh, Caunter and Beresford-Peirse were all on the best of terms, and pulled easily as a team with Wavell's firm but light hands on the reins. During CRUSADER these vital relationships began to go wrong. Morshead and the Australians and Freyberg and the New Zealanders both lost confidence in the all-British direction of the campaign, and in the fighting qualities of the British armour, whose constant repulses and painful losses had caused it to lose confidence in itself. (Montgomery has been the subject of much uninformed criticism for his alleged inability or reluctance to exploit success.

The fact is that he had no suitable instrument for the exploitation of a break-through, or a pursuit. The armoured brigades, moving from one extreme to the other, abandoned the practice of charging the enemy for one of extreme caution. They were easily stopped by the first sign of resistance; for example the 2nd Armoured Brigade at El Hamma, the 8th Armoured Brigade at the Wadi Akarit when Tuker's infantry had opened the way and, later in Tunisia, the 2nd again on the Goubellat Plain.) The centre of authority had shifted away from where it should be, the Commander-in-Chief and the Army Commander in the field. The Gazala battle was fought in an unhappy atmosphere of mistrust. Godwin-Austin, who had won CRUSADER, had been relieved as the result of a difference of opinion with Ritchie, the newly appointed army commander, over a matter where many thought him to be in the right. This led to Gott being appointed to the command of his corps, but not to improved relations. Norrie, the others corps commander, was Gott's close friend, and the two corps commanders practised a sort of joint command by confabulation, at one stage co-locating their headquarters. This was known to the staff and could only diminish the stature of the Eighth Army Commander, Ritchie. He, conscious of his lack of operational experience, was hesitant to assert his authority below, or to resist a flow of letters containing operational advice from his Chief, from above. His decisions were painfully slow. At the same time his subordinates suspected that their army commander was only the channel for the ideas of the commander-in-chief, and that these were in reality the ideas of Dorman-Smith, whose influence they distrusted.

The career of Dorman-Smith as a man of ideas outside the normal command structure was unusual but understandable. He was imaginative, full of ideas and extremely articulate, and he was able to exert his influence as the protégé of two successive commanders-in-chief whose minds were open to radical or novel ideas. His downfall was due partly to the misconception that all the bad tactical habits of the Eighth Army were due to his interference, and partly to a sharp tongue and a talent for making enemies. The prestige of Lieutenant-General W. H. E. Gott and his subtler but more powerful influence is harder to explain. He wrote no papers (or at least any that survive) nor left any memorable opinions on tactical doctrine, nor had he any great military successes to his credit after his brilliant debut as the commander of the 7th Armoured Division Support Group in the campaign against the Italians. On the contrary, he was involved in, if not responsible for, a string of failures. Yet he commanded universal respect, indeed affection, and other commanders often turned to him for advice. If there was a difficult or disagreeable task (such as the unpromising, limited counter-attack on Rommel in May 1941) it was apt to be handed to 'Strafer' Gott.

Gott's reputation rested on his personality. The punning nickname was quite inappropriate. There was nothing of the fire-eater or military bully 'strafing' the enemy or his subordinates in him.[226] He was always calm, good-humoured and courteous, and with a high sense of duty and loyalty which led him to assume any burden laid on his shoulders without complaint. In action he was seen at his best in adversity; courageous, clear-headed and 'unflappable'. When in March and April Rommel's first advance threw the British defences into hopeless confusion it was Gott, operating with a handful of small motorised columns and armoured cars, who held up Rommel's vanguards between Tobruk and the Egyptian frontier for the few vital days required to stabilise the situation.

Such tactics, basically an offensive-defensive kept up by wasp-like attacks from such columns with a hard core of often no more than a 'troop' (four guns) of artillery were peculiarly his own, and ideally adapted for the predicament in which he so often had found himself of having to contain a greatly superior force. He was quite clear in his own mind that in the open desert, where every position had an open flank, holding ground was of little significance and that both offensive and defensive operations had to be based on mobility and manoeuvre. This conviction was fortified by his experiences on the Western Front. He had a horror of battles of attrition 'where men stood shoulder to shoulder behind curtains of artillery fire.'[227] That a man of Gott's stature held such views, and that they were shared by his original comrades in arms of Support Group days, like Campbell and Renton, who in his turn was to command the 7th Armoured Division, was to ensure that they spread through the whole army, together with the weaknesses of fragmentation, endless regrouping ad hoc and wide dispersion. It is ironic that Dorman-Smith was, perhaps, sacked because he was wrongly believed to be the propagator of ideas originated by Gott, while Gott was chosen to command the Eighth Army.

How he would have coped with the task of breaking through the German position at Alamein, and whether he could have imposed his will on the fractious desert commanders, for there was a gentle side to Gott reminiscent of Robert E. Lee, can never be known, as he was killed when the aircraft in which he was travelling was shot down by an enemy fighter aircraft.

General Montgomery as a military commander and as a man

was the exact antithesis to Gott, and the ideas Gott stood for. Tactically there can be no comparison, for he never had to fight in the limitless desert. His resources were greater than any available to his predecessors and his immediate tactical problem, of breaking through a position whose flanks were secured, was different from anything they had had to face. He turned back to the methods of 1918, not because he was a reactionary, but because he was a realist. In his own way he was just as opposed to victory through effusion of blood as Gott. When he chose what to many appeared to be the tactics of attrition he saw to it that the attrition was efficient. Where Gott hoped to avoid casualties by manoeuvre Montgomery used fire-power to batter down his opponent and reduce his ability to inflict injury on his troops.

The change that came was one not so much of tactics but of style: the reinstitution of proper chains of command, regular formations, careful preparation and meticulous staff work. He also enforced one other change. Wellington once complained that the officers of his Peninsular Army paid no more attention to his order 'than if they were the pages of an amusing novel.' Montgomery was aware of the prevalent habit of disregarding, questioning or delay in complying with unpalatable orders and he was determined to be obeyed. He issued his famous order against 'belly-aching' and in due course sacked a general, the cavalryman Lumsden, to prove his point.

There is no need to describe Montgomery's methods. His opening battles, so carefully prepared and staged, have been dissected repeatedly. There is, however, one relatively insignificant action that is a perfect example of his style. By March 1943 the Eighth Army was 1,000 miles to the west of its desert arena, near the small town of Medenine, some twenty miles from the strong Axis position at Mareth, which Montgomery was preparing to attack. In the meantime he had to pause and built up his over-stretched lines of communication, and he was anxious about the security of forward supply dumps and airfields just to the east of Medenine. He had only two divisions forward, and he was determined not to expose himself to one of the sudden counter-offensives Rommel had twice used so disconcertingly in the past against his predecessors.

Accordingly, he ordered XXX Corps, reinforced by a third (infantry) division, to take up a solid defensive position on some suitable high ground covering all the roads from the west which conveniently converged on the town. The infantry of the 51st Highland and the 2nd New Zealand divisions together with the infantry brigade and the artillery of the 7th Armoured Division were deployed to cover a twenty-one mile front, with some 400 tanks in reserve. There were 500 anti-tank guns available, mainly 6-pounders, and a proportion of the new 17-pounders (with a performance slightly superior to the dreaded 88-mm at 1,000 yards, being able to defeat 113 mm of armour, just under 4½ inches, compared with the 88-mm's four). These were carefully sited in defilade with interlocking arcs of fire across the front, sometimes in front of the infantry. The field artillery, 192 25-pounders and thirty-two 4.5 and 5.5-inch, was controlled centrally and allotted prearranged defensive fire tasks.

When the expected attack materialised on 6 March it proved a forlorn hope, made by the elements of three depleted panzer divisions totalling only 100 tanks which were thrown frontally against XXX Corps' guns. The result was inevitable. One of the crews of the new 17-pounders destroyed six tanks with the first six shots fired in action. The German tanks and infantry, fighting with their usual courage and determination, made four separate attempts, withdrawing three times to what they hoped was the cover of a number of ravines in front of XXX Corps' position to reorganise, but there they came under the concentrated fire of the divisional artilleries, called down by the observers on the high ground, and the ravines became their graveyard. After the fourth attack the panzers withdrew, leaving fifty-two of their tanks wrecked or burning in front of the muzzles of the anti-tank guns.[228] There was no pursuit or exploitation by the British armour as they trailed back to Mareth; Montgomery was taking no risks.

Medenine lacks the cut and thrust, the oscillating fortunes and the excitement of the battles in the open desert which still fascinate the military student. Its outcome was never in doubt. The statement in a report made by the Eighth Army: that 'this action proved conclusively that if infantry are well dug in with their anti-tank guns properly concealed, and if they are well supported by artillery fire, they have nothing to fear from a tank attack even though they are not protected by wire and mines' was perhaps too sanguine. Medenine was a victory by cannonade: the Valmy of the war in North Africa. The real significance of the battle is the contrast in style with the battles of the desert era which, doctrine apart, were a series of desperate emergencies and improvisations. At Medenine the method was precisely adjusted to the goal, and the planning a model of Staff work. It revealed nothing new, but it can be seen as the terminus ad quem of the arguments about mobility of fire-power and dispersion and concentration that had been put to the test on the desert sands.

So ended one of the most exciting and bizarre chapters in the history of the British army. Montgomery was said to have added after his brutal opening remarks to his new staff that he had no intention of allowing himself to be defeated, but if he were, it would not be in detail. Lord Carver has expressed his doubt whether any commander arriving earlier could have reversed the trend. Perhaps he is right. Perhaps the reaction to the methods of the First World War were so strong and the desert generals so wedded to mobility, to everything that was the opposite to the cliche's of the Field Service Regulations, and the social habits and lack of professionalism so deeply deplored by Hobart were so firmly embedded in the desert soldiers that they had to be worked out of the British military system before anything else could be done. It was a valuable exercise, but it does seem to have been a costly way to have established some obvious truths.

CHAPTER 14

A Cybernetic Solution – I
The Artillery on the Ground

The command of any body of artillery should be centralised under the highest commander who can exercise control.
Field Service Regulations Volume II, 1935
(A. P. Wavell)

Cybernetics is the science of control and communication, with special reference to self-controlling or adaptive systems.[229]

THE secret of success of the blitzkrieg was that it dislocated the opposing communication, command and control system – the 'C3' system, in modern defence jargon. It availed little to design new weapons or adopt different tactics unless the C3 was radically improved. A new nervous system and a better brain were required if the lightning attack was to be met by as prompt a parry and as powerful a riposte. The whole tempo of warfare on land had increased. The Germans were as agile and as rapid in the defence as they were in the attack, and once tactics had been devised to defeat the blitzkrieg they would have to be extended to the attack: fire-power had to be combined with dexterity. It was a problem not to be resolved by restructuring divisions, mixing weapons in different proportions or ingenious manoeuvre. War is not a game of chess. It was a cybernetic question.

'Cybernetics' was not a word that would have meant anything to the hard-pressed and practical officers who in those days were busy with the application of artillery fire or airborne fire-power to the battlefield, but the underlying ideas were familiar to engineers who designed servo-mechanisms and automatic pilots. They were also inherent in the command structures of armies. The efficiency of a command system is defined by the rapidity of the flow of information and the smoothness of its reaction to the 'feed-back', i.e. fresh orders based on it. In modern jargon it must work in 'real time'. The machine must also be adaptive.[230]

Not even the most sophisticated cybernetic system is perfect; still less the complex one that goes to make up the components of an army. Machines do not have to contend with deliberately false information or attempts to damage them. The commander of an army has a rather different task, but nevertheless he acts in the same way; in jargon, 'heuristically'. That is, he uses his imagination and judgement to choose the most likely of his opponent's courses of action or his most likely posture, to construct a 'model' of the situation based on such information as he has, and then to alter it as the action goes on in the light of events.

It could have been possible, no doubt, to build a C3 machine for an army commander allowing him to manipulate all his units direct, without the need to go through the intervening chain-of-command or 'hierarchical' structure of corps, division, brigade and so on; on the lines of the system invented by the Royal Air Force. In that, all the information was gathered in to a central control room and orders were transmitted direct to airfields or to aircraft in the air. Nothing else would have served for the Battle of Britain, fought at hundreds of knots with combats lasting only minutes. It was not possible then to use an identical system for an army in the field, because communications technology was insufficiently advanced. Besides the hierarchical system is robust and matches the way an army is organised. If the subordinate commanders are properly trained and allowed to use their initiative an army can survive a degree of C3 blackout for some time, provided that they do not lose their nerve. Hence the old adages, dating from the days when the fog of war was almost permanent, 'if in doubt, attack', or 'march to the sound of the guns'. The chain of command therefore remained. In any case, a complete restructuring was not possible in the middle of a war. Instead the existing C3 was reinforced by degrees by superimposing new circuits on to the old, bypassing if necessary the retransmission points in the existing one.

Each of these circuits or systems served a specific purpose. As previously mentioned, Air Marshal Sir Arthur Barratt sent out his own radio-equipped contact patrols to the front to discover the situation and report direct to his headquarters. General Montgomery used a team of specially trained liaison officers permanently attached to his forward headquarters who acted as his own eyes on the battlefield. As C3 became more and more dependent on radio communications it became possible to 'listen' to a battle and 'read' it by monitoring the usually en clair orders and reports of the forward units in action and so supplement or anticipate the reports coming up the chain of command. (This was called the 'J' Service.) Parham, operating on a lower level, similarly jumped the breaks in the artillery communications by sending out his 'CRAs representatives' directly connected to him and able to give him first-hand information or call for fire from all his guns in his name.

The wider problems of controlling artillery and aircraft, in essence similar, were more difficult. There was the question of 'ownership' as regards the artillery, and the touchiness of the air officers, who were suspicious of any move leading even to the slightest infringement, or threat of infringement, to the autonomy of the Royal Air Force. In the middle period of the Desert War the infantry and tank brigade commanders won their battle to 'own' their artillery, a move not greatly resisted, it appears, by the senior artillery commanders, some of whom were converted to the idea that the desert demanded different methods. (As for the junior, they positively relished the freedom of action they enjoyed in the 'brigade groups' and Jock Columns.) When, however, some of the desert generals turned covetous eyes on the air force in the Middle East which, they felt, was being directed towards long term and strategic goals while the Luftwaffe was making its presence felt over the battle-field every day, they were rudely rebuffed. This was a question of priorities, and arguable. At the same time there were bitter (and often uninformed) complaints that the air effort was not going to the support of the field army; the trouble being that it was not visibly supporting the army.

The Royal Air Force, Middle East, was at that time unique because it had, a year or more ahead of the home forces, a prototype of what was later to become an officially established 'Tactical Air Force' in the shape of the Desert Air Force. The trouble in the Middle East was not a question of willingness but lack of machinery to convey the army's requirements to the air staff, and to control and direct air attacks on to ground targets amid the swirling, dust-shrouded manoeuvres of desert warfare. On one occasion during the bitter debate that continued for most of 1941 and part of 1942 Air Vice-Marshal Coningham, commanding the Desert Air Force, complained to his chief, Tedder, that even if he did place squadrons on standby for the army the army failed to use them. 'His fight . . . had not been with the enemy, but for targets . . . [on 10 December 1941] the whole of the enemy forces had been located in a comparatively small area south-west of Gazala, but for three days they had not been bombed at all . . . squadrons of bombers had been at call, but always their operations had had to be postponed because of lack of identification and the close contact of the enemy forces with our own.'[231] Clearly this difficulty was not resolved by handing over a few squadrons to each corps headquarters for their exclusive use.

Unlike the Commanders, Royal Artillery, who had no executive head of service, Tedder had the powerful support of the Chief of the Air Staff in England, and another way had to be found to resolve the difficulty, which in fact was purely one of 'C3'. The solution required intimate liaison with the 'client', rapid communication, rapid processing of the request and a rapid response. A control apparatus meeting these requirements was arrived at by a process of logical thought and brought into being in time to be used in conjunction with the Desert Air Force and the Eighth Army.

The artillery problem was similar, but the solution had to be rather different, because of the complexity of the army's organisation in the field and the ever-changing pattern of deployment. There was little experience on which to build, for in the First World War the circumstances were different and little thought had been given to the subject, although the special problem of providing continuous artillery support after a break-through had been studied after the war, and met by introducing short range close support batteries to accompany the infantry, giving battalions their own mortars, or relying on tanks.

To the infantry who fought on the Western Front the artillery seemed to be something lethal but remote, almost a separate army. There was, of course, some personal contact between infantry and artillery commanders, and in static conditions there were good communications through the dense and complex web of telephone cables linking all the units and headquarters. However, no official doctrine concerning close liaison existed, and the infantry and artillery co-operation varied from division to division and corps to corps. The heavy artillery relied principally on balloons, aeroplanes or acoustic methods ('sound ranging') for fire-control. It only sent ground observers forward for special tasks such as the registration of some troublesome strong point in the front line. In the divisional or field artillery all the officers including the subalterns (whose casualties were severe) took their turn at manning the battery observation post in the trenches. The position of the battery commander was his own decision, depending on his circumstances. Sometimes he manned his own observation post, but more often his responsibilities kept him at the gun position. In the New Armies, if he was a regular, he was often the only officer who understood how to carry out the technical duties of the 'gun position officer'. It was his duty to stay in the gun position, often as much the post of danger as the front line, when the gunners were working under the intense counter-battery fire of that war, when his battery was actually under attack by infantry or, in the later war, tanks. He, personally, had to supervise a withdrawal and to be the last man to leave the gun position; a tradition duly observed on many occasions both in 1918 and in the hectic armoured battles in the desert in 1941–2.

According to *Artillery Training* 'forward observing officers' (FOOs), usually subalterns, were detailed to accompany battalions in the attack so as to provide support when they passed out of view of the main observation posts. They went forward on foot with a party of signallers paying out a telephone line and carrying a daylight signalling lamp as a reserve, but the line was often cut, the lie of the land and the smoke of battle often made visual signalling impossible, and the FOOs were not infrequently killed or wounded. Lieutenant-Colonel Carrington recalls that in 1916 he was adjutant of his battalion when it was the extreme left-hand battalion of the VIII Corps. He had a good view of the attack by the London Scottish, the right-hand battalion of the VII Corps, on Gommecourt Wood, which they duly captured, only to be severely counter-attacked and thrown out again six hours later. No artillery defensive fire came down to protect the London Scottish on their objective. 'Telephoning in all directions,' Carrington says, 'by field lines that always went "dis" (disconnected), I tried to persuade some Gunners, any Gunners, to intervene. They all said, "not in their area".'[232] (The probable explanation being that the artillery units of VIII Corps were under orders not to fire blind across the inter-corps boundary.) This was a common enough situation on the Western Front. The inability to give continuous support to the attacking troops once they had disappeared into the depth of the German defensive system, alive with machine-gun nests and local counter-attacks, was the great stumbling block in artillery tactics until the FOOs became permanent, established officers equipped with portable radios.

In the inter-war years the rôles of majors and subalterns were reversed. The subalterns, educated at the Royal Military Academy and the School of Artillery, were perfectly capable of technical control; more so than most of their hippophile seniors, who had but the haziest notions of gunnery and survey. The battery observation post was manned by the battery commander, accompanied by an impressive cavalcade of assistants bearing directors, range-finders, signalling lamps or even heliographs, and their horse-holders. He had to choose a position with a good view, which was not necessarily near the battalion commander he was to support, nor had he any communication link with him in mobile warfare. If he wanted to see him he had to send for his horse and ride to battalion headquarters.

This was remedied by the introduction of radio communications and the reorganisation of field regiments in 1938, when batteries were subdivided into 'troops' of four guns commanded by captains. The troop commanders became the established observation post officers, the subalterns continued to command the guns, and the battery commander, now linked to his battery by radio, was free to position himself with his designated battalion commander. The 1938 organisation was unsatisfactory for a number of reasons, the chief one being that it did not 'fit' a three-battalion brigade, having only two large batteries, and only four of the six troop commanders being equipped as observing officers. The 'twelve-gun battery' had not been designed with tactical considerations in mind, only technical and saving of manpower. It was presented to the Royal Artillery as a fait accompli, and we then had to devise ways of working it in mobile warfare.

The artillery in the Western Desert was differently organised, the pre-war six-gun batteries being mated into double batteries, which in any case as often as not operated separately as six-gun troops, but there too there was the lack of fit with triangular brigades. This was eventually resolved in 1941 in the Home Forces, in 1942 in the desert, when all field artillery was organised into regiments of three eight-gun batteries each of two four-gun troops, with *six* troop commanders, providing two observation posts for each infantry battalion, a battery commander for each battalion headquarters and as a second in command had been added to regimental headquarters the regimental commander was free to attach himself permanently to the infantry brigadier.

These organisational details may seem too trivial to mention, but the system of 'affiliation', as it was called, when taken in conjunction with the elaborate network that came into being as sufficient radio sets came off the production lines, lay at the heart of the whole system developed by the Royal Artillery in the Second World War, unsurpassed for efficiency by any other army.

It was not, however, designed: it evolved. No directive, no training memorandum laid down that it was to be introduced. No one can claim to be its originator. It may in fact have grown up in different formations at the same time. The cradle was certainly the desert, and probably the 7th Armoured Division, whose young Royal Horse Artillery officers, very much of the same class and outlook as the cavalry and the Rifle Brigade, learnt the art of close co-operation in the Jock Columns. The brigade group, pernicious as it may have been, fostered a similar spirit. By 1941 artillery officers supporting armoured regiments were mounted in tanks and equipped with a second radio on the tank command network.[233] The earliest systematic use, however, appears to have arisen through force of circumstances during the siege of Tobruk.

The defence of Tobruk is of wide interest because it showed, even as early as 1941, that the dreaded panzers were vulnerable to a determined defence, and that artillery fire could be concentrated in the desert as it could anywhere else. Tobruk was not in any technical sense a 'fortress', although later its defensive positions were strongly entrenched and guarded by wire and deep minefields. It was an area occupied as a point d'appui from which the left flank of the Axis force pressing towards Egypt could be threatened. As a defensive position it was umpromising. Tobruk, whose uninterrupted working as a port was essential to the operation, was commanded by a semi-circular ridge of hills, along which the Italians had constructed a defensive perimeter thirty miles long consisting of little more than an anti-tank ditch, easily bridged, and pairs of concrete posts at intervals of about 800 yards.

The decision to hold Tobruk was made on 8 April 1941 and the first formal attack on it was mounted on the 14th. In the interval a garrison was hastily assembled from various units, some of whom were streaming back in confusion in front of Rommel's unexpected offensive. Fortunately the commander was Major-General L. Morshead, an outstanding commander and tactician, and his infantry, like him, were Australians not particularly impressed by the mystique of the panzers and the blitzkrieg. The artillery included four regiments of the élite Royal Horse Artillery, two of which had shot their way through Rommel's encircling columns with their own guns to reach Tobruk. Morshead's division had been sent forward without its guns, except his 2-pounder anti-tank regiment. His battalions and batteries, therefore, were strangers and had to learn to work together and trust each other. That this was successfully achieved in two or three days was revealed by the rude rebuff dealt to the first German attack.[234]

Briefly, Morshead's orders to his infantry were to hold their hastily occupied positions on the perimeter and, if attacked, to let the panzers through and concentrate on their accompanying infantry. If overrun they were to stay in their trenches and call for artillery fire on top of their own positions. The panzers were to be received in succession, by the anti-tank guns of the Australian regiment and the 3rd Regiment Horse Artillery, the latter manoeuvring in their 'portees', then by the 25-pounders, whose positions had been chosen with good direct fields of fire, and finally the anti-aircraft guns defending the base installations and wharves around the port itself. The four regiments of field artillery were deployed so that at least forty guns could cover any one vital sector of the perimeter. These sound but unpractised tactics were followed to the letter. The German pioneers bridged the anti-tank ditch in the dark early on the morning of the 14th and the 5th Panzer Regiment, followed by infantry, assaulted with their usual élan, but no German infantry succeeded in passing the forward posts, and the panzers on reaching the line of 25-pounders were beaten back. At 7.30 a.m. they retreated, leaving behind 17 tanks, 150 dead and 250 prisoners.

Rommel was furious. He complained that his infantry were poorly trained (the fact was that they had never encountered good British or Commonwealth infantry before, strongly posted and ready for them) and that his battle group commander did not understand the art of forcing an entry, rolling up the flanks and then rushing into the depth of the position. He was no more successful himself when he tried a fortnight later. He made a dent in the perimeter but the furious and repeated Australian counter-attacks stopped the *durchbruch*, and as for the *aufrollen*, when his assault groups tried to work right and left along the perimeter from the flanks of the dent they came under intense artillery fire that rolled with them, and gave it up. British gunners and Australian infantry had worked together perfectly.

Things might have gone very differently. There was little rapport between the Australian and British armies. Their system of command and the relations between ranks and approach to warfare was different. The British regarded the Australians as uncouth and undisciplined (as indeed some were) and on occasion treated them with a singular lack of tact, while the Australians thought the 'Poms' were inefficient and effete, and had not been impressed by their precipitate flight before Rommel's attack. Fortunately, the British CRA, Brigadier L. F. Thomas, immediately attracted Australian admiration: 'he at once displayed his capability by the excellence of his dispositions and arrangements'.[235] In Australian eyes the 'Pom' artillery was on trial, while the British officers, with a dozen things to do in all too little time – discovering the infantry layout, arranging communications, registering the zone of fire, introducing their observing officers to the forward companies and positioning them, planning defensive fire – had to make contact with their opposite numbers, find out what was required, and ensure that they in turn understood how the British batteries operated in defence and attack. The obvious thing to do was remain with them and see the battle through. It was not the action that was significant, but that as the siege wore on, these 'affiliations' were seen to work best if they were disturbed as little as possible. The two sides began to respect and trust one another. The horse artillerymen, very professional themselves, admired the professionalism of the Australians who, contrary to their image, had their own standards of strict discipline and no time for casual or careless soldiers. They in turn had been impressed by the speed and accuracy of the artillery fire, and the Royal Horse Artillery's staunchness in facing the panzers in fierce gun battles at short range. Soon troop commanders were known by their Christian names. All this was the secret of co-operation. (On an occasion later in Italy a Royal Artillery officer took command of an infantry battalion in an attack when all the British officers had fallen, and led it successfully to its objective. The significance of the story is that the troops were Indians, yet they knew him and trusted him as if he were one of their own officers.)

The system of permanent affiliations spread through the army by example and word of mouth. The later pamphlets refer to it as an established practice. For instance, commanders of armoured brigades are reminded that their affiliated regiments are not their 'private, inalienable property' and that affiliation 'did not imply a return to the old idea of brigade groups'.[236] When the British 70th Infantry Division relieved the Australians in Tobruk it also came without its own guns, so the same regiments and the same CRA initiated it in turn into the mysteries of affiliation, concentrated fire and intimate close support. All this had an instant appeal for the infantry who relied absolutely on their guns for support in both attack and defence. Such an impasse as faced Carrington on the Western Front was unthinkable. Every fire-plan contained a prearranged belt of defensive fire in front of the objective, immediately adjusted by the FOOs on arrival, and slammed down in the face of the invariable German counter-attack.

The armoured regiments were slower to learn. After Tobruk was relieved the 104th RHA went to support the cavalry regiments of the 1st Armoured Brigade, but having only two batteries affiliation was imperfect. Nevertheless, its officers made it work in training, 'but all that was thrown to the winds when we went back to the desert in support of the Bays, who were strangers to us, and used us in the old, casual way'.[237]

This chaotic state of affairs was remedied when the armoured division was finally reorganised on a rational basis with a divisional artillery commanded by the CRA, but even then in the new 10th Armoured Division the artillery regimental commanders grumbled at having to link themselves to his command radio net.[238]

By early 1943 the affiliation system was also well established in the British First Army, which had trained in England before it arrived in Tunisia in 1942, although it was not universal, as it had become in the Eighth. (The present writer, as the commander of a battery in a non-divisional medium regiment, had never heard of it, and was initiated as late as April 1943 when attached to the artillery of the 1st Armoured Division.) By 1944 it was what the Americans call a 'standard operating procedure' and working like clockwork.

An officer posted to command a field regiment in a division in Italy in that year describes his introduction as follows:

'As I drove up the Axis that day I found the infantry brigade commander and the acting field artillery regimental commander at the side of the road, their wireless sets chattering away and the pair of them jointly and effectively in touch with what was going on and in charge of the battle. From then on, I lived at Brigade headquarters, or brigade tactical headquarters, and accompanied the brigadier everywhere . . . sometimes I didn't see my guns for days on end. It was exactly the same at battery-battalion level. Living constantly together during the battle relationships became very close. The observation posts were deployed as required, and here again troop commanders and company commanders were as one. This enabled fire-plans to be developed quickly, to whatever level of support was required. Being located together, and having parallel communications extending up to the CRA and the divisional commander who were also working closely together, plans could be made and the action needed to implement them, such as the issue of orders and the registration of targets, taken almost simultaneously. The system was never more valuable than in 'sticky' situations as the consolidation on an objective, often a precarious position on a ridge, vulnerable to an immediate counter-attack. It became second nature to take joint action to select and register defensive fire tasks. . .'[239]

The remaining step was to bring the medium and heavy artillery and the reserve 25-pounder regiments into the system. On the Western Front the vast array of heavy guns had been either grouped under corps for the counter-battery battle or for massive preparatory bombardments of the German defences before an attack. It was organised into brigades or groups of brigades controlled at corps or army level: the exception being in fluid situations such as final advances of August 1918 when, as in 1914, some heavy batteries were decentralised to divisions. In 1939 there still existed the appointment of 'Commander, Corps Medium Artillery', a brigadier who controlled some of the antiquated equipments sent to France, and all lost there. After Dunkirk there was little left for him to command; only a few obsolete equipments such as converted 60-pounder guns and British 6-inch and United States 155-mm howitzers were parcelled out as convenient, and the CCMA became redundant. Medium regiments and batteries then led a masterless existence, wandering from division to division. In 1942 when the new medium and heavy guns became available in quantity it was decided to group them together once more under a brigadier and headquarters complete with organic signals unit, with the rôle of either reinforcing the divisional artillery by regiments, adding weight to the huge fire-plans that became the fashion from Alamein onwards or conducting the counter-battery battle on the corps front. Their composition varied, but were usually a heavy regiment (7.2-inch howitzers, 8-inch howitzers or 155-mm guns), three medium regiments (4.5 or 5.5-inch) and one or two reinforcing 25-pounder regiments. The obvious title was 'artillery brigade' (like the similar anti-aircraft artillery brigade) but the Army fell into one of its sematic confusions. 'Brigade' was rejected because the brigadier might regard his command as a homogenous fire-unit and make difficulties over attaching individual regiments to other formations. 'Royal Artillery Groups' might lead to a facetious or insulting interpretation of the acronym, so, as the original intention was to retain them under army control, the final title was 'Army Group, Royal Artillery', a pronounceable acronym, but in practice the 'AGRAs' were almost invariably deployed as corps troops.

All the AGRA regiments were as fully equipped and staffed to provide direct support as the divisional regiments, their observation posts were deployed in the front line and their communications cross-connected with the divisional units, so that the whole corps artillery virtually became one weapon-system, capable of being brought into action by the simple act of picking up a microphone. On one occasion, in Italy in the Spring of 1944, an emergency call for fire from an observation post was answered in thirty-five minutes by 600 guns. In Africa it was found that smaller but accurately delivered and closely concentrated bursts of fire could not only deter but inflict damage on the panzers if they attempted the characteristic massed attack they used in the desert.[240] For example, in Tunisia, at 'Hunt's

Gap' in March 1943, the artillery of the 46th Division reinforced by the 2nd Medium Regiment (seventy-two 25-pounders and sixteen 5.5-inch) battered the 10th Panzer Division to a halt, twenty-seven wrecks being counted later on the battlefield.[241]

It was these formidable bombardments that made a great impression on the infantry, and lingered in the memory after the war, but the real secret of success was the complex and sensitive machinery for command and control, by which one of these thunderclaps could be summoned, a counter-attack repelled, a battalion running into unexpected resistance helped forward, or an elaborate fire-plan modified in mid-battle. In this way the artillery was restored to its dominant position on the battlefield, which it had temporarily abdicated during the Desert War.

CHAPTER 15

A Cybernetic Solution – II
The Artillery of the Air

The Royal Air Force was concerned only to give the Army the greatest assistance in the most effective way. In order to do this our forces had to be concentrated under a single control.
Marshal of the Air Force Lord Tedder[242]

T HE struggle for the return to sound principles of artillery employment was a relatively painless affair. The artillery commanders had no ambition other than to be allowed to support the army in the field, using their own expert knowledge. No tank or infantry commander had to plead or argue for artillery support. The boot was on the other foot: it was the artillery commanders who had to educate the two other arms in its use. By contrast, the question of air support for the army in the field was fraught with conflicting aims, inter-service rivalries and misunderstandings arising from personal relationships.

The position of most senior army officers was simple enough. The events of 1940, and also the brief but effective impact of the Japanese air force on land operations in 1941, had brought home to them the effectiveness of air-power, rather belatedly, and they demanded (as the Royal Navy had) an air component for the direct support of the army over which they would have effective control.

The opinion of air officers was divided. There were those who believed that the only correct air strategy was a sustained attack on the enemy homeland with the twin objectives of wrecking his war industries and destroying civilian morale, and that any substantial diversion of resources from this aim was a violation of the principles of concentration and offensive action. At their head stood Air Marshal Sir Arthur Harris, the Chief of Bomber Command, whose views were so rigid that they were self-defeating. Clearly some air effort had to be devoted to the three-fold requirements of the army. These were reconnaissance ('tactical reconnaissance', or 'Tac R', and 'artillery reconnaissance', or 'Arty R'), strategic support, the word 'strategic' being used in the old fashioned sense of off but connected with the battlefield, and direct offensive support. Equally clearly there had to be a more flexible and sensitive system than one on which the air force fundamentalists insisted: for the army to state its requirements 'through the usual channels', and for the air force to meet them if it thought fit and in a manner only the air force could decide.

Not all the senior air officers shared the rigid, neo-Trenchardist views of Sir Arthur Harris. Fortunately, there was also a more flexible and open-minded group, whose most famous member was Arthur Tedder, then Air Officer-Commanding-in-Chief, Middle East Air Force. Tedder is the bête noire of some Army officers because of his strong personal dislike of Montgomery and the tone of his memoirs shows little affection for the khaki uniform he once wore in the Dorsetshire Regiment, but he was an eminent and clear-minded supporter of the tactical air force idea. His lieutenant, 'Maori' Coningham, commanded the Desert Air Force, and later the 2nd Tactical Air Force in direct support of 21st Army Group in Normandy. His Senior Air Staff Officer was Harry Broadhurst, who succeeded him in command of the Desert Air Force and later commanded No. 83 Group in 2nd TAF in direct support of the British Second Army. To these names must be added that of Sir Arthur Barratt, to whom we will return shortly. These officers saw and understood the Army's needs, but felt, just as did the senior artillery officers in their own field, that to be effective air-power must be under centralised control, and that it should be handled by those who were technically competent to do so. In the early part of the war their arguments were reinforced by a shortage of aircraft. Lack of resources dictates central control and strict determination of priorities, and the Army at first made little headway in its struggle to obtain some declaration from the air force of the degree of assistance they could expect on the actual battlefield.

The Army, which had suffered painfully from the attention of the Luftwaffe both in France and Belgium and the Mediterranean, understandably demanded not only that the Royal Air Force should defend it from the Luftwaffe's attentions, but that it should be given the means of retaliation, in the shape of an air component of bombers and other aircraft dedicated solely to ground support, under Army command and control and not deflected at the behest of the Air Staff to attack strategic targets remote from the land battlefield. This was pressed too

vehemently and, perhaps, with too little understanding of the air
officer's point of view, by two successive Chiefs of the Imperial
Staff, Dill and Brooke. They made little impression on the Chief
of the Air Staff, Portal, who in any case was short of resources.
(The Desert Air Force, the only tactical group in constant
contact with the enemy, only began to grow the necessary
muscle when the flow of good American light and fighter-
bombers began to reach it in 1942.)

It was a fraught situation, difficult for both sides, neither of
which were being wholly objective. The Air Staff at the time was
almost paranoid on the subject, seeing in every Army demand a
sinister move towards an 'Army Air Force' and a threat to the
hard won integrity of the Royal Air Force. Nothing illustrates
this frame of mind better than the early history of the Air
Observation Post squadrons. The 'air OP' was the invention of
Captain H. C. Bazeley, Royal Artillery, secretary of the Royal
Artillery Flying Club. In 1938 the only system for directing
artillery fire from the air still required specially trained Royal Air
Force officers using a special procedure flying in slow aircraft in
enemy air space and vertically, or thereabouts, over the target.
Briefly, Bazeley's idea was to provide batteries or brigades of the
Royal Artillery with the same sort of small, low-powered aircraft
that the officers of the flying club flew for pleasure, able to take
off from a meadow or a dirt strip close to the gun positions. The
aircraft was to be merely a mount or a flying platform for
artillery officers, who would use the ordinary artillery procedures
for ranging a battery. They would not fly over enemy territory,
but over their own guns or near them, gaining just enough
height to scc targets on ground dead to ground OPs. To
compress the saga of the Air OP and Bazeley's central part in it,
Bazeley, a single-minded and determined man, argued his case
patiently and persistently. He was able to give practical demon-
strations that it was workable and, vital to its acceptance, that
these tiny aircraft, flying at low altitude, would not attract the
attention of enemy fighters and would prove difficult targets if
they did. Considerable force was added to his arguments when in
1940 the new Lysander aircraft, specially designed for air
reconnaissance and artillery spotting were shot out of the sky.

The only air force solution was to use high performance
fighters for the task, with other fighters protecting them, but
with both fighters and fighter pilots at a premium this gave the
artillery only a distant and doubtful prospect of obtaining air
force assistance. It might have been thought that the Air Staff
would have seized on Bazeley's idea with joy, as the aircraft
were very cheap and the Royal Air Force would be relieved

from what was regarded as no more than a chore, but not a bit of it. Every objection was advanced against it: artillery officers could not be trained to the necessary standard of airmanship, the aircraft would all be shot down, and so on. 'Were these aircraft to be *armed*?' was a question revealing the Air Staff's fear that if the Army once got its hands on its own aircraft there would be a demand for more and better, the way opened for the resurrection of an Army air arm. (The objections, it must be understood, originated inside Army Co-operation Command, Royal Air Force: from the otherwise sympathetic Barratt himself.) In the end the Royal Air Force units were jointly manned by the Royal Artillery and the Royal Air Force and, an important concession, the pilots were all Royal Artillery officers remaining on the strength of the Army, and not seconded to the Royal Air Force for the duration of the war. They proved a great success in every theatre, confounding every hostile critic. Unfortunately, organised procrastination denied the Eighth Army their services in the desert, where they would have been invaluable. The first to see action were eight aircraft of 651 Squadron led by Bazeley himself in Tunisia in November 1942, and they were there only because of the insistence of Brigadier Parham, the Brigadier Royal Artillery, First Army, the innovator of rapid concentrations, himself an amateur pilot of the RA Flying Club and a strong supporter of Bazeley.[243]

The Air OP affair is of double interest. Artillery is as effective as its observation or target acquisition systems and the Air OPs increased that of the field and medium artillery by a factor difficult to quantify exactly but undoubtedly a large one. It also illustrates the deep prejudices and inter-service friction that had to be overcome by anyone attempting to organise 'army co-operation'. The only agreed doctrine for army/air co-operation, still taught at the Army Staff College in 1940, was the pre-war one. The army in the field would have direct control, but not command, of its tactical reconnaissance squadrons. Requests for all other tasks would be passed from army to air headquarters, where the Air Staff would study their feasibility and how they should be attacked. As a general rule the air force would not intervene on the battlefield except in a grave emergency; the boundary between the army and air spheres of operation being the limit of range of the army artillery.[244] This was the procedure in force governing the employment of the Air Component and British Air Forces France that Air Marshal Sir Arthur Barratt had found so unsatisfactory.

Barratt had a clear perception of the army's requirements, and his appointment as the Air Officer Commanding-in-Chief of the new Army Co-operation Command, formed in 1940, after he had returned from France, was fortunate. His task was not an easy one. Before the war 'Army Co-op' had not been a highly regarded activity, being confined to the 'Tac R' (reconnaissance) 'Arty R', (spotting for the guns), message dropping and snatching, and dropping small bombs or warning leaflets on recalcitrant tribesmen. New there were demands by the War Office for parachute training, transport aircraft, gliders, and aircraft to take the place of Lysanders. Above all there was the whole fraught question of direct offensive support for the army in the field, the provision of a suitable force and the formulation of the procedure for its control, all of which, whatever any diehards on the Air Staff may have felt, was inescapable. To this last and apparently intractable problem Barratt and his staff addressed themselves, and produced an outstandingly successful solution.

Unlike the reorganisation of the artillery control system which came about through individual effort and trial and error in different places and times, the army/air control system was created as a whole, by one man, as the result of logical analysis. When Barratt moved to his new command he took with him two army officers who had served him well in BAFF. One was Brigadier (now Lieutenant-General Sir John) Woodall. It was he who, assisted by Group Captain Wann, designed the scheme originally set out in what came to be known as the 'Wann-Woodall report'. Woodall not long afterwards left for other and higher appointments, leaving the work of realising the plan to his colleague, Brigadier C. C. Oxborrow, whose success in the task of explanation, persuasion and education of both sides in the art of army/air co-operation was such that he was kept at it for the rest of the war.

Woodall broke the problem down to four essentials. First there had to be an air formation suitably equipped and reserved for the direct support of an army in the field, but entirely under air force command. This had to be so because there were two separate but interconnected battles to be fought, apart from long range action against the enemy base and lines of communication. One was to shield the army from enemy air attack, which could not be done by providing constant fighter cover above it, an impractical method which for a time obsessed army officers, but by offensive action often out of the Army's sight altogether. The other was to bring the awe-inspiring weight of airborne fire-power to bear on the battlefield itself, closely co-ordinated with the Army's ground operations.

Second, there had to be a specially trained Army staff able to explain the air force method of operation and its limitations to the soldiers, and the army method of operation and the army's plan and situation to the pilots who were to fly the missions. This already existed in the form of 'Air liaison officers' or ALOs.

Third, there had to be a joint command post or control centre staffed by army and air officers.

Fourth, and this was central to the whole plan, there had to be a communication network linking the control centre directly to the 'clients', wherever they were, so that a brigade headquarters, for instance, could pass its request without going through the chain of command, and another connecting the control centre directly to the airfields, where ALOs with access to it, were positioned.

In practice the headquarters of the army and the 'Tactical Air Force', as the special forces were to be designated, were eventually co-located, and the control centre (the Army Air Control Centre, or AACC) was in a group of caravans drawn up in a quadrangle connected by telephone to each, with its own display charts of operational readiness and situation maps. The essence of the scheme lay in the structure of the communication nets. At all the headquarters in an army there was an outstation, complete with Royal Corps of Signals operators and a staff officer trained in air support, called a 'tentacle'. (A nickname, from the appearance of the net which became the official term.)

All the tentacles in each division were on a common frequency and, as can be seen from the net diagram, one from each division was positioned at corps headquarters. This enabled every interested party to be simultaneously informed and, if absolutely necessary, allowed him to object, on the grounds of duplication or troop safety for instance. Otherwise the staff at intermediate levels remained silent. Strictly speaking, final authority for answering the call for an air strike rested jointly with the army Chief of Staff and the Royal Air Force Group Senior Air Staff Officer, but in practice the decision was left to the control centre, where the request was checked against the situation on the map and the 'bomb-line' – the line, adjusted from day to day and based usually on some physical feature easily identifiable from the air, forward of which it was safe to attack enemy targets – squadrons allocated by the air side and army ALOs alerted at airfields to be ready to brief the pilots. There was simply not the time in modern battle for prolonged discussion, and even if there had to be reference back the speed of response was kept high by observing the basic staff principle of simultaneous preparatory work at all levels in anticipation of a decision.

The tentacles providing the communications were grouped into independent special units. These were first called 'Close

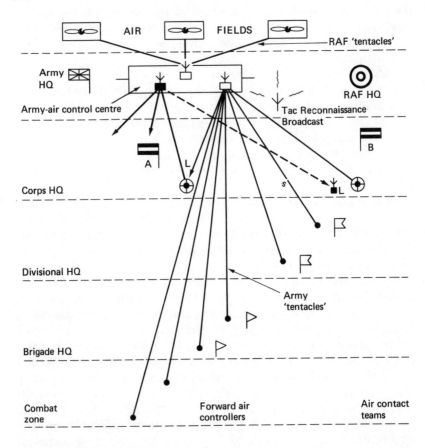

13.   *ASSU communication di.. .m. Note that all radio stations in one corps*
      and the tentacles (L) at the other corps HQ are on one frequency, so every
      HQ is simultaneously informed, and all have direct access to RAF
      reconnaissance results.

Support Bomber Control', then 'Army Air Support Control', to
be deployed on the scale of one per corps. They were mixed with
the signals operators from the Royal Corps of Signals and the
Air Liaison Officers from any arm or regiment. The liaison
officers in command of the tentacles were first discarded (it being
found that the Royal Signals sergeants could manage them satisfactorily) and in 1944 all the ALOs were removed, the whole
responsibility for operation transferred to the Royal Corps of
Signals and the units retitled 'Air Support Signals Units' (ASSUs).
The ALOs on the army side without changing position became
part of the 'G' (Operations) staff. There was a GSOI (Air) at
army headquarters, and a GSO2 at each Corps. Below this air
matters were the responsibility of the ordinary 'G' (Ops) staff.

Later refinements were the addition of special tentacles equipped with suitable radio sets for voice communication with aircraft in flight, 'Air Contact Teams' (ACTs) used to put out ground markers (flares, coloured smoke or strips laid out as arrows or letters) to indicate the position of friendly troops, and *Forward Control Posts* (FCPs). These last included an air force pilot (the *Forward Air Controller*, or FAC) and worked in the front line. They directed aircraft on to targets using the terms one pilot would use to another. As soon as returning reconnaissance pilots had been debriefed, a summary of their reports known as the 'Tac R' broadcast, was transmitted on a special frequency and picked up by the tentacles, and so reached all the interested headquarters without delay. Otherwise the Woodall system, soon to be put to the test in the desert, remained unchanged throughout the war and was copied almost exactly by the United States Army Air Force.

By 1943 the torch had passed from Woodall's hand, as he left on promotion, but not before the framework of the system had been constructed and the nucleus of what was to become the famous and immensely powerful 2nd Tactical Air Force was in being and exercising regularly with the Army. Brigadier Oxborrow took his place, to be joined by the third most important army figure in the history of air co-operation, Lieutenant-Colonel C. E. Carrington, whose intellect and powers of exposition were brought to bear on propagating the gospel of co-operation (Carrington is the author of a classic work describing the infantry experience on the Western Front, and was later to become the distinguished student and biographer of Rudyard Kipling.)[245] In October 1942 Oxborrow and he demonstrated the Woodall system and the working of a control centre to a number of high personages, and obtained the final seal of approval. Carrington wrote the two War Office pamphlets which were to be the guidelines on the subject for many years: *Army/ Air Co-operation*, No. 1, *General Principles and Organization* (March 1944) and No. 2, *Direct Support*, (April 1944).

While all this good work was going forward an AASC had been sent to Africa to gain experience. One of Woodall's far-sighted moves had been to insist on forging the tentacles into proper units with their own esprit de corps, and with the best officers he could obtain who would be able to train them, and also possess the necessary tact and firmness to educate the generals in their use. (It would have been too easy simply to have increased the establishment of formations to include the sets and operators, where they would have certainly been misused, misappropriated or used according to the commanders' own ideas.) Major (now Major-General) J. M. McNeill was, like Woodall, a Royal Artillery officer and late of the Royal Horse Artillery, who was also to spend his war in the vital field of air co-operation. He was appointed on emerging from a Camberley Short War Course in 1940, somewhat to his surprise, as he had no special qualifications except the fortuitous one that he had been the Royal Artillery instructor at the School of Signals and so was at home with signals matters. He was presented with a copy of the recently approved 'establishment' by Woodall, another artilleryman, and ordered to raise and train the new unit to 'Royal Horse Artillery standards'. This he did, beginning by sending out his subaltern officers, as they joined, to the ordnance depots with orders not to return until they had acquired every specified item of equipment in the table of organisation. It was the fashion then for formations to identify themselves by quasi-heraldic emblems painted on the vehicles. Inspired by his patronymic and the country in which the unit was raised he appropriated the Red Hand of Ulster. (A genuine piece of heraldry, as opposed to the curious animals and objects in most formation signs.)

McNeill and No. 2 AASC arrived in Africa in December 1941 and was sent up to the desert to attach himself to the XIII Corps, by then occupying the northern sector of the Gazala line, the misconceived and ill-fated system of isolated brigade localities marking the limit of the gains of the CRUSADER offensive. It had been planned as a jumping off line for the next Eighth Army offensive and a protective belt for the forward airfields and the numerous supply dumps being prepared in anticipation. Then, in May 1942, Rommel reopened the fighting before his opponent was ready. No more inauspicious test-bed for the Woodall system could have been chosen. The machinery was incomplete. There was no control centre, only the core of the system had been set up, and the rearward or RAF network of tentacles to the airfields did not exist except in rudimentary form. Most of the action took place in XXX Corps' sector, and the fighting there was extraordinarily confused. Brigades were overrun, generals captured, headquarters put to flight and as the Gazala defences collapsed the Desert Air Force had to leave its forward airfields and pull back to Egypt. The two sides were so intermingled that drawing bomb-lines and target recognition from the air was difficult and often impossible. As a result many rewarding targets went unpunished by air attack. Nevertheless, when it was possible to use the AASC channels the time of response, from first call to aircraft over target, was reduced from the two hours it had averaged during the CRUSADER battles to thirty minutes.[246]

It had been a valuable if exciting experience for the new unit, and once the situation had been stabilised at El Alamein it was possible for McNeill to take stock. The original idea had been to have a separate network of tentacles for each corps, but it seemed clear that it should be based on army headquarters, and that the control centre should be there. In any case it was sounder for the Desert Air Force, the equivalent of an RAF Group, to be controlled centrally, throwing its full weight on any corps front as appropriate. The reorganisation was greatly assisted by the arrival of General Montgomery in command of the Eighth Army. He was a firm believer in Army/Air co-operation and had been closely involved with its development in England. One of his first actions was to move Eighth Army headquarters to a new site chosen with the agreement of Air Vice-Marshal Coningham, who also moved his own headquarters there, which allowed the control centre to be in close touch with both the army and the air staff. The complete system was then built up in time for Montgomery's first battle, at Alam el Halfa.

The defensive battle of Alam el Halfa was won by the army holding its ground while its artillery and the Desert Air Force destroyed the enemy. The panzer columns were bombed, for the first time, by night and day; the targets being illuminated and identified by relays of Albacore aircraft dropping flares. McNeill, to obtain the airman's point of view, flew in one such sortie and took away a lasting impression of the long dense columns of the panzer army, pausing and closing up to negotiate the gaps their pioneers had made in the British minefields; 'just like a column of ants when they come up against an obstacle.' Alam el Halfa was a premeditated and carefully planned defensive battle. What is known variously as the battle of El Hamma, the Tebaga Gap or the 'left hook at Mareth' is a perfect example of the use of air power to support an attack.

When the Eighth Army resumed its advance in Tunisia after the battle of Medenine it was faced by a strong Axis position at Mareth, a fortified line with one flank on the sea and the other protected by a barrier of sandy desert and rocky hills, believed impassable to a mechanised army. British reconnaissance, however, discovered a possible route, although a very difficult one, leading round its right or inland flank to a pass in the hills – the 'Tebaga Gap' – and so to good tank country around the town of El Hamma in the rear of the Mareth Line. Montgomery decided to make the main attack frontally, and to send the 4th Indian Division to work on foot through the hills, and the 2nd New Zealand Division, reinforced by the British 8th Armoured

Brigade, to cross the desert and force the Tebaga Gap. Both these flank attacks were intended purely as diversions. The New Zealand commander, Lieutenant-General Freyberg, reached the gap but was held up there by the German 21st Panzer and 164th Infantry Divisions, both reduced to a fraction of their former strength by this date, but still capable of skilled and determined resistance. Conscious of the need to avoid unnecessary New Zealand casualties, he did not press an attack intended as a feint; he had played his part by attracting the Axis reserves, and so remained inactive where he was.

By 23 March the frontal attack had failed beyond redemption and Montgomery decided to shift his weight to the left. He sent the 1st Armoured Division to reinforce Freyberg, and Lieutenant-General Horrocks with his X Corps Headquarters to take all under command, with orders to break through the Tebaga Gap and encircle the Mareth position. Speed was essential, but it took the 1st Armoured Division until the 26th to struggle through the sand. Some of its wheeled artillery batteries toiling in the rear reached their positions only just in time to lay out the lines of fire, be handed the gun programmes for the Corps artillery fire-plan prepared already by the artillery advance parties, and be ready by H-hour to support the attack.

Horrocks, aware that if he failed the Eighth Army had failed, made a bold plan and attacked at the earliest moment possible – 4 p.m. on the 26th. The 8th Armoured Brigade was to lead the attack with orders to press on through the enemy position until nightfall, disregarding any resistance it could not crush itself and leave it to the New Zealand infantry following behind. In the meantime the 1st Armoured Division, accompanied by Horrocks and a small tactical headquarters, waited formed up in a solid phalanx with orders to advance, as soon as the moon rose, through the line secured by the New Zealanders and to drive on through the night to El Hamma, until daylight saw it out in the clear on the plain.

The artillery programme to cover the advance was fired by the three New Zealand field regiments, two Royal Horse Artillery regiments, a reserve field regiment and two medium regiments, altogether 144 25-pounders, sixteen 4.5-inch and sixteen 5.5-inch guns. Part of the programme was a thin creeping barrage, the shell bursts placed at hundred yard intervals, not intended to damage, but to create a line of dust and smoke to serve as a moving 'bomb-line' for the Desert Air Force.

By this time the Desert Air Force was commanded by Air Vice-Marshal (now Air Chief Marshal Sir Harry) Broadhurst, promoted to command from the appointment of its Senior Air

Staff Officer. He was an officer with the whole subject of air support for the army at his fingertips and an enthusiastic practitioner of the art. (His career continued to be linked with Montgomery and Horrocks, and he was to command the immensely powerful No. 83 Group RAF of 2nd RAF in support of the Second Army from the Normandy landings to the end of the war.) Broadhurst recalls that he had been repeatedly teased by Major-General de Guingand, Montgomery's Chief-of-Staff, over the exaggerated claims made by the Desert Air Force. Ground reconnaissance by the army showed significantly fewer wrecks than the results of debriefing. Broadhurst took all this in good part, but seriously. He was a great believer in accuracy of bombing and, as opportunity offered, he took his squadrons out of operations for some realistic training. Captured Axis vehicles and tanks provided by the army were set out in tactical dispositions, the aircraft being exercised were summoned through the AASC net and controlled by some of his own most experienced pilots in the new Forward Control Posts. Target recognition and accuracy was obviously easier at low altitude, and Broadhurst insisted that all attacks were to be made at very low level; so low in fact that Tedder, when he heard of it was alarmed and his former chief, Coningham both signalled him and sent his own chief staff officer to warn of the dangers he was incurring and how heavy his casualties were likely to be. (Coningham and Tedder had both moved out of the Middle East to General Eisenhower's command, where they were busy setting up a tactical air force.)

The air support plan demonstrated the Woodall system in its final, perfected form, and the closest integration between the air and the ground forces so far seen. The Desert Air Force had been largely reinforced and re-equipped. Broadhurst was able to dispose of three squadrons of twin-engined light bombers and no fewer than sixteen of American 'Kittybombers' (fighter-bombers). In addition he had five squadrons of Spitfire IXs for air control – freedom from interference by the Luftwaffe being, of course, a sine qua non of such ground-air operations – and a novelty in the shape of a 'tank-buster' squadron of Hurricanes armed with two 40-mm Vickers light anti-aircraft guns. (These were effective but awkward to fly, and the next and even more effective step in the air versus tank contest was the use of air-to-ground 5-inch rockets.) Some of the most experienced pilots in the Desert Air Force accompanied the tanks of the 8th Armoured Brigade as FACs, and another innovation was a 'flying FAC' able to monitor the whole battle.

The first phase of the plan was a softening-up programme

while X Corps completed its assembly and preparations. In the second the fighter-bombers scoured the ground ahead of the advancing tanks from H-hour until the light failed, swooping on demand on to any centre of resistance that came to life. Casualties proved mercifully light for, as any anti-aircraft gunner could have informed the doubters, a fighter-bomber tearing along at 'zero feet' is the most difficult and disconcerting of targets. Few aircraft were lost, and most of the pilots were picked up safely by the advancing troops. (A forced landing in the desert was relatively simple which was not the case in Europe.)

The attack was a complete success. There were some exciting incidents on 27 March, when the remnants of the defenders found themselves retreating in parallel and in company with the main body of the 1st Armoured Division as it went pelting along. Some unusual combats took place between fleeing panzers and Royal Artillery anti-tank guns, whose 'Number Ones' (the gun sergeants), not content to remain screening the flanks, limbered up to pursue and actually succeeded in shooting up some tanks, but the gallant von Liebenstein rallied enough troops to establish a gun line and hold off the threat of complete encirclement. All the same, the Horrocks-Broadhurst operation levered the Axis forces out of the Mareth Line and they were once more in full retreat.[247]

This is the first recorded use of FACs in battle. Later in 1943 when Wingate's 'Special Force', the Chindits, were being assembled and trained in India, Squadron-Leader R. (now Sir Robert) Thompson pressed for pilots to be attached to the Chindit columns to direct the attacks of United States No. 1 Air Commando, and such Royal Air Force squadrons as were allotted for support. There was no tentacle organisation or AACC; simply a direct radio link from the columns inside Burma to the airfields on which the Air Commando was based. The first strike was made by a Royal Air Force squadron in support of the 77th Brigade in March 1944. The Chindits had no artillery bigger than a 3-inch mortar, and depended entirely on the air for fire-power. In Burma the British and American pilots brought close, direct support to a fine art.[248]

Broadhurst and Horrocks planned the final breakthrough in Tunisia using similar methods on an even larger scale, described by the war correspondents as a 'Tedder Carpet', much to Broadhurst's amusement.

So, by the end of the war in Africa the whole vexed problem of air support for the army had been satisfactorily solved, a damaging difference of opinion between the two services settled, and the army provided with a weapon without which its future successes would not have been possible. Curiously, the actual nature of the solution seems to have escaped Tedder, a man normally alert to technical developments. All that he says in his memoirs is that the army had improved its signalling and introduced an 'operations room' on the air force model, and that the new army instructions on the subject had probably been drafted by Coningham.[249] In fact a training pamphlet, *Direct Air Support* (undated but probably drafted late in 1942 and issued in March 1943), was issued jointly by the army and Headquarters Royal Air Force Middle East, but bears evidence of army authorship. The importance that the army attached to the subject is shown by the issue shortly afterwards of another pamphlet, *The Employment of Air Forces in Support of Land Operations*, by 15th Army Group, with an introduction ordering that it was 'to be read by all ranks', over the facsimile signature of General Sir Harold Alexander.[250]

It might have been thought that no branch of the army had greater need of direct air support than the airborne forces, and if that is so and had not been immediately apparent the operational reports from South-East Asia on the second Chindit operation would have made the point clear. (In fact, the formal report was not published until 1945, but the facts should have been known in England well before September 1944.) The whole of the Arnhem phase of the MARKET GARDEN operation remains a tragic example of hasty planning and mismanagement, of which the failure to make satisfactory arrangements for direct air support for the 1st Airborne Division was but a single factor, although an important one.

The basic cause may have been that the airborne units were not only a superior and peculiar race, set apart from the rest of the army, but they also remained outside the main stream of military experience. Compared with the seasoned formations from Africa and Italy, their staffs were young and inexperienced and their staff work chaotic.[251] All that is as may be. The facts are as follows, and remain an awful warning.

Colonel Carrington recalls visiting General F. A. M. Browning and explaining the Woodall system, but no action to produce an airborne ASSU or FACs was taken. A staff officer from the 1st Airborne Division was sent to Normandy to learn how air support was arranged, and nothing resulted from that either.[252] The result was that the First Allied Airborne Army had no ASSU and no training in army/air co-operation; indeed, there is a strong presumption that neither the air forces concerned nor the airborne troops knew that such arrangements existed, or if they did, what they were. MARKET, the airborne phase of the operation, was planned in England, and involved three, or in fact, four headquarters: the Airborne Army, I British Airborne Corps, the United States Army Air Force Troop Carrier Command (which, together with Nos. 38 and 46 RAF Groups, was responsible for delivering the airborne troops to their objectives) and the United States 8th Air Force, which had no experience of ground support or familiarity with conditions in the chosen battle area. GARDEN was the ground operation of the British Second Army, led by General Horrocks' XXX Corps, supported by No. 83 Group of 2nd TAF. The airborne forces were to become part of GARDEN as they landed and their direct air support would be provided by Broadhurst, who could call at the shortest notice on 2nd TAF for extra support.

For some reason the two operations were planned separately, without any co-ordinating higher headquarters or arrangements for liaison. No one thought of consulting Oxborrow or McNeill at Headquarters 21st Army Group, and Broadhurst himself was informed of the details of the GARDEN plan only twenty-four hours in advance. It would have been perfectly possible to include some FACs equipped to communicate with No. 83 Group in the gliders destined for Arnhem (as was done the following year in VARSITY, the airborne part of the Rhine crossing), but instead some American air contact teams were attached to the British 1st Airborne Division, but those not lost during the fly-in proved hopelessly untrained, and a failure.[253] The only air support arranged by 8th Air Force was a preliminary bombardment of the German flak batteries along the route of the fly-in.

The lack of full ASSU communications could have been overcome, had it not been for the disastrous decision, taken in England by Headquarters which was wholly out of touch, to ban intervention by No. 83 Group during the period when the 1st Airborne Division was fighting for its life against the 9th and 10th SS Panzer Divisions. The communications of the 1st Airborne Division had completely broken down, but Broadhurst was well aware of what was happening through the 'Y' (army radio intercept service) monitoring the German transmissions, and he kept his Typhoons armed and ready with their tank-busting rockets, but to no avail. 'All our pleadings and protests' were disregarded until it was too late, said Broadhurst.[254] How matters would have turned out had he been given a free hand it is impossible to say, but at least he could have slowed down the panzer attacks and help to prolong the resistance of 1st Airborne Division. Major-General R. E. Urquhart in his own account, published fourteen years later, says rather helplessly that 'no direct signals link had been arranged' and that the absence of the Tactical Air Force was 'inexplicable'.[255] It remains a mysterious affair.

Arnhem was a special case, but the failure there illustrates a general principle to which we shall refer again when the heavy bombers of the strategic air force became involved in the battle on the ground. Co-operation of any kind, whether between artillery and infantry, tanks and infantry or air forces and the army is a slow-growing and delicate plant, requiring time, much good will, regular human contact and careful training. It is a mood, not to be conjured into existence by decree or at a moment's notice. Without it the most elaborate and sophisticated cybernetic machine is not of the slightest use.

Fire-Plan Statistics:
1940–1945

C HAPTER 5 described how the circumstances of the Western Front dictated the increasing weight and complexity of artillery fire-plans required to break into modern defensive positions, and Chapter 13 how the circumstances of the Western Desert misled some British commanders into reversing every sound principle of artillery employment, and indeed of tactics generally. This period ended in September and the return to better methods is marked by the battle of El Alamein in October, 1942.

Apart from this disastrous interregnum the history of fire-power in the Second World War followed the pattern of the First World War, but fortunately without the need to rediscover the methods worked out with so much pain and labour in 1915–17. They had been carefully preserved by the Royal Artillery, for which it can thank the successive commandants of its School, who refused to be seduced by any of the inter-war heresies, and were ready for use when the occasion demanded.[256] One of the most remarkable and unregarded feats of the artillery of the Eighth Army was to produce the Alamein fire-plans without a hitch or mistake after some eighteen months of motoring about the desert in independent troops, as it is only too easy to lose the knack of such detailed processes if they are not regularly exercised.

It would be otiose to describe every successful fire-plan between October, 1942 and the Combined Fire-Plan for D-day of the invasion of Normandy in full, because they only differed in matters of technical gunnery. The artillery statistics of the following engagements are the landmarks on the route leading from the early successes against the Italians to D-day, when the problems of an amphibious assault on a coastal fortress system demanded a completely fresh approach.

Attack on Nibeiwa and Tummar West Camp, 9 December 1940

A simple programme of timed concentrations fired by 25-pounders, 56; 60-pounders Mark II, 8; 6-inch howitzers, 8. Ammunition available, 42,272 all natures.

Bardia, 19 January 1941

As above, with 122 guns of all natures and 36,000 rounds available.

Tobruk, 21 January 1941

A well-thought-out fire-plan was made with four phases: 1. a four-day preliminary harassing bombardment by all the artillery, some warships and the Royal Air Force; 2. a preliminary counter-battery programme; 3. a programme of timed concentrations and a barrage; 4. a reversion to counter-battery fire once the perimeter of the defences had been successfully crossed by the tanks.

Keren, March 1941

Keren was a succession of small but bitter actions to force a long mountain pass against a tenacious opponent, by the 4th and 5th Indian divisions. No overall artillery commander (CCRA) was appointed, but the two CRAs co-operated perfectly, using their combined resources to support each division in turn. After a period of conventional mountain warfare to seize the peaks commanding the Dongolaas gorge leading to Keren had worn down the defenders the final and successful attack to capture the town was made along its floor behind a creeping barrage. The available artillery consisted of 92 guns and 110,000 rounds were expended.

Sidi Omar, 22–28 November 1941

This was an attack on two Axis fortified localities made by a brigade of the 4th Indian Infantry Division during the CRUSADER operation, with a well-arranged fire-plan and tanks. (*See Notes from the Theatres of War*, Cyrenaica November–December, issued 7 March 1941, p. 20). Had the bad policy of dispersing the artillery to every quarter not been in fashion the artillery employed would not have been limited to a single regiment and the operation terminated promptly and with far fewer casualties.

ABERDEEN, 4–6 June 1942

ABERDEEN is the code name given to the counter-attack on the Axis forces temporarily trapped east of the British minefields. This was the only attempt to use massed artillery during the period of open desert warfare, and a total fiasco. Ninety-two 25-pounders were assembled to fire a preliminary bombardment at what was thought to be the Axis outer defensive lines, but there was no reconnaissance of the target area and in fact the bombardment fell on empty desert. In the subsequent counter-attack by the panzers the artillery gun line was overrun after a hard fight lasting all day in which the crews for the greater part died round their guns, but heroism was no consolation for the loss of 64 field guns, and some 100 anti-tank and light anti-aircraft guns. (See S. Bidwell, *Gunners at War*, pp. 169–73.)

Ruweisat, 7–8 July 1942

The Ruweisat ridge was a feature of the Alamein position, and gives its name to the first defensive battle there, fought under the direction of General Auchinleck. The western end of the ridge was held by the tenacity of a field regiment engaging tanks over open sights, while to the north Rommel's attempts to bypass it were halted by repeated and heavy concentrations of fire from three regiments of South African 25-pounders and a British medium regiment. This concentration was, possibly, fortuitous and due to the fact that the reinforcements available were mainly artillery and the battle was fought on a narrow front, rather than a deliberate change of policy.

Alam el Halfa, 30 August – 6 September

This was a successful defensive battle and the first fruits of the return to sound principles and the full use of the Army/Air control system. It was decided by the centralised control of the fire of 400 tanks, 300 infantry and artillery anti-tank guns, 256 field guns of all natures, and the sustained attacks of the Desert Air Force.

El Alamein, 25 October – 5 November 1942

This, like the great First World War battles, was a sequence of sub-battles, each with an elaborate fire-plan using two or three hundred guns. The Axis defensive layout was very similar to the depth system adopted by the Germans in 1917, with mines in place of belts of wire, anti-tank guns in place of machine-guns as the principal menace, and panzer divisions as the counter-attack force, in place of the infantry *eingriefdivisionen*. Artillery policy was laid down by Brigadier (later General Sir Sidney) Kirkman acting with the authority of General Montgomery, who had summoned him to fill the position of BRA Eighth Army. (Armies in the First World War had major-generals in this post.) Attempts on the part of the artillery commanders of armoured divisions to dissent from centralised control were firmly suppressed. The opening fire-plan employed 824 25-pounders and 48 medium guns, and very large amounts of ammunition were dumped. The 25-pounders alone fired some 1,008,500 rounds during the battle; the three medium regiments, 83,500.

Tunis, final attack. 6 May 1943

As soon as the position in Tunisia had stabilised after a bold advance to seize Tunis by coup de main had failed the First Army resorted to large scale fire-plans. In the final battle the fire-plan employed 444 guns on the narrow frontage of 3,000 yards and was augmented by 2,000 sorties by the tactical air forces.

ITALY

Italy with its mountains, narrow river valleys running across the axis of any advance from north to south and its stoutly built villages was ideally suited to a delaying retreat. In a manner reminiscent of the earlier war ambitious operations designed to launch armour through a gap foundered, and the campaign proved an affair of limited attacks and massive artillery bombardments. The mountain mass of *Monte Camino* (29 December 1943), for instance, a natural bastion of the German defensive line, was gradually reduced by patient infantry attacks on small objectives after they had been pounded by artillery fire. No fewer than 1,329 tons of ammunition were fired at four groups of targets in the first seventy-five minutes of the opening phase.

Attack on the Gustav Line, 11 May – 17 May 1944

The offensive against the Gustav Line was undertaken by the Polish Corps, to whom fell the honour of finally reducing the famous strong-point in the monastery of Monte Cassino, the French and the British XIII Corps, commanded by the then Lieutenant-General S. Kirkman. It was supported by the largest fire-plan fired in Italy and one of the largest in the war. The defences were immensely strong and the assembly areas exposed to observation from the mountains opposite, so to conceal them 800 tons of smoke material was discharged from generators and 135,000 smoke shells fired in five days. The total number of guns used, including 3.7-inch anti-aircraft used to intensify the counter-battery programme was 1,060. The ammunition dumped, but not necessarily fired was in rounds per gun: the Polish artillery, 25-pounder and 105-mm, 1,090; medium, 700, and XIII Corps sector: 25-pounder and 105-mm, 600; medium, 350; heavy, 200.

BURMA

The India-Burma theatre of operations resembled Italy but with a tropical climate. Mountains covered with dense forest alternated with stretches of dry scrub. It seemed an unsuitable terrain in which to deploy massed artillery. Moreover, as the defensive practice of the Japanese was to hold to the bitter end 'bunkers' proof against anything less than a direct hit by a 5.5-inch shell or an armour-piercing shot, fire-plans based on neutralisation seemed unprofitable. Destructive shoots, some-times by single guns being pushed up to engage strong-points at point blank range was often the only effective way to use artillery. Nevertheless, as the CCRA of IV Corps reported (quoted in Pemberton, p. 313), 'the impact of 100 bombers, 100 or so guns, eighty 3-inch mortars and 100 tanks followed up by well-trained, determined infantry was too much even for the most fanatical and determined foe in his village positions.'

Crossing of the Irrawaddy, 12–13 February 1945

In a preliminary bombardment the Royal Air Force put down a carpet of bombs and incendiary material 2,000 yards square on the Japanese gun area. This was followed by an artillery counter-battery programme. To cover the crossing and expansion of the bridgehead the CCRA of XXXIII Corps formed a corps artillery group to support the successive assaults of the two divisions in the corps, made up of 25-pounders, 24; 105-mm self-propelled howitzers, 24; 5.5-inch, 12; 6-inch howitzers (the serviceable 6-inch 20 cwt of the previous war with short range but a formidable 100 pound shell), 8; 7.2-inch howitzers, 4 and 3.7-inch heavy anti-aircraft guns used as field artillery, 16. The fire of this group was switched to the support of either division, using the radio control system now universal throughout the Commonwealth forces.

CHAPTER 16

Ends and Means

*The general's skill lies in bringing his troops close
to the enemy without their being killed before
beginning the attack.*

Frederick the Great

So after much travail, many trials and many errors, the year
1944 saw the British in possession of a perfectly articulated
war machine, capable of dealing blows heavy enough to make
even German soldiers reel. In June it was to be put to the ultimate test. The invasion of Normandy was the most dangerous
and difficult operation ever attempted in the history of warfare.
From Louisburg, in the days of black powder and smooth-bore
artillery, down to Singapore, defended by modern guns fitted
with the most advanced fire-control systems, the proved strategy
was never to make a frontal attack on a coastal fortress, but to
go ashore elsewhere and attack its landward perimeter. Now the
whole Channel coast had been converted into what was virtually
a continuous fortress. General Sir Frederick Morgan, who planned
the operation, said in retrospect: 'The prospect of launching an
invasion out of England was little short of appalling. There was
no precedent in history for any such thing that must of necessity
be attempted here.' Small wonder that the British high command
refused to consider launching it before the Allied forces were
strong enough and skilled enough, or that there were those who
had the gravest doubts about attempting it at all.

These doubts were not confined to those in high places who
knew all the facts and upon whose shoulders rested the burden
of decision. The student body at the wartime Staff College at
Haifa was largely composed of young officers who had
experience of battle, a number of whom had already taken part
in the assault landings in Sicily and Salerno. They were perfectly
familiar with the technique and had worked out all the details in
many a paper exercise, but they certainly had no illusions about

the hazards of attempting the 'Atlantic Wall'. What they had heard about the Dieppe affair was hardly reassuring. All the same, as soldiers they were not nervous, and as emergent staff officers they knew that with adequate resources and good planning the most difficult obstacles could be overcome.

It was the custom at the British Staff Colleges for any student with special knowledge to speak on his topic. In January one such was an officer who had been intimately concerned with the planning of devices or weapons for breaching the Atlantic Wall. He knew his subject, he spoke well, and he had the close attention of a highly professional audience. His unfolding of the purely technical arrangements could only arouse confidence, but he concluded with rather a bad joke, aimed at the waverers. 'Well, gentlemen,' he said, 'There you are. Those are some of the factors in Operation BLOODBATH.' The reaction, in that particular audience, was significant. A collective shudder ran through it, followed by a low, wordless murmur, and then, instead of the usual buzz of conversation and lighting of pipes and cigarettes that preceded the general discussion, it remained silent and still.

Our reaction might have been even stronger had we known the closely guarded secrets of the invasion plan and the constraints within which it was made. Even had the approach been overland a defensive system like the Atlantic Wall would have been a tough proposition, comparable to the Axis defences at El Alamein, with the difference that the approach had to be by daylight over the open sea. A British planner would think in terms of five or six divisions whose whole force would be available at once, an American in nine or ten. But in the winter of 1944 the Germans assembled thirty divisions and some 1,400 armoured fighting vehicles to break through a fifty mile wide front in the Ardennes defended by five or six depleted or green American divisions and the Russians would have used some astronomical number of guns and tanks. The first wave of British and Canadian assault troops, on whose initial success the whole invasion plan rested, was limited by the number of available landing craft to five spearhead brigades, each of one battalion of tanks and two of infantry, which were to be landed at widely separated beaches along a twenty mile stretch of coast. (All the subsequent figures relate to the Canadian-British sector. The Americans faced the same type of defences and were subject to the same constraints.)[257]

The German defensive system was based on the principles developed in 1917; virtually a line of outposts backed by a main line of resistance supported by a mobile counter-attack force,

suitably modified for the defence of a coast line. Out at sea there
was a minefield and its landward edge was covered by fifteen
long range heavy batteries in steel and concrete emplacements.
(These, it will be understood, were 'coast defence', or anti-ship
guns, with the special fire-controls required to engage moving
targets, long regarded as the masters of naval guns firing from
unstable platforms.) The next belt of marine obstacles lay
between high and low watermark and consisted of steel
scaffolding with explosive devices attached. The beaches themselves were mined, and their exits blocked by wire and more
mines. Where there was no natural scarp or cliff an actual
concrete wall had been built. Behind this were more minefields
and an anti-tank ditch or system of ditches.

Only thirteen battalions had been allotted to the defence of
the British-Canadian sector, and only ten companies drawn from
them to beach defence, but they were well dug in or in the villas
and villages studding what was in peaceful times a holiday resort,
now converted into little forts.

The forward, or outpost line was thin in men but not short of
weapons. The beaches were swept by interlocking arcs of fire
from ninety 88-mm guns, fifty mortars and 500 machine-guns,
cunningly sited in enfilade and not easily spotted from seaward.
The main line of resistance consisted of a belt of strong points
manned by the balance of the infantry 1,000–1,500 yards inland,
covering more minefields and other obstacles and supported by
field artillery up to 150-mm calibre in gun-pits or concrete
shelters, all registered on the beaches. There was another
echelon of 88-mm anti-tank guns including thirty-eight of the
self-propelled armoured *panzerjagers*. Excluding the coast
artillery, the total number of guns was 260. A counter-attack
force of five panzer divisions, roughly equal in strength to the
five American, British and Canadian divisions to be landed on
D-day formed the mailed fist of the defence, poised to smash
any bridgehead before it could be hardened. This was the grim
military arithmetic faced by the invasion planners; only too
aware that a superiority of 4:1 is the least the attackers require at
the point of impact. They were cheered, however, by the great
truth that whatever advantages modern technology had conferred on the defence, technology could also take away.

The grand plan for NEPTUNE-OVERLORD was a master-
piece of staff work and technical and tactical ingenuity. A
deception plan concealed the choice of landing place and caused
four out of five of the panzer reserves to be held back from the
coast. The French resistance was alerted. In a month-long battle
the Luftwaffe was beaten into the ground and the whole French

railway system wrecked, isolating the invasion area, and the coast batteries all along the Channel coast regularly bombed. Three airborne divisions were to drop during the night before H-hour to protect the flanks of the seaborne landings. Amphibious battle tanks and specialised armoured vehicles for clearing mines and bridging the anti-tank ditches were to be the vanguard of the assault brigades. There still remained the problem of ferrying the assault units ashore in daylight and landing them unscathed, for the complex navigation and the business of breaching the wall and lifting the land mines could not be done in darkness. For this the planners contrived an operation gigantic in itself; the 'Combined Fire-Plan'.

Its first phase was a preliminary bombardment by heavy bombers of the Royal Air Force in which 500 tons of bombs were dropped on each of ten selected coast batteries. Channels were successfully swept through the deep sea minefield, and at daybreak ships of the Royal Navy steamed through to begin the second phase. Two battleships, a monitor, a gunboat and twelve cruisers, mounting a total of 115 guns of calibre from 5.25 to 15-inch anchored and began the task of silencing any coast batteries still active, their fire observed by pilots in Spitfires. Later, as the troops made progress inland they were able to switch their fire on to targets called for by specially equipped Royal Artillery observers trained to control naval gun fire. Thirty-two destroyers, variously armed with eight, six or four 4.7-inch and 4-inch guns cruised up and down closer inshore using direct fire in close support of the assault troops: a floating substitute for the divisional artillery. The third phase was another air attack, from fifteen to ten minutes before the landing craft were due to hit the beach, made by 1,000 United States heavy bombers on the main line of resistance across the whole Allied front.

For reasons of safety the naval guns had to stop firing on the beach defences while they were closed by the landing craft, and to bridge this gap eighty-one landing craft were converted to 'gunboats' by mounting on them every spare weapon in stock; naval 4.7-inch guns, 6 and 2-pounder anti-tank guns, 40-mm Bofors and mortars firing 60-pound bombs. These led the landing craft fleet and deluged the beach with fire. In the last few minutes twenty-two more craft armed with multi-barrel rocket launchers fired 20,000 5-inch rockets, and the specialised armour was to land closely followed by the infantry. In case there was any shortage of fire-power a Royal Marine bombardment group equipped with what sailors call a 'lash-up', self-propelled guns made by mounting 90-mm howitzers in obsolete tanks, were to join the army ashore.[258] The artillery of the assault divisions were equipped with the new self-propelled 25-pounders. These were to wait in their landing craft off the beaches until there was room for them to deploy. On the sound principle of never letting guns stand idle they were stowed in their craft so as to be able to fire broadsides and their Royal Artillery crews instructed in a rudimentary drill for shooting when afloat. History does not record whether they hit anything in particular, but some 200 guns firing 18,000 rounds into the 'brown' certainly added noise, smoke and terror to the suppressive effect of the final phase of that colossal bombardment.

Even this battering did not knock the fight out of all the allegedly 'second-rate' but brave German troops, though many were killed and wounded or simply but effectively stunned out of their wits. There was much hard fighting left to be done, and the ever more crowded beaches remained under indirect artillery fire for some hours. When the 25-pounders finally came ashore they went into action with the surf washing over their tracks. Yet, by nightfall all was well. Only on OMAHA beach had there been for some hours the kind of scene that had haunted the imagination of the timid and the resolute alike, but tragedy had been averted by the fire of the destroyers and American valour. There had been no massacres on the beaches, no dreadful repetitions of Tanga, Cape Helles or Dieppe. The British-Canadian casualties were mercifully light, 3,000, and the next day the battle to form a continuous bridgehead began.

Soon the armies had the direct support of the 2nd Tactical Air Force, a huge affair with no fewer than seventy-eight squadrons of the most up-to-date fighters, fighter-bombers and light bombers, together with a number of the Air OP squadrons. On 10 June three squadrons moved to France and operated from a strip only 1,000 yards from the front line. Air power had made the invasion possible and air power now helped to secure the bridgehead. The great panzer counter-attack never materialised. Rommel, who had the experience of fighting in an adverse air situation, not then shared so far by other German generals, would have broken up the panzer group and positioned the tanks where they could have intervened immediately, but he was overruled, except for one division, but that too proved ineffectual against the combination of artillery and aircraft.

The problem now facing the Allied commanders, and the 21st Army Group in particular, was quite a different manifestation of the tank. As the Germans were forced to turn from blitzkrieg to defensive warfare their tanks, following the natural history of weapons, had evolved into heavily armed and armoured tank-destroyers, proof against anything but a direct hit from a powerful anti-tank gun or a rocket, or heavy bombs and shells. The drives to break out of the bridgehead were met by successive cordons of infantry and anti-tank guns braced by a steel framework of Mark V Panthers and Mark VI Tigers, doubly protected by being dug into gun-pits, like artillery. Seen on an air photograph these defensive positions appeared to be no more than over-extended gun-lines, but this was in a way their strength, for there was little to hit and it was not easy to suppress the fire of the tanks – in effect, mobile pill boxes. It was difficult, if not impossible to dislodge them with infantry, and they out-gunned the Sherman and Cromwell tanks of the Allies. There was no room for manoeuvre and no time to waste. Once again the answer had to be attrition, in attack after attack, with yet more fire-power. Even the tactical air forces were insufficient, and it was necessary to invoke the heavy bombers of the Allied strategic air forces. They proved to be a far from perfect instrument, being designed for quite a different task and lacking the air/land control machinery now working so perfectly in the tactical groups. The pilots found it difficult to navigate to ill-defined military targets or to identify them if they arrived, and there was no ground to air communication, although the Royal Air Force adapted the 'OBOE' radio marker to indicate point of aim. Some costly errors were made, in particular by the United States bombers, who killed a number of their own troops, including a general. Nevertheless, without the aid of the heavy bombers the break-out would have been long delayed.

One example will suffice. On 8 August the Canadians devised fresh tactics to defeat the German tank-and-gun defence. The basic idea was to attack at night immediately after an air bombardment in the hope of penetrating the defences and beginning the 'dog-fight' while the defenders were still stunned and blinded by smoke and darkness. The novelty was that the whole attacking force was to be protected by armour, led by detachments of armoured engineers in flail tanks to deal with mines, tanks, and infantry in armoured carriers improvised from the hulls of self-propelled 25-pounders. The heavy bombers dropped 3,458 tons accurately on the defences in thirty minutes, and eight armoured columns advanced behind a fast barrage fired by 144 5.5-inch guns and 216 25-pounders. It was a bold move, and was rewarded with success, but, as had occurred so often in 1916–18 yet another defensive line was found 2,000–3,000 yards farther on and this one consisted of sixty tanks and ninety 88-mm guns, and the business of attrition had to be repeated.[259]

It seems strange that in 1980 an academic historian, and a distinguished one, can write: 'Virtually all British generals had a habit when they enjoyed a vast material superiority, of giving up military ingenuity and relying on crushing force applied in a somewhat unsubtle way,' adding '. . . that Montgomery's casualties at Alamein were actually higher, as a proportion of combatant strength, than Haig's on the Somme in 1916'.[260] (Whether this is to be read as a vindication of Haig or a condemnation of Montgomery is not clear.) But this was true of other generals and other armies. Even Patton, the American Murat, was forced to resort to the same methods when he came up to Metz and the Siegfried Line. As for the Russians, it seems strange that their generals have never attracted the same odium as the British, though they were still using the tactics of 1916 in 1944, with all the figures, casualties, numbers of guns and material resources multiplied by ten.

The generals of 1942–5 did not take long to discover that it was of little use to weave tactical arabesques round such soldiers as the Germans and Japanese. Tanks alone could no longer be used against an unshaken defence, and in spite of the growth in air-power and the gift of mobility conferred by armoured troops infantry, though so vulnerable, remained the most precious of military commodities. By 1945 even the mighty United States Army was running short of replacements. The generals, from Montgomery onward, together with his corps and army commanders, perceived that all their plans depended on protecting their infantry by one means or another until they were close enough to the enemy to use their own weapons. Their artillerymen, with almost unlimited resources, became adept at assembling a mass of guns, surveying them in, feeding them ammunition, digesting target intelligence and preparing the long and complicated fire-plans in such a form that by H-hour every 'Number One' (the sergeant commanding a gun) had in his hand a gun-programme detailing the range and bearing of every round his gun was to fire for the next two or three hours. All this was done at a speed that would have astonished the Kirke Committee.

The Royal Artillery commanders may well have been hippophil to a man, regrettably ignorant of any theories of war apart from those expressed in the Field Service Regulations (if they read at all they preferred Surtees to Liddell Hart, and *Horse and Hound* to the *Army Quarterly*) but they were practical men of strong common sense. Their motto, often on their lips, was 'shells save lives', and they considered it a professional crime to leave the infantry unsupported even for minutes, or leave a single piece of artillery standing idle during an attack. During the later stages of the war the new discipline of operational research, first used to evaluate aerial bombing and anti-submarine tactics, was applied to the less amenable and unquantifiable subject of land warfare. Using as a definition of intensity the parameter shells delivered per area per unit time connected with the rate of casualties of attackers and attacked, the somewhat obvious conclusions were reached concerning the weight of bombardment to an upper limit of usefulness; namely, the superior merits of a dense pattern of small shells to a fewer heavy shells or bombs, the brief duration of the stunning or 'neutralising effect', and that short bursts of intense fire were sometimes more effective than a prolonged bombardment. None of this was news to men who had been learning empirically for the previous two years. Nor was it an original thought that in the 'dog-fighting' inside the objective, enemy resistance could often be cleared up more expeditiously and economically by deft infantry action than by calling down huge concentrations. To be sure, but soldiers learn quickly, and the lesson most deeply ingrained in veterans is caution. On D-day the 1st South Lancashires had to clear up the combined strong-point and coast battery of La Brèche, which had been pounded by every weapon in the British armoury. It cost that fresh, well-trained and determined battalion thirteen officers (five killed) and ninety-six NCOs and rank and file. By November 1944 such sacrifices seemed unnecessary. When the weary and depleted 5th Dorsets were ordered to take the fortified village of Bauchem the CRA resorted to the methods of 1916 and preceded the time-programme with a four hour preliminary bombardment in which 1.8 tons per 100 yards square were delivered, followed more rapidly by another 149 tons. The Dorsets then rushed the village losing only seven men, four to their own artillery, so close were they to the bursts when it ceased.[261]

In 1945 Hitler's decision to defend the soil of the Reich west of the Rhine led to some of the hardest fighting in north-west Europe. Of the opening phase, led by XXX Corps, General Horrocks said later: 'There was no room for manoeuvre and no scope for cleverness. I had to blast my way through three defensive systems, the centre of which was the Siegfried Line.' The first, or outpost, line was held by the 84th Infantry Division, one of those 'low category' German formations composed of elderly or unfit men who so often disconcerted British intelligence assessments by their stout fighting in the defence. Horrocks' intention was to go through this in one rush, pause for a brief, close reconnaissance of the Siegfried Line, resume the attack at nightfall and secure a start-line for the next phase of the offensive, by the First Canadian Army, some 12,000 yards from his own. One thing he could not afford was a failure, for that would dislocate the whole army plan.

The artillery statistics of the fire-plan in support of operation VERITABLE are: 25-pounders, 576; 4.5 and 5.5-inch, 320; heavies, 155-mm, 7.2-inch, 8-inch and 240-mm, 82; twelve, 32-barrel rocket launchers: additional sources of fire-power; tanks with 75-mm guns, 60; 40-mm Bofors, 114; 3.7-inch anti-aircraft guns used as field artillery, 72; 17-pounder anti-tank guns, 24; .303 machine-guns, 188. Ammunition dumped in advance, approximately 11,000 tons; fired to support the break-in, 5,953 tons. German artillery supporting the 84th Division, 147 guns and howitzers. These were engaged in a preliminary bombardment by 616 guns; the average concentration, gun versus gun, was 20:1, the most intense 44:1. The front and flanks of the deep but narrow penetration were protected by smoke screens, one 8,000 yards long.[262]

In addition to this mass of artillery totalling 1,248 barrels, excluding the rocket-launchers and machine-guns, there was the invaluable assistance of the tactical air forces, the ASSUs by then employing further refinements such as artillery firing coloured smoke to indicate targets, and mobile radar control posts enabling targets to be attacked by night or through cloud.

This was no mindless regression to the methods of 1918, but the methods of 1918, themselves both scientific and effective, brought up to date, speeded up and made flexible. 'Every trick that had been learnt during the past two and a half years was brought into play, and several new ones added.' XXX Corps' casualties were light, and its advance was delayed by mud, floods and mines more than by the enemy, and by the evening of 9 February, D plus 1, Horrocks had fought, or 'blasted', his way through the Siegfried Line and was on his objectives. The casualties, excluding prisoners, of the 84th Division were also light; the operational research teams following up the battle estimated that only 3 per cent of the combat strength were casualties of the bombardment, but 'neutralisation' was complete. Fifty guns, about one third, were found damaged or abandoned intact in their pits. Headquarters were paralysed, communications cut, the defenders of strong-points stunned and driven into their shelters and best of all, the German officers and NCOs were prevented by the shell-storm from visiting their posts and cheering up their men.

It is strange that thirty years after those now remote battles the idea persists, and among men learned enough not to deceive themselves, that there is some elegant formula for the overthrow of a powerful opponent. The Allied war-machine in June 1944 was technically as great an improvement on the German combination of panzer divisions and air-power as that had been over the armies of 1918. The aim was to avoid unnecessary loss of life, and this vast expenditure of steel and high explosive had this supreme justification. The figures speak for themselves. The nine great battles in which Haig broke all German resistance between 8 August and 11 November 1918 cost the Australians, British and Canadians 3,645 casualties a day. (The 105 days of 'Passchendaele' cost 244,000, or 2,121 per day.) The battle of Normandy cost the 21st Army Group 1,333 casualties per day. Even so, with better shells, better fuzes, better target intelligence and better communications, the later war was not a cheap affair. The Reichswald battle, of which VERITABLE was the opening move, cost the First Canadian Army some 15,000 men. There was much talk before 1939 of the ability of air forces to overleap defences and avoid the slow battles of attrition on land, and there can be no doubt that the Allied air forces made the invasion of Normandy possible, but not without attrition. The same sort of battle took place, but several thousand feet above the ground. The cost for thirty-five days aerial fighting was 2,000 aircraft and 20,000 aircrew. As that redoubtable general of the First World War, General Mangin, once said: 'Quoi qu'on fasse, on perd beaucoup de monde.'[263] And casualty figures are absolute. It is not percentages that count, but the number of dead.

Epilogue

In March 1945 the British Second Army mounted the last great offensive battle it would ever fight – the passage of the Rhine. It committed five divisions, one airborne, supported by 706 guns and twelve thirty-barrel rocket launchers which fired 434,232 rounds. The fire-plan embodied every refinement, including a new departure in the form of a counter-battery programme intended to neutralise the anti-aircraft batteries before the arrival of the 6th Airborne Division. The direct air support was on the usual scale, and this time Broadhurst insisted on flying his Forward Air Controllers in the gliders of the airborne division. Ronald Lewin was to write of it later: 'Montgomery, the master-mathematician of the set-piece battle, had achieved a result which mathematicians, in their obscure calculations, describe as aesthetically elegant. Huge numbers of men, and much material, had produced a decisive result at small loss. Mass had not been wasted: there had been an economy of effort. By the 27th Montgomery was across the Rhine within a bridgehead 35 miles wide and 20 deep. The British Second Army had lost 3,968 casualties, and the Americans 2,813, but the lodgement was firm, and the prisoners taken were over 16,000.' 'The *Gotterdämmerung* was not ignoble,' Lewin added, referring not to the sordid and terrible end of the Third Reich, but to 'the last effective manifestation of such unquestionable power by the British'.[264]

The final rounds of battle, fired on 28 March, marked the end of an era. The technique had become obsolete. It was effective, but it was in a narrower sense inefficient. On the morning of D-day of the Normandy landings it had taken a cruiser 192 successive rounds to hit and silence one of the coast batteries. During the anti-flak programme which preceded the descent of the 6th Airborne Division beyond the Rhine 440 tons of artillery ammunition were fired at the anti-aircraft guns on the far bank, and the tactical air forces dropped *500 tons on each battery*, with the net result that only one bomb landed in a gun-pit. As Pemberton remarked: 'It might be questioned whether artillery preparations were not reaching uneconomical proportions.'[265] But that was not the main point. Britain would never again have the industrial and economic resources to engage in war on such a scale, even if there were not some more effective way to wage it. At first sight battlefield nuclear weapons seemed to promise an impregnable defence, and there was a rush to dismantle the conventional forces, but the briefest analysis revealed that to resort to such terrible weapons would be suicidal and should be reserved as the ultimate deterrent. A sane defence policy demanded powerful orthodox forces equipped with conventional fire-power.

In the meantime the British Army had undertaken the retreat from Empire terminating in the long drawn-out conflict in Ireland. Far from having been relieved of the need to prepare for both continental and imperial wars, as it had had to before 1914, both commitments continued in new forms. Yet it must be observed that the British Army was better prepared to deal with the vexations and conflicting demands that those commitments placed upon it. Its officers were not cynical and yawning with boredom, as they had been in the 1930s. The post-war breed, tempered by war and confronted with half-a-dozen military emergencies, and with clearly defined missions, were far more professional and ambitious than before the war. The professional journals regained the importance they had had between 1906 and 1914. Significantly, the Training directorate began to publish its own *British Army Review*, a forum for young officers. More important, the new establishments, of which general staff officers like James Edmonds had only dreamed in 1914, came into existence to provide a brain, a stream of ideas and a structure of inter-communicating agencies.

Liddell Hart's recommendation that a branch of the staff without any routine responsibilities be set up to consider the lessons of past operations and the impact of new weapon technology on future ones was more than fulfilled, although the historical dimension continued to be neglected. During the war the new technique of 'operational research', or 'operational analysis', mathematical in its approach, was applied first to naval and air force problems, and later to land warfare, growing into something far more elaborate than the simple 'think-tank' he had suggested. The Army now has arms directors, tactical employment wings at the great arms schools, the Royal Armaments Research and Development Establishment, the Defence Operational Analysis Establishment, and in the Ministry of Defence there is the old Training directorate and the new directorate for Combat Development. If anything the flow is too much with occasionally conflicting voices, so in 1980 the post of Director-General of Training was established to act as an overlord. This apparatus ensured that the Army had a clear idea of the nature of modern warfare, of its opponent and his tactics, and the most economical way to deploy its resources.

Indeed, it may be thought that the modernisation of the Army would have been guided if not by ideal solutions, at least by rational matching of resources to the most likely and greatest threat. This has not been achieved even remotely. The long road from the 1950s to 1974–5 is littered with the blueprints and prototypes of wonder weapons discarded for lack of money. The basic fighting formation of the Army, the division – the brick of which the Expeditionary Force of 1914 had been constructed, and defined as the smallest unit containing all the arms and resources required for sustained fighting – has undergone six reorganisations since 1945. None, except possibly the last, has betrayed any evidence of rational analysis and all reveal the British Army disease of semantic confusion and addiction to 'words of power': 'battle group', 'combat team'. There came in succession a post-war armoured and infantry division, each very powerful and reflecting the experience of the last two years of war; the abolition of the armoured division in all but name in favour of a strong armoured brigade group and an infantry division including its own tanks; the abolition of the division itself, except as a directing headquarters for a number of *brigade-groups*, the divisional artillery being abolished and the CRA being only narrowly saved, in a re-run of the attempted reorganisation in Africa in 1942. This proved unworkable and the division was restored, only to be drastically altered in the reorganisation ordered by the Labour government in 1974. On that occasion the *brigade* was abolished.[266]

In 1981 there was a return to the previous organisation.

Nothing illustrates better the confusion about the nature of modern warfare than continual changes in the organisation of the division. But all this confusion may be facilely explained by the conflicting needs of low intensity conflict and NATO, the restrictions of finance, the competition between the services and the rate of technological change. Yet the German army, like the Soviet army, despite all the traumatic events that were inflicted on it from 1910 to the present day, possesses a consistent doctrine derived from a continual rigorous analysis of its past experience. It is a professional body, not a number of loosely co-ordinated social groups which mirror the views of the society from which they derive their attitudes to military problems, as is still the case in the British Army. For example, no explanation has been offered for the present imbalance between the three arms, other than it represents the outcome of the last struggle for existence between these groups. The British Army is not an institution able to express views and to propose decisions on professional grounds alone, allowing the politicians both the right and the responsibility of disposal. To that extent, despite its achievements and reforms since 1906, the Army remains what it was then, *sans* doctrine and an unprofessional coalition of arms and services.

Fredericton, New Brunswick
and Wickham Market, Suffolk,
February, 1981

Notes

PROLOGUE

1 'The British Army and the modern conception of warfare', reprinted from *The Edinburgh Review* in *The RUSI Journal*, Vol. 55, September, 1911, p. 1181.
2 Brian Bond, *British Military Policy between the Two World Wars* (Oxford, Clarendon Press, 1980), p. 2.

CHAPTER 1

3 The reported comment of a German Great General Staff writer in 'The British Army and modern conceptions of war', reprinted from *The Edinburgh Review* in The *RUSI Journal*, Vol. 55, September 1911, p. 1181.
4 The material on artillery tactics and technology between 1904 and 1914 is contained in numerous articles in the *Journal of the Royal Artillery* and the *Journal of the Royal United Services Institution* (*RAJ* and *RUSI*) during those years and after 1918; Sir John Headlam's, *The History of the Royal Artillery*, Volume II, (1899–1914); and, in particular the following articles: Captain B. Vincent, 'Artillery in the Manchurian Campaign', *RUSI*, Vol. 52, 1908; Major R. H. Hare, 'The new shooting regulations in the German field artillery', and Lieutenant J. H. Marshall-Cornwall, 'The organisation and tactics of the French field artillery' both in *RAJ*, Vol. 38, 1911; H. W. Wynter, 'A comparison of British, French and German methods . . .', *RAJ*, Vol. 39, 1912. See also Philip Towle, 'The Russo-Japanese War in British military thought', *RUSI*, Vol. 116, 1971.
5 Lieutenant-General Sir John du Cane commanded XV Corps, and became senior liaison officer at Versailles in 1918: Sir William Furse commanded 9th Scottish Division on the Somme and succeeded Sir Stanley von Donop as Master-General of the Ordnance in 1916.
6 The Staff College Library, Camberley. *Minutes of the General Staff Conference of 1911.*
7 Du Cane took Kiggell's case apart in more detail in 'The co-operation of field artillery with infantry in the assault', *Army Review*, Vol. 1, July 1911, p. 97. In it he offered the battle of Taschichiao as an example of Russian indirect fire driving off Japanese infantry.
8 A semi-concealed position was one which allowed the enemy to see smoke, dust or the flash of the gun but not the gun itself. In flat or wooded country such positions were often not to be found.
9 Quoted by Lieutenant-Colonel A. F. Brooke, the future CIGS, in Part I of a series of articles 'The evolution of artillery', *Royal Artillery Journal*, Vol. 51, January 1925.
10 Later Lieutenant-General Sir Alexander H. Gordon commander IX Corps at Messines and during the offensives of 1918.
11 A Jewish officer was found guilty of selling military secrets to the Germans and sent to Devil's Island. After a long political storm an aristocrat turned out to be the culprit and Dreyfus was exonerated. The Army's class prejudice, anti-Semitism and system of justice were exposed and its confidence undermined.
12 But a survey reported in the *RUSI* Journal found that few poilus knew or cared anything about Alsace or Lorraine, the provinces lost in 1870 to Germany, when they entered the Army, so perhaps they needed political training.
13 The French recognised that southern Belgium would be invaded. The surprise was the width of the turning movement and its weight.
14 Comparative Divisional artillery strengths: French; German; British; 36 × 75-mm

guns versus 54 × 77-mm guns and 18 × 105-mm howitzers versus 54 × 18-pounder guns, 18 × 4.5-inch howitzers, 4 × 60-pounder heavy guns. Available from Corps artillery: 48 × 75-mm guns versus 12 × 150-mm howitzers versus nil. The British mobilized 24 × 6-inch howitzers, the nearest equivalent to the German 150-mm howitzer, for three corps in the autumn of 1914.

15 The General Staff really dates from 1908 as a conscious corps of élite soldiers, although the special training for which an entrance examination was necessary dates from the previous century's reforms.

16 The creation, in 1907, of divisions that would fight as divisions in war was new to the British. The division as a force of all arms required tactics to be centred around them and for them. The task was not completed by 1914.

17 There were three batteries each of six guns in howitzer and field gun brigades and four guns in a heavy battery.

CHAPTER 2

18 The Maxim could put ten bullets into a target in a few seconds. It was an example of overkill unless the target was a bunch of men such that every bullet might claim a separate victim.

19 In the 1914 German Army a regiment contained three battalions, a brigade two regiments and a division two brigades.

20 Jaegers were light infantry and usually fought with cavalry.

21 The information is in the 'Lobell Reports' of 1912 and 1913, in *RUSI*, Vol. 57, March 1913, and Vol. 58, May 1914. That they were correct, despite Sir James Edmonds assertion that German scales were, like the British, two machine-guns per battalion, is supported by reports from the field in 1914. According to the last 'Lobell Report', 233 machine-gun companies for about 651 active battalions were formed in 1914.

22 The handling of German machine-guns improved after 1910 when Captain C. A. L. Yates visited the Prussian Guard manoeuvres and reported adversely on it at an Aldershot Military Society lecture.

23 It is interesting that in 1909, before a counter-attack against indirect fire methods conceived in Manchuria, *Field Service Regulations Part I*, p. 16 read: 'Improved means of communication permit artillery commanders to exercise control over the fire of dispersed artillery, so that concentrations of guns is no longer necessary to ensure control of fire.'

24 Writing after the experience of the war, Alan Brooke, *op. cit.*, condemned the destructive rôle given to the artillery during the war as much as the accessory one that it had had in 1911.

25 Haig was in India in 1911 and returned to command I Corps in 1912. From India he corresponded with Kiggell, his successor as DSD, warning him to have no truck with the windbags who were trying to complicate tactics.

26 Haking was author of *Company Training* (1914), a Guards Officer, later Lieutenant-General Sir Richard, he was to command XI Corps at Loos with indifferent success. Subsequently he gained a reputation as 'a butcher' which Edmonds thought was unmerited.

27 *RUSI*, Vol. 59, November 1914, p. 381.

28 The Liddell Hart Centre, King's College, London, A. A. Montgomery-Massingberd Papers. Then Lieutenant-Colonel A. A. Montgomery an instructor at the Staff Colleges at Quetta and Camberley, Montgomery became Chief of General Staff to Sir Henry Rawlinson, commander Fourth Army, 1916. He succeeded Field Marshal Lord Milne as CIGS.

29 IWM, Bruce Williams Papers.

30 The CIGS announced this decision at the General Staff conference in January 1911.

31 IWM, Bruce Williams Papers contains much tactical material from before and during the war years. Included in the collection are course précis from Hythe and printed results of the trials with rifle and machine-guns carried out in 1908 and subsequently. Lieutenant-Colonel Bruce Williams was on the directing staff at the Staff College under Brigadier-General William Robertson as commandant.

Robertson served as QMG and Chief of General Staff in the Expeditionary Force, CIGS and Field Marshal. He rose from trooper. Williams commanded 37th Division in France and Belgium. His senior general staff officer was Lieutenant-Colonel Jack Dill, later CIGS in 1940 and Field Marshal.

32 The 'new' rifle was issued to the regular Army in 1913. The Cavalry started to receive the Vickers in 1912 and the infantry from 1913.

33 IWM, Bruce Williams Papers.

34 IWM, Maxse Papers, *Army Training Memoranda* of these years; PRO, Inspectors General *Annual Reports*; Staff College Library, Camberley, General Staff Conferences *Minutes*; *RUSI*, 'Lobel Reports'.

35 Brian Bond, 'Doctrine and Training in the British Cavalry, 1870–1914', in M. Howard, Ed., *The Theory and Practice of War* (London, 1965). Edward M. Spiers, 'The British Cavalry, 1902–14', *Journal of the Society for Army Research*, Vol. 57, Summer 1979. Erskine Childers, *War and the Arme Blanche* (London, 1910). '*War and the Arme Blanche*, the General Staff views on Mr Childers' Book', *RUSI*, Vol. 54, 1910, p. 1059. IWM, Bruce Williams Papers, *Memorandum on Army Training*, 1910. C. von Hutier, 'Military Notes', *RUSI*, Vol. 55, 1911, p. 352. Staff College, Camberley, General Staff Conference of 1910, *Minutes*.

36 Later Major-General and commander 14 Division. Earlier he was Brigadier-General Staff to Lieutenant-General Sir Walter Congreve, V.C., commander XIII Corps.

37 The 1st Cavalry Brigade was surprised by the German 4th Cavalry Division but, with N battery RHA, virtually destroyed its capacity to continue in the German advance. *OH* 1914, Vol. 1, 256–8.

38 In the autumn of 1914 the cavalry helped to save the Army at the battle of Ypres by using its weapons in the line.

39 The material in professional articles is mainly by middle rank officers and predominantly in favour of increasing the fire-power of the infantry and concerned with fire-support problems. Some examples are: R. V. K. Applin, 'Machine-gun tactics in our own and other armies', a lecture, *RUSI*, Vol. 54, 1910, p. 34. G. S. Tweedie, 'The call for higher efficiency in musketry', *RUSI*, Vol. 58, 1914, p. 652. A. H. C. Kearsey, 'The manner in which the infantry attack can best be supported . . .', *RUSI*, Vol. 54, 1910, p. 75. F. Culmann, 'French and German tendencies with regard to the preparation and development of an action', *RUSI*, Vol. 52, 1908, p. 690. G. H. J. Rooke, 'Shielded infantry and frontal attack', *RUSI*, Vol. 58, 1914, p. 771.

40 IWM, Maxse Papers. F. I. Maxse, 'Battalion organisation', *RUSI*, Vol. 56, 1912, p. 53. R. J. Kentish, 'The case for the eight company battalion', *op. cit.*, p. 891. 'Infantry Officer', 'A short plea in favour of the present organisation', *op. cit.*, p. 1579. G. J. Scovell, 'The organisation of a battalion in war and peace', *RUSI*, Vol. 55, 1911, p. 1293. Hereward Wake, 'The four company battalion in battle', *RUSI*, Vol. 59, 1914, p. 362.

CHAPTER 3

41 These lines were quoted by Brigadier-General Thomas Capper in a letter to Lieutenant-Colonel Bruce Williams when discussing the British habit of denigrating staff work and praising the physical aspects of soldiering (*c.* 1913). Capper was killed commanding 7th Division at Loos.

42 Edmonds, a Royal Engineer, became the Director of the Historical Section of the Committee of Imperial Defence. The fourteen volumes of narratives about the Western Front which he edited or 'compiled' were not completed until 1948.

43 The Liddell Hart Centre for Military Archives, King's College, London. The Liddell Hart Papers and the Edmonds Papers.

44 Divisional commanders killed in action by the end of 1915 included Lomax of 1st Division, Hamilton and Wing of 3rd, Capper of 7th, and Thesiger of 9th. The majors and captains who died were potential battalion and brigade commanders.

45 *OH*, Vol. 1, p. 9 fn.

46 A. J. Anthony Morris, 'Haldane's army reforms 1906–8: the deception of the radicals', *History*, Volume 56, No. 186, 1971.

47 John Terraine has attempted to counter-balance a popular opinion that the commanders were all incompetent. His has remained a minority view, on the whole, despite the skill and moderation with which he has presented his case.

48 The swingletree was a metal bar used to attach the traces of the wheel horses to the limbers. The expression refers to those whose interest was strictly limited to horses.

49 The Journal of the Royal United Service Institute was published monthly. The War Office published an Army Journal and military societies regularly published proceedings. The army officer had no excuse for being ill-informed about his own or foreign armies for articles in foreign journals were regularly translated and military correspondents were very active in the popular press.
    It is noteworthy that General Sir James Marshall-Cornwall, an active historian in his nineties, was translating foreign articles and writing historical articles as a Royal Artillery subaltern before 1914.

50 Brigadier-General John Headlam and others had been pressing for an artillery school to be established on the Plain.

51 *OH*, Vol. 1, p. 11.

52 The artillery and cavalry received three years training.

53 Public Record Office, 105/46 12 April 1911 and 105/47, n.d., The Roberts Papers.

54 A. J. A. Wright, 'The probable effects of compulsory service on recruiting for the Regular Army', *RUSI*, Vol. 51, December 1911.

55 *OH*, Vol. 1, p. 7.

56 Peter Paret, 'The history of war', *Daedalus*, Spring, 1971, p. 377.

57 The Treasury Board contracted for money and supplies other than those provided by the Ordnance Board.

58 'Army Administration', a lecture given at the *RUSI* by Lieutenant-General Sir H. S. Miles, November 1922.

59 John K. Dunlop, *The Development of the British Army, 1899–1914* (London, 1938), pp. 209–10, *passim*.

60 General G. F. Ellison, 'Higher control in war', *National Review*, Vol. 88, No. 524, October 1926, p. 205 and 'Imperial defence', *ibid.*, No. 527, January 1927, p. 685. Ellison had been principal private secretary to Mr J. B. S. Haldane.

61 Clive Trebilcock, 'War and the Failure of Industrial Mobilization: 1899 and 1914', in *War and Economic Development*, J. M. Winter, ed., Essays in Memory of David Joslin (Cambridge, 1975). The Imperial War Museum, The von Donop Papers. Sir Charles Harris, 'Army Finance' and 'Finance of the Army', lectures presented at the Staff College, 23 November 1907, and at the RUSI, 2 March 1921. Sir Charles Harris was Finance Member after the war and Permanent Head of the Financial Department before it. The text of the former lecture was found in the Bruce Williams Papers at the IWM. The latter is in *RUSI*, Vol. 66, 1921, p. 217.

62 IWM, von Donop Papers, 'The Supply of Munitions to the Army'.

63 The opposition in Campbell Bannerman's cabinet until 1908 and in Herbert Asquith's thereafter saw to the economy theme and dubbed Haldane 'Minister for Slaughter'. Haldane considered the Chancellor, David Lloyd George, 'an illiterate with an unbalanced mind'. Morris, *op. cit.*, p. 25.

64 *OH*, 1914, Vol. 2, p. 463.

65 An Australian told Edmonds that they were as much good as the cuneiform writing on a Babylonian brick to his soldiers. The Germans had a barrackroom level of publications which the British lacked. They were concrete and not abstract. Staff Conference *Minutes* of 1913.

66 It was at this conference that the CIGS pointed out that in the new *Infantry Training* the wording had been changed from 'The decision is obtained by superiority of fire' to 'A superiority of fire makes the decision possible'.

67 McMahon mentioned 'at least six in the battalion' which is probably the source of Edmonds' argument that the Army had asked for them. But Edmonds was referring to Maxims and McMahon to light weapons.

68 This was a reference to the obsolescence of the British rifle used in 1910 and its use of the Ogival bullet.

69 PRO WO 163/18 Precis 641, 653 and 663, on the capabilities and issue of a .276-inch rifle. WO 32/7067 minute sheets in 1911 between CIGS and MGO.

70   *RUSI*, 'Military Notes' for issues from 1911 refer to the increased scale of machine-guns in the German Army.

71   In 1914, to the surprise of Lord Kitchener and the Cabinet, the humble rifle proved to be a difficult item to mass-produce and orders had to be placed abroad. Von Donop's only success was with the Japanese. The London Scottish at Messines-Wytschaete, on 1 November 1914, reported that 50 per cent of their rifles were useless for rapid fire owing to the defective magazines of the old Mk I Lee Metford with which they and all the other Territorial Infantry were then armed. *OH*, 1914, Vol. 2, p. 350.

72   PRO WO 106/296, 24 October 1913 on the postponement of the .276 rifle and the issue of the SLE to the TF.
     WO 32/7100   On rearming with the SLE.
        32/7069   Automatic rifle trials with aircraft.
        32/7071   On automatic rifle trials.

73   LHC, Kiggell Papers.

74   Edward M. Spiers, 'The British Cavalry 1902–14', *Journal of the Society for Army Research*, Vol. LVII, Summer 1979, pp. 75–7.

CHAPTER 4

75   J. H. Boraston, ed., *Sir Douglas Haig's Despatches* (London, 1979). 'The Final Despatch', 21 March 1919, p. 319.

76   Martin Middlebrook, *The First Day on the Somme* (London, 1971), describes this day in the lives of the survivors in their own words.

CHAPTER 5

77   Quoted by Leon Wolff, *In Flanders Fields* (New York, 1960), p. 44.

78   Winston Churchill, *The World Crisis* (abridged and revised edition) (London, 1931), p. 641.

79   The special problems of fighting in close country had been discussed at a Staff Conference before the war. It had been proposed that a suitable training area be appropriated but lack of funds and the unpopularity of the acquisition of training areas caused the matter to be dropped.

80   The first 18-pounder HE shells were fired as a trial at Ypres in October. The research and development had been completed before the war.

81   Brent Wilson's unpublished thesis for the University of New Brunswick on British Army morale in the First World War and the Cabinet 45 series papers. Trench foot, widespread incidences of sentries sleeping at their posts, insubordination and drunkenness were the overt signs of poor morale.

82   PRO WO 158/17, 'G.S. Notes on Operations 1915'.

83   Like the 8th Division the 7th had been made up from regular battalions serving overseas.

84   Sir Henry Rawlinson was commissioned into the King's Royal Rifle Corps and had served in Sudan and in the South African War. He was commandant of the Staff College 1903–6 and then a divisional commander. He was appointed commander of the force formed for the abortive attempt to relieve Antwerp in October 1914, raised the 8th Division and was appointed commander of the new IV Corps formed from 7th and 8th Divisions. Early in 1916 he commanded the new Fourth Army. His HQ went into suspended animation when Rawlinson was transferred to the Versailles Council. He succeeded General Gough when that officer was relieved of command of the Fifth Army, which was renumbered the Fourth Army, and remained under Rawlinson's command until the end of the war.

85   National Library of Scotland, Edinburgh, The Haig Diaries, 2 March 1915.

86   Churchill College, Cambridge, The Rawlinson Diaries, 5 March 1915. Brigadier General A. H. Hussey was then IV Corps 'artillery adviser', an appointment that carried no command responsibilities. So the CRA of one of the divisions co-ordinated and commanded the corps artillery on an ad hoc basis.

87 Rawlinson blamed a battery of 6-inch howitzers that arrived late on the previous day and was unable to register accurately. The *OH* says that two batteries had arrived from the UK during the afternoon of the 9th and had been unable to complete their platforms in time. Yet it was the uncut wire that caused the casualties and that was the responsibility of the 18-pounders not the 6-inch howitzers.

88 Rawlinson Diaries, 16 March 1915.

89 The Germans had used cloud gas from cylinders placed in the front trenches in April 1915 at Ypres.

90 Gough, a cavalry officer, commanded a cavalry brigade in 1914, later rising to the command of the Reserve Army which was later the Fifth Army.

91 PRO Cabinet 45/120, the OH correspondence on Loos. Gough's letter of 12 July 1926. Also PRO WO 158/184, 95/711. LHC, AA Montgomery Papers and Edmonds Papers. IWM, Richard Butler Papers; Bruce Williams Papers. Churchill College, Cambridge, The Rawlinson Diaries. National Library of Scotland, The Haig Papers.

92 Sir William Robertson, French's Chief of the General Staff, became CIGS. Major-General Launcelot Kiggell became Haig's CGS.

93 Birch had commanded the 7th Division artillery at Neuve Chapelle and that of I Corps at Loos. He remained with Haig until the end of the war and, although he had problems with Haig's staff, satisfied Haig himself. He replaced Headlam at GHQ. Headlam went to the War Office.

94 Correspondence on the *OH*: Cabinet 45/140, 103/112 and 103/113. The various plans are in WO 158/18, 19, 38, 207, 214, 300. Rawlinson and Haig Diaries. Royal Artillery Library, Woolwich, 'Second Army Papers'. LHC, Edmonds Papers. A collection of documents on the political aspects of the plan are in John Terraine's *The Road to Passchendaele*.

95 *History of the Great War Military Operations 1918* (Macmillan, 1935) pp. 157–60.

96 Rudyard Kipling, 'Ubique (Royal Artillery)', *The Definitive Edition of Rudyard Kipling's Verse* (Hodder & Stoughton, 1946 p. 484).

97 Von Donop had been secretary of the Ordnance Committee in 1906, successively chief instructor at Lydd ranges, Assistant and Director of Artillery and MGO since 1913. He was sacked by Lloyd George in December 1916 and sent to command Humber District. He was disgracefully treated.

98 IWM, Von Donop Papers, 'The Supply of Munitions to the Army', 1919.

99 By May 1918 the British had 6,490 guns in the field on the Western Front of which 37 per cent were heavier than of field calibre. The French proportion was 50 per cent. RA Library, Woolwich, Rawlins Papers, File 14, 8 May 1918.

100 Lt-Col C. D. Stansfield, 'High Explosives', RA Institution Lecture, 13 November 1919, *RAJ*, Vol. 46, p. 407.

101 Herbert Cambell Uniacke established the New Army artillery school in 1914. He commanded 5 Bde RHA in October and, as a brigadier-general, No. 2 Group of Heavy Artillery, which was his first introduction to heavy artillery. In November 1915, he became GOC RA V Corps and in July MGRA Fifth Army. He was appointed MGGS, Deputy Director-General of Training, under Ivor Maxse in June 1918 and after the war he organised the Central Artillery School at Larkhill.

102 The account of the effort to have the senior RA officers at Army and Corps named as commanders is best explained in the papers of S. W. Rawlins, Senior Staff Officer to Noel Birch, MGRA at GHQ. Birch's papers include a letter from him on 9 July 1916 when the events of 1 July were being considered. He made the point that had artillerymen been consulted before the plan was made, they would have recommended alterations in it. He did not suggest, however, that the Fourth Army could have won a great victory.

103 Directorate of History, Ottawa, *Draft History of the Royal Canadian Air Force*, Volume I. Sections II, VI, VII, XVI, XVIII, PRO WO 95/631.

104 Kite balloons with baskets slung beneath them had been used as observation posts for years but it was not until 20 May 1915 that the first one ascended near Poperinghe. It was provided by the Royal Navy. *OH*, 1914, Vol. II, p. 303 fn.

105 This is not a trivial point. Battery commanders were very particular about who directed their guns and did not always accept what the airman advised.

106 This step was taken in early 1916 on the advice of the Artillery Adviser at GHQ, John Headlam, who tried but failed to have an extra artillery officer appointed.

107 Information for this section is derived from:
   a. *OH*, 1915, Vol. II, p. 83.
   b. *Report on Survey on the Western Front*, 1914–18 (HMSO, 1920).
   c. *Artillery Survey in the First World War*, Sir Lawrence Bragg, A. H. Dowson, and H. H. Hemming (Field Survey Association, 1971).
   d. H. StJ. L. Winterbotham, Lecture on Field Survey, Royal Artillery Institution, *RAJ*, Vol. 46, 1919–20.
   e. H. C. Harrison, 'Calibration and ranging', *RAJ*, Vol. 47 1920.
   f. N. M. McLeod, 'Survey work in modern war', *RAJ*, Vol. 48, 1921.
   g. Last, but not least, conversations with Lieutenant-Colonel Ralph Eastwood RA (Retd).

108 Sir Lawrence Bragg, 'Sound Ranging', in *Artillery Survey* in the *First World War*.

109 A German artillery group order of 23 June 1917 reads: 'In consequence of the excellent sound ranging of the English, I forbid any battery to fire alone when the whole section is quiet, especially in an east wind . . .' Bragg, *op. cit.*, 38.

110 Cf. PRO, Cabinet 45/133–7 containing the many hundreds of letters from participants to the historians of the Somme volumes and IWM, Maxse Papers, including analyses of the tactics used on the Somme.

111 G. C. Wynne, *If German Attacks: The Battle in Depth in the West* (Faber, 1940), p. 118 *et seq*.

112 LHC, A. A. Montgomery-Massinberd Papers.

113 *OH*, Vol. 1, 1915, p. 152.

114 *OH*, Vol. 1, 1916, p. 490. German monograph 'The focus of the battle in July, 1916'.

115 Stephens commanded 25 Brigade in 8 Division in September 1915 and went on to command X Corps by September 1918. He was Commandant, the Royal Military College, Sandhurst after the War. His views correspond with those expressed by Major-General W. C. G. Heneker, of 8 Division and Sir Ivor Maxse who commanded 18 Division and, later, XVIII Corps.

116 In January 1918, the soldier received fourteen weeks of actual training in the UK and could be drafted to France at 18½ years. New Army men had originally been trained in their units and for longer.

117 IWM, Stephens and Heneker Papers.

118 IWM, Lieutenant-Colonel Reynolds Papers.

119 *OH*, 1916, p. 64–5. But the increase in Lewis guns mentioned was not carried out by 1 July 1916.

120 *OH*, Vol. 2, 1916. Retrospect, 573–4 discusses some of these questions. Fourth Army Tactical Notes of May 1916 are in Appendix 18 1916.

121 RA Library, Woolwich, Uniacke Papers.

122 IWM, Horn Papers include material written by G. M. Lindsay.

123 IWM, Bruce Williams Papers.
    RA Library, Uniacke Papers.

124 IWM, Bruce Williams Papers.

125 IWM, Maxse Papers.

126 IWM, Maxse Papers, XVIII Corps, No. G.S. 70 Dated 21 August 1917.

CHAPTER 8

127 These points have been made elsewhere, in the *OH* for instance. But most recently they have been stated clearly by John Terraine in his *To Win a War: 1918 the Year of Victory* (Sidgwick and Jackson, 1978).

128 H. C. B. Rogers, *Tanks in Battle* (Seeley Service, 1965), presents a clear and accurate historical account of the period. Additional information has been gathered from the *OH*, the PRO War Office 95 series and from the extensive correspondence in Cabinet 45 between the Historical Section and participants.

129 John Terraine, *op. cit.*, p. 264.
130 Later Major-General Sir Ernest Swinton, Chichele Professor of War History, Swinton was the first 'Eyewitness' or official correspondent with the Army in France and Belgium.
131 On 8 August there were 630 tanks in the fifteen battalions of the Tank Corps. Between 8 and 31 August, in fourteen days of fighting, 1,184 tanks were engaged. On 31 August, 250 remained fit. In August and September, 582 tanks were recovered for repair. The total personnel strength of the Corps on 8 August was 7,200 of which 2,167 had become casualties by 27 September. *OH*, Vol. IV, 1918, p. 517 and 384–5 (Note 1).
132 The Kirke Committee reported on the lessons of the First World War in 1932.
133 GHQ had only eight Divisions in reserve in March 1918.
134 A political decision was taken to reduce the size of divisions rather than their number, despite the tactical implications of an unfamiliar three battalion brigade and nine battalion divisions.
135 Later Lieutenant-General Sir Aylmer Haldane Commander VI Corps. Haldane commanded the Tenth Brigade at Shorncliffe before the war. An old friend of Sir James Edmonds, he features in the Edmonds papers and kept a useful diary which is at the National Library of Scotland, Edinburgh.
136 Telephone lines were built up on a grid in positional warfare to allow lateral and alternative links. But in faster moving conditions, when lines had to be laid in linear fashion, lateral communications were more difficult and forward links liable to be cut.
137 Major W. Arthur Steel, 'Wireless Telegraphy in the Canadian Corps in France' published as a long series of articles in the Canadian Defence Quarterly starting in Volume IV, 1928.
138 Mr Brereton Greenhous, Senior Historian the Directorate of History, Ottawa, and the drafts *Canadian Airmen and the First World War* (Volume 1, the *History of the Royal Canadian Airforce*) published in 1980. Notes about artillery/air co-operation are also to be found in the Rawlins, Uniacke and Headlam papers at the RA Library, Woolwich.
139 Brigadier McMahon was killed by a stray shell when on his way to command a brigade in 1914.
140 Frederick Myatt, *History of the Small Arms School* (privately published, 1972).

CHAPTER 9

141 The *Gunner* magazine, February 1920, p. 7.
142 PRO, Kirke Committee report, WO/32/3116.
143 *RAJ*, Vol. LI, 1924–5.
144 All officers had to pass qualifying written examinations for promotion from lieutenant to captain and from captain to major in tactics, military history, military law, administration and political and commonwealth affairs. Entrance to the Staff College was via the captain to major examination, with extra subjects and more stiffly marked.
145 This valuable record is as yet unpublished, but available Royal Artillery Institution.
146 Eric Harrison, *Gunners, Game and Gardens* (Leo Cooper, 1979) p. 73.
147 G. B. Tatcher, in the *Gunner* magazine, October 1978.
148 Harrison, *op. cit.*, p. 63. In England officers' chargers, forage and soldier grooms were free perquisites. Government horses could be used for hunting on payment of a small fee for insurance, £9 p.a. in England and Rs90 in India.
149 'Station chukkas', or non-competitive polo in which civilians, infantry and artillery joined were played on any suitable piece of flat ground all over India.
150 'Poodle-faking', a curious slang word of unknown origin. To 'poodle-fake' was to dance, to go to parties, to play tennis with girls. A contemporary of the author was carpeted for taking a girl out riding instead of playing polo.
151 *RAJ*, Vol. L, 1923–4.
152 The exact wording is: 'In view of the improvements in mechanised transport likely

in the near future, discuss the possibilities of its use for all natures of field artillery, *including horse artillery*, in substitution for horse draught both on the road and across country.'

153 In the presence of most of the junior officers, including the author.
154 *RAJ*, Vol. L, 1924, p. 498. See also Maurice-Jones, *The Shop Story*, pp. 45–6.
155 See *Wingate in Peace and War* by D. Tulloch, pp. 26–7. The running was actually authorised by the commandant.
156 The Woolwich cadets had century old traditions of ragging and rioting, even of mutiny, but it was never vicious. The bullying of nonconformists and of one individual by many was a nasty feature of this particular period.
157 Formerly the 'Ordnance College', then the 'Artillery College' (1921). It became the Military College of Science in 1927 and was located at Woolwich and had a strong artillery bias.

CHAPTER 10

158 A. J. Trythall, *Boney Fuller, The Intellectual General* (Cassell), p. 87.
159 *History of the Royal Artillery 1919–1939 RA Historical Committee*, a compilation by various authors, unpublished, p. 159.
160 K. Macksey, *Armoured Crusader: Major-General Sir Percy Hobart* (Hutchinson), p. 109.
161 *RAJ* Vol. LVII, 1930–1, p. 183.
162 The author of FSR, 1924 was Aspinall-Oglander, with Fuller contributing the 'principles'. They embodied the negative lessons of past wars, such as the mistake of dissipating one's forces, adopting a defensive posture, failing to secure the base of operations, signalling one's intentions to the enemy and so on. Of themselves they were meaningless and mutually contradictory, but made sense when linked to actual operations, *vide* Sir F. Maurice's *British Strategy: A Study of the Applications of the Principles of War*.
163 *RAJ*, Vol. LIII, 1926–7, p. 350.
164 Trythall, *op. cit.*, p. 56.
165 Liddell Hart, *Thoughts of War* (Faber, 1944), pp. 248–51.
166 *RAJ*, Vol. LIII, 1926–7, p. 19. Lecture given by Rawlins in 1925, Birch in the chair.
167 Macksey, op. cit., p. 82.
168 *Ibid.*, p. 86.
169 *RAJ*, Vol. LII, 1925–6, p. 232. Later General Sir Frederick Pile.
170 R. M. Orgkiewicz, *Irmoured Forces* (Arms and Armour Press, 1960) pp. 228–9.
171 Macksey, *op. cit.*, pp. 162–3, 201, but also p. 221 when on being restored to the active list he takes a better view of Brooke.
172 Macksey, *op. cit.*, p. 126. It was a difficult decision. See Postan, Hay and Scott, *Design and Development of Weapons* (HMSO, 1964), chapter 3, esp. pp. 315–6 and 346.
173 See, for instance the essays by K. M. Loch Vol. LV, p. 139; G. E. A. Granet, Vol. LVI, p. 139; and Cherry, same vol. p. 263.
174 The D of A was concerned solely with weapon design. There was no 'arms' directors, and therefore no Director of Royal Artillery with a charter to *direct* (as opposed to inspecting and reporting) every aspect of artillery work.
175 Lecture by Rawlins, *op. cit.*
176 One of the authors commanded a battery of four Mark I 60-pounders with shrapnel ammunition in 1941. There was also a later Mark on a modernised carriage.
177 *RAJ*, Vol. LVI, 1929–30, pp. 129, 263.
178 *RAJ*, Vol. LV, 1928–9, Captain K. M. Loch, p. 139.
179 I. McLaine, *Ministry of Morale* (George Allen & Unwin, 1979). p. 26. The Air Staff calculation was 66,000 killed in the first week. Basil Collier, *A History of Air Power* (Weidenfeld & Nicolson, 1974), p. 97.
180 N. H. Gibbs, *History of the Second World War*, UK Series, Vol. I *Grand Strategy* (HMSO, 1976), p. 467.

181 Macksey, *op. cit.* p. 137, also p. 144.
182 Liddell Hart, *Thoughts on War* (Faber, 1964), p. 125.
183 PRO/WO32/3116.
184 J. Terraine, *The Smoke and the Fire* (Sidgwick & Jackson, 1980), p. 154.
185 Ogorkiewicz, *op. cit.* pp. 226–9.
186 B. H. Liddell Hart, *The Memoirs of Captain Liddell Hart* (Cassell, 1965), p. 178.
187 British nomenclature is unintelligible to outsiders, for the non-tactical 'regiment' is a tactical entity in the armoured troops and artillery. The artillery which is functionally a corps is collectively a 'Royal Regiment', while the former King's Royal Rifle Corps is an infantry regiment, and before 1938 artillery units were called 'brigades'. Some batteries of artillery are entitled troops, which is also used as the subdivision of a battery. The cavalry designation 'squadron' has been borrowed by the engineers and signals. 'Corps', as well as meaning a functional grouping, e.g. the Corps of Royal Engineers or Royal Corps of Signals, also means an 'army corps', i.e. a group of divisions.
188 *RAJ*, Vol. LVII, 1930–1, articles on pp. 45, 304 and 363. 'Mutt' and 'Jeff' were two stupid stereotypes in a comic strip of that era.
189 See the article by its inventor, Lieut.-Colonel A. J. Farfan, 'A compromise between "Mutt and Jeff",' *RAJ*, Vol. LVII, 1930–1, p. 363, on 'linked' batteries.
190 The essay awarded the Silver Medal in the Duncan Gold Medal Essay competition by Major R. G. Cherry suggested a new organisation for the field artillery closely resembling the one forced on Royal Artillery in 1938. *RAJ*, Vol. LIX, p. 131.
191 Based on statements made by the late Major-General Parham to the author. See also S. Bidwell, *Gunners at War* (Arms and Armour Press, 1970), pp. 129 and 138–41.

CHAPTER 12

192 For a full analysis see Barry A. Leach, *German Strategy Against Russia 1939–1941* (Oxford University Press, 1973), Chapter I, esp. pp. 20–37.
193 J. R. M. Butler, *Grand Strategy*, Volume II (HMSO), p. 14.
194 Anon (P. Gribble), *The Diary of a Staff Officer* (Methuen, 1941), p. 10.
195 *RAJ*, Vol. CVII, No. 1 March 1980, p. 21. F. M. Lord Ironside, article by R. Macleod.
196 H. Guderian, *Panzer Leader* (Michael Joseph, 1970), Appendix III, p. 472.
197 Except for the much debated order to halt Kleist's Panzer Group in May, instead of using it to crush the French and British divisions trapped between it and the Army Group driving them back to the coast.
198 See Len Deighton, *Blitzkrieg* (Cape, 1979), pp. 300–1.
199 From '*Sturz-Kampf-Flugzeug*', 'crash-dive military aircraft'.
200 Guderian, *op. cit.*, pp. 483–4.
201 *The Diary of a Staff Officer, op cit.*, pp. 29–31.
202 It was sometimes left out of battle, or as in the ill-fated BATTLEAXE operation in 1941, sent on a separate mission.
203 G. K. Zhukov, *Memoirs of Marshal Zhukov* (Cape, 1971), pp. 323–8.
204 D. Richards, *Royal Air Force 1939–1945*: Vol. I.
    The Fight at Odds (HMSO, 1953), p. 131.

CHAPTER 13

205 Mellenthin, *op. cit.*, pp. 52–3 and fn. Mellenthin's italics.
206 Apart from the many valuable works cited in the bibliography, the best analytic accounts are by two authors who served as staff officers during the campaign. For the German side I have relied mainly on F. W. von Mellenthin's *Panzer Battles 1939–1945*, (Cassell, 1955). R. M. P. Carver (Field Marshal Lord Carver) has covered the field three times, first in a series of articles under the general title of 'Desert Dilemmas' in the now defunct *Royal Armoured Corps Journal*, then in his *Tobruk* (Batsford, 1961). His biography, *Field Marshal Lord Harding of Petherton*, (Weidenfeld & Nicholson, 1978), is also a valuable source.

207 Related to the author by the late Lieutenant-Colonel M. T. G. Wood, RA, who was present.

208 R. M. P. Carver, RACJ, Vol. VI No. 2, 'Desert Dilemmas', Part 8, p. 93.

209 Diary of Major W. Blacker, RHA, comd 'I' Battery (Bull's Troop) Library of the Royal Artillery Institution. His whole diary is revealing on the confusion of tactics in the armoured division. For long periods his battery was split in two, the halves operating quite separately.

210 Guenther Blumentritt, *Rundstedt: the Soldier and the Man* (Odhams, 1952), pp. 53–4.

211 K. Macksey, *op. cit.*, p. 159.

212 Personal communication to author from General Sir S. Kirkman, then BRA Eighth Army.

213 R. M. P. Carver, RACJ, Vol. VI, No. 2, p. 94, 'Desert Dilemmas', Part 8.

214 *Notes from the Theatres of War*, No. 1. Also S. Nalder, *Signals in the Second World War*, Royal Signals Institution, 1953, pp. 49–55.

215 R. M. P. Carver, RACJ, Vol. V, No. 2 April 1951, 'Desert Dilemmas', Part 4. See also Ian V. Hogg, *The Guns 1939–1945.*, Purnell's History of the Second World War, Book II, (Macdonald, 1970), p. 58 *et seq* for a clear discussion of the technical aspects and the evolution of anti-tank guns.

216 The ordinary 88-mm FLAK was deadly as an anti-tank gun, which led to a number of them being appropriated and converted, sometimes in defiance of orders, as the anti-aircraft defences were correspondingly depleted.

217 A. L. Pemberton, *The Development of Artillery Tactics and Equipment* (Second World War, 1939–1945, Army), The War Office, 1951, p. 127.

218 Pemberton, *op. cit.* pp. 108–9.

219 The author was present.

220 Unidentified article quoted by Carver, *Tobruk*, pp. 254–5. This paradox of concentration through dispersion occurs frequently in Liddell Hart's work, e.g. his *Thoughts on War* (Faber, 1944), pp. 196–202.

221 Pemberton, *op. cit.* pp. 111–13.

222 Henry Maule, *Spearhead General, the Life of General Sir Frank Messervy* (Odhams, 1961), p. 204.

223 *Notes from the Theatres of War No. 16* North Africa, November 1942–May 1943 The War Office October 1943 pp. 62–3. The whole of this pamphlet dealing with the Army's experiences in Tunisia is enlightening, the First Army beginning by repeating many of the mistakes of the Eighth, except as regards the concentration of artillery, and then correcting them.

224 For the best account of Dorman-Smith see Correlli Barnett, *The Desert Generals* (William Kimber, 1960), *passim* and pp. 303–4. Dorman-Smith also communicated with the present author: S. Bidwell, *Gunners at War* (Arms and Armour Press, 1970), pp. 176–7. In May 1942, all *bouches inutiles* were sent back from the desert to Egypt, among them artillery commanders deprived of their commands by the policy of dispersion, among them the CRA of 50th Infantry Division. The BRA and the CCRAs of the Eighth Army seemed to have tamely acquiesced, and the Major-General RA in Cairo only learned the facts when informed by the indignant Brigade Major RA of 50th Division after the retreat. (Personal communication, Major-General W. D. E. Brown.)

225 Pemberton, *op. cit.*, pp. 118–9, 124–5.

226 From First World War slang, based on the Kaiser's alleged prayer, '*Gott strafe (punish) England*'. Hence 'strafe' for an artillery bombardment or a severe dressing-down.

227 Personal communications. Also R. M. P. Carver, *Tobruk*, p. 254.

228 Pemberton, *op. cit.*, pp. 150–2.

CHAPTER 14

229 F. H. George, *Cybernetics* (The English Universities Press, 1971).

230 *Ibid.*, pp. 8–9.

231 Tedder, *With Prejudice: Memoirs of Marshal of the Air Force Lord Tedder* (Cassell, 1966), p. 175 and the chapter 'November 1941', *passim*.
232 Lieutenant-Colonel C. E. Carrington, personal communication.
233 *Notes from the Theatres of War*, No. 1 (Cyrenaica), November 1941, p. 4.
234 For the best and most detailed account of the siege up to the relief of the Australians see Barton Maughan, *Australia in the War of 1939–1945*, Series 1, (Army) Vol. III *Tobruk and Alamein*, Canberra Australian War Memorial, 1966, or (Angus Wilson, 1967), pp. 149–56.
235 *Ibid.*
236 *Notes from the Theatres of War* No. 20 (Italy 1943–4), p. 34.
237 D. S. Graham, joint author, personal experience.
238 Lieutenant-Colonel P. S. Turner, personal communication.
239 Major-General N. L. Foster, personal communication.
240 *Notes from the Theatres of War*, No. 14, pp. 69–70; No. 16, p. 78.
241 S. Bidwell, joint author, was present at part of the action and made the count shortly after the war in Tunisia was over.

CHAPTER 15

This chapter is based primarily on verbal communications, contemporary training pamphlets and private papers given or lent to the author by Lieutenant-Colonel C. E. Carrington and Major-General J. M. McNeill, both of whom served for the whole of the Second World War in the vital field of army/air co-operation.

242 Tedder, *op. cit.*, p. 175.
243 For the history of the 'Air OP' see Parham H. J. and Bellfield E. M. G. *Unarmed into Battle*, (Warren & Sons, the Wykham Press, 1956), also S. Bidwell, *Gunners at War*, Chapter VIII. For some RAF reactions, see PRO Air 35/111, File 14111/Air/4.
244 McNeill, Staff College precis, 1940.
245 As 'Charles Edmonds', *A Subaltern's War* (Peter Davies, 1979).
246 *Notes from the Theatres of War*, No. 1. Unpublished history of No. 2 AASC unit, McNeill.
247 Current Reports from Overseas No. 6. Pemberton, *op. cit.*, pp. 163–4. Air Chief Marshal Sir Harry Broadhurst, personal communication.
248 Current Reports from Overseas No. 73, January, 1945.
249 Tedder, *op. cit.*, p. 355, p. 397.
250 It was drafted by McNeill, when GSO1 (Air Ops) in 15th Army Group, where he went on promotion from 2 AASC.
251 Private communication.
252 Article by the late Brigadier W. F. K. Thompson, *Airborne Operations* (Salamander, 1978), p. 114.
253 M. Hickey, *Out of the Sky: A History of Airborne Warfare* (Mills & Boon, 1979), p. 70.
254 Personal communication.
255 R. E. Urquhart, *Arnhem* (Cassell, 1958), index; 'Tactical Air Force, inexplicable absence of . . .'

INTERLUDE

256 I am grateful to Major-General E. K. G. Sixsmith for the information that the 'bible' of infantry commanders as regards fire-planning was the War Office pamphlet, *Preparation of an Attack with Special Reference to the Fire Plan*, published in 1932, and distributed to all units, and that its author was the future CIGS, Field Marshal Viscount Alanbrooke.

CHAPTER 16

257 All data concerning the Normandy landings are from L. F. Ellis, *History of the Second World War*, Vol I, *The Battle of Normandy* (HMSO, 1962), Chapter VII and pp. 197–8. Also A. L. Pemberton, *The Second World War 1939–1945, Army: The Development of Artillery Tactics and Equipment*, pp. 217–22.
258 Unfortunately many of the landing craft carrying them foundered, but enough arrived to make their presence felt. Ellis, *op. cit.*
259 Pemberton, *op. cit.*, pp. 227–8.
260 Norman Stone, *Hitler* (Hodder & Stoughton, 1980), p. 153.
261 Pemberton, *op. cit.*, p. 249.
262 Ibid, p. 263.
263 John Terraine, *The Smoke and the Fire* (Sidgwick & Jackson, 1980), p. 45 n., p. 46.

EPILOGUE

264 Ronald Lewin, *Montgomery* (Batsford, 1971), p. 252 and p. 249.
265 Pemberton, *op. cit.*, p. 273, p. 279.
266 Infantry battalions, 56, of which only twelve are armoured; armoured regiments (i.e. battalions), with main battle tanks, 10, and organised as light armoured reconnaissance units, 9; artillery regiments (also equivalent battalions), 22.

Bibliography

UNPUBLISHED SOURCES I. 1904–1918

1. Churchill College, Cambridge. The papers of General Lord Rawlinson of Trent and Sir Charles Bonham-Carter.
2. The Directorate of History, National Defence Headquarters, Ottawa. Draft narratives, the Official History of the Royal Canadian Air Force, Volume I.
3. The Imperial War Museum, Lambeth. The following private collections:
   Lieutenant-Colonel J. H. Boraston
   Lieutenant-General Sir Richard Butler
   General Sir Stanley von Donop
   Major-General W. G. C. Heneker
   General Lord Horne with those of G. M. Lindsay
   Lieutenant-General Sir Hugh Jeudwine
   General Sir Ivor Maxse
   Lieutenant-Colonel L. L. C. Reynolds
   General Sir R. B. Stephens
   Lieutenant-General Sir H. Bruce Williams
4. The Liddell Hart Centre for Military Archives, The Library, King's College, London. The papers of Sir Basil Liddell Hart, Sir James Edmonds, Field Marshal Sir Archibald Montgomery-Massingberd, Lieutenant-General Sir Launcelot Kiggell.
5. The Library, the Staff College, Camberley. The minutes of pre-1914 General Staff annual meetings.
6. The National Library of Scotland. The papers of Field Marshal Lord Haig and Lieutenant-General Sir Aylmer Haldane.
7. The Royal Artillery Institution Library, Woolwich. The papers of:
   Brigadier E. C. Anstey, including his draft history of the Royal Artillery, 1914–18.
   A. F. Becke (Member of the Historical Section)
   Captain William Bloor
   Lieutenant-Colonel A. H. Burne
   Major T. H. Davison
   Lieutenant-Colonel H. M. Davson
   Major-General Sir John Headlam
   Brigadier-General A. H. Hussey
   Colonel R. McLeod
   Brigadier E. Mockler-Ferryman
   Lieutenant-Colonel S. W. Rawlins (including papers of Lieutenant-General Sir Noel Birch and Rawlins draft 'A History of the development of the British Artillery in France, 1914–18'.)
   Major-General H. C. C. Uniacke
   'Second Army Papers, 1917–18'.
8. The Public Record Office, Kew and Portugal Street.
   1906–1914.
   WO 105/45   Mr Haldane's Memorandum, 30 July 1906, Comparison of German and British standards of military efficiency.

105/46–7 The Roberts Papers.
163/10–20 Army Council minutes and précis. Inspectors General annual reports.
32/ Papers of War Office committees
237 Digests of committee reports
WO 106/44–51 Correspondence of the Directorate of Military Operations.
/59 Brigadier H. Wilson's letter book.
WO 107 QMG's files. Raising of Kitchener divisions.
WO 159/ Kitchener Papers. Von Donop-Robertson correspondence.
WO 32/3116 'The Report of the Committee on the Lessons of the Great War', (The Kirke Committee, 13 October, 1931), dated October 1932. Also 'The Report on the Staff Conference to consider the Report'. 9–11 January, 1933.

1914–15 Cabinet 45/114, 129, 142, 145, 163–5, 182, 194–202. (The Historical Section correspondence and narratives)
I Corps, WO 95/588–590. First Army, WO 95/154, 181–2
II Corps, WO 95/629–631
Second Army, WO 95/268
III Corps, WO 95/668–70
IV Corps, WO 95/706–8, /1313
Cabinet 45/120–1 (Historical Section correspondence on Loos.)
IV Corps WO 95/711–12. GHQ, 158/184. First Army, 158/267–8
1916. Cabinet 45/132–8 (Historical Section correspondence on the battle of the Somme).
WO 158/234–6, /321, 333/4, WO95/431, 674 and 851. (Fourth Army papers concerning the Somme.) IV Corps, WO 95/714, XIII Corps, WO 95/995, X Corps, WO 95/851, III Corps, WO 95/896, 673, XIV Corps, WO 95/910–11, XV Corps, WO 95/922.
Fifth Army lessons: WO 158/344.
1917. Cabinet 45/116. (Historical Section correspondence on the battle of Arras).
Third Army WO 158/223–4, 311–16 (including Cambrai).
Cabinet 45/140 and 103/112 (Historical Section correspondence on the battle of 3rd Ypres).
McMullen Committee WO 158/38.
Second Army, WO 158/208–9 and 214
Fifth Army, 158/249–50, Fourth Army, 158–239
WO 95/275, 520, 643, 835, 853, 912–3, 951–2, 821.
Cabinet 45/316. (Historical Section correspondence on the battle of Cambrai).
WO 158/53–54 and 32/5095B (Cambrai enquiry).
Tank Corps files: WO 95/91 (Arras), 92 (Cambrai), 95–104, 93 (1918), 677, 952, 984, 986. GHQ on tanks, WO 158/200. MGO on tanks, WO 161/24.
1918. Cabinet 45/184–5 and 192 (Historical correspondence on Third and Fifth Armies).
1915–18 GHQ (Ops) GS Notes: WO 158/17–20
Secret (Ops) letters: WO 158/311.
Composition of infantry battalion, WO 158/90
MGO on New Armies arms and ammunition 1914–15
January 1915–December 1916. Tanks WO 158124, 25

SECONDARY SOURCES

Selected Works

Baynes, John, *Morale: a study of men and courage; the Second Scottish Rifles at the Battle of Neuve Chapelle, 1915* (Cassell, 1967).

Bidwell, R. G. Shelford, *Gunners at War* (Arms & Armour Press, 1970).

Bond, Brian, *Liddell Hart: a study of his military thought* (Cassell, 1977).

The Victorian Army and the Staff College (Eyre Methuen, 1972).

Boraston, J. H., *Haig's Despatches 1915–19* (Dent, 1919).

Davidson, Sir John H., *Haig, Master of the Field* (Peter Nevill, 1933).

Edmonds, Sir James E., (Compiler), *History of the Great War: Military Operations France and Belgium.* (14 Volumes) (HMSO, 1922–48).

Fraser-Tytler, Neil, *Field Guns in France* (London, 1922).

Hart, Basil H. Liddell, *The Real War, 1914–18* (Faber, 1930).

Headlam, Sir John, *The History of the Royal Artillery from the Indian Mutiny to the Great War, Volume II, 1899–1914* (RA Institution, Woolwich, 1936).

Luvaas, Jay, *The Education of an Army* (Cassell. 1964).

Terraine, John, *Douglas Haig: the Educated Soldier* (Hutchinson, 1963).

General Jack's Diary, ed. (Eyre & Spottiswoode, 1964).

The Road to Passchendaele: the Flanders offensive of 1917: a study in inevitability (Leo Cooper, 1977).

To Win a War: 1918, the year of victory (Sidgwick & Jackson, 1978).

Tyler, J. E., *The British Army and the Continent, 1904–14* (Edward Arnold, 1938).

Wynne, G. C., *If Germany Attacks: the battle in depth in the West* (Faber, 1940).

Other Works

Baker-Carr, C. D., *From Chauffeur to Brigadier* (Ernest Benn, 1920).

Beaumont, Harry, *Old Contemptible* (The Adventurers Club, 1968).

Becke, A. F., *The Royal Regiment of Artillery at Le Cateau* (RA Institution, 1919).

Behrend, Arthur, *As from Kemmel Hill* (Eyre & Spottiswoode, 1963).

Berdinner, H. F., *With the Heavies in Flanders* (1922).

Blake, Robert, *The Private Papers of Douglas Haig* (Eyre & Spottiswoode, 1952).

Blunden, Edmund, *Undertones of War* (Cobden-Sanderson, 1930).

Callwell, Sir C. E., *Field Marshal Sir Henry Wilson: his life and diaries* (Cassell, 1927).

Chapman, Guy, *A Passionate Prodigality* (MacGibbon & Kee, 1965).

Charteris, John, *At GHQ* (Cassell, 1931).

Churchill, Winston S., *The World Crisis, 1911–18* (Thornton Butterworth, 1931).

Crozier, F. P., *A Brass Hat in No Man's Land* (Jonathan Cape, 1930).

Currie, Sir Arthur W., *Canadian Corps Operations during the year 1918*, (Department of Militia and Defence, 1920).

Duff Cooper, A., *Haig* (Faber, 1935).

Dunlop, John K., *The Development of the British Army, 1899—1914* (Methuen, 1938).

Edmonds, Sir James E., *A Short History of World War 1* (Oxford UP, 1951).

Freytag-Loringhoven, Baron von, *Deductions from the World War* (Constable, 1918).

Fuller, J. F. C., *Tanks in the Great War* (John Murray, 1920).

On Future Warfare (Sifton Praed, 1928).

Memoirs of an Unconventional Soldier (Ivor Nicholson & Watson 1936).

Machine Warfare (The Infantry Journal, 1943).

Armament and History (Eyre & Spottiswoode, 1946).

Armoured Warfare (Military Service Publishing Company, 1955).

Geographical Section (General Staff), *Report on Survey on the Western Front, 1914–18* (HMSO, 1920).

Gooch, John, *The Plans of War: the General Staff and British Military Strategy, c. 1900–1916* (Routledge & Keegan Paul, 1973).

Gordon, Huntley, *The Unreturning Army* (Dent, 1967).

Gough, Sir Hubert, *Soldiering On* (Barker, 1954).

The Fifth Army (Hodder & Stoughton, 1931).

Graham, Stephen, *A Private in the Guards* (Macmillan, 1919).

Graves, Robert, *Goodbye to All That* (Cape, 1929).

Greenwell, Graham, *An Infant in Arms: War letters of a Company Officer* (n.d.).

Haigh, Richard, *Life in a Tank* (Houghton Mifflin, 1918).

Haking, R. C. B., *Company Training* (Hugh Rees, 1914).

Hankey, Donald, *A Student in Arms* (Dutton, 1917).

Harington, Sir Charles, *Plumer of Messines* (John Murray, 1935).

Hemming, H. H. (ed.), *Artillery Survey in the First World War* (Field Survey Association, 1971).

Hogg, Ian V., *The Guns, 1914–18*, (Ballantine, 1971).

Gas, (Ballantine, 1975).

Howard, Michael, *The Continental Commitment* (Temple Smith, 1972).

Junger, Ernst, *The Storm of Steel* (Chatto & Windus, 1929).

Copse 125 (Chatto & Windus, 1930).

Lloyd George, David, *War Memoirs*, (Ivor Nicholson & Watson, 1933–36).

Ludendorff, Erich, *My War Memories, 1914–18* (Hutchinson, 1919).

'Mark Severn', *The Gambardier: giving some account of the heavy and siege artillery in France, 1914–18* (Ernest Benn, 1930).

A Subaltern on the Somme in 1916 (Dutton, 1928).

Masefield, John, *The Old Front Line* (Macmillan, 1917).

Maurice, Sir Frederick, *Forty Days in 1914* (Constable, 1919).

The Last Four Months (Cassell, 1919).

British Strategy: a study of the application of the principles of war (Constable, 1929).

Haldane, 1856–1915 (Faber, 1937).

ed., *The Life of Lord Rawlinson of Trent*.

Maurice, Nancy, (ed.), *The Maurice Case* (Leo Cooper, 1972).

Middlebrook, Martin, *The First Day on the Somme* (Allen Lane, 1971).

Monash, Sir John, *The Australian Victories in France* (Angus Robertson, 1936).

Montgomery, Sir A. A., *The Story of the Fourth Army in the Battle of the Hundred Days*, (Hodder & Stoughton, 1920).

Nicholson, G. W. L., *Canadian Expeditionary Force, 1914–18* (Queen's Printer, Ottawa, 1964).

Oliver, F. S., *The Anvil of War* (Macmillan, 1936).

Ordeal by Battle (Macmillan, 1915).

d'Ombrain, Nicholas, *War Machinery and High Policy: defence administration in peacetime, 1902–14* (Oxford University Press, 1973).

Orgill, Douglas, *Armoured Onslaught, 8th August 1918* (Ballantine, 1972).

Priestley, R. E., *The Signal Service in the European War of 1914–18*, (France) (The Institution of Royal Engineers, 1921).

Repington, C A'C., *Imperial Strategy* (John Murray, 1906).

The First World War (Constable, 1920).

Robertson, Sir William, *Soldiers and Statesmen* (Scribners, 1926).

Rogers, H. C. B., *Tanks in Battle* (Seeley Service, 1965).

Sandilands, H. R., *The Fifth in the Great War: a history of the 1st and 2nd Northumberland Fusiliers, 1914–18* (Dover, 1938).

Sassoon, Siegfried, *Memoirs of an Infantry Officer* (Faber, 1930).

Siegfried's Journey 1916–20, (Faber, 1945).

Sixsmith, E. K. G., *British Generalship in the Twentieth Century* (Arms & Armour Press, 1970).

Spears, Sir Edward, *Liaison 1914* (Eyre & Spottiswoode, 1968).

Prelude to Victory (Cassell, 1956).

Swinton, Sir Ernest, *Eyewitness* (Hodder & Stoughton, 1932).

Tyndale-Biscoe, Julian, *Gunner Subaltern, 1914–18* (Leo Cooper, 1971).

Wade, Aubrey, *Gunner on the Western Front* (Batsford, 1959).

Weber, W. H. F., *A Field Artillery Group in Battle* (Royal Artillery Institution, 1923).

Wheldon, John, *Machine Age Armies* (Abelard-schuman, 1968).

Published Articles

1. **The Army Review**

Bird, M. H. C., 'Some duties of the Royal Garrison Artillery in War', Volume 2, 1912.

Du Cane, J. P., 'The cooperation of field artillery with infantry in the attack', Volume 1, 1911.

Carter, F. C., 'Our failings in the assault', Volume 3, 1912.

Clarke, R. G., 'Machine guns', Volume 4, 1913.

Ellison, G. F., 'Our Army system in theory and practice', Volume 3, 1912.

'Footslogger', 'War organisation of an infantry battalion', Volume 3, 1912.

Greenly, W.H., 'Employment of Cavalry in a retreat', Volume 4, 1913.

Haig, Douglas, 'Army training in India', Volume 2, 1912.

Monro, C. C., 'Fire and movement', Volume 1, 1911.

Montgomery, H. M. de F, 'Cooperation of infantry and artillery in the attack', Volume 5, 1914.

2. **The Army Quarterly**

Anon. (Historical Section), 'The Staff', Volume 1, 1920.

'A German account of the British offensive of August 1918', Volume 6, 1923.

'German defence during the battle of the Somme', Volume, 7, 1924.

'The organisation and administration of the Tank Corps during the Great War', Volume 8, 1925.

'German casualties in the Great War', Volume 16, 1928.

'The German Official History of the War' (The preparations), Volume 23, 1932.

'General Gough and the Fifth Army', a review, 1932.

'The question of the active policy' (the Somme), a review of the *OH*, 1916, Volume 1. Volume 24, 1932.

'The battle of Vimy Ridge: the German view', Volume 31, 1936.

'General Debeney's reflections', a review. Volume 36, 1938.

'The memoirs of General Messimy, minister of war 1911–14', Volume 36, 1938.

Birch, Sir Noel, 'Artillery development in the Great War', Volume 1, 1920.

Bird, Sir W. D., 'Mr Churchill's opinions: some other points of view', Volume 14, 1927.

Durrant, J. M. A., 'Mont St Quentin, August 1918', Volume 31, 1935.

Elles, Sir Hugh, 'Some notes on tank development during the war', Volume 2, 1921

Haig, W. B. W., 'Duff Cooper's *Haig*', a review. Volume 31, 1936.

Hart, B. Liddell, 'British and French doctrines on infantry in the attack', Volume 2, 1921.

Comments on his 'The defence in future war based on historical analysis' in *The Times*, 4 January 1938. Volume 36, 1938.

Piers, Sir Charles, 'A Corps in the making: the Canadian Expeditionary Force 1914–19', Volume 3, 1922.

Rowan-Robinson, H., 'The limited objective', Volume 2, 1921.

Smith, A. G. Baird, 'Open War', Volume, 5 1924.

Wade, E. W. N., 'From Maxim to Vickers', Volume 28, 1934.

Wright, R. M., 'Machine gun tactics and organisation', Volume 1, 1920.

Wynne, G. C., 'The development of the German defensive battle in 1917 and its influence on British defence tactics', (3 parts) Volumes 34 and 35, 1937.

'The chain of command', Volume 36, 1938.

3.   *The Journal of the Royal United Services Institute*

Anon. 'Some captured German documents-notes on the offensive', Volume 63, 1918.

'Frontal attack and infantry fire superiority', tr. from *Militar-Wochenblatt*, Volume 51, 1907.

'War and the *Arme Blanche*', the General Staff views on Mr Childers' book. Volume 54, 1910.

'Military Notes', 'Report of the air demonstration 12 May 1911'. Volume 55, 1911

'Machine gun scales in the German Army', Volume 57, 1912 and 1913.

'Notes on Army budgets past and present', The issue of the Vickers machine gun to the Cavalry', 'Further research on the .276-inch rifle'. Volume 58, 1914.

Applin R. V. K. 'Machine-gun experiments', Volume 54, 1909.

'Machine-gun tactics: our own and other armies', Volume 54, 1910.

Bortnovski, A., 'Hand grenades in the Russo-Japanese War', Volume 54, 1910.

Budworth, C. E. D., 'Training and action necessary to further co-operation between artillery and infantry', Volume 57, 1912.

Burke C. J., 'The aeroplane and strategy'.

'Aeroplanes of today and their use in war'. Volume 55, 1911.

Cadell, J. F., 'Shielded guns', Volume 51, 1907.

Carrington, C. E., 'Kitchener's Army: the Somme and after', Volume 122, 1977.

Culman F., 'French and German tendencies with regard to the preparation and development of an action', (tr.) from *Revue Militaire*.

Cunninghame, T. A. A. M., 'The supply of a division in the field with special reference to M.T.' Volume 56, 1912.

Degtyaret, A., 'Company and battalion tactics and the employment of artillery in battle' (tr.) from Voiennyi Sbornik, Volume 52, 1908.

Fuller, J. F. C., 'The tactics of penetration: a counterblast to German numerical superiority', and 'The procedure of the infantry attack'. Volume 59, 1914.

Hardcastle, J. H., 'The rifle: a weapon of precision', Volume 56, 1912.

Kearsey, A. H. C., 'Infantry attack supported by artillery', Volume 54, 1910.

Knapp, K. K., 'Pack artillery in the close support of infantry', Volume 52, 1908.

Langlois, H., 'The British Army in European conflict', Volume 54, 1910.

Von Lobell Reports: Infantry tactics in various armies, Volume 53, 1909. The co-operation of infantry and artillery, and centralised versus decentralised machine guns, Volume 56, 1912.

Armour and armour piercing bullets, Volume 59, 1914.

Miles, Sir H. S., 'Army administration', Volume 68, 1923.

'N', 'The organisation of a division', Volume 57, 1913.

Rawlinson, Sir H. S., 'Night operations', Volume 52, 1908.

Robinson, H. Rowan, 'More accurate methods in the field artillery', Volume 58, 1914.

Rohne H., 'The French and German field artillery: a comparison', (tr.) *from Jarhbucher für die Deutsche Armee und Marine*. Volume 52, 1908.

Rooke, G. H. J., 'Shielded infantry and the decisive frontal attack', Volume 58, 1914.

Soloviev, report in 'Military Notes', 'Impressions of a company commander in Manchuria', Volume 51, 1907.

Stone, F. G., 'Heavy artillery of a field army: a comparison', Volume 52, 1908.

Towle, Philip, 'The Russo-Japanese War and British Military Thought', Volume 116, 1971.

Tweedie, G. S., 'The call for higher efficiency in musketry', Volume 58, 1914.

Tudor, L. H., 'Collective fire', Volume 56, 1912.

Vincent, B., 'Artillery in the Manchurian campaign', Volume 52, 1908.

Wake, Hereward, 'The four company battalion in battle', Volume 59, 1914.

Wright, A. J. A., 'The probable effects of compulsory military training on recruiting in the regular army', Volume 55, 1911.

Other notes and unattributed articles:

'The British Army and modern conceptions of war', from The Edinburgh review. Translated from the German General Staff account of the South African War with comments. Volume 55, 1911.

Aeronautical Notes: 'The organisation of naval and military aviation', Volume 57, 1913.

4. *The Canadian Defence Quarterly*

Broad, C. N. F., 'The development of artillery tactics, 1914–18', Volume 1, (two parts), 1924.

'Editorial', 'G. C. Wynne and British tactical doctrine', Volume 15, 1938.

Heighington, Wilfrid, ' "Might have been – or as you were": Mr Lloyd George on British Generalship', Volume 11, 1936.

'Soldiers and Politicians', Volume 11, 1936.

Holland, R. T., 'Smoke as a weapon of war', Volume 1, 1924.

Long C. E., 'Ammunition supply during the Great War. . .' Volume 5, 1928.

McNaughton, A. G. L., 'Counter Battery Work', Volume 3, 1926.

'The development of artillery in the Great War', Volume 4, 1927.

Steel, W. Arthur, 'Wireless telegraphy in the Canadian Corps in France', Volumes 4, 8, 9 and 17 (8 articles).

Stuart, K., Basil Liddell Hart's *The Real War*, a review.

Basil Liddell Hart, '*The Real War:* a reply.'

5. *The Journal of the Royal Artillery*

Arbuthnot, A. G., 'Observation', Volume 53, 1927.

Atkinson, B., 'The employment of field artillery', (Duncan Silver Medal award), Volume 37, 1910.

Becke, A. F., 'The coming of the creeping barrage', Volume 58, 1931.

Body, O. G., 'Lessons of the Great War: the barrage versus concentrations on selected targets', Volume 53, 1926.

Brooke, A. F., 'The evolution of artillery' (Part 1 of a series), Volume 51, 1925.

Budworth, C. E. D., 'Tendencies of modern artillery', Volume 48, 1922.

'British and French QF field artillery', Volume 37, 1910–11.

Capper, J. E., 'The military aspects of dirigible balloons and aeroplanes', Volume 36, 1909.

Cherry, R. G., 'The Royal Air Force and Army Cooperations', Volume 52, 1926.

Cornwall, J. H. M., 'The organisation and tactics of the French field artillery', (tr.) from *Vierjahrschafte fur truppenfuhrung und heereskunden* No 2 of 1911, Volume 38, 1911–12.

Crowe, J. H. V., 'Artillery from an infantry point of view. . .' Volume 36, 1909–10.

Dare, J. A., 'The communications of the field artillery brigade', Volume 36, 1909–10.

Donop, Sir Stanley von, 'Artillery equipments', Volume 50, 1924.

Evans, W. (tr.) Capitaine Perre, 'Essay on anti-tank defence', Volume 51, 1924.

Ferguson, K. B., (tr.) Lieutenant Neuffer, 'Lessons learned concerning the employment of artillery to be drawn from the East Asian War, 1904–5'. (Prize essay in *Artillerische Monatsschafter*, November 1909), Volume 37, 1910.

Fitzwilliam, J. K. L. (tr.) 'The artillery duel' (from *Artillerische Monatsschafte*, June 1910), and 'Field guns versus howitzers for field artillery' (from the *Russian Artillery Journal*, June 1910), Volume 37.

Flare, R. H. (tr.) 'The new shooting regulations and the tendency of today in the German field artillery' (from *Revue Militaire des Armées Etrangères*, July 1911), Volume 38, 1911.

Flenley, Ralph, 'History of artillery', (Part 1 of a series), Volume 47, 1920.

Fuller, J. F. C., 'The tactics of penetration', Volume 53, 1927.

Goschen, A. A., 'Artillery tactics', Volume 52, 1924.

Harrison, H. C., 'Calibration and ranging', Volume 47, 1920.

Hartley, H., 'Gas warfare', Volume 46, 1919–20.

Hudson, N., 'Trench mortars in the Great War', Volume 47, 1920.

Ironside, Sir W. E., 'The course of future war', Volume 51, 1924.

Jarrett, A. F. V., 'The development of artillery survey', Volume 57, 1930.

McLeod, N. M., 'Survey work in modern war', Volume 48, 1921.

Neate, A. C. B. (tr.) 'The influence of field artillery on the issue of a modern battle' (from *Artillerische Monatsschafter*. April 1911), Volume 38, 1911.

Robertson, H. Rowan, 'Surprise, rapidity, concentration', Volume 47, 1921.

Stansfield, C. B., 'High explosives', Volume 46, 1919.

Stone, F. C., 'Aeroplanes in 1911', Volume 37, 1911.

Ward, C. F., 'A plan for more signallers', Volume 37, 1910–11.

Wilson, A. S., 'Artillery survey', Volume 58, 1931.

Wing, F. D. V., 'Observation on the employment of artillery in the field', Volume 36, 1909–10.

Winterbotham, H. StJ. L., 'Surveying in the Great War', Volume 46, 1919.

Wynter, H. W., 'A comparison of British, French and German methods of artillery in the field. . .'. (Duncan Gold Medal), Volume 39, 1912.

Other articles:

G.S.C., 'Shrapnel and HE', Volume 54, 1927.

Anon. Reprint from US Army *Coast Artillery Journal*, 'Statistics on the effect of artillery neutralisation and destructive fire', (March 1924), Volume 51, 1924.

'Outsider', 'Artillery Training', Volume 38, 1911.

6. *The Royal Engineers Journal*

Edmonds, Sir James E., 'The conception and birth of some of the War babies, 1914–18', Volume 58, 1944.

Jack, E. M., 'Survey in France during the war', Volume 30, 1919.

'The Experimental Section, RE', from *Work of the Royal Engineers in the European War, 1914–19*, September 1924–September 1925.

7. *Miscellaneous Articles*

Bond, Brian, 'Doctrine and Training in the British Cavalry, 1870–1914', *The Theory and Practice of War: Essays presented to Captain B. H. Liddell Hart on his seventieth birthday*, Michael Howard, ed., (Praeger, 1966).

Campbell, J., 'Fire Action', *Aldershot Military Society Publication*, 14 March 1911.

Campbell, John P., 'Refighting Britain's Great Patriotic War', *International Journal*, Volume 26, 1970–1.

Chenevix Trench, Charles, 'From Arquebus to Rifle: the pursuit of perfection', *History Today*, Volume 23, 1973.

Cowley, Robert, 'The Bloodiest Battle in History', *Horizon*, Volume 14, 1972.

Davidson Sir John, and Boraston, J. H., 'Douglas Haig', *Army Quarterly*, April 1928.

Ellison, G. F., 'Higher Control in war', *The National Review*, Volume 88, October 1926.

Falls, Cyril, 'From the last war to the present: the mobility of 1918 and its influence between the wars', *The Times*, July 26 1940.

Gamage, W., 'Sir John Monash: a military review', *Historical studies*, Volume 16 1974–5.

Greenhous, Brereton, 'Close support aeroplanes in the First World War: the counter-attack role', *Aerospace Historian*, Volume 21, 1974.
'Evolution of close ground-support role for aircraft in World War 1', *Military Affairs*, Volume 39, 1975.

House, Jonathan, M., 'The decisive attack: a new look at French infantry tactics on the eve of World War 1', *Military Affairs*, Volume 40, December 1976.

Keegan, John, 'Men in Battle', *Human Nature*, Volume 1, June 1978.

Morris, A. J. Anthony, 'Haldane's Army Reform, 1906–8: the deception of the radicals', *History*, Volume 56, 1971.

Porch, Douglas, 'The French Army and the spirit of the offensive, 1900–1914', *War and Society*, Brian Bond and Ian Roy eds., (Croom Helm, 1975).

Spiers, Edward M., 'The British Cavalry, 1902–14', *Journal of the Society for Army Historical Research*, Volume 57, 1979.

Travers, T. H. E., 'The Offensive and the problem of innovation in British Military thought, 1870–1915', *The Journal of Contemporary History*, Volume 13, 1978.

Trebilcock, Clive, 'War and the failure of industrial mobilisation: 1899 and 1914', *Essays in memory of David Joslin* (Cambridge University Press, 1975).

Williams, M. J., 'The First World War on land', *A Guide to the Sources of British Military History*, Robin Higham ed., (Berkeley, University of California Press 1971).

Wolff, Leon, *In Flanders Fields: the 1917 Campaign* (Ballantine, 1958).

Woollcombe, Robert, *The First Tank Battle: Cambrai 1917* (Arthur Barker, 1967).

Yates, C. A. L., 'The manoeuvres of the Prussian Guard in 1910', *Aldershot Military Society*, 1910.

II. 1919–1945

The Gunner magazine (see chapter notes).

Royal Artillery Journal (see chapter notes).

Various authors, *History of the Royal Regiment of Artillery 1919–1939*, ed. RA Historical Committee, RA Institution, unpublished.

Various authors, *Airborne Operations* (Salamander, 1978).

Various authors, *The Soviet War Machine* (Salamander, 1980).

Anonymous, *Notes from the Theatres of War*; series of pamphlets issued under the authority of the Chief of the Imperial General Staff by the War Office London, 1941–1945.

Anonymous, *Current Reports from Overseas*, Ibid.

Anonymous (P. Gribble), *The Diary of a Staff Officer* (Methuen, 1941).

Anonymous (in fact Alanbrooke) War Office Training pamphlet 43/Training/128 (MT 3), *The preparation of an Attack with Special Reference to the Fire Plan*, 1932.

Barnett, Correlli, *The Desert Generals* (William Kimber, 1960).

Bidwell, S., *Gunners at War: A Tactical Study of the Royal Artillery in the 20th Century* (Arms & Armour Press, 1970).

Blumentritt, G., *Rundstedt: The Soldier and the Man* (Odhams, 1952).

Bond, B., *British Military Policy between the Two World Wars* (Clarendon Press, 1980).

Butler, J. R. M., *History of the Second World War United Kingdom* Series, Vol. II *Grand Strategy* (HMSO, 1957).

Carver, Michael, 'Desert Dilemmas', Parts 1–8, Royal Armoured Corps Journal Vols. IV–VI, 1950–1952.
Tobruk (Batsford, 1961).
Field Marshal Lord Harding of Petherton (Weidenfeld & Nicolson, 1978).

Collier, B., *A History of Air Power* (Weidenfeld & Nicolson, 1974).

Deighton, L., *Blitzkrieg* (Cape, 1979).

Edmonds, Charles, *A Subaltern's Way* (Peter Davies, 1979).

Ellis, L. F., *History of the Second World War*, Vol. I *The Battle of Normandy* (HMSO, 1962).

Gibbs, N. H., *History of the Second World War United Kingdom* Series, Vol. 1 *Grand Strategy* (HMSO, 1976).

Guderian, H., *Panzer Leader* (Michael Joseph, 1970).

Hamilton, H., *Monty: The Making of a General 1887–1942* (London, 1981).

Harrison, Eric, *Gunners, Game and Garden* (Leo Cooper, 1979).

Hart, B. Liddell, *The Memoirs of Captain Liddell Hart* (Cassell, 1965).

Hart, B. Liddell, *Thoughts on War* (Faber, 1964).

Hickey, S. M. W., *Out of the Sky: A History of Airborne Warfare* (Mills & Boon, 1979).

Hogg, Ian V., *The Guns 1939–1945*. Purnell's *History of the Second World War*, Book II, (Macdonald, 1970).

Leach, B. A., *German Strategy Against Russia* (Oxford University Press, 1973).

Lewin, R., *Montgomery* (Batsford, 1971).

McIlwaine, I., *Ministry of Morale* (George Allen & Unwin, 1979).

Macksey, K., *Armoured Crusader: Major General Sir Percy Hobart* (Hutchinson, 1967).

Macksey, K., *The Tank Pioneers* (London, 1981).

Maughan, Barton, *Australia in the War of 1939–1945*, Series I (Army), Vol. III, Tobruk and Alamein (Canberra, Australian War Memorial, 1966 and Angus Wilson, London, 1967).

Maule, Henry, *Spearhead General: The Life of General Sir Frank Messervy* (Odhams, 1961).

Maurice-Jones, K. M., *The Shop Story 1900–1939* (Woolwich, RA Institute, 1954).

Mellenthin, F. W., *Panzer Battles 1939–1945* (Cassell, 1955).

Nalder, S., *Signals in the Second World War* (Royal Signals Institution, 1953).

Nicol, G., *Uncle George* Field Marshal Lord Milne of Salonika & Rubislaw (Reedminster, 1976).

Orgkiewicz, R. M., *Armoured Forces* (Arms & Armour Press, 1970).

Parham, H. J. and Bellfield, E. M. G., *Unarmed into Battle* (Warren & Sons, The Wykeham Press, 1956).

Pemberton, A. L., *The Development of Artillery Tactics and Equipment*, (Second World War, Army, 1939–1945 (The War Office, 1951).

Postan, Hay and Scott, *Design and Development of Weapons* (HMSO, 1964).

Richard, D., *Royal Air Force 1939–1945* Vol. 1 *The Fight at Odds* (HMSO, 1953).

Stanhope, H., *The Soldiers* (Hamish Hamilton, 1979).

Tedder, Lord, *With Prejudice: Memoirs of the Marshal of the Air Force Lord Tedder* (Cassell, 1966).

Terraine, J., *The Smoke and the Fire: Myth and Anti-Myths of War 1861–1945* (Sidgwick & Jackson, 1980).

Trythall, A. J., *Boney Fuller: The Intellectual General* (Cassell, 1977).

Tulloch, D., *Wingate in Peace and War* (Macdonald, 1972).
Urquhart, R. E., *Arnhem* (Cassell, 1958).
Zhukov, G. K., *Memoirs of Marshal Zhukov* (Cape, 1971).

Index